HUMAN
BEHAVIOR

A Program for Self-instruction

HUMAN BEHAVIOR

A Program for Self-instruction

Leslie F. Malpass (*Editor*)
Max O. Hocutt
Edwin P. Martin
Paul R. Givens

University of South Florida

McGRAW-HILL BOOK COMPANY
New York   St. Louis   San Francisco   Toronto   London   Sydney

HUMAN BEHAVIOR: A Program for Self-instruction

LIBRARY OF CONGRESS CATALOG CARD NUMBER 65-17494

1234567890 HD 7210698765

preface

Human behavior is everybody's concern. Its study is challenging but frustrating, seemingly simple but actually very complex, open to inspection by all but never fully understood by anyone. It is discussed freely by poets and politicians, by teachers and tradesmen, by ministers and menials. In short, all of us have some interest in human behavior, and none of us, for our own good and that of others, can know too much about it.

The primary intent of this self-instructional program is to supply some basic information about human activities derived from biology, psychology, psychiatry, anthropology, sociology, and philosophy. These disciplines—at least those aspects of them which investigate behavior—are for convenience included under the general heading of the behavioral sciences. This book does not pretend to summarize all the available data from the behavioral sciences, but it draws significant material from each discipline mentioned in order to help you to understand more about various types of behavior and the reasons for their occurrence.

After completing this book, you should have a reasonably good grasp of the principles which underlie the systematic study of behavior, as well as some helpful information about different aspects of behavior. The text is divided into six major parts. In common with some other books about behavior, Part I presents scientific methods by which inferences are drawn about human activities. Part II deals with biological bases for behavior—the contributions of heredity and descriptions of how the brain, the nervous system, and endocrine glands mediate behavior. Part III of the program deals with two models for analyzing how behavior is learned. These models were developed mostly from laboratory investigations of infrahuman animals and have been found to be applicable to human learning.

Part IV combines information from human biology, learning theory, and social psychology in order to demonstrate how behavior develops during prenatal life, childhood, adolescence, and early adulthood. This part is followed in turn by one about personality. It deals with concepts from psychoanalysis and other personality theories. One of the units in this section also describes some common mechanisms we all use in adjusting to the stress of everyday living. Part VI presents some major philosophical considerations about the nature of man and his behavior. This unit also provides an overview of major concepts presented in other sections of the book.

As you read through the program, you will note that there is a progression from the study of specific aspects of behavior to more general concepts. However, material for each of the units is rooted in empirical observations. It is this emphasis on the systematic study of behavior which provides a unifying principle for the program as a whole.

LESLIE F. MALPASS

Use of the Book

This self-instructional program has been developed primarily for use in undergraduate college courses dealing with material from the behavioral sciences. It may be used as the primary textbook for courses of interdisciplinary studies or as a supplementary text for introductory psychology, for educational or developmental psychology courses, or for a course emphasizing personality and human relations. The table on the inside cover of the book cross-references the units in this program with chapters of some selected textbooks for such courses. A bibliography for these textbooks is given in a succeeding section.

If the program is used as a supplement to other books, it should not be utilized as a workbook. That is, you should read the self-instructional material *before*, not after, related material in a conventional text. By doing this, you will be better prepared to further your knowledge from the other sources.

In presenting basic facts, studies, and concepts about behavior in a programmed format, this book should enable you to learn the related material in other textbooks more easily. It should enable you also to participate more effectively in discussions about the science of behavior and about the fascinating topic of human behavior itself.

The parts of the program have been prepared so they can be studied independently, or in an order different from that given in the book. For example, it is possible to read any part (except perhaps Parts IV and VI) without reference to any of the other parts. Or, if it is preferred, the units about personality can be read prior to the parts on human biology and learning. This feature enables the program to be used in different kinds of courses. The prose introductions to each major section of the book, however, serve as conceptual bridges from one area of study to another, and should facilitate the use of the book as the major reading resource in a course of study.

Programmed Instruction in the Book

The contents of each unit in the program are presented in a standard manner. Introductions and summaries for each section are written in prose style. However, the presentation of the major content material is in the form of sentences or short paragraphs called information frames. Each of these frames has an important word or phrase missing, or else the reader is required to make a choice among alternative responses or to answer a direct question.

In the information frames, missing words are indicated by blank lines like this: _____. Missing phrases are indicated by +++++. You should have no difficulty in understanding the type of response which is required in each information frame. Furthermore, if you study the frames carefully, you will find that you will make very few errors. We strongly recommend that you *write your responses* to the information frames on a piece of paper. You will find it easy to "fudge" if you do not write the answer, and you will thereby lose much of the advantage of the programmed format.

In the left margin of each page is a column of answers. In order to obtain best results from the program, you should cover the column of answers with a mask when you begin each page. As you complete each information frame and write down your answer, lower the mask so that you can check your response with the answer given on the left. The requirements of giving an active response to each unit of information given, and then getting immediate information about the correctness of your answer, are unique and significant differences between programmed instruction and conventional study procedures.

The frames given below illustrate the format used in the program. They serve to introduce you to the technique of programmed instruction.

1 In order to use this book correctly, you should cover the responses in the left-hand margin. *Cover them now.* Each frame in this program presents some information which requires a(n) _____ from you.

response
(answer)

2 Do not uncover the answer which corresponds to this information frame until after you have _____ down your response on a piece of paper.

written

3 A missing word is signified by a blank line. A required phrase is indicated by five +'s. When you encounter +++++, you know that a _____ is necessary for the correct response.

phrase

4 When your response is different from that given in the answer, check to see if your **(1)** _____ is a reasonable synonym. If it is not, correct your response before going on to the next information **(2)** _____.

(1) response
(answer)
(2) frame

5 Programmed instruction is based on empirically derived principles of learning. There are several basic components of programmed instruction based on these _____ of learning.

principles

6 (a) The sequential presentation of information (b) in small units, each of which (c) requires an active response from the reader, with said responses (d) being confirmed or corrected immediately, promotes effective study. The preceding sentence is a description of the basic components of _____ instruction.

programmed

7 Can you give the basic components of an effective program of self-instruction? +++++.

If you cannot, reread frame 6 carefully.

As you read through the program, you will come upon bibliographical references in the information frames. They will be given in parentheses, usually including the name of an author and the date of his publication. A list of these references is given at the end of each unit. The references themselves provide extended discussions of specific points made in the program.

At the end of each unit you will also find a self-review quiz. Answers for each quiz are given at the end of the book. The self-review quizzes have been prepared so that they cover the major points made in the unit. They should help you to review the material. They also provide an index of how well you understand the material. Take the quizzes as often as desirable for study purposes.

REVIEW

Once you have completed a programmed unit, a quick and thorough review can be made by following these suggestions:

1. Reread the introductory paragraphs.
2. Reread the summary paragraphs for each subsection and for the entire unit.
3. Check the answers within the unit. If you cannot spontaneously associate a given response with a concept or bit of information, read the corresponding information frame.
4. Complete the self-review quiz. If you cannot answer an item correctly, go back to the program and study

the relevant information frames again. You will find it advantageous to do this immediately.

By following these procedures, your retention of the material in a unit should increase significantly. Comprehension, not speed, is the *sine qua non* of learning. By reviewing carefully, you will find that both your retention and your comprehension will be facilitated.

USING STUDY TIME EFFECTIVELY

Self-pacing is much more important than most people realize in using study time effectively. Like any other textbook, this program will permit you to progress at your own rate. Research with this program indicates that some people take much longer than others to complete a given part. There will also be some variation in your own pace from unit to unit. It is wise, therefore, to find a study pace that is most appropriate for the time you have available. Do not try to crowd too much into one study period.

Most of the units consist of approximately two hundred frames, and they are subdivided into several sections, each with a topical heading. A majority of college students who used a prior edition of this program found that they could study effectively from sixty to one hundred frames in thirty to seventy minutes. Consequently, an entire unit should take from about one hour to a little more than two hours to complete.

Most people find they cannot concentrate on programmed material for more than thirty to forty minutes at a time (and some people cannot do so for that long). It is recommended, therefore, that you do *not* try to complete any given unit in one study period. Rather, divide the unit into convenient sections for study periods of twenty to forty minutes each. If you review each preceding section before beginning the next one, you will probably remember better both the old and the new material. In turn, this procedure should make review of each complete unit much easier for you and thus enable you to use your study time most effectively.

RELATED TEXTBOOKS

It was pointed out earlier that a cross-reference to some textbooks in related areas is provided on the inside front cover of this book. Included are representative books used for interdisciplinary courses in behavioral science and for courses in introductory psychology, educational and developmental psychology, and personality and human relations. This does not mean that the units in this program and the areas in the books listed can be used interchangeably. Rather, this self-instructional program supplements information given in the cross-references and provides a different means of studying related material.

The numbers under each of the books in the table refer to the chapters associated with the units and topics of this program. The full bibliographical references for the reference books are given below.[1]

Interdisciplinary behavioral science and human adjustment:

Berelson, B., and G. A. Steiner: *Human Behavior: An Inventory of Scientific Findings,* Harcourt, Brace & World, Inc., New York, 1964.

Coleman, J. C.: *Personality Dynamics and Effective Behavior,* Scott, Foresman and Company, Chicago, 1960.

Dewey, R., and W. J. Humber: *The Development of Human Behavior,* The Macmillan Company, New York, 1951.

Shaffer, L., and E. Shoben: *The Psychology of Adjustment,* Houghton Mifflin Company, Boston, 1956.

Introductory psychology:

Hilgard, E.: *Introduction to Psychology,* 3d ed., Harcourt, Brace & World, Inc., New York, 1962.

Morgan, C. T.: *Introduction to Psychology,* 2d ed., McGraw-Hill Book Company, New York, 1961.

Ruch, F. L.: *Psychology and Life,* 6th ed., Scott, Foresman and Company, Chicago, 1963.

Sartain, A. Q., A. J. North, J. R. Strange, and H. M. Chapman: *Psychology: Understanding Human Behavior,* 2d ed., McGraw-Hill Book Company, New York, 1962.

Educational and developmental psychology:

Baller, W. R., and D. C. Charles: *Psychology of Human Growth and Development,* Holt, Rinehart and Winston, Inc., New York, 1961.

McDonald, J.: *Educational Psychology,* Wadsworth Publishing Company, San Francisco, 1959.

Smith, L. M., and B. B. Hudgens: *Educational Psychology,* Alfred A. Knopf, Inc., New York, 1964.

Stephens, J. M.: *Educational Psychology,* rev. ed., Holt, Rinehart and Winston, Inc., New York, 1956.

---

[1] Other textbooks can be analyzed, of course, to see whether this program can be used in conjunction with them.

ACKNOWLEDGMENTS

The authors wish to acknowledge their debt to many individuals who helped in the preparation of the book. In particular, we are indebted to E. J. Kormondy, Harry F. Harlow, Calvin Hall, John Barlow, Wendell Smith, and J. W. Moore for their helpful observations about content and programming style and to the faculty members of Bucknell University, Emory University, the University of Tennessee, the University of California (Berkeley), San Francisco State College, and Whittier Junior College, who helped to evaluate a previous version of the book. Several faculty members at the University of South Florida served as script reviewers. Many students helped by reading drafts of the different sections, thereby making feasible revisions based on student learning. Miss Joyce McKee and Mrs. Jo Duncan typed the manuscript. Mrs. Marie Clark provided able secretarial assistance.

contents

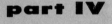

part 1

Methods of
Behavioral
Science

Max O. Hocutt

This part is both more and less than the title suggests. It is more in that the methods considered are applicable to all the sciences, not just to the behavioral sciences. It is less in that the account is truncated and leaves out much which ought to be considered if the aim were to cover all the essential features of the behavioral method.

The purpose of the part is not, however, to explain fully what scientific method is, nor to make experimental virtuosos out of its readers. For the first, a treatise would be required. For the second, much practice in laboratories or in the field would be necessary. The aim is to introduce the reader to some of the highlights of scientific procedure and to suggest something of the critical care with which an investigation can be conducted. The reader, we hope, will approach the topics of behavioral science, which constitute the rest of this book, with this part in mind.

Observation, generalization, and experimentation are the general topic headings. Under observation comes the verifiability criterion and a statement of the need for critical and careful observation. It is the point of this part to make clear that accurate empirical evidence is the *sine qua non* of the scientific value of any assertion. Under generalization comes a brief statement of the ways of securing reliable generalizations from accurate empirical data. It is asserted that taking a large enough random sample will increase the probability of obtaining a representative sample and hence a correct generalization. (Variations on random sampling, such as stratified and sequential sampling, are not considered.) Under experimentation falls a discussion of the predictive function of a hypothesis, a statement that prediction of an event requires specification of the antecedent conditions for the occurrence of the event, and a definition of experimentation as observation undertaken in order to confirm or disconfirm hypotheses. Independent and dependent variables are defined, and the importance of controlling variables is briefly stated and illustrated. Correlation is defined in such a way that it includes agreement and concomitant variation. (There is no discussion here of the statistics of correlation.)

The examples and illustrations are largely imaginary. Where they have been suggested by actual investigations in the behavioral sciences, it has been necessary to simplify these investigations in order to illustrate the points in question. Thus the reader would be well advised to follow up any reference to an actual work, in order to enrich his understanding of the procedures actually used.

Observation

1 Science, Whitehead once said, takes off from observation, makes a flight into the thin air of generalization, and lands for renewed observation. This suggests that the theories of science are of value just to the extent to which they are grounded in _____.

observation

2 To look, to listen, to touch, or to taste, and to notice what one sees, hears, feels, or tastes is to _____.

observe

3 To base assertions on observations is to be empirical. Science, as we know it today, is _____.

empirical

4 Assert any generalization, and a person of scientific temper will invariably ask you for your evidence. The only kind of evidence he regards as relevant is *empirical* evidence, that is, evidence derived from _____.

observations

5 The person who asserts that Scotchmen are frugal but who has observed very few Scots and has not observed them with any care, is making an assertion for which he has little _____ _____.

empirical evidence

6 Mothers commonly assert such propositions as "spare the rod and spoil the child." Often they are only repeating what they have heard and have very little _____ _____ for such an assertion.

empirical evidence

7 Suppose it is asserted that all socialists are "communists in sheep's clothing." Suppose this statement is justified by the assertion that the professor said so. The justification is not scientifically acceptable because it is not relevant _____ _____.

empirical evidence

8 An assertion for which there is good empirical evidence is said to be confirmed. An assertion against which there is good empirical evidence is said to be disconfirmed. The proposition that organisms tend to become less robust as they reach the ends of their lives has _____ [been confirmed/not been confirmed/been disconfirmed].

been confirmed

9 The proposition that there are manlike animals living on Mars has _____ [been confirmed/not been confirmed/been disconfirmed].

not been confirmed

10 The theory of the biological transmission of acquired traits _____ [has been confirmed/has not been confirmed/has been disconfirmed].

has been disconfirmed

false

11 A proposition which has not been confirmed has been disconfirmed. [T or F]

false

12 A proposition which has not been disconfirmed has been confirmed. [T or F]

13 Confirmation is a matter of degree. Which of the following would constitute least confirmation of the proposition that "sparing the rod spoils the child"? Which most?
- a. The testimony of mothers that they believe this proposition to be true
- b. The comparison of a few children on whom the rod has been spared with a few on whom the rod has been used freely and the observation that those who were whipped less were more "spoiled"
- c. The comparison of many children on whom the rod has been spared with many on whom the rod has been used freely and the observation that those whipped less were more "spoiled"

a would give no confirmation that is relevant; *c* would give greatest confirmation.

14 We often express the fact that the confirmation of a proposition is a matter of degree by saying that the proposition is true with such and such a *probability*. The proposition that two plus two equals four is necessarily true. By contrast, the proposition that the children of intelligent parents are also intelligent is true only with some _____.

probability

15 Confirmation of an assertion ordinarily establishes that the assertion is _____ [necessarily true/probably true].

probably true

16 Confirmation of an assertion consists in giving _____ _____ in favor of the assertion.

empirical evidence

17 To say that we have good empirical evidence for a proposition and none against it is to say that the proposition is _____ [possibly/probably/necessarily] true.

probably

18 Seldom is a scientist heard to state that a proposition has been proved to be *certainly* true (true beyond all possible doubt). More likely he will be heard to state that a proposition has been shown to be _____ true.

probably

19 The more empirical evidence there is for a proposition the _____ [greater/lesser] the probability of the truth of the proposition.

greater

20 A proposition for which there is no empirical evidence is a proposition which cannot be justifiably asserted in the sciences. [T or F]

true

21 If a proposition is capable in principle of being confirmed or disconfirmed, we say that it is verifiable. If it is not, we say that it is unverifiable. The proposition that there are little elves dancing on the table top, but that no one can see, hear, or in any way observe them is _____.

unverifiable

22 Since it is possible for us to make observations which would confirm the assertion that there are printed words on this page, it is _____.

verifiable

23 Since it is possible to make observations of the page which will disconfirm the assertion that there is a tiny animal lying on this page, it is _____.

verifiable

24 Consider the theory that everything in the entire universe is expanding at a constant rate. Since instruments of measurement would also be expanding at the same rate, this theory is _____ [verifiable/unverifiable].

unverifiable

25 The first criterion for scientific acceptability of a hypothesis is that it be verifiable, that is, that it be possible to make some observations which would either confirm or _____ the hypothesis.

disconfirm

26 Since there are considerable limitations on our ability to measure the intelligence of neonates, statements that one group is innately inferior in intelligence to another should be regarded with some misgivings because they have limited _____.

verifiability

Suppose someone says that there is an intangible, invisible, inaudible, spiritual being inside each of us called the "conscience," which "tells us" what is right and what is wrong but does not tell us with a voice which can be literally heard ("a still, small voice").

27 A behavioral scientist is likely to be suspicious of any such assertion because it is _____.

unverifiable

28 Suppose that someone proposes the theory that every human being has a soul but that this soul is unobservable and that we must take its existence on faith. While this proposition may have a great deal of *religious* value, it has little *scientific* value because the existence of such entities is _____.

unverifiable

29 Contemporary sciences of man (e.g., psychology, sociology, anthropology) tend to occupy themselves almost exclusively with man's behavior and to leave out of consideration such occult entities as souls. This is because assertions about behavior and its causes are **(1)** _____, while assertions about spiritual entities are **(2)** _____.

(1) verifiable
(2) unverifiable

30 It is interesting and important to notice that, although the term "psychology" means, etymologically speaking, "science of the mind," a good many psychologists now believe that unless the mind is defined in terms of observable behavior or equated with the brain, it is not a proper subject for a science of psychology. The reason given is that, if the mind is conceived as intangible and invisible, anything said about it would be _____.

unverifiable

A qualification must be made. When we say that the scientist requires that any hypothesis be verifiable, we must distinguish between verifiability in *principle* and verifiability in *practice*. By "verifiable in practice" we mean that we have the means to verify the hypothesis. By "verifiable in principle," we mean that we may someday have the means, even if we do not yet have them.

31 For example, a statement about what is on the other side of the planet Mercury is not verifiable in **(1)** _____, since we do not have the means to verify it; but it is verifiable in **(2)** _____, since we may someday have the means.

(1) practice
(2) principle

32 "Inside every man there is a spiritual substance which science is incapable of studying and which makes man uniquely what he is." This statement is unverifiable in _____ [principle/practice/both].

both. (It is unverifiable in principle and also, therefore, unverifiable in practice.)

33 "Let two people be placed in separate rooms. Though they cannot communicate in ordinary ways, subtle impulses are transmitted from one to the other. These are too slight to be measured by instruments yet available, but more refined techniques would allow us to measure them." These assertions are not verifiable in **(1)** _____, but they appear to be verifiable in **(2)** _____.

(1) practice
(2) principle

34 A scientist will refuse to discuss a question such as "How many angels are dancing on the head of this pin?" because this sort of question is unverifiable in **(1)** _____. He has no such objections to questions about whether there are men on Mars, since such questions, while not verifiable in **(2)** _____, are verifiable in **(3)** _____.

(1) principle
(2) practice
(3) principle

51 The orientation of most contemporary psychologists is toward external behavior and away from mental states. They regard behavior as a more fruitful and reliable source of data because behavior is _____ observable while private mental states are not.

52 The verifiability criterion of science consists in the requirement that an assertion, to be considered a legitimate scientific hypothesis, must be:

a. _____ [directly/directly or indirectly] verifiable

b. _____ [verifiable in principle/in practice]

c. _____ [publicly verifiable/privately verifiable]

53 The scientific insistence upon verification is simply the insistence that every assertion be backed up by _____ _____.

54 The data of the sciences are obtained by making _____.

55 It will be remembered that we have defined verification as either confirmation or disconfirmation of a theory. When a theory has observational evidence in its support then it has been, to that extent, (1) _____, but when it has evidence against it, it is, to that extent, (2) _____.

Despite the fact that there could be no science without observation, a person of scientific temper is not uncritical about observation. Observation is fallible. Consider the conflicting testimonies of witnesses to an accident. The driver of car A says car B ran the light. The driver of car B says car A ran the light. Both witnesses may be telling what they believe to be the truth.

56 The explanation of the conflict in testimony is that the two drivers _____ the same situation differently.

57 One of the factors affecting the accuracy of observation is bias. In the example of the preceding frame, the different observations made by the two witnesses were probably due to different _____.

58 If Negroes and Caucasians give different accounts of what went on during a race riot, then the difference may not be due to the fact that one is deliberately lying. It will probably be due to the fact that they have different _____.

publicly

a. directly or indirectly
b. in principle
c. publicly

empirical evidence (observations)

observations

(1) confirmed (verified won't do)
(2) disconfirmed

observed

biases

biases

Bias makes for selectivity in observation. Persons tend to observe and remember whatever bolsters their preconceived notions. A person with strong racial prejudices therefore tends to notice distasteful characteristics of another race and to ignore admirable characteristics.

selectivity

59 This is an illustration of _____ in observation due to bias.

Many experiments have been performed in which arguments for and against a certain ideology were presented to subjects. Those who already favored the ideology tended to remember more of the arguments for it. Those who already disapproved of the ideology tended to remember more of the arguments presented against it. The subjects also showed less understanding of arguments contrary to their positions.

selectivity

60 This is an illustration of how bias makes for _____ in perception.[1]

Bias also tends to distort perception. In one well-known experiment a picture was presented to subjects having prejudice against Negroes. The picture portrayed a white man standing on a bus next to a colored man. The Caucasian was holding a knife. When the pictures were taken away and the subjects were asked to describe what they saw, many of them asserted that the knife was in the hands of the Negro.

distortion

61 This is an illustration of how bias makes for _____ in observation.[2]

distortion

62 If my brother hits a person whom I dislike very much, I may subsequently convince myself that that person began the fight with my brother. This is an example of how bias results in _____ of what is observed and remembered.

[1] See, for example, Jerome M. Levine and Gardner Murphy, "Learning and Forgetting of Controversial Material," *Journal of Abnormal Social Psychology*, 507–517, 1943.

[2] See Gordon W. Allport and Leo F. Postman, "Basic Psychology of Rumor," reprinted in Maccoby, Newcomb, and Hartley (eds.), *Readings in Social Psychology*, 3d ed., Holt, Rinehart and Winston, Inc., New York, 1958, pp. 54–65.

Expectation (referred to as "set" in Part III, Unit I) also affects what we observe. We tend to see not only what we want to see but what we expect to see. One picture presented to subjects portrayed a placard advertising cigarettes named "Lucy Smile." (The picture contained many other details.) When the picture was taken away, many subjects reported having seen an advertisement for "Lucky Strike" cigarettes.

expectation (set)

63 This is an illustration of how _____ affects the way in which we observe.

expectation (set)

64 A chemist is expecting a reading of 98.7 because it would confirm his theory, and as a result, he observes a reading of 97.7 as 98.7. This illustrates how _____ affects observation.

carelessness

65 Another factor affecting observation is carelessness. A scientist in a hurry or distracted by noise is less likely to make reliable observations. This is because hurry and distraction make for _____.

bias (prejudice)

66 Consider a person who is prejudiced against Negroes. In making a study of the comparative intelligence of Negroes and whites, such a person will have to be careful lest his _____ affect the reliability of his observations.

observations

67 The data of the sciences are empirical data, that is, they are the result of making _____.

empirical (observational)

68 The only kind of evidence admitted as relevant in science is _____ evidence.

In summary, observation is essential to science in two ways:
First, if a proposition is to be considered worthy of investigation, it must be verifiable. That is, it must be possible to make some observations which would tend either to confirm or disconfirm the proposition. We need not have the means of verification at hand, but they should be such as can exist; that is, the proposition must, at least, be verifiable in principle if not also in practice. We need not directly observe the entities or facts alleged by the proposition to exist, but at least we should be able to observe their effects; that is, the proposition should at least be indirectly verifiable. Also, the proposition should

be such that more than one person could verify it; that is, public verification is desirable.

Second, if a proposition is to be considered true, it must have considerable empirical evidence in its favor and very little, or none, against it. Ordinarily, gaining evidence for a significant scientific theory is a protracted endeavor. Consequently, instead of saying that a theory has been proved beyond all possible doubt, it is more appropriate to say that it has been shown to be true with some probability. Theories having greater probability are those supported by more evidence.

Without observation, there is no science in the modern sense of the word. Yet, to be useful, observation must be accurate. Bias, carelessness, and other factors adversely affect the objectivity and reliability of our observations and the data resulting from them.

Generalization

69 Generalization consists of inferring a general rule from specific cases. For example, "Professors X, Y, and Z were absent-minded; therefore, professors are absent-minded," is a _____.

generalization

70 "Smith, Jones, Simmons, and Johnson are the New Yorkers I know. They are all bad drivers. Therefore, New Yorkers must be bad drivers." This is a _____.

generalization

71 When we derive a general rule from specific cases, we are _____.

generalizing

72 Professors X, Y, and Z can be known to be absent-minded only if someone has watched them. The specific cases from which a generalization is derived can be known only as a result of _____.

observation

73 "I have known artists A, B, and C. They were temperamental." Here the conclusion is a (1) _____ from specific instances. That the artists mentioned are temperamental is known, if at all, by (2) _____ them.

(1) generalization

(2) observing

74 The facts (or data) upon which a scientist bases his theories are the particular instances which he knows by making observations. If I have observed that Professors X, Y, and Z are absent-minded, then these are the _____ with which I have to deal.

facts (data)

observation	75 For our purposes, facts may be defined as particular instances known by _____.
(1) fact (2) observation	76 That some men (A, B, C, . . .) have died is a (1) _____ known by (2) _____.
(1) theory (general rule) (2) generalization	77 Let us define theories as general rules. On this definition, the proposition that all men are mortal is not a fact but a (1) _____ arrived at by (2) _____ from observing men die.
(1) facts (2) theory	78 "These animals (A, B, C, . . .) became restless as they were deprived of food. Therefore, deprivation tends to increase random activity." The first sentence states some (1) _____ known by observation. The second states a (2) _____ arrived at by generalization from the facts.
facts (observations, evidence, data)	79 Obviously, theories are of value just to the extent to which they are based on _____.
empirical evidence	80 Facts give us reasons to believe or disbelieve a theory; that is to say, they constitute _____ _____ for or against a theory.
good (much, adequate, etc.)	81 The facts which are available may be good evidence for a theory, or they may be poor evidence for it. If I have observed only one or two professors and assert that professors are absent-minded, then I have some evidence for my theory, but I do not have _____ evidence.
evidence (facts, data, etc.)	82 The value of a generalization depends on the value of the _____ for it.
not very good in either case	83 Suppose that I have been careless in making my observations. What will be the value of my evidence? What will be the value of the theory I base on my evidence? +++++.
are accurate (carefully made, etc.)	84 Obviously, one necessary condition for the value of a generalization is that the observations on which it is based +++++.
fallacious (wrong, etc.)	85 Even if the observations are accurate, the generalization from them may be faulty. If I have had very few Latin acquaintances and if I generalize that all Latins are passionate, then my generalization may be _____.

86 Some generalizations are better established by the evidence at hand than others. Consider the following:
  a. X was a sociology professor, and X was absent-minded. Therefore, professors are absent-minded.
  b. W was a sociology professor; Y was a chemistry professor; V was a philosophy professor; X was a history professor; and Z was a psychology professor. V, W, X, Y, and Z were all absent-minded. Therefore, professors are absent-minded.
Which of these gives best support to the generalization?

b

87 Rank the following generalizations according to the degree to which they are supported by the evidence:
  a. "I traveled in Brazil. The Brazilians were hot-blooded. Therefore, Latins are hot-blooded."
  b. "I had a Cuban roommate. He was hot-blooded. Therefore, I believe Latins are hot-blooded."
  c. "I have spent many years traveling through South America and Western Europe. The French, Spanish, Italians, Cubans, and Brazilians were hot-blooded. Therefore, I say that Latins are hot-blooded." +++++.

b has weakest support
c has strongest support

88 One common source of bad generalization is hasty generalization. Hasty generalization exists when we generalize from too few instances. For example, a person concludes from observations of the few Latins of his acquaintance that Latins are passionate. Such a person is guilty of _____ _____.

hasty generalization[3]

89 If we generalize regarding the personality of a person after having met him only once or twice, then we are guilty of _____ _____.

hasty generalization

A stereotype is a generalization about a social group which is rigidly applied to every member of the group. For example, "Latins are passionate" is a fairly common stereotype.

90 "Artists are temperamental," "professors are absent-minded," and "Italians are gangsters" are also _____.

stereotypes

---

[3] Some persons will prefer the term "overgeneralization." I make no distinction here, but we could mark out a class of fallacious generalizations which involve drawing a generalization for a larger class than the data will justify and call them overgeneralizations. For example, if we observe that something is true of a random sample of rats and then infer that it is true of all animals, we shall overgeneralize.

91 Sometimes prejudice against a group is rationalized by appeal to a general picture of the group. For example, antisemitism may be "justified" by the _____ that "Jews are grasping."

stereotype

92 Stereotypes are frequently the result of _____ _____ from observations of few, if any, of the members of the stereotyped group.

hasty generalization

93 It is an unfortunate and illogical habit of many persons to jump from a few observations to sweeping generalizations. This is the fault known as _____ _____.

hasty generalization

94 A generalization is made from *some* of the members of a group to *all* the members. The "some" is termed a "sample." The entire group is termed the "population" (or "universe"). Thus, a generalization is an inference from a **(1)** _____ to the total **(2)** _____ of which it is a part.

(1) sample
(2) population

95 In public-opinion polls, every available individual is not asked his opinion, but conclusions are drawn regarding the general opinion. Those persons who are actually asked for an opinion in such a poll are termed the **(1)** _____. The public as a whole is termed the **(2)** _____.

(1) sample
(2) population

96 If a sociologist wishes to discover whether a given type of personality (say, authoritarian personality) is characteristic of certain religious groups, it will obviously be impracticable to administer tests to every person belonging to these groups. Instead, the sociologist will have to content himself with taking a _____.

sample

97 We may define a hasty generalization as a generalization about a population which is based on too _____ a sample.

small
  (limited, etc.)

98 The way to avoid hasty generalization is to take a _____ sample.

large

99 Other things being equal, a generalization is more likely to be correct, the _____ the sample.

larger

Even though taking a large sample is important, and even though it is true that, all things being equal, the larger the sample the more reliable the generalization, there is a point at which taking a larger sample is not worth the labor which it entails. Books on statistics contain formulas for determining what that point is. In general, we may say that when the values of the sample stabilize or begin to fluctuate in a narrow range around some value, then the sample is large enough. For example, if I am tossing dice to determine the probability of getting sixes (something which it is unnecessary to do, incidentally), I will know that I have taken a large enough sample when the ratio of sixes to the total number of throws begins to stabilize (which will be at five-thirty-sixths).

It is important to take a large enough sample if generalizations are to have the likelihood of being correct. It is perhaps more important, however, to take a random sample. We may define a random sample as a sample taken in such a way as to give every member of the population an equal chance of being a member of the sample. Suppose our population is a bag of white and red beans. Suppose that the white beans were poured into the bag first. Suppose that the red beans were poured into the bag on top of the white beans.

100 Will the white beans have an equal chance with the red of being picked from the bag if we simply reach into the bag and pull beans off the top? _____

obviously not

101 See the preceding paragraph. Since we do not give every bean an equal chance of being chosen, we do not take a _____ sample.

random

102 Suppose that the red and white beans in our bag are thoroughly stirred so that the white beans are well mixed in with the red beans. Will such a procedure equalize the chances of each bean being a part of the sample?

Yes

103 By stirring the beans thoroughly we give each bean an equal chance of being a member of the sample; that is, if we take a sample from a thoroughly stirred bag of beans, we take a _____ sample.

random

104 Suppose that I want to find out how the country will vote in the coming presidential election and poll a group of persons in the Texas Panhandle. Since this sample does not give every potential voter in the United States an **(1)** _____ chance of being a part of the sample, it is not **(2)** _____.

(1) equal
(2) random

A sample that is not random will be said to be "biased." Obviously, then, a biased sample is a sample in which some members of the population are given a greater chance of being chosen than others. Consider the following example: Suppose you desire to know how many citizens in the United States are atheists. In order to arrive at a conclusion, suppose you poll a number of your fellow students.

biased

105 Since you have given only students a chance of being members of your sample, your sample is _____.

biased

106 Suppose a psychologist wishes to know the average time it takes a seventh-grader to learn a series of nonsense syllables. In order to find this out, he goes only to a special school for very bright children. Obviously, his sample will be _____.

random

107 Whenever we give every member of the population an equal chance of becoming a member of the sample, then we take a _____ sample.

biased

108 Whenever we give some members of the population a greater chance than others of becoming members of the sample, then we take a _____ sample.

The minister says, "This is totally unlike George! Why, he has attended my church for years. I have had a chat with him almost every Sunday. Never would I believe that he would desert his wife." This sample is biased because the minister sees George only in very special situations. (The population is George's personality; the sample is the minister's experience of George's personality.)

The sample is not random. Only certain persons frequent feed stores.

109 Is the following sample random? Explain your answer. "I know a good deal about people. I have run a feed store all my life and have there met countless people." +++++.

Random samples should not be confused with haphazard samples. If you desire to poll the students on your campus, and, in order to do so, you wander about the campus for a couple of hours interviewing whomever you happen upon, you will be taking a haphazard sample, but you will not be taking a random sample.

equal

Merely haphazard.
(Sizable portions
of the population
do not appear on
the streets at
10 p.m.)

It will be
haphazard.

b

110 Suppose that you wander into the coffee shop. Then you will be sampling those who spend time drinking coffee and chatting. Those who do not drink coffee will not have been given an _____ chance of being part of your sample.

111 Suppose you wish to find out how many persons in a town approve of socialized medicine. Suppose that you go down on the street corner at 10 p.m. and ask whoever happens by. Will your sample be random or merely haphazard? Why? ++++.

112 Suppose you wish to poll student opinion on your campus. Suppose you wander about from place to place asking questions. Will your sample be random or haphazard?

The best way to get a random sample is to assign each member of the population a number and use a table of random numbers. Such tables, with their explanations, may be found in elementary books on statistics. Essentially, a table of random numbers is a set of numbers which has been thoroughly and systematically "shuffled" to guarantee its randomness. A degree of randomness may also be achieved in less satisfactory ways. If, for example, your population is students and you can list their names by alphabetical order and take every *n*th name, then you can achieve some randomness, or you can achieve a degree of randomness by shuffling your population in some thorough manner. With populations that are exceedingly large, more complicated means must be used to ensure randomness.

113 Which procedure would be the best for getting a random sample from a bag of beans: (*a*) sticking your hand in the bag and pulling out a bean from wherever your hand may stop, or (*b*) stirring and mixing the beans thoroughly and then drawing a sample? _____

Suppose a telephone company wishes to know whether its customers would like to see some new service introduced. (*a*) It may have the operators call up the first 100 subscribers who answer at 12 to 1 p.m. on the fifth of July. (*b*) It may have operators call at several intervals spaced equally throughout the year and at several intervals spaced equally throughout the day, to interview subscribers spaced equally throughout its alphabetical listing of subscribers.

Obviously b would be more random.

114 Which procedure described above would be more nearly random? _____.

Those who were at work or those away for a luncheon with friends, etc.

115 Consider the preceding example. Can you think of any group of persons which might be eliminated by calling at 12 noon? +++++.

Those who were taking vacations or who were at the beach, etc.

116 Consider the same example. Can you think of any group of persons which might be eliminated by calling on the fifth of July? +++++.

random

117 Consider the same example. It is a haphazard sample, but not a _____ sample.

give some group a greater chance of being a part of the sample

118 Haphazard samples fail to be random because they are taken in ways which unwittingly +++++.

119 We have considered two ways to increase the probability that a generalization will be correct:

(1) large

(1) Avoid hasty generalization by taking a _____ enough sample.

(2) random

(2) Avoid biased samples by taking a _____ sample.

(1) take a large enough sample
(2) take a random sample

120 What are the two ways in which we increase the probability that a generalization from a sample will be correct? +++++

A generalization is correct if and only if the sample on which the generalization is based is representative of the population. Roughly speaking, a sample is representative if and only if it has the same characters as the whole. For example, suppose our population is a bag of beans, one-half of which are white and one-half of which are black. Suppose that someone who is unaware of this proportion draws a sample of beans from the bag.

representative

121 Suppose that two-thirds of this sample are black and one-third are white. If he infers from his sample that two-thirds of the beans in the bag are black and one-third white, he will be mistaken, for his sample is not _____ of the total population.

122 Suppose that, as a matter of fact, 60 per cent of college professors are Democrats. Now suppose that we interview a sample of college professors and find that only 45 per cent of our sample are Democrats. Obviously our sample is not _____ of the total population of professors.

representative

123 Suppose that we take a pre-election poll and find that 60 per cent of those interviewed say that they will vote for the Democratic candidate. Suppose that in the actual election, 60 per cent vote for the Republican candidate. Obviously, either the persons polled were lying or did not know their own minds or changed them (or followed some such procedure), or else the sample was not _____ of the population.

representative

124 Suppose the average IQ of some social group is between 90 and 110. Suppose that intelligence tests are given to a sample of that group. Suppose the average IQ of the sample is between 90 and 110. Then the sample is _____ of the social group in question.

representative

125 In order for a generalization to be certain of correctness, the sample must have the same properties as the population. That is, it must be _____.

representative

126 A generalization is correct only if the sample is representative. For example, suppose your population is a bag of beans, three-fourths of which are white and one-fourth of which are green. If you take a sample from this bag, your generalization will be correct only if **(1)** _____ of the beans in your sample are white and **(2)** _____ of the beans in your sample are green.

(1) three-fourths
(2) one-fourth

127 Suppose that 30 per cent of the business population has ulcers. Suppose that in order to find out what proportion of businessmen have ulcers, you take a sample. Your generalization will be correct only if your sample is such that _____ (a quantity) of the sample has ulcers.

30 per cent

128 A sample which has the same characters as the population is a representative sample. A sample which is taken in such a way as to give every member of the population an equal chance of being chosen is a _____ sample.

random

Obviously, we do not usually know in advance of examining an entire population whether a sample is representative or not. We could know this only by comparing the entire population with the sample. Nevertheless we can *increase the probability* that we will take a representative sample (and obtain a correct generalization) by taking a random sample. Suppose that the population is a bag of beans, one-half of which are red and the other one-half of which are green.

probable

129 If I take a random sample of these beans (say, by stirring them well) then it is _____ that I will take a representative sample.

Suppose my population is a bag of beans, two-thirds of which are white and one-third of which are green. Suppose I give every bean an equal chance of being chosen. Since there are twice as many white as green beans in the population, there are likely to be twice as many in the sample.

(1) random
(2) representative

130 This example shows why taking a **(1)** _____ sample increases the probability of getting a **(2)** _____ sample.

If I have a bag of beans (one-half white and one-half black) and thoroughly stir them, then it is *possible* that all the white beans will end up on top of the bag, so that when I sample the bag, I will get only white beans.

probable

131 However, it is not very _____ that such an event will occur.

(1) possible

(2) probable

132 If I take a random sample, it is **(1)** _____ that I will get an unrepresentative sample, but it is not very **(2)** _____.

Read the following statements carefully:
  a. A random sample is the same as a representative sample.
  b. Taking a random sample guarantees a representative sample.
  c. Taking a random sample has nothing to do with getting a representative sample.
  d. Taking a random sample makes it probable that one will get a representative sample.

d

133 Which of these statements is true? _____

134 A sample taken in such a way as to give every member of the population an equal chance of being chosen is a (1) _____ sample. A sample having the same relevant characteristics as the population is a (2) _____ sample.

(1) random
(2) representative

135 Taking a random sample is a procedure by which we attempt to increase the _____ of getting a representative sample.

probability

136 If I have a bag of beans, one-half of which are white and one-half of which are black, and if the white beans have been put into the bag first and the black beans poured over them, and if they have not been stirred, then it is unlikely that I shall get a representative sample if I start to draw beans off the top. This is because my sample will be _____.

biased

137 Remember that the opposite of "random sample" is "biased sample." If taking a random sample increases the probability of a representative sample, then taking a _____ sample decreases it.

biased

If we are to arrive at correct generalizations, biased samples are obviously to be avoided. Sometimes prior knowledge will help us to avoid biasing a sample. Consider the following generalization:
Sample: This student's handwriting on an examination
Population: This student's handwriting
Generalization: This student's handwriting is poor.

138 The sample is obviously (1) _____. Therefore, the generalization (2) _____ [is certainly/is probably] incorrect.[4]

(1) biased
(2) is probably

139 Refer to the preceding example. We know that the sample is biased and will probably be unrepresentative because we know that handwriting on examinations is +++++.

poorer than usual handwriting

Consider the following generalization:

Sample: Several cities in this state observed from a railroad car

[4] The problems in frames 138 to 143 are from Monroe C. Beardsley, *Practical Logic*, © Prentice-Hall, Inc., Englewood Cliffs, N.J., 1950. (Used by permission.)

Population: Cities in this state
Generalization: Most of the cities in this state are just collections of ugly factories.

140 Since railroads tend to run through factory sections, the sample is _____.

biased

141 Consider the following:

Sample: 200 Centerville adults interviewed on the streets between 7 and 9 p.m.
Population: Centerville adults
Generalization: 79 per cent of those in Centerville prefer movies to television.
What do you know about the habits of television watchers as opposed to movie goers which indicates that this sample is biased? +++++.

that TV watchers would not usually be downtown to see movies, while movie goers would be. (This, after all, is TV prime time.)

142 Consider the following:

Sample: Senators and Representatives whose opinions were featured in large front-page headlines in 1950
Population: Senators and Representatives
Generalization: Most members of Congress in 1950 believed that the administration contained a large number of subversive characters.
There is some reason to believe that this sample is biased, because what gets into the headlines is which of the following:
   a. Ordinary run-of-the-mill events
   b. Comparatively sensational items

b

143 Consider the following:

Sample: American citizens interviewed on airplanes and at airfields
Population: American citizens
Generalization: 75 per cent of all Americans disapprove of governmental health programs for the aged. What do you know about travelers which would suggest that this sample is biased? +++++.

that not all types of travelers go by air. (You might add that they tend to be of upper socioeconomic groups and more conservative.)

144 By taking a random sample we avoid a _____ sample.

biased (unrepresentative)

145 By taking a large sample we avoid _____ _____.

hasty generalization

(1) take a large
enough sample.
(2) take a random
sample.

observations

omitted
relevant data

biased

neglecting
relevant data

No response required

146 Two rules for increasing the probability of getting a representative sample, and, hence, a correct generalization are:
(1) +++++.
(2) +++++.

147 Even if our sample is large and random, the generalization may still be incorrect if the data on which it is based are incorrect. That is, even if the reasoning is good, the conclusion may be false if the _____ have not been accurately made.

148 One common way of biasing the sample is to leave out some of the data. For example, if the dispute is about whether prayer is effective and a person mentions all the times his prayers were "answered" but forgets about the times prayer did not seem to have the desired results, his sample is biased because he has +++++.

149 Suppose a person supports his view that Federal government is generally less efficient than private enterprise by citing a few particularly striking instances of waste in government. Even if his conclusion is correct, the evidence he is using to support it is probably _____.

150 See the preceding frame. Suppose the person involved forgets or fails to mention comparative cases of waste in private enterprise or striking cases of efficiency in government. He is biasing his sample by +++++.

151 We may bias samples by neglecting relevant data without doing so deliberately. It is important, therefore, to be careful lest we unconsciously bias a sample in this manner.

". . . Science, though it starts from observation of the particular, is not concerned essentially with the particular, but with the general. A fact, in science, is not a mere fact, but an instance."[5]
The process of inferring a general rule from particular cases is known as generalization (or induction). The particular cases upon which such an inference is based are termed the sample. The class of things about which the generalization is made is known as the population or universe. If a generalization is to be correct, the sample must have the same relevant characteristics as the total popula-

[5]Bertrand Russell, *Scientific Outlook*, George Allen & Unwin, Ltd., London, 1954, pp. 58–59.

tion from which it is drawn; it must be representative of, or typify, the population.

The procedure by which we increase the probability that a sample will be representative is known as random sampling. It consists in taking a sample in such a way as to give every member of the population an equal chance of being chosen. This procedure is not a guarantee of a representative sample, but it offers the best chance of securing one. Random sampling is best accomplished in some mechanical way, such as using a table of random numbers or drawing out of a well-shuffled pile. Less formal procedures involve deliberately avoiding selecting all members of the sample from any one subgroup of the population. A biased sample is a sample which gives some members of the population a greater chance than others of being chosen.

An important rule is: "Take a large enough sample." All things being equal, the larger the sample, the more likely it is to be representative. Generalizations based on samples that are too small are known as hasty generalizations. Unfortunately, a good many of our beliefs are the results of either hasty generalization or generalization from biased samples.

Experimentation

152 We may define experimentation as observation under controlled conditions for the purpose of confirming or disconfirming a hypothesis. Put less technically, an empirical test of an hypothesis is an _____.

experiment

153 Roughly speaking, any procedure for ascertaining whether a given hypothesis is true or not may be called an _____.

experiment

154 Suppose we have observed that some laboratory rats increased their random activity with food deprivation and have inferred that, therefore, all animals become restless as they are deprived. This inference, you know from the preceding section, is a _____.

generalization
(and a very
hasty one)

155 When, in order to test the preceding generalization, we take some species of animals not included in our original sample and observe whether their restlessness increases with deprivation, we are performing _____.

experiments

156 A generalization which has not been tested will be termed an "hypothesis." An **(1)** _____ then, is a test of an **(2)** _____.

(1) experiment
(2) hypothesis

If, after rewarding some rats with food for performing certain tasks, I notice that they learned the tasks faster than rats not so rewarded, I may be led to suppose that a good way to teach behavior is to reward it.

157 If, in order to test this idea, I take some animals and reward them for performing assigned tasks, then I am performing **(1)** _____ in order to test an **(2)** _____.

(1) experiments
(2) hypothesis

158 An hypothesis is a _____ before it is tested.

generalization

159 Hypotheses form the bases of predictions. Let the hypothesis be that redheads are temperamental. If this hypothesis is true, then we may _____ that Mary and Jim, who are redheads, will be temperamental.

predict

160 Let the hypothesis be that religious fundamentalists are likely to be politically conservative. If the hypothesis is true, then we may _____ that a random sample of religious fundamentalists will contain a preponderance of political conservatives.

predict

If the predictions made on the basis of an hypothesis are not borne out by subsequent observations, then the hypothesis is disconfirmed. Let the hypothesis be that food deprivation increases random activity.

161 Deprive a group of animals of food. If they do not become restless, then the proposition that deprivation causes restlessness is _____.

disconfirmed

162 If an hypothesis leads us to make predictions which do not come true, then the hypothesis has been _____.

disconfirmed

163 Observations undertaken for the purpose of verifying hypotheses are termed _____.

experiments

164 Clearly, an experiment tests an hypothesis by ascertaining whether the _____ made on the basis of the hypothesis come true.

predictions

165 Prediction amounts to the deduction of some of the *logical consequences* of an hypothesis (or general rule). Given the proposition that all men are mortal, we may predict that you will eventually die. This is because your dying is a _____ _____ of the propositions that all men are mortal and that you are a man.

logical consequence

166 If redheads are temperamental and if Mary is a redhead, then we may predict that Mary will be temperamental. That is to say, Mary's temperamental nature is a

logical consequence

_____ _____ of the hypothesis.

logical consequence

167 If P implies Q, then Q is a _____ _____ of P.

168 If any of the logical consequences of an hypothesis are false, then the hypothesis is _____.

false

169 If P implies Q and if Q is false, then P is _____.

false

170 To assert that Q will be true because P is true, and P implies Q is to _____ the occurrence of Q.

predict
  (or deduce)

171 If a logical consequence of an hypothesis is false, then the hypothesis is _____.

false

172 If the predictions made on the basis of an hypothesis are not borne out by subsequent observation, then the hypothesis has been _____.

falsified, shown
  to be probably
  false, etc.

Suppose the hypothesis is that a rat can be conditioned to blink its eyes in response to a sound if we present the sound shortly before flashing a bright light in its eyes. Suppose that, in order to verify this hypothesis, we repeatedly sound a buzzer immediately before flashing a bright light in a rat's eyes and then see if the sound of the buzzer alone produces eyeblinks.

experiment

173 Such a procedure may be called an _____.

predict

174 See the preceding frame. On the basis of our hypothesis we _____ that the rat will blink his eyes at the sound of the buzzer alone.

logical
  consequence

175 We make this prediction because it is a _____ _____ of the hypothesis.

disconfirmed

176 If the rat does not blink his eyes at the sound of the buzzer alone, then the hypothesis has been _____.

experimentation

177 The attempt to ascertain whether the predictions made on the basis of an hypothesis are true is termed _____.

178 Ability to predict often depends on ability to specify the *conditions* under which the predicted event may be expected to occur. If human beings learn faster when rewarded with praise, then one _____ under which it may be predicted that human beings will learn faster is verbal praise.

condition

179 If food deprivation tends to increase random activity, then one condition under which random activity may be predicted is _____ _____.

food deprivation

180 We do not merely predict. We predict that something will happen, *given* that something else happens. That is, prediction entails specifying the _____ under which the predicted event may be expected to occur.

conditions

181 When the meteorologist predicts that it will rain tomorrow, he does so because clouds are forming, the barometer is falling, etc. These constitute _____ for rain.

conditions

182 Let us define a "variable" as anything which can be present or absent, or, if present, present in greater or lesser degree. Since a person may be older or younger, age is a _____.

variable

183 A person may be a member of an upper, middle, or lower social class. The variable considered here is _____ _____.

social class

184 Whatever can vary in its value is called a _____.

variable

185 One person may be more intelligent than another. The variable here is _____.

intelligence

186 Let the hypothesis be that intelligent persons are more successful than unintelligent ones. The variables are _____ and _____.

intelligence
success

187 Two kinds of variables may be distinguished: dependent and independent variables. Independent variables are the conditions under which predictions may be made. If success can be predicted, given greater intelligence, then intelligence is the _____ variable.

independent

188 The dependent variable is so named because it "depends" on the independent variable. If success is dependent on intelligence, then success is a _____ variable.

dependent

189 A variation in the independent variable is the condition under which a variation in the dependent variable can be predicted. As conflict increases, the frequency of ulcers increases. Here, conflict is the **(1)** _____ variable, and ulcers is the **(2)** _____ variable.

(1) independent
(2) dependent

190 If higher social status increases the probability that you will get more education, then education is the **(1)** _____ variable, and social status is the **(2)** _____ variable.

(1) dependent
(2) independent

191 If an increase in the frequency of conflict situations increases the probability that a person will become neurotic, then the dependent variable is **(1)** _____, and the independent variable is **(2)** _____.

(1) neurosis
(2) conflict

192 A variation in the **(1)** _____ variable is the condition under which a variation in the **(2)** _____ variable may be predicted.

(1) independent
(2) dependent

193 (a) It is often said that the aim of the behavioral sciences is to predict behavior. This is not quite true. The aim is rather to acquire the ability to predict behavior. This means, however, that the aim is to state the conditions which will produce various behaviors. Or, put otherwise, the aim of the behavioral sciences is to relate conditions and behavior in such a way that behavior is the _____ variable. (b) If the aim of the behavioral sciences is to specify the conditions under which behavior will occur, then its aim is to express _____ as a dependent variable.

(a) dependent

(b) behavior

194 Let any given type of behavior be termed a response. Let any antecedent situation producing that type of behavior be termed a stimulus. Then the **(1)** _____ is the independent variable, and the **(2)** _____ is the dependent variable.

(1) stimulus
(2) response

195 Let S be the stimulus which produces a response R. For example, let S be a bright flash of light and let R be an eye blink. Then **(1)** _____ is the dependent variable, and **(2)** _____ is the independent variable.

(1) R—blink
(response)
(2) S—flash of
light (stimulus)

One of the basic types of law in the behavioral sciences is known as S-R law. S stands for any stimulus (antecedent condition) and R stands for a response which occurs subsequently to S. Such laws state that R will be produced by S.

(1) response (R)	**196** That is to say, S-R laws state that **(1)** _____ is
(2) stimulus (S)	the dependent variable and that **(2)** _____ is the
	independent variable.[6]

(1) random activity
(2) food deprivation

197 If food deprivation increases random activity, then the dependent variable is **(1)** _____, and the independent variable is **(2)** _____.

(1) frustration
(2) aggression

198 If frustration results in aggression, the S (independent variable) is **(1)** _____, and the R (dependent) variable is **(2)** _____.

responses (behavior)

199 Another type of law frequently found in the behavioral sciences has the form R-R. In this type of law, one kind of behavior is expressed as a function of another. That is, both the dependent and the independent variable are types of _____.

responses (behavior, performance)

200 If a person performs well on a standard intelligence test, then we may predict that he will perform well in the classroom (all other things being equal). This is an example of an R-R law, since performing in the classroom and performing on an intelligence test are both types of _____.

(1) classroom

(2) test

201 See the preceding frame. Since the response of performing well in the classroom may be predicted, given the response of performing well on an intelligence test (all else being equal), then **(1)** performance in the _____ is a dependent variable, and **(2)** performance on the _____ is an independent variable.

(1) independent
(2) dependent

202 "A person who will steal candy from a baby will murder his own grandmother." This is probably a false R-R generalization. It asserts that the response of stealing candy is the **(1)** _____ variable from which can be predicted the **(2)** _____ variable of murdering your own grandmother.

(1) responses
(2) stimuli

203 S-R laws state that **(1)** _____ are the dependent variables and **(2)** _____ are the independent variables.

[6] The terms "stimulus" and "response" are used here in very broad senses, which do not correspond to the rather special and narrow meanings frequently attached to these terms by behavioral scientists. In many contexts, for example, deprivation would not be referred to as a stimulus. No confusion should result from the present usage, however, if it is kept in mind that here stimulus means any antecedent condition and response means any behavior resulting from such a condition.

204 R-R laws state that both the dependent and independent variables are _____.

responses

205 True S-R laws allow us to predict behavior because they specify which _____ will produce that behavior.

S (stimulus, antecedent condition, independent variable)

206 To specify the S which will produce a response is to specify the _____ under which that response may be expected to occur.

conditions

207 Obviously, the condition under which an event may be expected to occur is a(n) _____ [dependent/ independent] variable.

independent

208 We may say either that the aim of the behavioral sciences is to express behavior as a (1) _____ variable or that it is to find the (2) _____ variables which are the conditions for the occurrence of given kinds of behavior.

(1) dependent
(2) independent

209 Observed correlations between two variables provide the basis for a belief that the two are related as dependent and independent variables. We believe that intelligence has something to do with success, for example, because of the _____ which has been observed to exist between success and intelligence.

correlation

210 Two variables are correlated when, as the one varies, so does the other. As the amount of formal education increases, so does the level of social class. That is to say, education and social status are _____.[7]

correlated

211 We say that there is a correlation between two variables whenever they +++++.

occur together
(vary together, etc.)

212 As conflict increases, so does the incidence of peptic ulcers. That is to say, avoidance behavior and peptic ulcers are _____.

correlated

[7] The term "correlation" is here used in a way which does not exactly correspond to the meaning frequently given it in scientific discussion. Here two events are said to be correlated if they frequently occur together. Correlation often means, however, a *measure* of the concomitant variation of two variables which ranges from -1 to $+1$ as computed by some standard statistical formula.

Two kinds of correlation may be distinguished: negative (or inverse) and positive (or direct) correlation. Two variables are positively correlated, when, one being present, so is the other, or when, as one increases, so does the other.

213 If peptic ulcers increase with conflict situations, there is a _____ _____ between these two variables.

positive correlation

214 As frustration increases, so does aggressive behavior. That is, there is a positive correlation between _____ and _____.

frustration
aggression

Negative correlation is the reverse of positive correlation. Two variables are negatively correlated when, if one is present, the other is absent, or when, as one increases, the other decreases.

215 Since fear stimuli tend to be accompanied by inhibitions in speech, there is a _____ _____ between fear and fluent speech.

negative correlation

216 As social class goes up, the incidence of diagnosed psychoses goes down. This is an example of _____ _____.

negative
  correlation

217 If we have observed that two variables have been correlated in the past, then we have some grounds for belief that we can _____ the occurrence of one, given the occurrence of the other.

predict

218 If two variables are related in such a way that, given the occurrence of one, the occurrence of the second can be predicted, then the first is an **(1)** _____ variable, and the second is a **(2)** _____ variable.

(1) independent
(2) dependent

219 We come to believe that two variables are related as dependent and independent variables when we have observed a _____ between them.

correlation

220 The hypothesis that two variables stand in the relation of dependence is frequently a generalization from observed correlations. That is, we infer that two variables, say A and B, will always be associated in the future because we have observed their association in the past. The observed associations constitute the _____ upon which we base our generalization.

sample (data)

221 We often arrive at an hypothesis that two variables are related by _____ from observed correlations.

generalization

222 If hypotheses expressing one variable as the function of another are generalizations, the same rules apply to such hypotheses as apply to any generalization. If we assert that one variable depends on another, after having observed only a very few associations between the two variables, then we are guilty of the fallacy of _____ generalization.

hasty

223 To assert that two variables will be associated in the future when we have observed them as being associated only one or two times in the past is to commit the fallacy of _____ _____ .

hasty generalization

224 Hasty generalization regarding the dependence of one variable on another is given the special name of *post hoc ergo propter hoc* fallacy. (*Post hoc ergo propter hoc* is Latin for "after this, therefore because of this.")

If I am playing poker and happen to have my girl friend's letter in my pocket, and if I win, and if I then make a practice of putting a letter from my girl friend in my pocket with the belief that this will help me win at poker, I am guilty of the $+++++$ fallacy.

post hoc ergo propter hoc

225 *Post hoc ergo propter hoc* reasoning consists in asserting that, because two variables have been observed to be associated on a *few* occasions in the past, therefore they may be expected to be associated on other occasions in the future. This is simply _____ _____ from too small a sample.

hasty generalization

226 Hypotheses are tested by _____ .

experiments

227 Once we have arrived at the hypothesis that variable *A* depends on variable *B*, because of an observed correlation between *A* and *B*, we must _____ this hypothesis.

test (verify)

The fact that a correlation between two variables has been observed does not, however, prove that one of these is the independent variable, although it constitutes some evidence for a hypothesis asserting that it is. Suppose that a psychologist has two groups of rats, *A* and *B*. He has deprived the rats in group *A* of food for forty-eight hours. He has not deprived the rats in group *B*. Group *A* learns to run a maze faster than does group *B* when both are rewarded with food for their efforts.

228 The psychologist in the example given above may be led to suppose that the deprivation was the cause of the higher rate of learning because of the correlation which exists between _____ _____ and _____.

food deprivation
learning

229 See the preceding example. Suppose that, unknown to the experimenter, the rats in group A were all offspring of a rat called "Einstein," while the rats in group B were progeny of a rat named "Mortimer Snerd" (after the stupid dummy of the ventriloquist, Edgar Bergen). Then there will also be a _____ between the intelligence of the parent and the rate of learning.

correlation

230 Reread the preceding two frames. Can the psychologist legitimately conclude that the difference in rate of learning between A and B was due exclusively to the deprivation of A?

no

231 See the preceding frame. Suppose the psychologist discovers his oversight. Can he correct his mistake and test his hypothesis by using two new groups of rats, C and D, both of which have the same parents but one of which has been deprived and the other not?

Yes

See the preceding frame. This is an illustration of the use of "control." Control is the essence of experimentation. It consists in holding some variables constant while allowing others to vary. In the preceding example, the two groups, C and D, both have the same parents. They differ in that C is deprived while D is not.

(1) parents
(2) deprivation
(or food
consumption)

232 Thus, the variable held constant is **(1)** _____, while the variable allowed (or made) to vary is **(2)** _____.

We control variables when we hold some constant while varying others. Suppose my hypothesis is that food deprivation increases learning when the animal is rewarded with food for performance. Suppose I hold intelligence, general health, and previous training constant and vary only the amount of food that I give to the animal prior to the trials.

controlling

233 Under these circumstances, I am _____ variables.

allowing others to vary (others vary, etc.)	**234** We are controlling variables when we hold some constant while +++++. Suppose there is a dispute as to whether intelligence is innate or the result of education. (Correlations of intelligence with both family members and educational level exist: Those with more education tend to score better on intelligence tests. Those with more intelligent parents tend to score better on intelligence tests.) In order to determine whether intelligence is due to innate factors, I take a group of identical twins who have been raised separately and have received different amounts of formal education.
controlling	**235** In this example I am _____ variables. (Identical twins have the same genetic constitution.)[8]
(1) native (inherited) capacities **(2)** training	**236** In the examples in the preceding frame, (1) which variable is being held constant? _____ (2) Which variable is allowed to vary? _____.
That it is probably false.	**237** See the preceding example. Suppose that, as a result of such an experiment, I discover that there is no significant difference in the intelligences of the sets of identical twins despite the fact that they have different amounts of education. What must I conclude regarding the hypothesis that intelligence is due to education? +++++.
experimental	**238** Let us term the variable which is varied the "experimental variable." If I wish to determine the effect of food deprivation on learning and if I attempt to do this by holding everything constant except the amount of food given the experimental animals, then the amount of food dispensed is the _____ variable.

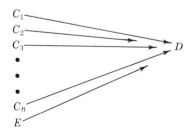

[8] This example is suggested by the famous twin studies of Newman, Freeman, and Holzinger. See H. H. Newman, R. N. Freeman, and K. J. Holzinger, *Twins: A Study of Heredity and Environment*, The University of Chicago Press, Chicago, 1937.

239 In the above diagram, the C's are independent variables which are held constant. D is the dependent variable. E is the independent variable which is allowed to vary. That is, E is the _____ variable.

experimental

240 By controlling variables, we eliminate the possibility that any variation in the dependent variable is due to those variables which were held constant. If we have kept the inheritance of our subjects constant while varying the amount of education they have received and if the scores of these subjects on intelligence tests are variable, then we have eliminated the possibility that this variation is due to any variation in _____ (since there is no such variation).

inheritance
(heredity)

If we take two groups of rats of equal health before an experiment and require them, in order to obtain food, to cross a grill which will give them an electric shock, and if the incidence of ulcers in that group tends to run significantly higher than it does in a group which was not placed in this conflict situation, then we can conclude that the higher incidence of ulcers was not due to a difference in the *health* of the two groups.

241 If the difference in the incidence of ulcers between the two groups was not due to a difference in health, and if it was due to *either* a difference in health or to the difference in stimulus (conflict situation), then we may conclude that it was due to a difference in _____.

stimulus
(conflict
situation)

242 The ideal of experimentation is to keep all variables constant except one. This variable is known as the _____ variable.

experimental

The point of keeping all independent variables constant except one is to eliminate the possibility that any variation in the dependent variable is due to any except the experimental variable. Let the independent variables held constant be $C_1, C_2, C_3 \ldots C_n$. E is the independent variable which is varied, that is, the experimental variable. D is the dependent variable.

cannot (if they have
really been held
constant, then
there is no varia-
tion in them.)

243 In this example, if there is any variation in D, then it _____ [can/cannot] be attributed to any variation in $C_1, C_2, C_3, \ldots$ or C_n. Justify your answer. $+++++$

E (experimental
variable)

244 See the preceding frame. If the variation in D must be attributed to one or the other of the independent variables, then since it cannot be attributed to either of the C's, it must be attributed to _____.

experiments

245 Hypotheses are tested by _____.

246 Good experiments involve the attempt to hold some variables constant while allowing others to vary. This is known as the use of _____.

control

247 The variables allowed to vary are known as _____ variables.

experimental

248 In an experiment, how shall we choose what is to be our experimental variable? The answer is that it should be the one which, according to our hypothesis, accounts for variation in the dependent variable. Suppose the hypothesis is that I_1 results in D. Let the other independent variables be $I_1 \ldots I_n$. Since what we want to know is whether a variation in I_1 will result in a variation in D, the experimental variable will be _____.

I_1

249 If the hypothesis is that brand Y of toothpaste can reduce the incidence of cavities, and if the other variables are frequency and method of brushing teeth, diet, etc., then the experimental variable will be _____.

brand of
toothpaste

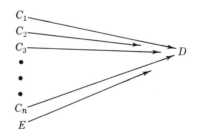

E, because this is
the only one
varied.

250 Here the C's are held constant. E is varied. D is the dependent variable. If there is any variation in D, then it must be attributed to _____. Why? $+++++$.

251 If the hypothesis asserts that intelligence increases the probability of success, then the independent variable, which will be our experimental variable, will be _____.

intelligence

One way to secure controls is to use the method of control groups. This method has been used in the examples so far considered. It consists of taking two groups, alike in all respects except one. One way to ensure that the two groups are alike is to *match* them. For example, if I wish to be sure that the intelligence of two groups of persons is the same, I may give intelligence tests to a number of persons and then choose two groups of persons which have the same average intelligence as shown by the test.

252 If I take two groups and be sure they are the same in some respect by comparing them in advance, then I am _____ them.

matching

Matching is difficult when the number of variables increases. When matching becomes impractical, the alternative is to use two groups which are both randomly chosen from the same population. Since there is a probability that random samples will be like the population, then there is a probability that they will be like each other.

controlling (matching will do)

253 If a psychologist uses two groups of rats randomly chosen from the rats in his laboratory, then he is _____ variables by the use of random sampling.

254 If two groups from the same population cannot be matched, then their similarity can be made more probable if each of the two groups is a _____ sample.

random

255 The two basic ways of increasing the probability that the two groups to be used in an experiment are alike in relevant respects are:
(1) +++++
(2) +++++

(1) to match them
(2) to choose both groups randomly from the sample population

SUMMARY

If men are ever to arrive at anything like the truth about human behavior and its causes, they must proceed as scientists. This means that they must employ the methods of science.

In broad outline, these methods are obvious, simple, and easily stated; one need only reason well from accurate and relevant data. To practice them successfully and to specify them in greater detail are, however, considerably more difficult undertakings.

Getting accurate and relevant data entails knowing what to observe and observing it with skill, with care, and without bias. This is easier said than done, particularly when it is ourselves that we are investigating. Nevertheless, empirical data are a desideratum of science, and no scientist will countenance a theory which lacks observational warrant. Every serious scientific hypothesis must be publicly verifiable, at least indirectly and in principle.

Reasoning well is a matter of following certain rules. Generalization, for example, should be premised on a sufficiently large sample randomly selected from the population. This requires systematic and careful procedure, not haphazardness. Only with system and care is there any probability that generalization will be correct.

Observation and generalization are only the beginning. They pose the problem of explanation: Why (under what conditions) do human beings behave as they do? It is the business of behavioral scientists eventually to attempt to express behavior as the function of specified conditions— that is, to suggest hypotheses in which responses are dependent variables and antecedent conditions are the independent variables. Hypotheses of the right kind permit prediction and thereby experimentation. For if they are true and if we experimentally control the variables, then certain results should ensue—a principle which defines the scientist's methods of confirming and disconfirming theories.

REFERENCES

Cohen, Morris R., and Ernest Nagel: *Introduction to Logic and Scientific Method,* book II, Harcourt, Brace & World, Inc., New York, 1934.

Copi, Irving M.: *Introduction to Logic,* part III, the Macmillan Company, New York, 1961.

Feigl, Herbert, and May Brodbeck (eds.): *Readings in the Philosophy of Science,* Appleton-Century-Crofts, Inc., New York, 1953.

Kimble, Gregory A.: *Principles of General Psychology,* chap. 2, The Ronald Press Company, New York, 1956.

Little, Winston W., W. Harold Wilson, and W. Edgar Moore: *Applied Logic,* part III, Houghton Mifflin Company, Boston, 1955.

Madden, Edward H.: *The Structure of Scientific Thought,* esp. Introduction, Houghton Mifflin Company, Boston, 1960.

SELF-REVIEW QUIZ

1 If we have the means to verify an hypothesis, we say it is verifiable in (a) _____; even though we may not have the means, if they are such as could conceivably become available, we say the hypothesis is verifiable in (b) _____.

2 Verification which consists of observation of the thing itself is (a) _____ verification; verification which consists of observing the effects is (b) _____ verification.

3 Verification by one person is (a) _____verification; verification by many is (b) _____ verification.

4 As we have here used the term, to verify (test) an hypothesis is (a) to confirm it, (b) to disconfirm it, or (c) to confirm or disconfirm it.

5 Suppose four-fifths of laboring men who are questioned say that they approve of social security. It is then inferred that four-fifths of all laboring men approve of social security. Then the laboring men questioned constitute the (a) _____, laboring men as a whole constitute the (b) _____, and the inference from (a) to (b) is known as a (c) _____.

6 Suppose that we carefully employ procedures designed to give every laboring man an equal chance with every other of being questioned. Then we are taking what is known as a (a) _____ _____.
Suppose on the other hand, that we, deliberately or unwittingly, exclude all carpenters. Since we shall be giving some laborers more chance than others of being selected, we shall be taking a (b) _____ _____.

7 Suppose that, although only four-fifths of those questioned approve of social security, fully 95 per cent of all laborers approve of social security. In such a case, we cannot claim to have taken a _____ _____, that is, one with the same relevant characteristics as the entire group of laboring men.

8 If we have given every laboring man an equal chance with every other of being questioned, then it is _____ [(a) impossible/(b) possible/(c) probable/(d) improbable/(e) certain] that the group questioned will divide on social security in the same way as do laboring men in general.

9 In order to ensure that every laboring man has an equal chance of being questioned, it is best to proceed by choosing whomever you will question in (a) a very offhand, haphazard manner; (b) in some systematically mechanical manner.

10 If we question only a very, very few laboring men but draw an inference regarding all laboring men, then we commit the fallacy known as _____ _____.

11 That which can have different values at different times and places (e.g., age) is known as a _____.

12 Suppose that social status goes up with educational level. Then social status and education have (a) _____ _____. Suppose, on the other hand, that, as one goes up, the other goes down. Then they have (b) _____ _____.

13 A test of an hypothesis which consists of observations made under controlled conditions for the purpose of ascertaining whether the predictions made on the basis of the hypothesis come true is termed an

_____.

14 Let the hypothesis be that alcohol produces a reduction in fear response. In order to test this hypothesis, we shall want to hold everything constant except the quantity of (a) _____; what we thus vary is known as the (b) _____ _____.

15 The procedure of holding some variables constant while allowing others to vary is known as _____.

16 In laws of the S-R form, the stimulus is the antecedent condition which produces a response. In such laws, the stimulus is therefore known as the (a) _____ variable; the response is the (b) _____.

17 Suppose the result of an experiment in which the hypothesis is of the form S-R is that there is no variation in R upon a variation in S. Then the hypothesis is said to be _____ by that experiment.

part II

The Biological Bases of Behavior

Edwin P. Martin

The importance of knowing how the body regulates human behavior is readily apparent. The purpose of this unit is to provide such information. Specifically, it is concerned with the mechanisms of heredity and the nervous and endocrine systems.

The way that most people interpret adages like "Great oaks from little acorns grow" and "Like father, like son" suggests that the importance of heredity is well recognized. The student of human behavior should be reasonably familiar with the ways that inherited characteristics are transmitted. He should also understand how heredity and environment interact to influence behavior. These topics are presented in Unit 1.

Unit 2 provides information about the biological integration of behavior. The brain serves as a reception center for incoming sensory stimuli, as a repository for experienced events, and as a relay center for transmitting information to various parts of the body. The central nervous system is primarily concerned with volitional activity. The decision to do something or to learn something involves deliberate activity. The central nervous system is concerned with such activity. The autonomic nervous system is more concerned with behavior over which the individual has little volitional control. Digestion, respiration, and most emotional reactions are examples of such behavior.

Knowledge of these body systems permits a wider understanding of human learning. Two major types of learning, operant (instrumental) conditioning and classical Pavlovian (emotional) conditioning, are dependent on different aspects of nervous-system activity. Material included in this unit will enable you to understand learning concepts better when you are introduced to them. It should also enable you to understand better some of the concepts presented in later sections about human development and emotional behavior.

unit 1

Heredity and Behavior

All the divergent views of the nature of man include some biological statements. Man is, at least, a biological object. He may be a biological object plus a variety of non-biological traits, but he cannot avoid his biological self, although many people think that he may transcend it.

In order to investigate human behavior, therefore, we begin with a consideration of its biological foundations. You know something about biology already; you should learn a bit more as you work through the next two units. The biological concepts of these units will help you to investigate, describe, analyze, and explain many of the problems considered later in the book.

Unit 1 is concerned primarily with heredity; it presents the relations between the biological properties transmitted from one generation to another and human behavior. It also considers the relations between heredity and environment as factors affecting behavior. Before examining heredity, you will study a short section dealing with homeostasis, or steady state. Homeostasis is a goal of much low-order behavior (shared with other animals), and the feedback type of regulation so common in biological homeostasis is an important type of regulatory mechanism for things as different as body temperature, missile trajectories, and, according to some people, learning.

When you finish Unit 1, we hope you will understand the following concepts:

1. The form of simple feedback systems
2. The simple mechanisms by which information is transferred from parents to children
3. The form of the interaction of heredity and environment
4. The simpler elements of the pattern relating genes and behavior
5. The usefulness of a knowledge of genetics to a student of human behavior, as well as the limits of the present state of that knowledge

Homeostasis

1 All sorts of life have relatively narrow ranges of environmental factors, e.g., temperature, within which they can _____ .

exist (survive)

2 In order to exist, living things must either find a place where the environment remains within the appropriate limits, or they must, by their own activities, hold the _____ within these limits.

environment

3 Biologists use the word "homeostasis" (steady state) for a situation in which the internal _____ fluctuations are held within tolerable limits.

environmental

4 Since man endures widely fluctuating external environments, he achieves _____ primarily by maintaining a steady internal environment.

homeostasis

5 The homeostatic condition does not mean that an environmental factor is unchanging. Rather, small controlled variations around a central value are typical of _____ .

homeostasis

6 Since homeostasis is necessary for life and a primary goal of behavior is to maintain life in an optimum state, a secondary goal of _____ is the maintenance of homeostasis.

behavior

7 In order to maintain homeostasis, any deviation from homeostasis must stimulate _____ which changes the environmental factor back toward the homeostatic value.

behavior

8 To maintain a homeostatic value, behavior must change the value of an environmental factor in a direction _____ to that of the deviation from homeostasis.

opposite

9 For example, if the blood-sugar concentration increases above the "normal" value, homeostatic mechanisms must cause it to _____ .

decrease

10 When the blood sugar increases in response to an environmental stimulus, this response becomes, in turn, a stimulus for a new set of responses which _____ the blood sugar.

decrease

11 A thermostat in a house is a simple example of a homeostatic system. When the temperature in the house decreases, the thermostat responds by +++++.

turning on the heat

12 When the heat is turned on, the temperature **(1)** _____; i.e., the value of the environmental factor concerned changes in a direction **(2)** _____ to the original deviation.

(1) rises (increases)
(2) opposite

13 As the heat continues to raise the temperature, the point at which the thermostat is set is passed, the heat is turned off, and the temperature begins to _____.

fall (decrease)

14 In the thermostatically controlled house, the thermostat responds to a decreasing temperature by causing it to **(1)** _____, and to an **(2)** _____ temperature by causing it to fall.

(1) rise
(2) increasing

15 In a thermostatic system, the response, a change in temperature, is fed back into the system as a stimulus to _____ the direction of the change.

reverse

16 In any homeostatic system, a response is fed back into the system as a _____ for homeostasis, and the result is a state in which the value concerned fluctuates around the optimum value. Such systems are often called "feedback systems."

stimulus

17 Some behavior by which man adjusts to his external environment can be explained as efforts to maintain _____.

homeostasis

18 The adding and removing of coats and sweaters as the external temperature varies is an effort to be comfortable, or to maintain an acceptable external _____. This is a crude example of mechanisms used to maintain homeostasis.

temperature (or,
environment)

19 A student with a reputation as a good student responds to an announcement of a test by extra work in an effort to maintain his status. His behavior might be described as analogous to a _____ mechanism.

homeostatic

20 *Review:* It is clear that one of the goals of _____ is homeostasis.

behavior

21 Homeostasis, at least in the biological sense, is maintained by feedbacks, i.e., feeding a response back into the system as a _____.

stimulus

22 Some overt behavior may be explained as a complex series of feedbacks aimed at maintaining biological or psychological _____.

homeostasis

You have now learned that organisms need to maintain a steady internal environment and, in a rudimentary way, that the principle of negative feedback is the basis for the systems which regulate internal conditions. Can you identify both similarities and differences between a thermostat regulating temperature in a house and an organism regulating its internal environment?

The Hereditary Material

Behavior is partly determined by constitutional factors which are received from parents. An elementary knowledge of the processes by which offspring receive these factors from parents should be helpful as you pursue your study of behavior. We shall begin with a brief look at the material basis of heredity.

inherit

23 Plants and animals usually resemble their ancestors because they _____ characteristics from them.

development

24 The fertilized egg from which an organism arises does not show the characteristics of the parents but acquires them by a *developmental* process. What is inherited is not the characteristics, per se, but a set of *instructions* for their _____.

instructions

25 When sperm and egg cells are formed, the nuclear material behaves with precision, while the cytoplasm behaves in a less predictable fashion. It seems, therefore, that the set of _____ for development must be primarily nuclear.

instructions

26 One substance, found only and always in nuclei, is DNA (deoxyribonucleic acid). The *substance* which is inherited and which carries the _____ for development is DNA.

development

27 A DNA molecule has no arms or legs. The information it carries is coded; i.e., an instruction for _____ corresponds to a molecular configuration.

unit

28 The fact that characteristics can be treated separately in an analysis of heredity indicates that the DNA is inherited in units. Each hereditary _____ of DNA is called a gene.

29 Genes cannot be seen in cells. At cell division, how- ever, bodies called chromosomes can be seen in the nuclei; these visible bodies are carefully divided. The distribution of characteristics from parents to offspring fits the assump- tion that the genes are on the _____.

chromosomes

30 Although _____ cannot be seen, the pattern of their distribution among eggs and sperms can be inferred from the distribution of the chromosomes.

genes

31 Since characteristics vary, e.g., eyes may be blue or brown, genes must also vary. For example, the process by which a gene for brown eyes changes to a _____ for blue eyes is called mutation.

gene

32 The variety of genes for a trait, which can be dis- tributed by reproduction, is one of the major sources of individual differences. This variety has occurred as a re- sult of _____.

mutation

33 The development of each biochemical form in the body is affected by one or more genes, i.e., molecules of _____.

DNA

34 Form and function are inseparable biologically. The effect of genes on form means that genes also affect _____.

function

Human behavior is the behavior of a particular kind of biological object. It is partly determined, therefore, by heredity.

Chromosomes in Reproduction

Egg cells and sperm cells are formed by a maturational process so that each gamete (sex cell) has half as many chromosomes as an ordinary body cell. Since the genes are on the chromosomes, each gamete has half of the genes of the persons involved. In the cells other than gametes, including fertilized eggs, chromosomes occur in pairs. One member of each pair comes from the father and one from the mother.

35 The paired chromosomes mean that for each char- acteristic an individual has at least _____ genes.

two

one	**36** As a result of the processes of gamete formation, one member of each chromosome pair goes to each gamete. Every gamete contains at least _____ gene for each characteristic.
genes	**37** Each gamete is a selection of one-half of the genes available, and is a sample of the total population of _____.
pair	**38** Each sample of genes, i.e., gamete, must contain one member of each _____ of genes, and thus contains a complete set, i.e., at least one gene for each characteristic.
will not	**39** Let us consider a simple sampling process. If several samples of fifty students are randomly drawn from a group of one hundred students, the percentage of boys _____ [will/will not] be the same in all samples.
samples	**40** The differences in percentage of boys in the _____ are not due to variation in the population sampled, since they were all drawn from the same population.
population	**41** Since the differences in percentage of boys are not due to variation in _____, they must be a function of the sampling process.
sampling	**42** Gametes possess variability because they are also formed by a _____ process.
chromosomes	**43** Since the genes are on chromosomes, it is not the genes but the _____ that are actually distributed during reduction division.
chromosomes	**44** There are two possible kinds of gametes for each pair of _____ in an adult individual.
four (two to the second power)[1]	**45** For an organism with two pairs of chromosomes, there are _____ kinds of gametes possible.
eight (two to the third power)	**46** For an individual with three pairs of chromosomes there are _____ kinds of gametes possible.
2^{23}	**47** For man, with twenty-three pairs of chromosomes, there are _____ kinds of gametes possible. This is a very large number (8,402,608 specifically).

[1] Two to the second power, written 2^2, means two times two, or four. Two to the third power, written 2^3, is eight. The use of the exponent is convenient for large numbers, such as those in some of the frames to follow.

gametes

variation

differ

resemble

behavior

48 In sexual reproduction, additional variation in off-spring occurs because of the fusion of varied _____ from two parents in fertilization.

49 When _____ due to mutation, reduction division, and fertilization are summed, the number of possible types of men is greater than the population of the world.

50 *Review:* Just as human beings differ in many details of body type, so do they _____ in many details of behavior.

51 Nonetheless, just as human beings resemble each other physically in fundamental structure, so they _____ each other in fundamental patterns of behavior.

52 Both the differences and the resemblances, in structure and in _____, are partly based on genetic factors.

Single-factor Inheritance

In the following section, you will apply your knowledge of the material basis of heredity to some patterns of distribution of traits among generations. Since many of the items in this section refer, directly or by implication, to Figure 1, you should study it carefully before you begin. Recent research has shown that the inheritance of phenylketonuria is considerably more complex than is indicated by the pedigree shown. However, the simplified pattern is useful to help you learn about hereditary processes.

Phenylketonuria is a metabolic deficiency which causes a type of mental deficiency. Since it is a genetic trait, a genetically simple trait (i.e., apparently controlled by one gene), and a behavioral trait, it will serve us well as an example.

Our example also illustrates the concepts of dominance and recessiveness. Your understanding of these concepts will be developed as you work the program, but a brief preparatory explanation may be helpful. A recessive trait is one which is expressed only when two genes for it are present. If the gene for the recessive trait is present with the gene for the dominant trait, the dominant trait will be expressed. For instance, if red flowers are dominant and white flowers recessive, only plants with two genes for white flowers will in fact have white flowers. Plants with one of each of the genes for flower color, as well as plants with two genes for red flowers, will in fact have red flowers.

To be sure you understand the pedigree in Figure 1, answer a couple of simple questions.

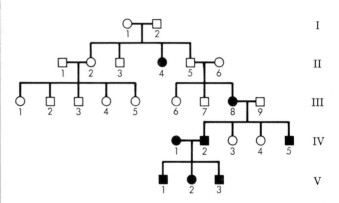

Figure 1. Pedigree of mental deficiency due to phenylketonuria. In this pedigree, generations are numbered with Roman numerals and individuals within a generation by Arabic numerals. Squares represent males and circles represent females. A horizontal line connecting a square with a circle indicates a marriage. A vertical line extending from a marriage line connects the parents with the offspring of that marriage. Blackened symbols represent persons with the mental deficiency; open symbols represent persons normal with respect to phenylketonuria.

uncle

53 What relation is II–3 to III–1?

grandmother

54 What relation is I–1 to III–8?

sister

55 What relation is III–1 to III–5?

mental deficiency

56 Individual II–4 was mentally deficient. This means (in this particular kind of mental deficiency) that II–4 has a gene for _____ _____.

I–2

57 Since II–4 has at least one gene for mental deficiency, either I–1 or _____ must also have a gene for mental deficiency.

gene

58 Since neither I–1 nor I–2 is mentally deficient, it is possible to have a _____ without it being evident.

more than one (two)

59 If one gene for mental deficiency does not make a person mentally deficient, II–4 must have +++++ genes for the symptoms.

more than once (twice)	**60** The gene for this type of mental deficiency, then, is one which expresses itself only when present +++++.
one	**61** A person with only _____ gene(s) for the trait does not show it but can transmit it to his offspring.
100	**62** Of the offspring of the marriage between IV–1 and IV–2, _____ per cent will be mentally deficient.
Yes	**63** Does III–9 have a gene for mental deficiency?
Yes	**64** Does IV–4 have a gene for mental deficiency?
Yes	**65** Could IV–5 have normal children?
Marriage to a woman with two normal genes.	**66** How could IV–5 have normal children when no normal gene is present? +++++
Either 1–1 or 1–2.	**67** Where in the ancestry of III–3 do you know a gene for mental deficiency to be? +++++
Some descendants of I–1 and I–2 are mentally deficient.	**68** How do you know? +++++
genetic	**69** From this example, you have learned that at least one kind of mental deficiency has a simple _____ basis.
genetic	**70** It follows, then, that at least some traits we usually call behavioral have a _____ basis.
gene	**71** From this example, you have also learned that an individual may have a _____ without showing it.
transmit	**72** An individual possessing a gene which is not apparent may nonetheless be genetically important because he may _____ the gene to his children.
genetic	**73** *Review:* In general, we may say (generalizing from this example) that the _____ basis of traits, be-
genetic	havioral and otherwise, is not always obvious, and careful study may be required to elucidate even simple _____ mechanisms.
genes	**74** Although eye color in human beings is quite varied, it is possible to identify two basic classes—blue and brown. Studies have shown that, like phenylketonuria (Figure 1), the basic class of eye color is controlled by a single pair of _____.

75 Since blue eyes constitute a single-gene character, which is expressed only when an individual has two genes for it, Figure 1 could also be a pedigree of eye color with the blackened symbols representing _____ persons.

blue-eyed

The inheritance of eye color and phenylketonuria can be studied together. Such studies show that the two characters are inherited independently of each other. Thus, in a marriage between a brown-eyed, mentally deficient man and a blue-eyed, normal woman who carries a gene for the mental deficiency, four kinds of children (with respect to the two characteristics) might be produced.

76 Of the four kinds of children produced, two will be different from the **(1)** _____ and two will be **(2)** _____ to the parents.

(1) parents
(2) similar

77 The above example shows that the complex of factors making up a human being is not inherited as a single package, but is _____ as a large number of genetic factors which may be combined in a variety of packages.

inherited

78 No genetic trait can be present in a child which was not present in one of its parents (whether expressed or hidden) but new combinations of _____ may produce children quite different from either parent.

genes

79 *Review:* These examples illustrate the point made earlier in this chapter, that variety is enhanced by recombination of existing **(1)** _____ as well as by the large number of **(2)** _____ genes in the human race.

(1) genes
(2) different

80 So far, we have considered only characteristics which had only _____ [two/four/eight] different genes which could affect them.

two

Multiple-allelic Inheritance

You can now, we hope, give simple but useful answers to the questions of why children resemble their parents in some ways, but not in others, and why some children resemble their parents more than others. Clearly, much of human inheritance is more complex than the examples you have studied. Although an extensive knowledge of genetics is unnecessary for the purposes of this book, it will help you to study some examples of slightly more complicated patterns.

The letters in Tables 1 and 2 each symbolize a gene. If the gene pair involves dominance, the capital letters represent dominant genes and the small letters recessive genes. In Table 1, neither A nor B is dominant relative to each other, but both are dominant relative to O.

Table 1. Blood Types and Genotypes

Blood type	Genotypes (One gene from each parent)
A	AA, AO
B	BB, BO
AB	AB
O	OO

81 Human blood types clearly depend on at least three genes, A, B, and O, with no more than two of them present in any one individual. Such a characteristic is like phenylketonuria or eye color in that a person inherits _____ gene for the trait from each of his parents.

82 Such a characteristic differs from phenylketonuria or eye color because there are more than _____ possible genes which can be inherited from a parent.

83 Table 1 shows the various genotypes that may cause each blood type. Gene O behaves as did the genes for mental deficiency and blue eyes, i.e., it is expressed only when +++++ are present.

84 Although both gene A and B are able to mask gene _____ (see Table 1), neither can mask the other.

85 If both gene A and gene B are present, both will be _____.

86 If a type-A woman married a type-A man, you know that they could not have a type-_____ child.

87 (Refer to Table 1) If a type-A woman married a type-B man, you know that they *might* have a child with the following blood types: _____.

one

two

two genes

O

expressed (apparent)

B

A, B, AB, O

To summarize the last several items, some characteristics may be affected by two or more kinds of genes. Such traits are described as multiple-allelic traits. Multiple-allelic traits differ from traits controlled by two possible alternate genes by showing more variability.

Quantitative Inheritance

The types of heredity so far studied have dealt with easily defined classes of individuals. It is obvious, however, that many important kinds of characteristics are not inherited by the genetic mechanisms so far described. You will recall, from the mental-deficiency example, that an individual with two different genes expressed only one of them.

88 If an individual with two different genes expresses only _____ of them, we call the expressed gene dominant.

one

89 The gene which is not _____ in an individual, such as the one described above, is labeled a recessive gene.

expressed

90 For a trait with a dominant and recessive gene, then, there are two combinations of _____ which produce the dominant trait.

genes

91 The two gene combinations referred to above are: (1) two dominant genes; and (2) one dominant and one _____ gene.

recessive

92 In the example on blood types, dominance was exemplified when either gene _____ or gene _____ was combined with gene O.

A or B

93 However, when gene A was combined with gene B, the blood type was _____.

AB

94 When gene A and gene B are combined, then, neither is dominant and _____ _____ are expressed. Such a phenomenon is often called blending inheritance.

both genes

95 All of these examples refer to traits which are discontinuous; i.e., each trait may be easily divided into _____ or more distinct classes (e.g., eye color, extra digits, deafness).

two

96 Many traits, some of them of considerable significance, vary continuously, i.e., they cannot be easily divided into _____ classes.

discrete (distinct)

97 In man, height, intelligence, skin color, and resistance to disease are examples of traits which vary _____.

continuously

98 Although, at first glance, a theory of inheritance by units (i.e., by _____) seems unable to explain the distribution of a trait which varies continuously, we shall show how it can.

genes

99 As stated above, and as is also evident from your observation, human skin color is an example of a trait which varies _____.

continuously

Table 2. Gene Combinations for Skin Color in Man (on hypothesis of two pairs of relevant genes)

Color class	Possible gene combinations
White	aabb
Light mulatto	Aabb, aaBb
Mulatto	AAbb, aaBB, AaBb
Dark mulatto	AABb, AaBB
Black	AABB

100 The fact that skin color _____ with environmental change, e.g., exposure to sun, is also common knowledge.

varies

101 We shall explore variation due to environment later. At the moment, let us consider that part of the variation in skin color is due to _____ factors.

genetic

102 The left-hand column of Table 2 shows five classes of skin color. Such a division of skin color into _____ classes is to some extent arbitrary.

five

103 If the color of skin is a really continuous variable, the number of classes is an _____ choice.

arbitrary

104 The number, five, in Table 2, although _____, is based on observation and represents the best inductive judgment of investigators.

arbitrary

105 In order to explain the theory of _____ of skin color which results in five classes, an hypothesis of two pairs of genes, inherited independently, is required.

inheritance

106 The right column of Table 2 shows all the possible gene combinations for each of the five _____ of skin color.

classes

107 The two extreme classes, black and white, can each be produced by _____ gene combination.

one

108 The classes "light mulatto" and "dark mulatto" can each be produced by _____ combinations of genes.

two

109 The class "mulatto" can be produced by _____ [one/two/three/four] different combinations of genes.

three

110 An examination of Table 2 shows that the critical genetic factor, i.e., the property of the gene combinations which determines the color, is represented by the number of _____ letters.

capital

111 The more capital letters present, the _____ the skin color.

darker

112 Genes A and _____ affect the skin color in the same way.

B

113 The genes indicated by the capital letters appear to add their effects on _____ _____.

skin color

114 *Review:* Each color class, therefore, is determined by the _____ of capital letters present, not by the kind of capital letters present.

number

Let us now determine the kinds of gametes which can be derived from the various combinations of genes. If you have forgotten the mechanisms of gamete formation, go back to frames 35 to 52 and review them before proceeding.

115 How many kinds of gametes can a white person produce? _____

one

116 A cross between two white persons (see Table 2) can produce _____ kind(s) of child(ren).

one

117 How many kinds of gametes can a black person produce? _____.

one

118 A cross between a white person and a black person can produce children with _____ kind(s) of skin color.

one

119 Children from a cross between a white person and a black person would belong to the color class(es) _____.

120 How many kinds of gametes could possibly come from a population of light mulattos? (See Table 2.) _____

121 What are the types (in terms of letters) of gametes possible from the class light mulatto? (Remember that each gamete must have one of the *a* genes and one of the *b* genes.)

122 How many types of gametes could a *single* light mulatto individual produce?

123 How many capital letters are in each of the kinds of gametes referred to in frame 122? +++++

124 How many different color classes could the children of two light mulattos include? _____

125 The three classes referred to in frame 124 have skin colors of white, light mulatto, and _____.

126 Without continuing through the rest of Table 2 in the same detail, let us consider a couple of questions to make sure you have understood the last several items. How many kinds of gametes could a population of dark mulattos produce? _____

127 What is the maximum number of color classes of children that could be produced by a cross between two mulattos? _____

Such traits as intelligence and height, which appear to vary continuously, are inherited in ways similar to, but more complex than, that described for skin color. Any hypothesis to explain these requires many more classes and therefore more genes. In addition, the genetic factor is modified by the environment, a phenomenon that you will study later in the unit.

Sex and Inheritance

128 One of the obvious and basic differences among human beings is that of sex. Two classes are easily defined. Since there are but two basic classes, we would expect the difference to be due to a _____ gene.

Left margin answers:

mulatto

three

Ab, aB, ab

two

one and none

three

mulatto

three

five

single

gene

129 Biologists have been unable to find a single sex _____, but they have discovered a difference between the sexes in chromosomes.

females

130 Males and females have twenty-two pairs of chromosomes in common, but the twenty-third pair differs. Males have a pair of chromosomes labeled XY, and _____ have a pair labeled XX.

chromosome

131 Thus, the basic difference between the sexes is due to a single _____, although an enormous number of genes affect sex in one way or another.

one

132 Females can produce _____ kind(s) of gamete, as far as the sex chromosomes are concerned.

X, Y

133 Males produce two kinds of gamete, as far as the sex chromosomes are concerned, one with an _____ chromosome and one with a _____ chromosome.

XX

134 In the laboratory, manipulation of hormones in embryos can override the chromosomal determination of sex and produce XY females and _____ males.

sex

135 Such experiments indicate that the genes determining _____ act via hormones, at least in part.

genetics (inheritance)

136 Such overriding of genetic factors by external factors also indicates that sex is only partly determined by _____ and that it is also affected by environment.

female

137 In addition to the two sexes, it is clear from observation that there are many anatomical and behavioral differences within the classes of male and _____.

138 Since there is so much variation within each sex, it seems that although maleness or femaleness may be determined by a single chromosome difference, the total pattern of sexuality is determined by a large number of _____ pairs.

gene

skin color

139 This kind of inheritance is basically like that studied in connection with _____ _____.

gene

140 Review: Like skin color, sexuality is partly a function of the environment and partly a function of _____ combinations.

141 Some genes are carried on the X chromosome. If these genes are recessive, their expression will _____ in the two sexes.

differ (be different)

142 A recessive gene on the X chromosome in a female would be expressed only if it were present in both _____ chromosomes.

X

143 A recessive gene on the X chromosome in a male would always be expressed. There can be no dominant gene to mask it, since there is no other _____ chromosome.

X

144 Genes on the X chromosome are called sex-linked, and the traits affected will be inherited differently from those controlled by _____ on other chromosomes.

genes

145 Behavioral differences between sexes are partly due to the social environment, but appear to be partly due to _____ factors as well.

genetic

As mentioned above, many characteristics are partly hereditary and partly environmental. Since the environment will be prominent as you continue your study of behavior throughout the book, the next section is directly concerned with the interaction between genetic endowment and environment as they affect an organism.

Heredity and Environment

146 All organisms have genes, and all organisms exist in an environment. We have already established the idea that people vary, in part, because of the effects of the genes. We now need to investigate the role of the _____.

environment

147 Since both genes and environment are always present, we can expect each individual to be affected by both _____ and environment.

genes (heredity)

148 We might repeat the same thing in other words. Early in this unit we said that the _____ were a code which partially determined the structure and behavior of organisms.

genes

149 We can say that the decoding process occurs in an environment and that variations in the environment would cause _____ in the way the code was translated into structure and behavior.

variations

genes	**150** The directions for the development of an organism encoded in the _____ are directions of an "if . . . then" sort.
if, then	**151** To say that they are "if . . . then" directions can be expanded to say that the genetic instructions are that _____ the environment provides certain items, _____ specified developmental events will occur.
gene	**152** Let us now examine a few specific examples of the relations between genes and environment. In chickens, it has been established that yellow legs are hereditary and that there is a single _____ for yellow legs.
dominant	**153** In the absence of the gene for yellow legs, the leg color is gray. If the yellow gene and the gray gene are both present, the legs will be yellow, i.e., the gene for yellow is _____ and the one for gray is recessive.
gene	**154** Some chickens, known to carry the _____ for yellow legs, fail to develop the yellow color.
yellow	**155** Investigation of these cases has showed that a yellow pigment, xanthin, was absent from the chickens' diet. If xanthin is added to the diet, the _____ color develops.
(1) gene (2) environmental (dietary)	**156** Yellow legs, then, require that the **(1)** _____ for yellow legs be inherited from parents, and also that a specific **(2)** _____ factor be present.
the characteristic (yellow legs)	**157** In the example cited, neither the environmental factor nor the genetic factor can produce $+++++$ alone.
gene	**158** Let us look now at a more complex example. Japanese couples who moved to California produced children whose height, as a group, was significantly greater than that of the parents, as a group. This shift in a population measurement was much too sudden to be due to shifts in the _____ combinations involved.
environmental	**159** Since the genetic endowment was essentially unchanged, the cause of the variation in height between the two groups must have been an _____ factor.
environmental	**160** In this case, we can probably determine the relevant _____ factors from our knowledge of human biology and of cultural differences between Japan and California.

161 Japanese eat markedly less, as well as different kinds of, protein than do Californians, and protein is known to be closely related to growth. The part of the environment causing the variation in height was probably +++++.

the protein in the diet

162 Clearly, the _____ instructions for the development of height were "if . . . then" instructions.

genetic

163 *Review:* The relations between genes and environment in this example might be stated thus: _____ the environment provides proper nutrition, _____ the height permitted by the genetic endowment will be achieved.

if, then

164 As a final example, let us examine the situation of intelligence. If a population of rats is tested with a maze problem, some of them will solve it better than others. The better ones can be called more _____ than their less successful colleagues.

intelligent

If bright rats are mated with each other and dull rats are also mated with each other, the offspring of the two matings will overlap extensively as far as their ability to solve the maze problem is concerned. This wide and continuous variation of the trait is reminiscent of our earlier example of the inheritance of skin color and suggests that many genes are involved with the trait.

165 After several generations of such selective matings, however, the overlap is practically eliminated, and we have a population of bright rats and one of _____ rats.

dull

166 Since all the rats shared essentially the same environment, the variation in problem-solving ability must be due to _____ factors.

genetic

167 Consider now the expression of intelligence in people. No matter how bright a person may be he cannot use his intelligence fully without appropriate education. Educational opportunities are not genetic, of course. They constitute an _____ factor that causes intelligence to vary.

environmental

168 Among the studies designed to measure the influence of heredity and of environment on intelligence, analyses of similarities of intelligence among persons of varying _____ relations and varying environments have been prominent.

genetic (or family)

genetic

169 As we would expect from the example of the bright and dull rats, evidence of a _____ factor for intelligence has been reported.

more

170 The presence of an hereditary factor for intelligence means that, as a group, brothers and sisters will be _____ alike in intelligence than unrelated persons. This is true.

more

171 The hereditary component further means that identical twins will be _____ alike in intelligence than nontwin brothers and sisters. This is also true.

less

172 If identical twins are reared in different environments, their measured intelligence will be _____ alike than if they were reared together.

environmental

173 This difference in intelligence due to separate environments shows the _____ component responsible for intelligence.

intelligence

174 Identical-twin studies (and other studies) establish that _____ is a function of both heredity and environment.

environment
genetic

175 *Review:* These data can be summarized by the statement that *if* the _____ permits, *then* the _____ potential intelligence will be developed.

SUMMARY

In this unit, you have studied the mechanisms by which personal characteristics are transmitted from one generation to another. The first part of the unit, however, was a study of simple feedback systems, a very common sort of regulatory mechanism in organisms. Perhaps the example of a thermostat will help you to remember how such a system works.

Next, you studied the genetic material. You learned of genes and chromosomes and of the DNA (deoxyribonucleic acid) of which they are made. You also learned that the genes, i.e., the material actually transmitted from one generation to another, function as instructions for developmental processes.

After a brief review of the formation of gametes, you studied some of the simpler mechanisms of heredity. You learned of characters controlled by variants of a single gene (e.g., phenylketonuria), of characters controlled by a few genes (e.g., blood type), and of characters controlled by the combined effect of several genes (e.g., skin color). You also studied the genetic basis of sex.

One of the very difficult problems for the student of behavior is the relation between hereditary or constitutional factors and environmental factors as they interact to affect behavior. You have worked through a number of items designed to help you to understand that relation.

Finally, you studied a brief statement of the kinds of knowledge we have concerning human genetics. You should now be ready to apply your knowledge to the analysis of behavior. You should always be conscious of the genetic factor, which is necessarily present and affects all human behavior.

REFERENCES

Bonner, D.: Heredity, Prentice-Hall, Inc., Englewood Cliffs, N.J., 1961.

Ingram, V.: "How Do Genes Act?" Scientific American, 198: 68–74, 1958.

Jukes, T.: "The Genetic Code," American Scientist, 51:227–245, 1963.

Neel, J., and W. Schulls: Human Heredity, The University of Chicago Press, Chicago, 1954.

Stern, C.: Human Genetics, W. H. Freeman and Company, San Francisco, 1950.

Tyron, R.: "Genetic Differences in Maze Learning in Rats," 39th Yearbook, National Society for the Study of Education, 1940, pp. 111–119.

Weisz, P.: The Science of Biology, 2d ed., McGraw-Hill Book Company, New York, 1963, chap. 18.

SELF-REVIEW QUIZ

1 What does the word "homeostasis" mean when used in a biological context?

2 How can one determine whether a given gene is dominant or not?

3 What are the major sources of genetic variability among people?

4 If gene X is dominant over gene x, and a person with XX marries a person with Xx, how many apparent kinds of children are possible? If Xx marries Xx? If XX marries xx?

5 How many kinds of gametes can a parent with a gene combination of AaBb produce? What are they?

6 In what way can the shape of a nose be passed from father to son in a sperm cell?

7 What sort of a genetic mechanism can account for complex and continuously varying properties such as intelligence?

8   What is the genetic difference between males and females?

9   Why are identical twins good subjects for study of the relationship between heredity and environment?

10 State briefly the relationship between heredity and environment as factors affecting behavior.

11 What is the significance of DNA (deoxyribonucleic acid)?

12 Why is direct knowledge of human genetics so scanty?

13 How do we learn about human genetics indirectly?

14 How reliable is our knowledge of human genetics? What evidence can you present to support your answer?

15 Why should a student of behavior study genetics?

unit 2

Biological Mechanisms and Functions

This unit continues the investigation of biological foundations of behavior. It is concerned with an exploration of the biological mechanisms by which man relates himself to his environment, including other men. These mechanisms—receptors, nervous system, and endocrine system—constitute the biological machinery of all behavior, no matter how complex it may be. To some extent, they determine the potential for, and the limits of, human behavior. As was the case with Unit 1, a good understanding of the materials in Unit 2 will be useful as you proceed to investigate human behavior through the remainder of the course.

When you finish this unit, you should understand the following concepts:

1. The basic biological principles by which man secures information about his environment
2. The nature of the nerve impulse which carries information within the body
3. The division of labor among the parts of the nervous system, including the basic differences in the relations of each part to behavior
4. The role of the endocrine system as it affects behavior

The Biological Basis of Integrated Behavior

One of the obvious properties of human behavior is that it is integrated, i.e., the individual behaves as a unit. The mechanisms of integration are complex and not completely understood, but for pedagogical reasons we can simplify and identify them with the nervous system and the endocrine system. The general purpose of these two systems, then, is to integrate behavior.

integrated

1 Some behavioral scientists think that _____ behavior can be understood only and completely by explanations of the biochemical events in the nervous system.

2 Other behavioral scientists think that overt behavior must be studied as a separate class of phenomena, and that knowledge of the _____ system is not of primary importance.

nervous

3 We shall adopt an intermediate view. We believe that integrated behavior can be understood only with the help of knowledge of the _____ system.

nervous

behavior

4 On the other hand, we are aware that some _____ cannot be explained by our present knowledge of the nervous system.

5 Before beginning our analysis of the integrating mechanisms, let us try to relate behavior, the _____ system, and the environment with a simplified scheme.

nervous

6 The direct causes of behavior are stimuli. A change in some part of the environment, which is perceptible to an individual, is defined as a _____.

stimulus

7 The environmental changes, or _____, deliver a quantity of energy which results in a response on the part of the individual.

stimuli

8 Because of the energy, certain events occur within the individual as a _____ to the stimulus.

response (reaction)

9 Not all parts of the human body are equally able to respond to the various stimuli or _____ changes which occur.

environmental

10 For example, a small amount of light energy delivered to the back of our hands elicits no obvious _____.

response

11 The same amount of light energy delivered to the eye, however, elicits a sensation of _____.

sight (vision)

12 Parts of the body capable of responding to _____ from the environment are called receptors.

stimuli (energy)

13 Receptors are classified by the sorts of _____ to which they respond.

energy (stimuli)

14 Thus the eye is called a light receptor and the _____ a sound receptor.

ear

15 The receptors, as a group, constitute a link between the individual and his _____.

environment

(1) environment (2) individual	**16** In this relation between an individual and environment, the energy moves from the (1) _____ to the (2) _____.
receptors	**17** The acquisition of information about the environment is the result of this energy input via the _____.
nerve fiber	**18** The receptors, activated by the energy input, transmit energy to nerve fibers. Regardless of the sort of energy received from the environment, it is measured as electrical energy when it is converted to an impulse on a _____ _____.
sound (or sound waves)	**19** To some extent, this process is analogous to the transformation of _____ into electrical energy by a microphone.
nerve	**20** To change the vocabulary, the transformation of the stimulus into a _____ impulse via a receptor amounts to encoding the information received from the environment.
information	**21** These coded bits of _____ are delivered to the brain by the system of nerve fibers.
nerve fibers	**22** In the brain, these bits of information received from the _____ _____ are integrated.
integration	**23** This process of _____ by the brain is complex and not well understood.
integration	**24** Brain activities, which we may call analysis, interpretation, relation to other information, and evaluation, must be involved in the _____ processes.
brain	**25** As a result of these processes, some sort of decision is reached by the _____.
brain	**26** If the decision is to act, the _____ delivers some energy to an outbound nerve fiber.
nerve fibers	**27** The impulse travels along _____ _____ until it arrives at an effector.
effectors	**28** These _____ are either muscles or glands.
effectors	**29** As _____, muscles allow an individual to act on his environment.

30 The effect exerted on the environment by an individual requires a transfer of energy from the individual to the _____.

environment

31 This transfer of energy from an _____ to his environment alters it in some way.

individual

32 This alteration of the _____ by an individual is one way to define behavior.

environment

33 *Review:* Our sequence of events, which began with an environmental change, has ended with _____ returned to the environment to change it.

energy

34 The environmental change caused by behavior can, of course, become a stimulus for further _____.

behavior
  (response)

35 The nervous system is the mechanism, then, which relates an individual to his _____.

environment

The Nerve Impulse

Now that you have learned, in a general way, the procedures by which individuals receive information from the environment and, after a complex series of events, act appropriately on the environment, we shall investigate some of the internal events in more detail. Let us begin with the nerve impulse and its transmission along the fibers of the peripheral nervous system.

Table 3. Relation between Magnitude of Stimulus and Magnitude of Response in a Hypothetical Single Neuron*

Stimulus strength	Response strength
0	0
1	0
2	1
3	1
4	1
5	0

* Both stimulus and response are measured as electrical energy, but not in the same units (i.e., response strength of 1 is not the same amount of energy as stimulus strength of 1).

Let us now turn our attention to the events in that portion of the nervous system which connects the brain with the receptors and effectors.

nerve

36 Energy is transmitted to and from the brain on _____ fibers.

nerve

37 The cells which bear the fibers are called neurons, or _____ cells.

impulses

38 The protoplasm of neurons is highly specialized to respond to stimuli and to transmit nerve _____.

nerve

39 In addition to constituting the transmission network, the _____ cells also constitute the brain. In this section we shall concentrate on the network of fibers and defer consideration of the brain until the next section.

neuron (or nerve cell)

40 Each _____ has a cell body which contains a nucleus.

cell body (or nerve cell)

41 Extending the _____ _____ in one or more directions are the fibers, which are sometimes called axons and dendrites.

cell body

42 We shall consider the transmission of nerve impulses on the fibers. Transmission through cell bodies is not well understood; we shall think of the _____ _____ as primarily responsible for the maintenance of the neuron.

effectors

43 Neurons occur in a variety of types. Transmission neurons, connecting the central nervous system with the receptors and _____, have at least one very long fiber and usually several short fibers.

neuron

44 If a transmission neuron connects a receptor to the central nervous system, it is called a sensory _____.

central

45 If a transmission neuron connects an effector with the _____ nervous system, it is called a motor neuron.

two

46 In addition to the _____ kinds of transmission neurons, there are, especially within the central nervous system, many neurons with many short fibers which serve a connecting function and are called connecting or association neurons.

Nerve

47 _____ fibers vary in length, diameter, and in some other structural details.

variations (changes)

48 As you would expect, these variations of structure are correlated with _____ of function.

variations (changes)	**49** The _____ in function are of two primary kinds: variation in the threshold of irritability and variation in the rate of transmission.
greater	**50** The threshold of irritability is an important concept, and we must examine it further. When one strikes a nail with a hammer, the harder the strike, the _____ the response of the nail.
response	**51** The nail displays no threshold; the magnitude of the _____ is proportional to the magnitude of the stimulus.
no	**52** Table 3 is a set of data from a hypothetical experiment in which increasing stimuli were applied to a fiber and the responses measured. Notice that with a stimulus intensity less than 2, _____ response is given.
2	**53** The threshold of irritability of the fiber in the example is, therefore, _____.
stimulation (irritability)	**54** Generalizing from the example, we can say that the intensity of _____ sufficient to elicit a response is the threshold of a nerve fiber.
response	**55** A stimulus below threshold intensity elicits no _____ and is called a subminimal stimulus.
stimulus	**56** In the subminimal range, consequently, the strength of the response is not proportional to the strength of the _____, but is a function of the nerve fiber.
1	**57** In Table 3, stimuli of strength 2, 3, and 4 all elicit a response of strength _____.
nerve fiber	**58** To generalize this example, we can say that once the threshold is exceeded, the _____ _____ responds completely.
nerve fiber	**59** In other words, within the range of irritability, the response is not proportional to the stimulus but is a property of the _____ _____.
0	**60** In Table 3, a stimulus of strength 5 elicits a response of strength _____.
nerve fiber	**61** This illustrates the fact that a stimulus of sufficient strength may damage a _____ _____ and make it unable to respond.

62 It is obvious that an individual often responds to stimulation in a way that is roughly proportional to the _____ of the stimulus.

strength
(intensity)

How can this be explained in the light of what we have learned about single fibers? The answer lies partly in the number of fibers stimulated. Table 4 illustrates the mechanism. For a stimulus of strength 1, one fiber responds.

Table 4. Response of Groups of Nerve Fibers to Stimuli of Varying Strength

Stimulus strength	Fiber A (Threshold 1)	Fiber B (Threshold 2)	Fiber C (Threshold 3)	Total fibers responding
0	. . . .	. . . .	. . . .	0
1	Respond	. . . .	. . . .	1
2	Respond	Respond	. . . .	2
3	Respond	Respond	Respond	3

63 A stimulus of strength 1 is below the _____ of fibers B and C and thus they do not respond.

threshold

64 To a stimulus of strength 2, fiber A responds as it did to the weaker stimulus, and fiber _____ also responds.

B

65 An additional fiber responds when the stimulus strength is raised to _____.

3

66 As you can see, the response of any one of the fibers is independent of the intensity of the stimulus (once the threshold is reached), but the response of the complex of three fibers is proportional to the _____ of stimulation.

intensity

67 To generalize, when stimuli are coded into nerve impulses, the intensity of the stimulus is coded by the number of _____ activated.

fibers

68 Let us look now at the nerve impulse itself. Its presence can be detected with a galvanometer; i.e., it is an electrical charge traveling along a _____ _____. (A galvanometer detects the presence, direction, and magnitude of an electric current.)

nerve fiber

electrical

69 The mechanisms by which this _____ charge propagates itself need not concern us here, but some of its properties do interest us.

70 The first property of interest we have already established; the amplitude of the electrical charge is a property of the particular fiber involved, and is not proportional

intensity (strength)

to the _____ of the stimulus.

71 Secondly, the rate of transmission of nerve impulses varies. This variation is also independent of the stimulus and is a property of the diameter and structure of the

fibers

_____ involved.

impulses

72 Rates of transmission of _____ in the human body vary from speeds of about 2 meters per second (about 4.5 mph) to 100 meters per second (about 225 mph).

73 A third interesting property of the nerve impulse is that, in itself, it is *not directional*. An impulse can be generated at any point on a nerve fiber, and it will spread

directions

in both _____ at equal rates.

neurons (nerve cells)

74 It is evident, from the fact that _____ can be labeled motor and sensory, that nerve impulses in the body do, in fact, normally travel in only one direction.

75 Somewhere in the nervous system we must find a directional mechanism. If we examine a sequence of several fibers, we see that an impulse, started in the

fibers

middle of one of the _____, spreads to both ends of the fiber stimulated.

impulse

76 As the _____ reaches one end of the fiber, it stops. At the opposite end, however, it somehow generates an impulse on the adjacent fiber on the other side of a gap, called a synapse.

77 The directional factor, then, is found at the ends of a

nerve fiber

_____ _____.

impulse

78 Studies have shown that the end of the fiber capable of passing an _____ to an adjacent fiber responds to the impulse by secreting a hormone, which diffuses across the synapse and stimulates the adjacent fiber.

79 Since only one end of a fiber can do this, an impulse can leave a fiber in only one direction, and the _____

directional

property of impulses is explained.

Information entering the body and encoded as nerve impulses is still chaotic. The organization of this information into meaningful patterns, which may elicit action by the organism, is accomplished by the central nervous system, which consists of the brain and the spinal cord. We shall now examine some of the properties of the central nervous system.

The Central Nervous System

Let us now turn to the central nervous system, which receives impulses from sensory fibers and transmits impulses to motor fibers. Between reception and transmission of impulses, the central nervous system performs the complex of functions which we have called integration.

fibers

80 Between the brain and the nerve _____ connecting with various parts of the body lies the spinal cord.

spinal

81 The _____ cord is composed of two kinds of nervous tissue, gray matter and white matter.

impulses

82 The white matter, lying on the outside of the cord, is made of sheathed fibers which transmit _____ rapidly and for relatively long distances.

impulses

83 In the center of the spinal cord is gray matter. Gray matter consists of cell bodies and naked fibers which serve as connecting neurons and which transmit _____ relatively slowly.

spinal cord

84 In lower vertebrates, and to a limited extent in man, the _____ _____ serves as a reflex center.

motor

85 By reflex center, we mean a place where impulses are transferred from sensory neurons to _____ neurons without volition being involved.

spinal cord

86 In man, however, the most important function of the gray matter of the _____ _____ is to connect the parts of the body with the brain and with each other.

gray

87 Through the connecting neurons in the _____ matter of the cord, the right side of the body is connected to the left side.

connecting

88 Also, various levels of the body are connected through _____ neurons in the gray matter of the cord.

89 On the other hand, on the long fibers in the white matter of the cord, impulses pass to and from the brain. The most interesting and most complicated part of the nervous system of man is the _____.

brain

90 Anatomists have classified the brain into many areas, but for our purposes we can consider it as having three main subdivisions: the brain stem, the cerebellum, and the cerebrum. (See Figure 2.) Our term, brain stem, includes the thalamus, hypothalamus, midbrain, and medulla of the diagram. The brain stem is really a modified extension of the _____ _____ into the cranial cavity.

spinal cord

91 The cerebrum and the cerebellum are expansions of the brain stem, the cerebrum at the anterior (front) end of the stem and the _____ on the back side of the stem.

cerebellum

92 Let us look first at the brain stem. The neat segregation of gray matter and white matter, characteristic of the higher brain centers as well as of the _____ _____, is not present in the brain stem.

spinal cord

93 The cell bodies and short, naked fibers, which constitute the _____ matter, are broken up into several separate masses which are called ganglia or nuclei.

gray

94 Sheathed fibers, which transmit _____ rapidly and over long distances and which constitute the white matter, weave around and among the ganglia in a complex fashion.

impulses

95 Of the twelve pairs of large cranial nerves connected to the brain directly, eleven are connected to the brain stem. Within the brain stem, _____ neurons tie the fibers of the cranial nerves to all parts of the brain.

connecting

96 (Refer to the diagram of the brain.) The brain stem serves two major functions. First, it transmits impulses between the _____ cord and the cranial nerves and to all parts of the brain. It appears to have some regulatory effect on some of these impulses.

spinal

97 Second, several reflex centers regulate such basic biological activities as breathing and heart rate in the _____ stem.

brain

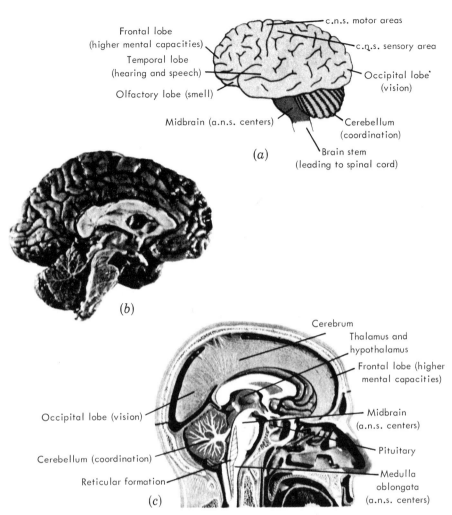

Frontal lobe
(higher mental capacities)
Temporal lobe
(hearing and speech)
Olfactory lobe (smell)

c.n.s. motor areas
c.n.s. sensory area
Occipital lobe
(vision)

Midbrain (a.n.s. centers)

Cerebellum
(coordination)

(a)

Brain stem
(leading to spinal cord)

(b)

Cerebrum
Thalamus and
hypothalamus
Frontal lobe (higher
mental capacities)

Occipital lobe (vision)

Midbrain
(a.n.s. centers)

Pituitary

Cerebellum (coordination)

Reticular formation

(c)

Medulla
oblongata
(a.n.s. centers)

Figure 2. (a) The left half of the brain, viewed from the outside; the functions of the various labeled parts are indicated in parentheses. (b) The left half of the brain, viewed from the inner cut side. (c) Model showing the various parts and their functions. (b, Photographic Department, Rhode Island Hospital; c, detail of model designed by Dr. J. F. Mueller, Ward's Natural Science Establishment, Inc., reticular formation added; Paul B. Weisz, *The Science of Biology*, p. 548, McGraw-Hill Book Company, 1963.)

In addition to these two general sorts of activities, additional important and interesting functions have been discovered in the brain stem by recent researches. These investigations are continuing by such means as the implantation of electrodes in the brain. These electrodes permit the variations in electrical activity of small parts of the brain to be studied and to be related to behavior. Partly as a result of these studies, we have learned to speak of centers in the brain for such things as sex, hunger, thirst, and even pleasure. In a sense, these centers seem to be some sort of reward mechanism, and animals will alter their behavior to get them stimulated. For example, rats will suffer pain, or will learn quickly to solve problems in order to get a stimulus in the pleasure center.

Also in the lower brain is the reticular system. Long known anatomically, its functions are only now becoming evident. All sensory nerve trunks send branches into the reticular system. It responds to all sensory impulses alike, not differentiating, e.g., between sight and sound. The response is to send impulses to all parts of the brain, and the reticular system somehow arouses the brain. Experiments on sleeping animals show that direct stimulation of higher brain centers will not arouse the animal; the reticular system must be activated first.

Although our understanding of the functions of these so-called lower brain centers is meager as compared with our knowledge of the cerebral cortex, contemporary investigators are adding to it rapidly. It is already clear that these parts of the brain play a more important part in human behavior than we had realized.

98   The cerebellum is on the back side of the brain stem. (See Figure 2.) In the cerebellum, the gray matter and white matter are again segregated, but in a way different from the segregation in the _____ cord.

spinal

99   In the cerebellum, the gray matter forms a mantle surrounding a central core of fibrous _____ matter.

white

100   The shift of the gray matter to the outside, where the area is greater, means that the ratio of _____ matter to white matter can be larger.

gray

101   The relative increase in gray matter means an increase in the number of connections possible. The increased number of connections means _____ complexity and flexibility in impulse transmission routes.

increased (greater)

102   The increased anatomical complexity makes possible more _____ and flexible behavior.

complex

103   The cerebellum receives fibers from the cerebrum and sends out _____ to the skeletal muscles. It is, therefore, involved in muscular adjustment of the body.

fibers

equilibrium

muscles

muscular

cerebrum

gray

gray

convolutions

convolutions

fibers

cerebrum

cerebral

104 Loss of the cerebellum, or parts of it, results in an inability to maintain equilibrium. The muscular adjustments necessary for _____ become uncoordinated and hence ineffective.

105 In addition, cerebellar damage destroys voluntary muscular coordination so that activities involving the co-ordinated effort of several _____ become jerky and ineffective.

106 Apparently, the cerebellum has no effect on the so-called mental activities of the brain. It does not partici-pate in sensations, memory, problem solving, or the initia-tion of muscular acts. It is concerned, rather, with the co-ordination of _____ acts initiated by the cerebral cortex.

107 The cerebrum (see Figure 2) is the "highest" part of the brain, lying at the top of the brain stem. The _____ is the largest portion of the brain.

108 In the cerebrum, as in the cerebellum, the white matter is surrounded by _____ matter. The gray matter is called the cerebral cortex.

109 The cortex further increases the _____ matter by folding in complex folds called convolutions.

110 Among the mammals, groups (e.g., cats) with more convolutions are usually considered more intelligent than groups (e.g., opossums) with fewer _____.

111 Within a species (e.g., man), however, variations in intelligence do not seem to be correlated with the number of _____.

112 In addition, the cerebral white matter contains a very large number of _____ connecting the right and left hemispheres and the various areas within each hemisphere.

113 Like its anatomy, the functioning of the cerebrum is extremely complex. First of all, the _____ is the sensory brain.

114 In the cerebrum are areas concerned with each of the specialized sensory receptors, e.g., a visual area, an auditory area, etc. (see Figure 2). All sensation, i.e., infor-mation consciously received from the environment, is put into the _____ cortex.

115 Some information, received without consciousness, may be handled at brain centers below the _____, in the brain stem (e.g., carbon-dioxide content of blood).

cerebrum

116 Secondly, all voluntary and some involuntary muscular activity is initiated in the cerebral _____.

cortex

117 These muscular activities are in response to information received, i.e., they are adaptive. Their adaptive quality requires that an integration occur between sensory input and motor discharge. This must occur in the _____ cortex.

cerebral

118 The cerebral cortex, then, is the part of the brain concerned with conscious sensory input, with voluntary motor output, and with their _____.

integration

119 Cerebral integration is not well understood. Several different kinds of activity must be involved in the cerebral _____, and they are often called mental activities.

cortex

120 First of all, the cerebral cortex makes possible what might be called selective attention. The environment sends a steady stream of _____ to the cortex from all the receptors.

impulses (information)

121 Only by selecting some stimuli for attention can mental chaos be avoided. Somehow, the _____ _____ performs such selection functions.

cerebral cortex

122 The act of enhancing this selective power of the _____ _____ and focusing attention on a narrow range of stimuli we call concentration.

cerebral cortex

123 In addition to selecting some stimuli for attention, the cortex mediates new information and relevant past experience. This recall of past _____ is, of course, memory.

experience

124 While memory is not the same thing as intelligence, intelligent behavior requires effective _____.

memory

125 In addition to sensation and memory, the _____ cortex also makes possible the activity often called problem solving.

cerebral

126 Problem solving involves sensation and memory but also goes beyond them. The mechanisms of _____ _____ are not understood, but neuron activity within the cerebral cortex is its physiological correlate.

problem solving

127 When an organism is confronted with a new problem, then, the cerebral cortex becomes active in a way we call _____ _____, which involves _____ and _____ as well as less-understood operations.

problem solving
memory
sensation

Even less well understood are the cortical functions of imagination, creative thought, and emotional responses. About all we know for sure about them, neurologically speaking, is that the cerebral cortex is involved. In short, then, all the integrating functions of the body are concentrated in the central nervous system and especially in the brain. Investigations of the brain are currently adding to our knowledge at a rapid rate and constitute one of the most active frontiers of science. Practical implications for mental health, for education, and for more effective use of our intelligence are tremendously exciting.

The Autonomic Nervous System

So far, we have studied the nervous system as it helps us to adapt to changes in the external environment. Equally important, although less evident, is its role in adjusting to changes in the internal environment and thereby helping to maintain homeostasis. The part of the nervous system primarily concerned with this kind of adaptation is called the autonomic nervous system.

homeostasis

128 The part of the nervous system which is principally involved in the maintenance of _____ is called the autonomic nervous system. (See Figure 3.)

muscles

129 The autonomic system innervates the muscles and glands of the viscera, and homeostatic adjustments are made by the activity of these visceral _____ and glands.

autonomic

130 The detailed anatomy of the autonomic system need not concern us. Functionally, there are two divisions to the _____ system, the sympathetic and the parasympathetic divisions.

sympathetic

131 Nearly all of the visceral muscles and glands are innervated by fibers from both the _____ and the parasympathetic divisions.

parasympathetic

slowed

132 Usually, for those organs which have the dual innervation, the results of sympathetic stimulation are opposite to the results of _____ stimulation.

133 For example, the heart is accelerated by sympathetic stimulation and _____ by parasympathetic stimulation.

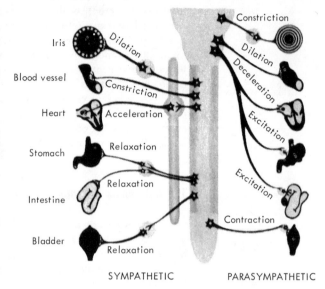

Figure 3. Some of the motor pathways of the autonomic nervous system. The column left of the spinal cord represents sympathetic chain ganglia. Each neural path shown occurs pairwise, one on the left and one on the right side of the body. Similarly, sympathetic chain ganglia occur to both the left and the right of the spinal cord. For simplicity, however, only one side is indicated in each case. (Paul B. Weisz, *The Science of Biology*, p. 531, McGraw-Hill Book Company, 1963.)

decreased or
slowed

134 On the other hand, activity of the stomach is increased by parasympathetic stimulation and _____ by sympathetic stimulation.

We can make a rough generalization, which includes the above two examples and most other cases of dual innervation, and say that sympathetic stimulation accelerates those body processes concerned with the mobilization and/or expenditure of energy. We can further say that parasympathetic stimulation accelerates those body processes concerned with the conservation of energy.

135 One of the most important roles of the sympathetic system is to prepare the body to meet an emergency. In this role, the _____ system works in cooperation with a hormone, adrenalin.

sympathetic

136 The rate and direction of activity of any of these dually innervated structures is a function of the balance between sympathetic and _____ stimulation.

parasympathetic

137 By shifts in this balance, in response to changes in the internal environment, the relatively stable state called _____ is maintained.

homeostasis

138 The integrating processes which regulate the balance between the two divisions of the _____ nervous system are located in the brain.

autonomic

139 In some manner not well understood, the _____ system is involved in emotional reactions of human beings.

autonomic

140 This involvement is illustrated by the reaction to purely emotional emergencies as if they were physical. Thus excitement makes our heart beat _____ even though we have no intention of running or fighting.

faster

141 Experiments studying the physiological effects of overcrowding, of anxiety, of overloads of responsibility, all show the intimate relation between emotional reactions and the _____ nervous system.

autonomic

The events studied in the preceding section begin when the organism is stimulated by its environment. The devices responding directly to stimulation are called receptors. They should be studied briefly before you conclude your examination of the nervous system.

Receptors

We have already mentioned several times that integrated behavior begins with the reception of information from both the external and internal environment. Information from the external environment enters the body by the stimulation of receptors.

142 Organs which are especially irritable to one kind of stimulus are called _____; e.g., the eye is very sensitive to light.

receptors

143 Sensation, however, does not result from stimulation of a receptor alone but requires the transmission of impulses to the _____ cortex of the brain.

cerebral

It is convenient to divide receptors into two main groups. Those which are stimulated by changes outside the body are called exteroceptors and those which are stimulated by changes inside the body are called interoceptors.

144 The receptors of the homeostatic mechanisms previously studied in connection with the autonomic nervous system are called _____.

interoceptors

145 The exteroceptors can be further classified according to the kind of _____ to which they are especially sensitive.

stimulus

146 For example, we can identify, among others, chemoreceptors (taste buds) and photoreceptors (_____).

eyes

147 Ordinarily, stimulation by light results in a sensation of vision. However, pressure on the eye similarly results in a sensation of _____ (seeing stars).

vision (sight)

148 Further, experiments have shown that direct electrical stimulation of the visual area of the brain causes a sensation of _____.

vision

149 Many experiments have confirmed that the type of sensation experienced is not a function of the type of stimulus or receptor, but is actually a function of the part of the _____ activated.

brain (cerebral cortex)

150 Thus both dream sensations and hallucinations involve an appropriate part of the _____, even though normal stimulation of receptors does not occur.

brain (cerebral cortex)

151 Few people have any difficulty in distinguishing between two types of sensation, e.g., sight and sound. Other properties of _____, however, present greater difficulties of discrimination.

sensations

For example, color-blind people are unable to discriminate red from green, and humans vary over a wide range of sensitivity to slight differences in color. This variation in the ability to discriminate among the qualities of a given kind of sensation is an important variable in the study of behavior. For example, differences in discrimination of the pitch of sound is one of the basic differences between musical and nonmusical people. The characteristics of sensation and stimulus discrimination will be discussed further in Part III, Unit 1.

152 The section on the brain discussed selectivity of stimuli. This selectivity is enhanced by a property of rec_____ called adaptation.

receptors

153 If a hair on your arm is bent, you experience a sensation; if the hair remains bent, however, the _____ disappears. (Try it.)

sensation

154 This disappearance of _____ while the stimulus continues is called adaptation.

sensation

155 Ignoring what might be called "background noise" is called _____.

adaptation

156 Not all receptors adapt equally well. The eye, for example, shows very little power of _____.

adaptation

157 On the other hand, the fact that we do not ordinarily "feel" our clothes shows that touch receptors _____ quickly.

adapt

158 Although we need not study all the different types of receptors, let us look briefly at some of them. Let us first look at the light receptor, the _____.

eye

159 The eye is able to convert a small amount of _____ energy into nerve impulses.

light

160 A large part of the eye is a device for focusing light on the light-sensitive cells. This part of the eye works like a camera and concentrates _____ energy on the cells of the retina.

light

161 The mechanism involved in focusing is flexible and is able to adjust to light entering the eye from varying distances. It is this _____ function of the eye that can be helped by glasses.

focusing

162 The focused light stimulates the light-sensitive cells in the back of the eye; their response to stimulation is to generate a nerve _____ on the optic nerve.

impulse

163 The light-sensitive cells vary in their sensitivity, not only to the intensity of the incident light but to its wave length. This differential _____ is the basis for color discrimination.

sensitivity

164 As a result of these activities, impulses correlated with the type of light stimulus are sent to the visual areas of the brain, where they are interpreted as _____ sensations.

visual

165 To repeat, the eye is a mechanism for translating light energy into nerve impulses. The interpretation is a function, not of the eye, but of the _____.

brain

166 Similarly, other receptors translate some particular kind of energy from the environment into nerve impulses; while correlated with the environmental phenomena, the sensation is a function of the _____.

brain

167 In spite of the fact that all sensations occur in the _____, we locate them elsewhere.

brain

168 Sensations of pressure and taste are located by us on the surface of our body; such _____ as sight and smell we project to spots distant from our body.

sensations

169 *Review:* Although sensations are not a perfectly reliable guide to the condition of our environment, they are the only source of information about the _____ we have.

environment

In addition to the nervous system, integration of our behavior is facilitated by the endocrine system. This system, consisting of several ductless glands, regulates somewhat different kinds of adaptive responses than does the nervous system. In the following section, we shall examine some of the differences in the functions of the two systems.

The Endocrine Glands

170 A number of glands which discharge their secretions directly into the blood stream constitute the _____ system.

endocrine

171 These _____ are called hormones and serve as regulators of body processes.

secretions

Table 5. The Principal Vertebrate Endocrine Glands and Their Hormones

Gland	Hormones	Chief functions	Effects of deficiency or excess
Pituitary, anterior lobe	TTH GTH ACTH Lactogenic Growth	Stimulates thyroid Stimulates gonads Stimulates adrenal cortex Stimulates milk secretion Promotes cell metabolism	Dwarfism; gigantism; acromegaly
Pituitary, mid-lobe	Intermedin	Controls adjustable skin-pigment cells (e.g., frogs)	
Pituitary, posterior	At least five distinct fractions	Controls water metabolism, blood pressure, kidney function, smooth-muscle action	Increased or reduced water excretion
Thyroid	Thyroxin	Stimulates respiration; inhibits TTH secretion	Goiter; cretinism; myxedema
Parathyroid	Parathormone	Controls Ca metabolism	Nerve, muscle abnormalities; bone thickening or weakening
Adrenal cortex	Cortisone, other sterol hormones	Controls metabolism of water, minerals, carbohydrates; controls kidney function; inhibits ACTH secretion; duplicates sex-hormone functions	Addison's disease
Adrenal medulla	Adrenalin	Alarm reaction, e.g., raises blood pressure, heart rate	Inability to cope with stress
Pancreas	Insulin	Glucose → glycogen	Diabetes
Testis	Testosterone, other androgens	Promote cell respiration, blood circulation; maintain primary and secondary sex characteristics, sex urge; inhibit GTH secretions	Atrophy of reproductive system; decline of secondary sex characteristics
Ovary	Estradiol, other estrogens		

SOURCE: Paul B. Weisz, *The Science of Biology*, p. 499, McGraw-Hill Book Company, New York, 1963.

homeostasis

172 Their regulatory activities help to maintain stability in the internal environment and thus contribute to the "steady state" referred to as _____.

hormones

173 Processes regulated by hormones differ from those regulated by the nervous system in three major ways. First, _____ usually act much more slowly than nervous-control mechanisms (compare changes in the uterus during the menstrual cycle with withdrawal from a burn stimulus).

nervous

174 Second, many hormones act over relatively wide areas of the body, whereas _____ controls are specifically localized.

nervous

175 Third, the effects of hormonal stimulation are generally longer lasting than the effects of _____ stimulation.

176 Review: Processes regulated by the endocrine system differ from those of the nervous system by:

(1) _____

(2) _____

(3) _____

Refer to frames 173 to 175.

177 Thus nervous mechanisms regulate the adjustments to sudden and temporary changes in the environment, while _____ in the endocrine system are more concerned with the regulation of longer-lasting responses.

hormones

178 Examples of slow and long-enduring processes are growth, sexual development, and sexual cycles. These are regulated by _____.

hormones

179 The various _____ glands have specific functions which we shall not list here (see Table 5). They all work together, however, under the general control of the pituitary gland.

endocrine

180 Changes in the activity of any endocrine gland are reflected in disturbances of the whole _____ system and the hormonal balance of the body.

endocrine

181 Many of the symptoms shown by some women during the menopause are due to an upset _____ balance caused by the cessation of activity of the ovaries.

hormonal

In summary, hormones appear to have some influence on behavior patterns and personality, although the mechanisms are not clearly understood. It is important to remember that the hormones and the nervous system work together to integrate the functions of the body.

SUMMARY

One of the most obvious properties of human behavior is that it is integrated, that is, the organism behaves as a unit. Such integration requires the acquisition of information from the environment, the analysis and interpretation of the information, and the selection of appropriate responses. The whole process of integration involves the nervous system and the endocrine system, and includes the maintenance of homeostasis.

Information from the environment enters the body through the receptors, e.g., eyes, touch receptors. Each receptor is especially sensitive to one kind of energy, e.g., photic, thermal, and responds to changes in the level of that kind of energy by generating a nerve impulse.

The nerve impulse, an electrical disturbance, travels along the fiber of a sensory nerve cell and enters the central nervous system. In the central nervous system—the spinal cord and brain—the impulse is distributed over a variety of fibers which connect the central nervous system to all parts of the body and, within the central nervous system, form a complex set of connections.

Analysis and interpretation of information occur in the brain by processes which are not well understood. More about them is being learned almost daily, however, as hundreds of scientists are currently investigating the human brain. The so-called higher mental activities, e.g., problem solving and memory, are part of the integration process occurring in the brain, and we are now learning that emotions, involving the autonomic nervous system and "lower" brain centers, are also important.

From the brain, impulses are sent on the fibers of motor nerve cells to the effectors, either muscles or glands. These effectors make adaptive responses to the changes of the environment which constituted the original stimulus. Many slow and enduring adaptations are mediated by the system of endocrine glands.

Behavior, then, rests on the biological base of the nervous system, with assistance from the endocrine system. In the present state of knowledge, an understanding of the nervous system is far from sufficient to explain behavior, but it is a necessary ingredient of any explanation.

REFERENCES

Katz, B.: "The Nerve Impulse," Scientific American, 187:55–64, 1952.

Pfeiffer, J.: The Human Brain, Harper and Row Publishers, Incorporated, New York, 1955.

Tustin, A.: "Feedback," Scientific American, 187:48–55, 1952.

Weisz, P.: The Science of Biology, 2d ed., McGraw-Hill Book Company, New York, 1963, chaps. 20 and 22.

Zuckerman, S.: "Hormones," Scientific American, 196:76–87, 1957.

SELF-REVIEW QUIZ

1 What is a stimulus?
2 How does information concerning the environment enter the body?
3 Differentiate among motor neurons, sensory neurons, and connecting or association neurons.

4   What is the threshold of irritability? Why is it important?

5   If nerve cells obey an all-or-none law, how are responses varied in intensity to be appropriate to the stimuli?

6   What is a synapse? What does it contribute to the operation of the nervous system?

7   What functions are served by the spinal cord?

8   What might occur to behavior in a man whose brain stem was damaged?

9   What might occur to behavior in a man whose cerebellum was damaged?

10 What might occur to behavior in a man whose cerebrum was damaged?

11 What parts of the body are innervated by the autonomic nervous system?

12 Illustrate the regulatory mechanism of an organ receiving both sympathetic and parasympathetic fibers.

13 What is the relation between the retina and a sensation of sight? Between the visual cortex and a sensation of sight?

14 How do bodily processes regulated by endocrine glands differ from those regulated by nerve fibers?

15 Is a knowledge of the nervous system necessary to explain behavior? Is it sufficient? Why did you answer the way you did?

part III

Principles of Learned Behavior

Leslie F. Malpass

For many years social scientists debated sharply with biologists about the importance of biological versus environmental conditions in the acquisition and maintenance of behavior. Although some individuals continue to invest energy in this debate, most behavioral scientists now agree that there is more profit in determining the processes by which behavior is acquired and extinguished than in continuing a fruitless argument. Both biological and environmental conditions affect behavior. The preceding section has suggested ways in which heredity, the nervous systems, and endocrine functions influence behavior. This section deals with fundamental aspects of learning, or conditioning.

Everyone is familiar with simple reflexive behavior. Blinking occurs in the presence of sudden, intense light; your leg straightens out suddenly when your knee is struck sharply; saliva accumulates when food is placed in the mouth. These responses occur automatically in the presence of appropriate stimuli.

Reflexes can be conditioned to occur in the presence of stimuli other than those which ordinarily cause them. Pavlov's famous experiments dealt with conditioning the salivary reflex to different sounds and visual stimuli. Unit 2 of Part III will describe some principles of reflex conditioning in detail.

Most human behavior involves more complex learning than the simple association of stimuli (such as food and sounds) which characterizes reflex, or respondent, conditioning. Principles of respondent learning can be used to demonstrate how emotional behavior is conditioned. Other principles are required to explain how we acquire complicated skills such as reading and writing, or how we learn to manipulate machinery and operate automobiles, and why we conform to the rules and regulations of our society.

Several theories have been offered to explain how

learning and conditioning occur (Hilgard, 1956). At the risk of oversimplification, we can say that all of them depend on a few basic principles. For example, all theories deal in some way with stimulus discrimination, although some prefer to use the terms sensation and perception instead.[1] Stimulus discrimination refers to the idea that some agent, usually in the external environment, is related to a change in behavior, i.e., a response. Some theories stress the interpretive, i.e., perceptual, aspects of stimulus discrimination; others deal only with observable and measurable relationships between the stimulus and response. In either case, all learning theories stress the importance of stimulus conditions antecedent to the behavior to be learned. This principle can be symbolized as follows: $S - O - R$, where O stands for conditions of the organism which may affect learning.

Some theories of conditioning stress what follows the response, i.e., the consequences of behavior, rather than its antecedents. If a response consequent works toward the recurrence of the response, it is called a reinforcing stimulus, or reinforcement (S^r). When a child is taught to say "Please" in order to obtain food, the word "please" is the response which works toward the obtaining of food which is the reinforcement for learning this particular verbal behavior. Reinforcement theories emphasize relationships between an expressed behavior (R) and its consequent.

Several concomitant principles associated with stimulus discrimination, organismic conditions, and reinforcement, as these affect learning, will be presented in this section.

[1] Sensation usually refers to the stimulation of a particular set of sensory receptors; perception refers to the interpretation of sensory events.

unit 1

Principles of
Learning—I

Learning refers to "a more or less permanent modification in behavior which results from activity, special training, or observation" (Munn, 1961, p. 716). This chapter deals principally with the response antecedents involved in learning. Their importance has been pointed out already in Part I and Part II, Unit 1, particularly with reference to the role of the stimulus in behavioral reactions. Aspects of stimulus discrimination and generalization, and how these processes are affected by stimulus properties themselves, are presented here. Information about predisposing biological and psychological conditions which may affect learning is also included. Knowledge of these response antecedents should assist you in understanding the actual conditioning processes described in the next unit.

Stimulus Discrimination

1 A stimulus is anything in the environment which causes a reaction in a sense organ. Stimulus discrimination occurs when an organism responds to a particular stimulus which is presented along with another similar stimulus. Observing the change in color when a traffic signal changes from red to green illustrates stimulus _____.

discrimination

2 Discrimination of "green light" means that the driver responds to that particular stimulus rather than to another _____ with similar properties.

stimulus

3 The green light serves as the stimulus for the _____ of the event, "light changing."

discrimination

4 We presume that discrimination occurs because there is a change in the driver's _____.

behavior (response, activity)

5 The absence of any other observable change in the environment suggests that the change in behavior is a function of the discriminated stimulus. The symbol S^d is used to identify a _____ _____.

discriminated stimulus

S^d (discriminated stimulus)

6 Let's say that Joe was used to sleeping in his darkened room until 8 a.m. One night his roommate did not pull down the blinds. When the sun rose at 6:30 a.m., Joe woke up. The sunlight is the _____ for his waking behavior.

related

7 The importance of the stimulus in learning is that it is functionally related to behavior. Learning theory presumes that a particular response does not occur except as it is _____ to an S^d.

change (difference)

8 In shaking someone's hand, you become aware of a change in the pressure on your hand. The stimulus in this case is the _____ of the pressure of the handshake from that of other handshakes.

temperature

9 A person walks out of the hot and humid outside air into an air-conditioned room. The stimulus in this instance is the change in _____.

stimulus

10 The individual's discrimination of the light on eye receptors or pressure on the pain receptors is related to a change in properties of the _____.

interpretation (perception)

11 Perception is usually defined as the process of interpreting stimuli. Discriminating a tree as a tree or a particular person as someone you know involves the _____ of stimuli.

perception

12 The process by which stimuli are interpreted is called _____.

stimuli

13 Because perception as a process is not open to observation by others, many behavioral scientists prefer to analyze behavior simply as it is related to _____.

changes

14 Perception refers to the interpretation of stimuli, as in the examples given below. Stimulus discrimination itself depends on the stimulation of sense organs by _____ in the environment.

(1) eyes
(2) ears
(3) taste buds

15 The sense organs employed in visual stimulus discrimination are **(1)** _____; those in audition are **(2)** _____; those in gustation (taste) are **(3)** _____ _____, and so on.

Stimulus discrimination depends on two things. One deals with the condition of the organism, the other with the properties of the stimulus. We have defined an S^d as a discriminated stimulus which is related to behavior. You can see that any event which occurs is not necessarily a stimulus for a learned response. A stimulus does not occur outside of a context of other sensory events. One rarely, if ever, discriminates a single stimulus; he discriminates among stimuli. What is important is that we should be able to specify the event which governs the behavior we are interested in. If a given stimulus is functionally related to a given response, other stimuli present can be called S^Δ (S-delta).

A diagram of the relationships between the S^d (a bar), some S^Δ's and a particular behavior (pressing the bar) in a laboratory rat's behavior serves to illustrate the distinction between S^d and S^Δ's.

S^Δ (floor of the cage)
S^d (bar on wall of cage) ⟶ R (bar press)
S^Δ (sides of cage)

In this example, we are interested in relating the S^d to the response, designated by R (in this case, the bar press).

16 In the example above, the S^d is not the only stimulus present. S^Δ is used to represent the idea that other stimuli may be present, but they are unimportant to the _____ in question.

response
(behavior)

17 *Review:* The process by which a particular stimulus becomes functionally related to a given response is termed _____ _____. It is basic to the total learning process.

stimulus
discrimination

Stimulus Generalization

18 Sometimes stimuli with similar properties tend to elicit the same response; i.e., there is a generalization effect. The tendency to respond to events which have properties similar to a stimulus already related to the response is called stimulus _____.

generalization

19 Pavlov found that dogs which had learned to salivate at the sound of a particular bell tone would also salivate when similar _____ were presented.

bell tones
(sounds)

Watson and Raynor (1920) described an experiment in which an infant learned to fear a white rat. The child cried when the rat was present. When a white rabbit was introduced into the room, the child also cried. Presumably the child cried because the rat and the rabbit had similar stimulus properties; i.e., both were small, white furry animals.

20 In this study, stimulus generalization was demonstrated because the animals had similar _____ properties.

stimulus

21 The child also reacted to other objects having similar color and texture properties as the white rat, e.g., a Santa Claus beard. This illustrates the principle of _____ _____.

stimulus generalization

22 Instead of similar stimuli being S^{Δ}'s, under stimulus generalization they take on the properties of the original _____ (or S^d).

stimulus

We can designate a generalized stimulus by S^g. The following diagram demonstrates how stimulus generalization operates for the preceding example.

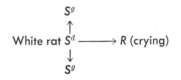

23 Now substitute "white rabbit" and "white beard" for the S^g's and complete the diagram. +++++.

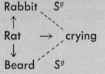

24 A child learned to like spinach but not yellow vegetables. Taken to a cafeteria, he sees collard greens for the first time. All the other vegetables are yellow. The principle of stimulus generalization suggests he would select _____ _____.

collard greens

25 Stimulus generalization is most likely to occur with stimuli which are highly similar to the original. Mistaking a person as a friend because he has red hair, a body build, and a gait like those of your friend is a common example of _____ _____.

stimulus generalization

26 You use stimulus discrimination to identify differences among stimuli; stimulus generalization occurs when stimulus properties are _____.

similar

27 In most everyday behaviors stimulus discrimination and generalization occur together. The process of learning what is appropriate behavior and what is not involves both _____ _____ and _____ _____.

stimulus discrimination
stimulus generalization
(either order)

28 A year-old infant learns to call his father "daddy." Suppose that, when other men come near him, he also calls them "daddy." Calling others "daddy" represents _____ _____.

stimulus generalization

29 The Goldstein-Scheerer tests of concept formation (Goldstein and Scheerer, 1941) consist of many objects of different size, shape, color, and use. The idea is to group them according to any of the ways they might go together. This grouping represents concept formation. The subject is asked to classify test objects together so that his ability to form _____ can be measured.

concepts

30 The classification process represents a complex series of responses to a variety of stimuli. In the process, the test objects first of all must be visually _____.

discriminated

31 When test objects which have common properties are placed together, the grouping is usually based on the process of _____ (S^g)

generalization

32 For instance, knives, forks, and spoons are discriminated as objects which share a common property; i.e., they are all used for eating. Stimulus discrimination permits selection of each utensil; they are grouped together because of the principle of _____ _____.

stimulus generalization

33 Mathematical "set theory" also emphasizes the necessity for making stimulus generalizations, but this in turn is dependent on distinguishing common properties that go together. The abstraction of common characteristics in mathematics requires determining events that have common stimulus _____, i.e., that form sets.

properties

34 Rules for set theory involve manipulation of events that occur together or which have _____ properties.

similar (common)

In summary, the basic processes of stimulus discrimination and stimulus generalization are involved in practically all the activities we participate in. In order to understand better the bases of these fundamental processes, we might well examine some of the characteristics of visual and auditory stimuli. Size, proximity, illumination, and color are all stimulus properties of visual stimuli; volume, pitch, and timbre contribute to the clarity of audition. Characteristics of these two types of stimuli emphasize the importance of stimulus properties for understanding human behavior.

Stimulus Properties

1. Visual Stimuli

35 In general, the larger an item is, the easier it is to discriminate. There is a positive relationship between _____ of an item and its discriminability.

size

36 Other things being equal, a quarter is easier to see than a dime. Even without considering monetary valuation (which might also affect discrimination) this is true because of differences in _____ of the coins.

size

37 The size of lettering in textbooks is carefully determined in order to try to maximize visual discrimination. Type one-half the size of that used in this book obviously provides smaller _____ stimuli than standard-size type used here.

visual

38 These examples are used to emphasize the point that, other things being equal, the larger an item is, the easier it is to _____.

see (discriminate)

39 Proximity, or nearness, is another stimulus property which affects our interpretation of events. Proximity refers to the _____ of a stimulus.

nearness

40 If you take a picture of a man holding a cigar in his fingers, and his arm is extended toward the camera, the cigar will look much _____ [larger/smaller] than if he had it in his mouth.

larger

41 This difference in stimulus discrimination is due principally to the _____ of the cigar to the camera.

proximity (nearness)

42 In addition to size, then, another stimulus characteristic which affects response behavior is _____.

proximity

43 Illumination is still another stimulus property which affects response to a given stimulus. In general, the more light reflected from an object the _____ it is to see.

easier

44 Illumination is due in part to the amplitude of the light waves which are reflected by a given object. The magnitude, or size, of light waves refers to their _____.

amplitude

45 The brighter an object appears, the greater the amplitude of the _____ _____ it is reflecting.

light waves

46 At night, sand does not appear as "white" as it does in the daytime. In large part this is a function of the _____ of the light waves which are reflected from the sand.

amplitude

47 In general, then, visual acuity (that is, the ability to make visual discriminations) increases with _____ as well as with size and proximity.

illumination

48 *Review:* Visual acuity increases with _____, _____, and _____.

size
proximity
illumination

49 Achromatic colors (black through gray to white) have only the dimension of brightness. A pure gray would be designated technically as not having color, i.e., it is _____.

achromatic

50 A pure gray (like black or white) has only the dimension of _____.

brightness

51 Most objects that we see reflect electromagnetic wave lengths of light between 400 and 700 millimicrons (a millimicron is one-millionth of a millimeter). This range includes those wave lengths for seeing chromatic _____.

color

52 Hue is the technical term for the quality of redness, greenness, or yellowness that we discriminate as _____ color.

chromatic

53 We discriminate between different colors because of the differences in wave _____ properties that objects have.

length

54 The color range, called the solar spectrum, goes from deep purple (about 400 millimicrons) to bright red (about 700 millimicrons). Blue and yellow have intermediate wave lengths. The technical term for the range of color we see is the solar _____.

spectrum

55 Parts of the solar spectrum are visible as colored because of different wave lengths of light which they reflect. The component colors of the _____ _____ contribute hue to an object.

solar spectrum

56 Objects which reflect only achromatic colors have only the dimension of brightness; those with chromatic colors have a brightness dimension plus _____.

hue

57 Brightness and hue are two aspects of color. A third is saturation. Apparent purity of color is referred to as _____.

saturation

58 The saturation of a color can be reduced by mixing gray with it. Increasing or decreasing the brightness of a pure color will also reduce _____.

saturation

59 We discriminate between objects having different colors in terms of the different wave lengths of light they reflect. Chromatic colors have characteristic _____ _____.

wave lengths

60 In addition to the brightness dimension of illumination, then, two dimensions of color contribute to the stimulus properties an object may have. They are _____ and _____.

hue
saturation

61 The aspects of illumination which permit us to differentiate between a red and a green apple, or a purple and a green coat, are _____, hue, and saturation.

brightness

62 Brightness, hue, and saturation are aspects of _____. In addition to illumination, size and proximity are two stimulus properties affecting visual discrimination.

illumination

63 *Review:* Three general properties of visual stimuli affect their discrimination. They are _____, _____, and _____.

size
proximity
illumination

Another property which affects visual discrimination is the context in which an event appears. You probably have observed that the moon looks larger on the horizon than when it is directly overhead. Obviously, the moon does not change in size as it revolves around the earth.

64 The reason for the apparent size discrepancy described above is the differences in environmental _____ in which the moon is viewed.

context (condition)

Look at this drawing and decide what it represents. The connected vertical lines represent a fence. Does this alter your interpretation of the figure? (If you are already familiar with this example go to Frame 66.) Can you accommodate the idea that the jagged line could be the end of a soldier's rifle, with bayonet attached?

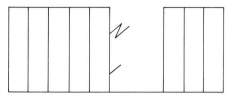

65 You can probably agree that the line below the soldier's gun is the tail of an _____.

animal (dog, etc.)

66 By now perhaps you have already altered your interpretation of the drawing so that you see this as a soldier and an animal walking past +++++.

a hole in a fence

The next example may require some audible reading on your part in order to combine the separate stimuli into a different type of context. First, read the words slowly. On succeeding trials read them progressively faster.

FORCE   CORE   ANTS   HEAVEN   EARS   EGO

67 If you read the words slowly, they probably bore no relation to each other. As you read them more quickly, you should have heard yourself reading the opening words of Lincoln's famous _____ _____.

Gettysburg
Address

One more example might serve to emphasize the idea that stimulus discrimination is affected by the context in which the stimulus occurs. Which of the three horizontal lines below appears to be the longest?

(1) ———————————————
(2) >———————————————<
(3) <———————————————>

Which line appears to be the shortest?

68 Actually, all the lines are of the same length. If the so-called Muller-Lyer illusions occur in lines **(2)** and **(3)**, they can be attributed to the _____ in which the lines appear.

context

69 This section dealt with some properties of visual stimuli. Visual discrimination is affected by the size, proximity, illumination, and color of stimuli, and by the _____ in which stimuli appear.

context

70 *Review:* In addition to context, the other stimulus properties discussed in this section were _____, _____, _____, and _____.

size
proximity
illumination
color

71 Stimulus properties are important conditions for visual discrimination, but the stimulus properties themselves do not ensure that any two observers will _____ to them in the same way.

respond (react)

72 Individual differences among people obviously affect visual discrimination. Two different people may respond to the same stimulus in quite different ways. Conditions of the organism, including background of experience, contribute to _____ _____ in visual discrimination.

individual
differences

Stimulus properties permit common response; individual differences in conditions of the organism permit differences in response. This is true for all kinds of stimuli—visual, gustatory, tactile, and so forth. It might be well to compare visual and auditory stimuli to see how common principles operate for both types.

2. Auditory Stimuli

73 Some of the generalizations that were made about visual discrimination of stimuli hold true for auditory stimuli. Stimuli mediated through the ears and then transmitted to the brain are called _____ _____.

auditory
stimuli

74 Auditory stimuli, like visual stimuli, consist of waves. Sound waves are caused by displacement of the existing _____ or water. When these waves stimulate the eardrums, they set up vibrations.

air

75 Consecutive displacement of air sets up vibrations which stimulate the _____.

eardrum

76 Sound waves, or air vibrations, are the actual auditory stimuli. It is the peculiar _____ _____ set up by a whistle that distinguish them from those of a human voice.

sound waves
(air vibrations)

77 "Oh, those screeching brakes!" means that friction created between brakes and pavement sets up vibrations which provide an auditory _____ for the listener.

78 Sound waves, like light waves, have several dimensions. Pitch, loudness, and timbre are the three most important dimensions of _____ _____.

79 The frequency of sound waves determines the pitch of a sound. Sound waves which provide stimuli for humans vary from 16 to 20,000 cycles per second in _____.

80 Frequency determines the _____ of a sound.

81 Pitch refers to the _____ of sound waves.

82 The higher the vibration frequency, the higher the _____ we discriminate.

83 A piano produces sound frequencies from about 30 per second to 4,600 per second. A flute produces frequencies similar to the upper register of piano _____.

84 A high-pitched sound would represent a _____ _____ of vibrations.

85 So-called "pure" tones have only one frequency. "White noise" (such as the sound of a racing car going by) is composed of many complex _____.

86 An electronic pure tone represents only one **(1)** _____; the sounds at the Indianapolis Speedway represent many **(2)** _____ frequencies.

87 Pitch and loudness are ordinarily considered together. Amplitude of sound waves is to loudness as frequency of sound waves is to _____.

88 If loudness refers to amplitude of sound waves, you might infer that the louder the sound, the _____ the amplitude of sound waves.

89 *Review:* The higher the vibration frequency, the higher the **(1)** _____; the greater the amplitude, the **(2)** _____ the sound.

90 It is not difficult to discriminate between "loud" and "soft" sounds. However, these words are not precise in denoting subjective auditory _____.

stimulus

sound (air) waves

frequency

pitch

frequency

pitch

tones (sounds; frequencies)

high frequency

frequencies

(1) frequency
(2) complex

pitch

greater

(1) pitch
(2) louder

discrimination

91 In order to assign values to sounds of varying loudness, acoustical engineers use a scale composed of decibels, which are tones of defined loudness. One-tenth of a bel is a _____.

decibel

92 Decibels are used to measure _____ of sounds.

loudness

93 Decibels actually are measures of physical pressures on the eardrum. Loudness of sounds thus refers to _____ of sound waves exerted on the eardrums.

pressure

94 A tympani player beats with various degrees of pressure on his drums. The resulting vibrations vary in frequency and amplitude on our eardrums, and we perceive them as variations in _____ and _____.

pitch
loudness

95 It is actually the (1) _____ on the eardrums which provides the S^d for loudness, just as it is the frequency of sound waves which provides the S^d for (2) _____.[2]

(1) pressure

(2) pitch

96 Human voices and musical instruments vary in more than just pitch and loudness. Their distinctive tonal characteristics are also due in part to timbre. Quality of tone is referred to as _____.

timbre

97 Timbre actually depends on impurities in sounds, such as overtones. An overtone, as the name implies, is some multiple of the fundamental sound frequency which is higher in _____.

frequency

98 Timbre really refers to mixtures of different tones, much as saturation is a _____ of color.

mixture

99 A trumpet has a characteristic timbre because of the _____ which are peculiar to it. The same can be said of other musical instruments.

overtones

100 An overtone, by definition, is some multiple of the fundamental sound frequency which is _____ in pitch than the fundamental tone.

higher

101 An auditory stimulus, then, is composed of sound waves which have characteristic pitch, loudness, and _____.

timbre

[2] It has ben determined that human beings can discriminate sounds varying from 0.002 dynes per square centimeter to 20,000 dynes per square centimeter in pressure. A dyne is the amount of energy required to move 1 gram the distance of 1 centimeter per second.

(1) amplitude
(2) frequency

stimulus

frequency

amplitude

mixture

(a)—2
(b)—3
(c)—1

stimulus

not harmonize
(go together)

consonants

dissonants

102 Timbre is to quality of tone as loudness is to **(1)** _____ and as pitch is to **(2)** _____ of sound waves.

103 It is the combination of pitch, loudness, and timbre which enables us to identify a particular auditory _____ as, e.g., a human voice, an automobile horn, or a saxophone.

104 In a sense, hue and pitch are functions of wave _____.

105 Brightness and loudness are functions of wave _____.

106 Saturation and timbre are the results of a _____ of light or sound wave properties.

107 *Review:* The three dimensions of auditory stimuli correspond to three dimensions of visual stimuli. Match the following:
    (a) pitch   1. saturation
    (b) loudness   2. hue
    (c) timbre   3. brightness
Review frames 54 to 60 if you do not recall what items 1, 2, and 3 represent.

108 When colors are mixed together, they tend to lose their identities in the mixing process. Tones also tend to mix together to form a new auditory _____.

109 Tones sounded together are either consonant (their frequencies and amplitudes go together, i.e., harmonize) or dissonant (i.e., their frequencies and amplitudes do _____ _____).

110 Tones which harmonize are called _____.

111 Tones which do not harmonize are called _____.

Unlike the mixing of colors, when tones are sounded together, it is usually possible to discriminate particular tones. The analogy of color and tonal mixing breaks down at this point, but it is nonetheless useful for descriptive purposes. Other types of stimulus properties are attached to particular types of sensory stimuli (e.g., odors, flavors, etc.). The illustrations provided by properties of visual and auditory stimuli should be sufficient to demonstrate the major idea of this section, namely, that behavior is in part a function of the properties of the stimuli to which it is related.

Conditions That Affect Learning

Following the original suggestion of Robert Woodworth (1938), O. Hobart Mowrer (1960), along with many authorities, has reiterated that the *S — R* paradigm is an oversimplification of why and how behavior occurs. Mowrer has suggested that the state of the organism has a great deal to do both with discriminating stimuli and making responses. He proposes that the paradigm would be more appropriate if it read: *S — O — R*, where O stands for organism.

Some dedicated behaviorists have rejected this suggestion because, they say, only the functional relationships between stimuli and behavior are significant for behavioral analysis. Yet a large body of research indicates that biological and psychological conditions can dramatically affect both stimulus discrimination and behavioral response. This section suggests how body conditions, emotions, and other psychosocial conditions can influence learning.

Body Conditions

biological

112 When a person is debilitated or weakened because of the effects of illness, fatigue, intoxication, or trauma, he is obviously not operating under normal _____ conditions.

learning

113 Invasion of the body system by infectious diseases usually results in lowered energy output and reports of malaise. Such conditions obviously can affect _____.

healthy person
(someone without
these symptoms)

114 Elevated temperature, rhinitis (runny nose), and lethargy are typical symptoms of influenza. Under these conditions, you would hardly expect a person to discriminate stimuli in a learning situation as well as a _____
_____.

diseases

115 Influenza and other infectious _____ obviously can affect both stimulus discrimination and behavioral responses.

fatigue

116 Fatigue is another condition which can affect behavior adversely. All those conditions which are harmful or debilitating, which occur because of duration or amount of effort, and which are recoverable by rest, can be defined as _____.

During and after World War II, many experiments were run to determine the effects of fatigue on learning and performance of complex skills. Munn (1961, pp. 679–680) describes the results of a study done at Cambridge University by Davis. Subjects were placed in a simulated cockpit and told to "fly" correctly. Close attention and precise motor acts overtime were required. Subjects were forced to "fly" until fatigue occurred.

fatigue

117 In this study, as performance progressed without rest, the pilot became less responsive to signals that he was "off course." The signals were not responded to effectively because of _____.

tired (fatigued)

118 Reactions to signals were usually delayed under conditions of fatigue. Mistakes occurred, and pilots complained that they felt _____.

stimuli (signals)

119 In this study inappropriate response to _____ was used to assess fatigue.

decrease

120 Decrease in work performance has been used to assess fatigue. One of the most common measures of fatigue is a _____ in work or performance.

increase

121 Acute sleep deprivation (from twenty-four to one hundred hours) results in decrease in speed of reaction as well as impairment of vigilance (Williams, Lubin, and Goodman, 1959). Conversely, there is a sharp _____ in error rate in the performance of motor skills.

(1) speed of
 reaction
(2) errors
 (error rate)

122 *Review:* Two behavior changes common under conditions of fatigue are (1) decrease in +++++ and (2) an increase in _____ during work performance. A third characteristic of fatigue occurs when a person reports that he feels tired.

self-reports
 ("feeling tired")

123 Which of the three characteristics of fatigue given in the preceding frame cannot be measured precisely? _____.

124 One of the interesting findings of the Cambridge cockpit studies was that knowledge of results seemed to attenuate the effects of fatigue. In other words, work decrement was delayed and error rates were reduced by giving subjects _____ of their work.

knowledge (results)

125 Ill health has often been used as an explanation for lowered output or efficiency. This is a term that has perhaps even more vague connotations than _____.

fatigue

126 As a matter of record, one physician has reported that somewhere between one-third and two-thirds of all patients who seek medical help are actually suffering from nervousness and/or _____ (Wilbur, 1949).

fatigue

Deprivation of food or water may also produce biological conditions which affect behavior. An interesting study of men who voluntarily participated in a semistarvation experiment revealed that consistent reduction in food intake produced alterations in behavior (Keys, et al., 1950). For six months the men in the semistarvation study were placed on restricted diets so that their daily caloric intake was reduced to less than one-half that of normal (from 3,500 to 1,570 calories). Their average weights dropped from about 155 to 120 pounds. They seemed to be preoccupied with food continuously. These men would have long discussions about food-related implements (utensils, crockery, cookbooks, etc.), and walking past a hardware store was likely to cause them to stop and discuss any object that was related to food.

127 Evidently, the preoccupation with food was a function of _____ of food.

deprivation

128 Severe food deprivation can affect behavior in much the same way as other abnormal biological conditions such as (1) infectious _____ and (2) _____.

(1) disease
(2) fatigue

Drugs, including alcohol, provide another means for altering normal biological functioning. The effects of alcoholic beverages on the body depend on the concentration of alcohol in the body tissues (see Table 6). Thus the amount of alcohol in common beverages may be of some interest. This amount is denoted in given beverages by dividing by one-half the amount of the "proof" of the beverage. That is, 100-proof whisky contains 50 per cent of alcohol by volume.

129 How much alcohol is ingested by a person who drinks a double shot (2 ounces) of 100-proof whisky? _____.

1 ounce

130 Ingested alcohol must be absorbed before it can affect the tissues. Absorption rate varies with concentration of alcohol, contents of the stomach, and biological differences among individuals (Wenger, et al., 1956, p. 392). Other things being equal, the stronger the drink, the greater the _____ rate of alcohol.

absorption

131 Other things being equal, the emptier the stomach, the faster the _____ of alcohol.

absorption

Table 6. Relationships between Blood-alcohol Percentages and Behavior

Per cent of Blood Alcohol	Behavior
Less than 0.1	Dry and decent
0.1–0.2	Delighted and devilish
0.2–0.3	Disgusting and delinquent
0.3–0.4	Dizzy and delirious
0.4–0.5	Dazed and dejected
0.5–0.6	Dead drunk

SOURCE: R. W. Husband, *Applied Psychology*, p. 428, Harper & Row, Publishers, Incorporated, New York, 1949. Permission to reprint granted.

132 The percentages in the table may be slightly high for the behaviors they represent. If they are approximately correct, however, they suggest that body conditions and social behavior are increasingly affected by _____ amounts of alcohol in the blood.

increased

133 The increase in blood alcohol is related to the parts of the brain affected. Since rational behavior is mediated primarily by the cerebral cortex, and vegetative functions are mediated primarily by the "old brain" (specifically, the medulla), you can see that the **(1)** cerebral _____ is affected by smaller quantities of alcohol than the **(2)** _____ _____.

(1) cortex

(2) old brain

134 Alcohol has anesthetizing effects at about 0.5 per cent of blood volume. This _____ effect probably protects many people from death from overdrinking.

anesthetizing

Other drugs, such as morphine, heroin, and caffeine, also affect stimulus discrimination and other behavior. Extended descriptions of such effects can be found in Uhr and Miller's book, *Drugs and Behavior* (1960).

135 Congenital disorders or traumatic brain injury also may affect the ability to learn different kinds of skills. Many forms of mental retardation occur because of **(1)** _____ or **(2)** traumatic _____ disorders. These obviously affect learning capabilities.

(1) congenital
(2) brain

136 There is some evidence that the basic perceptual processes of retarded children are not very different from those of _____ children.

normal (non-retarded)

137 However, the response repertoire, i.e., the observed behavior of _____ children, differs considerably from that of normals. They learn much more slowly and cannot perform as adequately as most normal children of their age.

retarded

As far as traumatic brain injury is concerned, the location, extent, and nature of tissue damage determine the degree to which various types of behavior (e.g., motor, language) are affected (Halstead, 1945; Reitan, 1958).

138 Figure 4 represents the location and extent of a brain lesion. The _____ and _____ of brain damage determine what behavior is affected.

location
extent

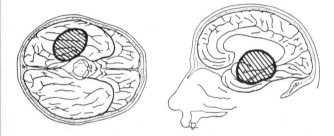

Figure 4. Lesions in the right hemisphere of the brain. (After Reitan, 1960.)

139 The patient represented in Figure 4 suffered symptoms of aphasia, a difficulty in communication. The brain lesion is _____ in the right hemisphere of the brain.

located

140 In addition to the location of the damage, behavior is affected by the _____ of the lesion.

extent (amount)

141 The lesion represented in Figure 4 involved a considerable portion of the right hemisphere. The amount of behavior affected was proportional to the _____ and _____ of the brain involved.

extent
location

142 The nature of the tissue damaged by the lesion also influences the type and extent of behavior involved. This lesion was located in the cortex, which accounts for the fact that difficulties in _____ were involved.[3]

communication
(i.e., aphasia)

143 *Review:* The type and amount of behavior affected varies to a considerable extent with the _____, _____, and _____ of the tissue damage.

location
extent
nature
(any order)

damage

144 Thus, _____ to the brain, as well as other conditions mentioned heretofore, can affect learning.

Debilitation due to disease, fatigue, deprivation of food or water, traumatic brain damage, and drugs can upset biological homeostasis and result in interference with stimulus discrimination and responses to stimuli. This, in turn, affects learning.

Emotions

This section describes emotions as patterns of biological responses and as patterns of subjective experience. No matter how emotions are defined (and there is disagreement about what the term represents), most authorities agree that they may affect learning and conditioning. Information about the development of emotional behavior in children will be given in Part IV, Unit 2. Long-term effects of emotions on behavior will be discussed in Part V, Unit 2.

145 Biological response patterns in intense "flight-or-fight" behavior represent particular kinds of _____. That is, they represent intense fear or rage reactions.

emotions

146 Under stimulus conditions demanding an intense emotional response, rapid mobilization of _____ resources can be observed and measured.

body
(biological)

147 Both "flight" and "fight" reactions include certain well-known physiological changes. These _____ changes themselves are related to specific activities of the anterior pituitary gland and the adrenal cortex.

physiological

148 Increases in heartbeat, blood pressure, and respiration rate are typical physiological _____ observed.

changes

[3] Refer to Part II, Unit 2 for a discussion of different types of brain tissue.

149 Capillaries in the brain and large muscles expand during strong emotion. This permits quicker and more intense _____ to the stimulus which provokes the change.

reaction (response)

150 On the other hand, capillaries in the digestive tract constrict, and muscle action diminishes, so that _____ of food slows down during the emotional reaction.

digestion

151 Production of sugar and red blood cells is increased during strong emotion. Increases in production of _____ and +++++ is related to increased energy required by the body for intense emotional reactions.

sugar
red blood cells

152 The physiological changes described in the preceding frames are common both to intense "_____" and "_____" reactions, i.e., behavior representing strong anger or fear.

"fight"
"flight"

153 These increases in body activity are not observed in depressive emotional reactions. Rather, pulse, blood pressure, respiration, and sugar production either remain about the same or actually _____.

decrease (lessen)

154 In other words, when the body-action potentials for emotion are depressed under certain stimulus conditions, they provide a criterion for a _____ emotional reaction.

depressive

155 Review: The biological reactions described above are normal adaptive procedures to temporary emotional situations. If prolonged, these reactions can result in impairment to the _____.

body (person)

156 Selye (1956) describes three stages of body reaction to _____ stress. They are the *alarm reaction*, the *resistance stage*, and the *exhaustion stage*.

emotional

157 In the initial stage, the biochemical changes described above are mediated by the autonomic nervous system. They constitute the _____ reaction.

alarm

158 The body is mobilized for activity by the _____ reaction.

alarm

159 In the second stage, Selye reports that an increase in activity of the anterior pituitary and adrenal cortex, along with other biochemical changes, enables the individual to adapt to, or resist, emotional _____.

stress

resistance

160 Thus the second stage is called the _____ stage.

physiological
(body)

161 During the resistance stage, there is a resumption of normal functioning of the _____ processes described previously, even though stress continues.

(1) pituitary
(2) adrenal

162 If the anterior (1) _____ and (2) _____ cortex are unable to compensate for the prolonged and severe stress encountered, exhaustion occurs.

exhaustion

163 The third stage of Selye's adaptation theory is called the _____ stage.

exhaustion

164 In the exhaustion stage, the original symptoms typically reappear in a more severe form and other ailments may be reported. Severe and prolonged emotion may result finally in _____ of body resources originally capable of resisting stress.

alarm
resistance
exhaustion

165 Review: The three stages of adaptation to stress are termed by Selye the _____, _____, and _____ stages. If you cannot identify the characteristics of these stages, review frames 157 to 164.

As mentioned earlier, biological concomitants of severe emotion are well known. Emotions are also classified according to subjective experience. We "feel" afraid, or angry, or guilty, or affectionate, as the case may be. That is, we are aware of our reaction to particular stimuli.

fear

166 A normal emotional reaction to danger is _____.

behavior (responses,
learning)

167 When it is interpreted as cowardice, or when it leads to irrational behavior, fear can inhibit effective _____.

fear

168 Anxiety is a term used to describe vague and diffuse _____. It will be discussed further in Part IV, Unit 3.

hostility

169 Hostility is a typical (though not the only) reaction to frustration. Anger and resentment are forms of _____.

frustration

170 It is quite normal to respond to _____ with hostility.

behavior
(learning)

171 However, to the degree that hostility is persistent or uncontrolled, it may inhibit effective _____.

guilt

behavior
(reaction)

emotions

severe

observation
(experience)

one-trial

emotional

learning

(1) physiological
(biological)
(2) responses (reac-
tions, feelings)

172 Similarly, guilt can be a useful or a crippling emotion. A subjective reaction against one's violation of conditioned standards of value is a definition of _____.

173 Irrational guilt can lead to depressive _____. This, too, will be discussed more fully in Part IV, Unit 3.

174 Our point here is that subjective emotional experiences such as fear, hostility, and guilt, if excessive and persistent, can give rise to ineffective behavior. Plutchik (1962) and others have summarized experiments which show how these _____ can affect learning.

175 In general, severity of emotional reaction is related to learning and conditioning. The more _____ the reaction, the greater the relationship to learning (other things being equal).

176 Some severe emotional reactions result in "one-trial learning." This has been demonstrated in many aversive conditioning experiments with lower animals and humans, and is often confirmed by personal _____.

177 Animals can be conditioned to avoid electrified grids in Skinner boxes, and humans often learn to avoid deep water or high places as a function of _____-_____ learning.

178 One-trial learning usually involves a strong _____ reaction to some aspect of the learning situation.

179 Similarly, the stronger and more persistent the emotional reaction (using either body condition or subjective experience as the criterion for emotion), the greater the likelihood that _____, in the usual sense, will be affected.

180 *Review:* This section emphasizes that emotions can affect learning and conditioning. Emotions can be designated in terms of (1) _____ changes or in terms of subjective (2) _____ to stress.

Other Conditions That Affect Learning

At any given time, the number of sensory stimuli which bombard us is enormous. Light rays are reflected from many discrete objects; a variety of sound waves impinge on our eardrums; a great diversity of odors are wafted to us;

clothing exerts pressure on different parts of our bodies. We have already seen that stimulus properties such as size, intensity, proximity, and clarity cause some stimuli to be perceived instead of others. The characteristics of the stimuli and the biological conditions of the organism are important in determining what is perceived. Other conditions also affect what stimuli are discriminated and how they are perceived. For example, the psychological "set" we have for seeing or hearing something, the familiarity we have with similar stimuli, and the voluntary attention we pay to an event also determine the way it is perceived and reacted to. This section deals with such conditions.

181 When a track star prepares for the beginning of a race, he places his feet in starting blocks and prepares for, or "gets set," for the starter's gun. His anticipation of the starting signal is part of his preparatory _____.

set

182 In this instance, the runner is enabled to leave the starting line more quickly because of _____ _____.

preparatory set

The influence of set on human behavior has been demonstrated in a number of experiments. One of these involved identification of playing cards that were briefly exposed in a tachistoscope, a projection device with a controlled time exposure (Bruner and Postman, 1949). The subject had to identify common playing cards, but some unusual cards were introduced as well.

183 When a black four of hearts or a red six of spades was introduced, most subjects called them something different, e.g., a red four of hearts or a black four of spades. In other words, the cards were not _____ correctly.

identified (called)

184 When the incongruous cards were pointed out to the subjects, they reported fewer false identifications. Presumably, they had developed a _____ for incongruities.

set

185 These two examples, preparation for a starting signal and change in response as a function of anticipating incongruity, demonstrate how _____ set can affect behavior.

preparatory

186 Set is demonstrated at a basketball game by both spectators and players just _____ the opening whistle.

before

187 Preparatory set involves some familiarity with a perceived event. If the spectators had no _____ with the game, they would not respond as they do at the opening whistle (or thereafter, for that matter).

familiarity

188 The symbol 𝄞 carries no meaning for the person who cannot read Chinese. Familiarity with this symbol enables one to _____ it as "man."

interpret (perceive, read)

189 People who have been blinded early in life and who later recover their eyesight have difficulty in identifying objects visually, even though they may have familiarized themselves with their shape, size, and other characteristics through other kinds of sensory _____ with them.

contact (familiarity)

190 Boys who are adept with a basketball may be very awkward with a baseball or football, if they have little prior experience with them. In this case, specific skill or performance is affected by _____.

experience (familiarity)

191 *Review:* We have said that preparatory _____ for an event and _____ with the event tend to enhance the probability of learning about that event.

set
familiarity

192 The social conditions under which behavior occurs also affect _____.

learning

193 Soldiers commonly use profanity when by themselves. Frequency of usage drops when the social conditions change, e.g., when women are present. This suggests that _____ conditions affect behavior.

social

194 Stimulus generalization occurs under appropriate social conditions. For example, Seward (1946) reports that a rat that is badly beaten by another rat will then respond submissively to rats over which he previously had been dominant. This demonstrates how stimulus _____ is related to social conditions.

generalization

195 A man despised his boss, who had red hair. Previously he had not disliked red-haired people, but after working under his obnoxious superior, he reported, "Red hair makes me sick." This exemplified the principle that social conditions affect stimulus _____.

generalization

196 If a person's behavior changes because of variations in the social situation, it may be safely inferred that the _____ conditions are affecting behavior.

social

197 *Review:* The foregoing section points out that psychosocial conditions affect learning. Specifically, the particular psychosocial conditions referred to include **(1)** preparatory _____, **(2)** _____ with the event to be learned, and the **(3)** _____ conditions under which learning takes place. The last-named condition is discussed more fully in a companion volume, *Social Behavior,* to be published by the McGraw-Hill Book Company.

(1) set
(2) familiarity
(3) social

SUMMARY

Learning is one of the most fundamental of human activities. It affects virtually every aspect of our behavior. Learning depends, in part, on the processes of stimulus discrimination and generalization. The first refers to the ability to distinguish a particular stimulus from among other stimuli. It is exemplified by learning to notice a red light (among other visual stimuli); to see or to touch appropriate typewriter keys for spelling particular words; or to distinguish, among a host of other auditory stimuli, the sound of someone calling your name. Generalization refers to the tendency to respond in the same way to different stimuli with similar properties. For example, a child who has learned to fear a white rat may respond in the same way to white cats.

Discrimination of visual stimuli is affected in part by their saturation, hue, and brightness, as well as by the context in which they appear. Auditory stimuli are actually sound waves of different pitch, loudness, and timbre (quality). It is the combination of these properties that enables us to identify particular sights and sounds. Stimulus properties permit common responses from different people. Individual differences in people permit unique stimulus discrimination and, subsequently, unique behavior.

Illness, traumatic injury, and fatigue are body conditions which can affect learning adversely. Alcohol and drugs also tend to inhibit maximum learning potential. Excessive emotions, psychological "set," and familiarity with the material to be learned are other conditions which determine in part the ease with which particular events are learned or whether they are learned at all.

Knowledge of stimulus discrimination and generalization and of other conditions which affect learning is of value in understanding the principles of respondent and operant conditioning described in the next unit.

REFERENCES

Bruner, J., and L. Postman: "On the Perception of Incongruity: A Paradigm," *Journal of Personality*, 18:206–223, 1949.

Delgado, J., H. E. Roswell, and E. Looney: "Evoking Conditional Fear by Electrical Stimulation of Subcortical Structures in the Monkey Brain," *Journal of Comparative and Physiological Psychology*, 49:373–380, 1956.

Dews, P. B.: "Psychopharmacology," in A. J. Bachrach (ed.), *Experimental Foundations of Clinical Psychology*, chap. 12, Basic Books, Inc., Publishers, New York, 1962.

Goldiamond, I.: "Visual Signal Detection and Perception in Retarded Children," in C. Atkinson, I. Goldiamond, and L. Malpass, *Perceptual and Response Abilities of Retarded Children*, Southern Illinois University Press, Carbondale, Illinois, 1960.

Goldstein, K., and M. Scheerer: "Abstract and Concrete Behavior: An Experimental Study with Special Tests," *Psychological Monographs*, vol. 53, no. 2, 1941.

Halstead, W.: *Brain and Intelligence*, The University of Chicago Press, Chicago, 1945.

Keys, A. B., et al.: *The Biology of Human Starvation*, The University of Minnesota Press, Minneapolis, Minnesota, 1950.

Mowrer, O. H.: *Learning Theory and Behavior*, John Wiley & Sons, Inc., New York, 1960.

Munn, N.: *Psychology*, 4th ed., Houghton Mifflin Company, Boston, 1961.

Olds, James: "Pleasure Centers in the Brain," *Scientific American*, 195:108–118, 1956.

Pavlov, I.: *Conditioned Reflexes*, trans. by G. Vanrep, Oxford University Press, London, 1927.

Plutchik, R.: *The Emotions: Facts, Theories and a New Model*, Random House, Inc., New York, 1962.

Reitan, R.: "Qualitative and Quantitative Mental Changes following Brain Lesions," *Journal of Psychology*, 46:339–346, 1958.

Ronchi, N.: *Optics: The Science of Vision*, New York University Press, New York, 1957.

Ryan, T. A., and P. C. Smith: *Principles of Industrial Psychology*, The Ronald Press Company, New York, 1954.

Selye, H.: *The Stress of Life*, McGraw-Hill Book Company, New York, 1956.

Seward, J. P.: "Aggressive Behavior in the Rat," *Journal of Comparative and Physiological Psychology*, 39:51–76, 1946.

Skinner, B. F.: *Science and Human Behavior*, The Macmillan Company, New York, 1953.

Uhr, L., and J. P. Miller (eds.): *Drugs and Behavior*, John Wiley & Sons, Inc., New York, 1960.

Watson, J. B., and R. Raynor: "Conditioned Emotional Reactions," *Journal of Experimental Psychology*, 3:1–4, 1920.

Wenger, M. W., F. N. Jones, and M. H. Jones: *Physiological Psychology*, Holt, Rinehart and Winston, Inc., New York, 1956.

Wilbur, D. L.: "Clinical Management of the Patient with Fatigue and Nervousness," *Jour-nal of the American Medical Association*, 141:1199–1204, 1949.

Williams, H. L., A. Lubin, and J. J. Goodwin: "Impaired Performance with Acute Sleep Loss," *Psychological Monographs*, no. 14, 1959.

Woodworth, R. S.: *Experimental Psychology*, Holt, Rinehart and Winston, Inc., New York, 1938.

SELF-REVIEW QUIZ

1 What is the technical term applied to the process whereby an organism responds to a particular stimulus rather than to others that are present at the same time?

2 The actual interpretation of stimuli involves a process known as _____.

3 Define stimulus generalization.

4 The amount of light reflected by an object is an index of its _____. Name three aspects of this property.

5 The Muller-Lyer illusion and similar illusions demonstrate that stimulus discrimination is affected by the _____ in which the stimulus occurs.

6 Auditory stimuli actually are _____ _____.

7 Frequency of sound waves is to (a) _____ as amplitude of sound waves is to (b) _____.

8 Colors which "mix well" and tones which, when sounded together, "sound well" are said to be _____.

9 Name three types of body conditions which tend to influence learning.

10 Which glands are most often associated with emotional reactions?

11 Selye describes three stages of body reaction to stress. Name and describe each.

12 In contrast to physiological manifestations of emotion, guilt, hostility, and fear may be conceived of as _____ aspects of emotion.

13 Getting ready to take an exam, to study, or to do any other learned activity refers to the principle of _____ _____.

14 Stimulus discrimination and generalization are fundamental to the process of acquiring and maintaining new behavior, which we call _____.

unit 2

**Principle of
Learning—II**

Respondent (Classical) Conditioning

Conditioning, which is a basic form of learning, may involve a very simple response or a complex series of responses. The process of conditioning depends on stimulus discrimination and predisposing conditions of the organism which affect behavior. It also depends on whether something is obtained as a function of behavioral response. Reinforcement is a general term often used to designate the consequences of behavior. However, reinforcement will be redefined later in the unit as a particular type of behavior consequent. Not all consequents of behavior are reinforcing, as we shall see. In this unit we shall specify quite precisely how behavioral consequents affect learning.

For convenience, two types of conditioning will be described in this book.[1] The first is called respondent or classical conditioning. Sometimes it is called Pavlovian conditioning, after the Russian physiologist who first suggested it. Respondent conditioning is principally concerned with relationships between the antecedent stimulus and response. It is useful for explaining how involuntary behavior and emotional reactions are conditioned. Operant or instrumental conditioning, the second type to be presented, describes another type of learning. It emphasizes relationships between the behavior to be learned and its consequents. Because it is principally concerned with reinforcing stimuli, it is sometimes called reinforcement learning. This type of learning is useful for explaining how voluntary behaviors of all types are conditioned. Sometimes the respondent- and operant-conditioning explanatory constructs are combined into one general theory, called a two-factor theory of learning. It should be pointed out that not all learning theorists subscribe to this break-

[1] For extended discussions of respondent and operant conditioning and other theories of learning, the reader is referred to Kimble (1961), Lawson (1960), and/or Mowrer (1960).

down of conditioning concepts. As stated earlier, it introduces the concepts in a convenient way.

Let us begin with a description of respondent conditioning. Pavlov (1928) has described how his interest in learning was generated. He was studying certain physiological reactions related to salivation. He would strap a dog in a harness, insert a fistula (small tube) in its cheek in order to measure precise amounts of saliva, and then present food and other stimuli to the animal. His observations of the effects of associated stimuli on the salivary response generated much interest in the formal investigations of the learning process.

Acquisition

1 When food is presented to a dog which has not been fed for several hours, salivation occurs "naturally," i.e., without prior _____. This kind of behavior Pavlov called an unconditioned reflex.

learning or
conditioning

2 If a puff of air is directed onto the exposed eyeball, blinking "naturally" occurs. If one's hand suddenly comes into contact with a very hot object, sudden withdrawal of the hand is almost sure to follow. These are other examples of the unconditioned _____.

reflex

3 The salivary, blinking, and withdrawal responses are called unconditioned reflexes. Similarly, the presentation of food (or air jet or hot object) is called an _____ stimulus.

unconditioned

4 The unconditioned stimulus (US) evokes, or elicits, an unconditioned response (UR). When Pavlov presented his dog food, as an unconditioned (1) _____, the food evoked a salivating response, which was an (2) _____.

(1) stimulus
(2) unconditioned
response

5 So far this is no different from the simple S-R paradigm described in the last section. But Pavlov was interested in teaching the dog to demonstrate the same response to another stimulus, i.e., for the dog to _____ to respond to a bell tone in the same way he had responded to the food.

learn

6 By presenting the bell tone at almost exactly the same time as the food, Pavlov conditioned the dog to salivate when the _____ _____ was sounded.

bell tone

salivation

US = unconditioned
  stimulus
CS = conditioned
  stimulus
CR = conditioned
  response

7 In this study, the food was the unconditioned stimulus (US); the bell tone was the conditioned stimulus (CS); the conditioned response (CR) to the bell tone was _____.

8 Define the symbols

$$US \longrightarrow CR \qquad US = \text{_____}$$
$$CS \longrightarrow UR \qquad CS = \text{_____}$$
$$CR = \text{_____}$$

Now substitute the appropriate words for the preceding frame for the symbols in the diagram.

unconditioned
  stimulus

9 In respondent conditioning, essentially the same response is elicited by a previously neutral stimulus when it has been paired (usually several times) with an _____ _____ which "naturally" was able to elicit the response.

US = loud sound
CR = fear

10 John Watson, an American psychologist, applied principles of Pavlovian conditioning to humans. In one study, he conditioned an eleven-month-old infant to fear a white rat by presenting the animal at the same time as a very loud sound (Watson, 1920). In this instance, what was (a) the US? _____ (b) The CR? _____.

neutral

11 Prior to the study, the infant had never seen a rat (assumed to be a neutral stimulus for fear). He responded with no fear when it was presented. In this instance, the rat was a _____ stimulus for the fear response.

CS (conditioned
  stimulus)

12 It was only after being paired with the US that the rat became a _____ _____.

conditioned (CS)

If you cannot, refer
  to frame 13 again

13 When a neutral stimulus is paired with a stimulus which already is related to a particular response, so that presentation of the neutral stimulus elicits the same response as the US, it can be called a _____ stimulus.

14 In your own words, state the basic principles involved in respondent conditioning. +++++

acquisition

15 When a previously neutral stimulus evokes the same response as the unconditioned stimulus, we say acquisition has occurred. The bell tone for Pavlov's dog demonstrates _____ of properties originally maintained by the sight of food.

16 The class of behavior which has been discussed so far is called respondent behavior. "Automatic" body activities, such as salivation, digestion, and perspiration, are mediated by the autonomic nervous system. They are examples of _____ behavior.

respondent

17 These behaviors are mediated by the _____ nervous system and presumably have survival value.

autonomic

18 Respondent behavior includes the relatively simple reflex behavior studied by Pavlov. Salivation is an example of the _____ as a form of respondent behavior.

reflex

19 Much behavior we term emotional results from a conditioning of relatively simple physiological reflexes. Expressions of pain are sometimes simply examples of reflexes; sometimes they represent _____ behavior.

emotional

20 Simple reflexes and some comparatively complex emotional behavior constitute the two major types of the larger class of _____ behavior.

respondent

21 The development of many examples of emotional behavior (e.g., the fear "reflex") can be conveniently explained by the paradigm of _____ _____. (The explanation of complex emotional behavior sometimes requires additional use of operant-conditioning principles.)

respondent conditioning

22 Emotional behavior ordinarily involves autonomic nervous-system activity and occurs "automatically" in the presence of the conditioned stimulus. Consequent emotional behavior is sometimes used as a synonym for _____ behavior.

respondent

23 Because it helps to explain how emotional behavior is learned, respondent conditioning is often termed _____ conditioning.

emotional

24 Because respondent or emotional conditioning is the time-honored classical theory of conditioning, it is also referred to in some textbooks as _____ conditioning.

classical

25 Understanding the labels in conditioning is far less important than understanding the processes involved. You will avoid confusion if you know that the processes involved in respondent conditioning refer to the same as those in emotional or _____ conditioning.

classical

26 Respondent conditioning is principally concerned with substitution of stimuli, where both stimuli evoke approximately the same _____.

response

27 Perhaps by now it has occurred to you why respondent conditioning bears that name. It refers to responses elicited by a _____ stimulus.

conditioned

unconditioned stimulus (US)

28 Respondent conditioning involves pairing a conditioned stimulus (CS) with an _____ _____ in order to elicit the same response from the conditioned stimulus.

substitution

29 Respondent or classical conditioning emphasizes stimulus _____ and is ordinarily concerned with involuntary behavior.

conditioned

30 Children often develop food aversions and preferences remarkably like those of their parents. If a child refuses tomatoes and you know his mother also dislikes tomatoes, you might reasonably infer that tomatoes for the child represents a _____ stimulus for the mother's aversion to tomatoes (the US in this case).

stimulus substitution

31 It may well be that practically all learned emotional behavior—hating animals, revulsion against spiders, fearing high places—involves _____ _____ as the basis for its demonstration.

involuntary

32 Classical conditioning is concerned with stimulus substitution of _____ [voluntary/involuntary] behavior.

respondent

33 Whenever behavior can best be analyzed by reference to the Pavlovian paradigm, it can be called classical or _____ conditioning.

Extinction and Counterconditioning

34 Let us refer again to the Pavlov experiment. Suppose that Pavlov's dog, after being conditioned to salivate when the bell sounded, then had not been given food for many trials after the bell sounded. Do you think it would have continued to salivate? +++++

As a matter of fact, it did not.

35 In Pavlov's experiment, food was the reinforcement for salivation. When a previously conditioned stimulus is no longer reinforced by pairing with an unconditioned stimulus, there is a tendency for extinction to occur. In this case, cessation of a response is the criterion for _____.

extinction

College sophomores have been conditioned to blink their eyes at many things (including members of the opposite sex). In laboratory experiments, the usual procedure is to administer a puff of air into their eyes as they are simultaneously exposed to a CS such as a light turned on at the same time.

36 The actual conditioning of the blink to other events is called _____ of a response.

acquisition

37 In a demonstration conducted by the author, students were conditioned to blink when a blue light was turned on. Having acquired this conditioned response, the air puff was discontinued when the light went on. As exposure without US continued over many trials, what do you predict happened to the blinking behavior? + + + + +

In most cases it stopped.

38 Once conditioning has been established, extinction usually results when the reinforcing effects of the US are omitted, as in the example above, when the _____ _____ no longer was directed at the eyeball.

air puff

39 When a CS fails to evoke the conditioned response, _____ has occurred.

extinction

40 The curves for acquisition and extinction are represented in Figure 5. You can see that the shapes are reversed. Fill in the names of the curves, (1) curve for _____ (2) curve for _____.

(1) acquisition
(2) extinction

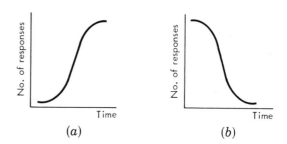

Figure 5. Curves for (a) acquisition and (b) extinction of responses.

41 The criterion for extinction is the _____ of a response or behavior.

cessation (stopping; interruption)

42 Many laboratory investigations of acquisition and extinction indicate that, other things being equal, the more times an event occurs, the harder it is to extinguish it. Accordingly, one should expect that the greater the number of pairings of US and CS, the greater the probability that _____ of the CS will not occur.

extinction

43 Stated in other terms, resistance to extinction provides a criterion of strength of conditioning. If subject A continues to blink at a blue light over twenty-eight trials without US-CS pairing, but subjects B, C, D no longer blink after fifteen, twenty-one, and thirteen trials respectively, subject A's score represents greater + + + + +.

resistance to extinction

Increase the number of pairings between CS and US in the acquisition phase of conditioning

44 Suppose you wanted to increase the number of trials over which a person would blink without the US present. How would you increase the strength of the conditioned response? +++++

45 A child's fear of water may be increased if you threaten to throw him in every time he goes near water. The repetition of verbal threat may well increase the child's _____ response. (It may well extinguish his tendency to go near the water, too.)

fear

46 Not infrequently, investigators have found that a response extinguished in one laboratory session recurs spontaneously at another session. In these instances, it is apparent that complete _____ of the conditioned response had not occurred.

extinction

When a previously conditioned response recurs spontaneously (i.e., without reinforcement from pairing with the US), the event is called "spontaneous recovery." Pavlov's dog was "extinguished" for producing saliva to the tone of the bell. Every so often, thereafter, particularly early in a laboratory session, he would produce small quantities of saliva.

47 The apparently spontaneous salivary activity, occurring after cessation of this conditioned response, represents _____ _____.

spontaneous recovery

48 It seems unlikely that any strongly conditioned response is ever completely extinguished. Occurrence of spontaneous recovery suggests that resistance to _____ is strong even in simple responses.

extinction

49 In the eyeblink-conditioning procedure described earlier, resistance to extinction would be demonstrated if blinking were observed when the blue light went on *after* a criterion for _____ had been met.

extinction

By recurrence of a response after extinction had presumably occurred

50 How would spontaneous recovery be demonstrated? +++++

51 Many variables affect resistance to extinction, some of which will be discussed in the next section. The major point here is that strength of conditioning can be evaluated by resistance to _____ as well as by rate of response.

extinction

52 In respondent conditioning, extinction occurs because of the *lack* of either (1) pairing of US and CS, or (2) obtaining of _____.

reinforcement

Principles of extinction have been widely used in the treatment of stuttering. Many people who stutter claim that their speech disability is compounded by other people laughing at, being impatient with, or acting embarrassed about their speech. Eliminating such reactions by other people sometimes leads to extinction (at least, in this case, reduction) of stuttering.

The US for stuttering initially may be feelings of self-consciousness or inadequacy. (These are very hard to determine.) The CS would be the reaction of others. Thus "other people" become stimuli for stuttering.

very difficult

53 Extinction of stuttering is usually _____ [very difficult/easy/impossible]. Do you see why?

drinking
(alcoholism)

54 In treating alcoholism, physicians sometimes utilize counterconditioning principles and isolation to try to reduce or extinguish drinking. By isolating the alcoholic over time, the _____ is presumably extinguished.

counterconditioning

55 Counterconditioning is a method which is sometimes more effective in the extinction of alcoholism than is isolation. When an incompatible response replaces an existing response, _____ has occurred.

incompatible

56 Counterconditioning occurs when an _____ response replaces an existing one.

57 In the treatment of alcoholics, two types of counterconditioning are often used. One involves physiological stimuli, the other psychological ones. Both types of stimuli presumably are incompatible with the existing behavior, i.e., _____ behavior.

drinking

58 Consider the effects of administering an emetic (a substance which produces vomiting and nausea) at the same time that alcohol is presented. The responses to the emetic and alcohol are _____.

incompatible

(1) existing
(2) incompatible

59 Counterconditioning of alcoholism involves the replacement of an **(1)** _____ response (drinking) with an **(2)** _____ response (nausea).

counterconditioning

60 Some mothers attempt to countercondition their children against bad-tasting medicine by accompanying the dosage with other desired things, such as candy or verbal praise. By so doing, they are using principles of _____.

(1) conditioned
stimulus
(2) countercondi-
tioning

61 *Review:* Extinction of a respondently conditioned behavior may be accomplished by two major methods: **(1)** by discontinuation of pairings of the unconditioned stimulus with the _____ _____; **(2)** by using _____.

This section has dealt with the acquisition and extinction of respondently conditioned behavior. The paradigm for respondent, or classical, conditioning can be used to explain how much emotional behavior is acquired and how it might be suppressed, if not extinguished. A great deal needs to be learned before principles of respondent conditioning can be extrapolated safely to complex behavior, such as alcoholism. As a matter of fact, although counterconditioning sometimes works with alcoholics, most results are disappointing.

Operant (Instrumental) Conditioning

Much of our behavior can be partially explained by principles of respondent conditioning. This is particularly true of involuntary behavior mediated by the autonomic nervous system, including simple reflexes and much of which is termed emotional behavior. Other aspects of everyday human behavior can be more clearly accounted for by principles of operant conditioning. This includes our repertoire of voluntary acts or behavior that once depended on voluntary acts. The distinctions between respondent and operant conditioning are given because they help to distinguish between ways that different behavior is learned, and thus one or the other may be applied more appropriately to behavior which the reader himself may wish to condition.

conditioned stimulus

62 Respondent behavior involves stimulus substitution. The learned response is evoked by the _____ _____.

63 Respondent behavior is primarily controlled by stimuli that occur _____ the response.

before (prior to)

64 Often a behavioral response itself causes changes in the environment. The changes subsequently determine whether the response will recur. In other words, stimuli which _____ the response are more important in operant conditioning.

follow (occur after)

65 In this kind of conditioning, any emitted behavior may operate on the environment to produce a change in it.[2] Operant conditioning thus refers to a response which operates on the _____.

environment

66 Operant conditioning involves a response instrumental in obtaining change. This is why operant conditioning is often called _____ _____.

instrumental
   conditioning

67 In respondent conditioning, the stimulus which precedes the response controls it. In operant conditioning, the stimulus which _____ an emitted response controls it.

follows

68 Heretofore we have used the S—R model to represent _____ conditioning. We have used S^d to represent a discriminated stimulus, i.e., one which elicits or evokes a response.

respondent (Pav-
   lovian, classical)

69 The model for operant conditioning involves representing both the antecedent stimulus and a stimulus which follows the _____.

response

70 The response consequent, i.e., the stimulus following the response, is called a reinforcing stimulus if it conforms to certain principles. Reinforcement is a general term used to describe a **(1)** _____ stimulus or, to use the synonym, the response- **(2)** _____.

(1) reinforcing
(2) consequent

71 The symbol S^r is often used as a convenient symbol for _____ _____.

reinforcing stimulus

Reinforcement

Because principles of reinforcement are basic to operant conditioning, it is advisable to look at them in some detail.

[2] A distinction is made between an "emitted" response and an "evoked" or "elicited" response. An emitted response is one that is not functionally related to an antecedent stimulus. An evoked or elicited response is one which is related to an antecedent stimulus in the usual S—R sense.

Let us use a common laboratory situation. Figure 6 represents a Skinner box, which is a cage used for studying learning processes in laboratory animals. The cage affords a very limited environment. Certain kinds of events can be controlled and their effects measured.

behavior (response)

72 Refer to Figure 6. For convenience, let's say that our problem is to condition a rat to press the lever or bar. Lever pressing is the _____ we plan to condition.

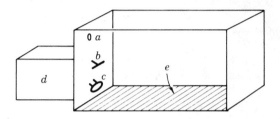

Figure 6. Diagram of a Skinner box. It contains a light *a*, which can be turned on and off automatically, a small metal bar or lever *b*, extending from the wall of the cage, a small cup *c* into which controlled amounts are supplied from *d*, which is the housing for the motor that activates a food dispenser when the bar is pressed. Pressing the bar serves to close electrical switches which may activate the dispenser or electricity in the metal grid floor *e* of the cage.

press

73 We can teach the animal to press the lever indiscriminately or lead him to _____ it under different conditions (e.g., only when the light is on or under other conditions to be presented later).

food

74 When a food-deprived rat is put into the Skinner box, there is very little it can do except wander around or lie down. Deprivation of _____ is used to activate behavior so that movement will occur.

stimulus

75 Food, then, can be used as a reinforcing _____ in this situation.

Food

76 As the rat explores this environment, it happens to press the bar. See step *d* in Figure 6 to determine what occurs then. _____ is made available to the animal.

press

77 Since the amount of food that the rat receives from the dispenser is very small, most animals will again _____ the bar (or lever).

reinforcement (reinforcing stimulus; S^r)	**78** The bar-pressing behavior "procures" food from the environment and is repeated. The food serves as a _____ for bar pressing.
continues (repeats)	**79** We can say the animal has learned the bar-pressing behavior if it _____ to press the bar.
learn (continue)	**80** If nothing happens after the bar is pressed, the animal does not _____ to press it.
reinforcement (S^r)	**81** The important consideration here, as in all operant conditioning, is the consequent of the response, i.e., the _____.
follows	**82** In operant conditioning, a reinforcement is a functionally related stimulus which _____ the response and serves to increase the probability of response repetition.
reinforcement (reinforcing stimulus; S^r)	**83** If a response consequent serves to maintain or increase a response repertoire, it can be called a _____.
response	**84** On the other hand, if the response rate is not maintained, we can say that the response consequent has decreased in power to control the _____.
response rate	**85** Response rate is one criterion used to evaluate strength of reinforcement. In our illustration, if the animal continues to press the bar the same number of times per minute or if he increases the number of bar presses, the reinforcement (food) is maintaining or increasing _____ _____.
strength	**86** Response rate is one criterion for evaluating the _____ of a reinforcement. In our example, the rate of bar pressing indicates the value of food as a reinforcement.
reinforcement	**87** The number of times a boy runs to a water cooler during a baseball game can serve to denote the "strength" of water as a kind of _____ on "water-deprived behavior" for that boy.
reinforcing stimulus (reinforcement; S^r)	**88** In addition to response rate, there is another commonly used criterion of reinforcement strength. It is called resistance to extinction. Presumably, the longer it takes to extinguish a previously reinforced response, the greater the strength of the _____ _____.

89 *Review:* Two criteria commonly used to assess the effectiveness of a given reinforcement on a given behavior are (1) the acquisition and maintenance of response _____ and (2) the resistance to the _____ of a previously reinforced response.

(1) rate
(2) extinction

The laboratory example referred to in frames 72 to 81 demonstrates how a particular reinforcement affects a given response. Now suppose you are interested in a more complex learning problem, such as training the rat to press the Skinner box lever only when the cage light is on. (This is analogous, in a highly simplified way, to teaching school children to stop talking when the teacher enters the room.)

90 Refer to Figure 6. The first step would be to connect the food dispenser so that it would be activated only when the _____ is on.

light

91 If the animal presses the bar when the light is off, what happens?

Nothing; the rat gets only exercise

92 The light serves as a conditioned S^d for responding; nothing happens unless the rat $+++++$ when the light is on.

presses the bar

93 Obtaining food serves as a reinforcement for a rat's bar pressing. Analogously, a paycheck serves as a _____ for a man's working, although many more variables are involved.

reinforcement

Refer to Figure 6 again. The cage has a metal grid floor. If the controls are properly set, the grid can be electrified with a very weak current so that the rat is uncomfortable but not endangered. The bar can be arranged so that a bar press will turn off the electric current.

94 When the current is turned on, the rat ordinarily begins to move about rapidly. If the rat happens to press the bar, the current is turned _____.

off

95 The electric current is turned off only when the bar is pressed. The rat can _____ the shock by pressing the bar.

remove (terminate; turn off)

96 Obviously, bar pressing as a response leads to consequences in this situation as well as in the food-getting situation. In the shock-reduction situation, the bar press serves to strengthen a behavior designed to _____ a stimulus.

remove (terminate)

97 Stimuli which serve to strengthen behavior when they are removed are called negative reinforcements.[3] Terminating the shock by pressing the bar constitutes a _____ _____.

negative reinforcement

98 Human beings turn on fans or air conditioners to terminate the consequences of heat and humidity. Pushing the appliance button serves as the response; the negative reinforcement is _____ heat and humidity.

terminating

Negative reinforcement occurs when a response consequent enables the organism to terminate or avoid some condition. To denote the aversive or negative aspects of reinforcement the symbol S^a is sometimes used. Now refer again to Figure 6. A rat is placed in the Skinner box, and an electric current is turned on so that the floor of the cage is "hot." The animal presses the bar, presumably obtains relief from pain, and continues to press the bar.

because it enables the animal to avoid pain.

99 Why is the response consequent termed negative reinforcement in this situation? $+++++$.

The use of food or water as reinforcing stimuli, or of pain avoidance as an aversive stimulus, is convenient for laboratory demonstrations. Another dramatic technique has been used by several investigators (e.g., Delgado et al., 1955; Olds, 1958; N. E. Miller, 1961; and others) to demonstrate reinforcement properties. This is the technique of electrical brain stimulation.

Basing their procedure on methods originally reported by W. R. Hess (1954), these investigators have implanted tiny electrodes in the lower parts of the midline system

[3] Negative reinforcement is distinguished from positive reinforcement. Up to this point we have been omitting the word positive in referring to reinforcement. It should be pointed out that negative reinforcement is not the opposite of positive reinforcement. Negative reinforcement causes different, but not necessarily converse, responses than positive reinforcement. Nonreinforcement of a previously reinforced response brings the opposite of a response that has been either positively or negatively reinforced.

in the "old-brain" areas (see Part II, Unit 2). Stimulation gives rise to complex responses. For example, Delgado et al. and Miller have trained animals to avoid pain from stimulation of the midline region by pressing levers in a Skinner-box type of apparatus. Olds reported that elevation of the probes slightly higher in the midline region would cause opposite effects to occur. Animals would press levers as many as 5,000 times per hour—a fantastically high response rate—in order to receive electrical brain stimulation in their "pleasure centers." Miller and others have also investigated the reinforcing effects of brain stimulation on hunger and thirst. Similar kinds of reports about chemical stimulation of the brain are also available (Russell, 1964).

100 Olds (1958) reported that rats will "work harder" to get brain stimulation than to obtain food. When pleasure shock was dependent on bar presses, the rats ran faster to reach an electrical brain stimulator than they would to reach _____.

food

101 Not infrequently, rats deprived of food for more than twenty hours would ignore food in order to obtain electrical _____ stimulation.

brain

102 Olds points out that rats do not become satiated (or satisfied) with electrical brain stimulation as they do when food or water is used to _____ their hunger or thirst.

satiate (satisfy)

103 Some rats continued to stimulate themselves for forty-eight hours without any reduction in rate of bar presses. Electrical stimulation of the "pleasure center" can serve as a very powerful _____ _____ for bar pressing.

reinforcing stimulus

104 In a sense, the laboratory investigations of reinforcing and aversive stimulation are codifications of the long-accepted principle that we work to obtain pleasure and avoid pain. They suggest, however, how the processes of obtaining _____ and avoiding _____ may operate.

pleasure; pain

105 In this way, experimental analysis of reinforcing and aversive stimuli leads to the possibility of better prediction and control of _____.

behavior

106 Another aspect of reinforcement that deserves consideration has to do with *why* a reinforcer reinforces a _____ (Lundin, 1961, pp. 64 to 65).

response (behavior)

107 In laboratory demonstrations of reinforcement, food, sexual contact, and pain avoidance typically are used to reinforce behavior. These types of S^r's have _____ importance.

biological

108 Reinforcers that have survival functions or are of biological importance are called primary reinforcers. If water is used to induce a thirsty person to do something one desires him to do, it is then used as a _____ _____.

primary reinforcer

109 For the learning of most human activities, primary reinforcers are not as important as secondary reinforcers. Water, food, and shelter are ordinarily available if we have the means to obtain them. In our society, people work for something (money) that is used to obtain these primary reinforcers. Money is not a primary reinforcer; it is a _____ reinforcer.

secondary

110 In a very real sense, secondary reinforcers are conditioned reinforcers; i.e., we have learned to associate responses elicited by a primary reinforcer to another reinforcer _____ with it.

associated (paired)

111 Money, of course, is only one example of a secondary reinforcer. Anything which accompanies a primary reinforcer and acquires reinforcing values of its own can be termed a _____ _____.

secondary reinforcement

112 A secondary reinforcement is positive when the accompanying primary reinforcement is positive; it is negative when the accompanying primary reinforcer is _____.

negative

113 Secondary reinforcers may come to exert a powerful control over behavior. Generally, however, behavioral scientists agree that primary reinforcers, because they deal with survival or have other biological importance, are more basically motivating than _____ reinforcers.

secondary

Let's return to the question posed in frame 106. Why is a reinforcer reinforcing? We can speculate that survival and biological satisfactions provide some of the ultimate answers. Certainly, these aspects of behavior seem more basic and pervasive than does conditioned behavior. Yet there is evidence that some secondary reinforcers come into play early in childhood and strongly influence behavior thereafter. As yet we have no empirical answer to the question, and additional information is badly needed.

Some studies and suggestions about this topic will be presented in succeeding units.

Schedules of Reinforcement

114 It is of some practical value to know how the presentation of reinforcement affects learning. The term "schedules of reinforcement" refers to the procedures used to _____ reinforcements (in this case, either positive or aversive stimulation).

present (or schedule)

115 Refer to Figure 7. Every time the rat presses the bar, he obtains food or avoids pain. This represents a regular or continuous reinforcement for responding. When a child's hand is slapped *every* time he puts his thumb in his mouth, a _____ reinforcement schedule is being used.

regular (continuous)

116 The TV set goes on every time we flip a switch. That is, we get reinforced regularly for $+++++$.

flipping a switch

117 Perhaps this accounts for the fact that we call a repairman so quickly when a picture does not immediately flash on the screen. Nonreinforcement of a response that has been regularly _____ quickly alters the response.

reinforced (rewarded)

118 A new behavior repertoire is most easily acquired by reinforcing the behavior _____.

regularly (continuously; every time it occurs)

119 Suppose you want to train your dog to roll over on command. It will learn this behavior most quickly if you reward (i.e., reinforce) the animal _____.

regularly (continuously)

120 Regular reinforcement can be arranged in laboratory situations, but it is not observed very often in everyday situations. Rather, sometimes a behavior is reinforced and sometimes it is not. That is, most everyday behavior is reinforced _____.

irregularly (inconsistently, etc.)

121 Under conditions where reinforcement is applied on some other basis than a continuous one, it is referred to as an intermittent or partial schedule. Rewarding a dog every other time it rolls over on command would be following a(n) _____ schedule.

intermittent (partial)

Fixed-ratio Reinforcement

Various types of intermittent schedules have been studied under laboratory and real-life conditions (Ferster and Skinner, 1957). Principles have been established about

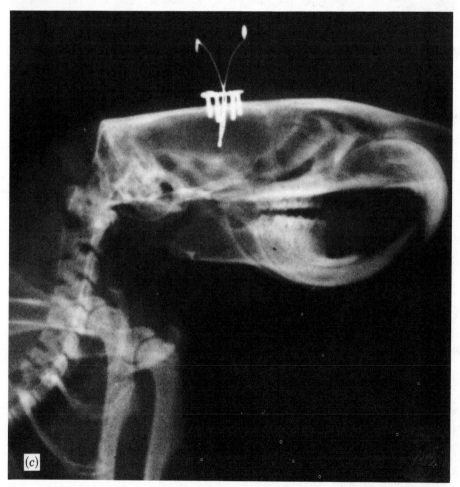

Figure 7. Electrical brain stimulation. (a) Animal with implanted electrode in Skinner box; (b) external detail of implanted electrode; (c) internal detail of implanted electrode. (Photographs a and b courtesy of David H. Long; x-ray photograph c courtesy of James Olds.)

acquisition, maintenance, and extinction of individual responses under such conditions. We shall examine two general classes of intermittent schedules. One deals with amount of reinforcement proportional to response rate. The other deals with the time intervals between reinforcements.

reinforced

122 For our discussion, ratio refers to the number of times a response must be made in order to be _____.

fixed-ratio

123 Under a fixed-ratio (FR) schedule, a response is reinforced only after it has been made a specified number of times. In a sense, then, continuous reinforcement is the simplest type of _____-_____ schedule.

three

124 A FR of 3:1 means that the response must be made _____ times before reinforcement occurs.

high

125 Curve a in Figure 8 is the response acquisition-and-maintenance curve (cumulative response curve[4]). It is almost vertical. It represents a very _____ rate of responding.

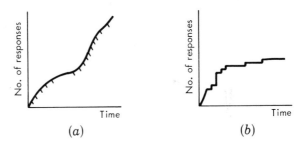

(a) (b)

Figure 8. Smoothed cumulative response curves representing (a) acquisition and (b) extinction of an animal responding under fixed-ratio reinforcement. Hatch marks in a designate occurrence of reinforcement.

ten

126 The ratio of reinforcement to response was 10:1 in this particular experiment. This means that the animal received food for pressing the bar after every _____ responses.

reinforcement

127 Curve b in Figure 8 is the extinction curve. Notice that there are no hatch marks representing _____.

[4] Cumulative response curves are obtained by having an automatic recorder attached to the response bar and reinforcement dispenser. Every bar press and reinforcement is thus recorded on a continuously moving sheet of paper. The response curves used in this book are smoothed out; the reinforcements are indicated by a hatch mark diagonal to the curve. Ferster and Skinner (1957) give a full description of cumulative records.

rate

decrease

reinforcement

fixed-ratio (FR)

number

5:1

number

vary (differ)

variable

128 The first part of the curve retains a reasonably sharp vertical slope. This suggests that the animal had been reinforced at a fairly _____ rate.

129 Decrease in slope means decrease in response _____.

130 Under extinction conditions, FR response rate initially continues to be high, but then a rather sudden _____ in response rate occurs.

131 Laboratory demonstrations indicate that, under a fixed-ratio schedule, response rates tend to exceed even a regular _____ schedule.

132 Extremely high fixed ratios can be established by increasing the ratio gradually. Starting with a 3:1 ratio and going to a 6:1, then 12:1, etc., rats, pigeons, and men can be induced to respond to appropriate reinforcements at a very high _____-_____ schedule (e.g., even at 500:1 to 3,000:1).

133 The rate or speed of response is not important for obtaining reinforcement in FR conditioning; it is the _____ of responses made that determines the payoff.

134 There are numerous applications of FR reinforcement to human behavior. Salesmen operating on a bonus system often are on FR schedules. If a bonus is offered for every five cars sold, the FR is _____.

135 Fruit pickers often work on an incentive plan. Pay is contingent on the _____ of baskets picked.

FR schedules can be extremely effective if the amount of work necessary is within reasonable limits for the rewards offered. People will not work very hard (if at all) if the reward is too small. An effective reinforcer generates a very high rate, for men and other animals, under a FR schedule.

Variable-ratio Reinforcement

136 As the term implies, under a variable-ratio (VR) schedule, the number of responses required for a given reinforcement will _____.

137 Under the VR schedule in Figure 9, the rat was reinforced on a random schedule of responses from 3:1 to 30:1. There was no particular order in the schedule; within these limits the ratio of responses to reinforcement was _____.

138 Notice that the acquisition response rate is very high. You can tell this by the _____ of curve *a*. Notice also that there is no regularity to the hatch marks which denote when reinforcement was given.

139 Under a VR schedule, very high _____ rates can be built up quickly, especially if the ratios at the beginning are small.

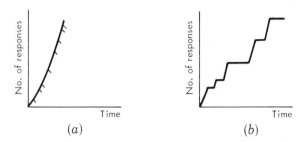

(*a*)   (*b*)

Figure 9. Smoothed cumulative response curves representing (*a*) acquisition and (*b*) extinction of an animal responding under variable-ratio reinforcement. Hatch marks in *a* designate occurrence of reinforcement.

140 The extinction curve *b* looks somewhat like the FR extinction curve. Initially there is a high _____ _____, which levels off quite abruptly.

141 Under curve *b*, there are fewer responses as time increases, and _____ is more rapid and complete.

142 In a sense, VR is the schedule that gamblers operate under. Since payoffs occur, but not in any predetermined order, gambling as a response rate continues to be _____.

143 The nature of gambling requires continued playing, though winnings are distributed in an irregular manner. Winnings, of course, are the _____ for continued gambling.

144 If losing and winning represent the intervals between payoffs, which of these tend to represent the longer intervals? _____.

145 Most slot machines are adjusted to different systems, according to their location. The payoff schedule in a Reno gambling club is usually higher than that in a transportation terminal, because people who may play the terminal machines play only a few times and do not _____.

slope (steepness)

response

response rate

extinction

high (consistent)

reinforcements

losing

continue (or return)

146 All-night poker games are played under conditions of _____-_____ reinforcement.

variable-ratio (VR)

147 A variable-ratio schedule is determined by the irregularity of the reinforcement proportional to the _____ of reinforcement.

ratio

148 Most "Sunday golfers" keep on playing because of VR reinforcement. The one or two good holes per round they earn keeps them $+++++$.

coming back (playing, seeking reinforcement, etc.)

149 The same is true for many college students. Take a student who rarely earns an A when he hands in his papers for grading. If he has received some A's and they are important to him, he continues to study at a reasonably _____ rate in the hope of obtaining others.

high

150 Outstanding marks, like beating the slot machines or playing par golf, are reinforcements which occur _____ for most people. In our culture, they seem to be strongly reinforcing.

irregularly (unpredictably, inconsistently)

151 Some bonus systems operate on a VR schedule. The president of General Motors gets a bonus based on the number of cars sold each year. His bonus varies each year on a _____-_____ schedule.

variable-ratio (VR)

152 The VR schedule is a powerful deterrent against extinction. That is, when the ratios are varied appropriately, the resistance to _____ is usually very strong.

extinction

153 For both fixed-ratio and variable-ratio schedules, it is important to remember that it is the _____ of responding proportional to reinforcement that is in question.

ratio (amount)

154 Ratio reinforcement can occur on either a **(1)** _____ or on a **(2)** _____ schedule.

(1) fixed
(2) variable

Fixed-interval Reinforcement

The essential difference between ratio and interval reinforcement is that the latter is concerned with the interval of time between responses and reinforcement rather than with the ratio of responses proportional to reinforcement.

155 As the term suggests, a fixed-interval (FI) schedule means that there is a _____ period of time that must elapse before a response is reinforced.

fixed

156 Figure 10 indicates that the animal's response rate for acquisition is _____ than for either VR or VI schedules.

157 As time increases under a FI schedule, pauses between responding also tend to _____. (Pauses are represented by horizontal lines in Figure 10.)

158 The increase in response rate just prior to payoff time (represented by the steep slopes just before the hatch marks) suggests that the animal knows when he will be _____, i.e., he is estimating the time interval.

159 The pauses also might suggest that the animal has learned to "tell _____."

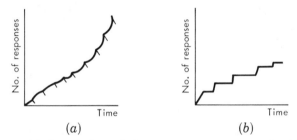

(a)   *(b)*

Figure 10. Smoothed cumulative response curves representing (a) acquisition and (b) extinction of an animal responding under fixed-interval reinforcement. Hatch marks in a designate occurrence of reinforcement.

160 As a matter of record, Ferster and Skinner (1957) describe typical "clock-watching" behavior in pigeons that is remarkably like that of humans. Clock watching is of course based on principles of discrimination of _____ intervals.

161 In one sense, an FI schedule tends to promote economy of responding. Unnecessary responses are not made during much of the time before reinforcement. The sharply vertical lines following the horizontal lines which are characteristic of fixed-interval schedules show this typical _____ of response rate.

162 Humans learn to anticipate time by watching actual clocks or by adjusting body conditions so that they can discriminate _____ intervals.

163 If reinforcements occur at periodic intervals, a _____-_____ schedule tends to be established.

---

lower

increase (get longer)

reinforced (paid off)

time

time

economy

time

fixed-interval (FI)

164 It was pointed out earlier that a bonus-payment system illustrates a fixed-ratio schedule. Analogously, payment by a salary system represents a _____-_____ schedule. This is because salaries are paid at weekly or monthly, i.e., fixed or regular, intervals.

fixed-interval

165 Obviously, humans do not demonstrate exactly the same characteristic response curves under salary conditions that rats do under _____-_____ schedules.

fixed-interval (FI)

166 Humans tend to work steadily between paydays, perhaps more so than do rats in a Skinner box. That is because other types of _____ are operating on humans.

reinforcements

167 What might some of these other reinforcements be for a salaried employee? +++++.

verbal S^r from the boss and other workers; advantage of spacing work, etc.

168 If absenteeism might be one criterion of the effectiveness of an FI schedule, when would you expect the lowest rate of absenteeism? +++++.

On payday.

169 If students know their instructor will give a quiz every Monday but not at any other time during the week, when do they tend to study? +++++.

Sunday night just before the quiz.

170 In this instance, the response curves of these students would look much like those in Figure 10, i.e., long periods of no study with a short burst of intense _____ just before the quiz.

study

171 Regarding resistance to extinction as a criterion of reinforcement strength, FI reinforcement tends to strengthen +++++.

resistance to extinction

172 Children as well as adults demonstrate characteristic FI response curves. It has been demonstrated that children will work longer after cessation of reinforcement under a _____-_____ schedule than under regular reinforcement.

fixed-interval (FI)

173 Other things being equal, an FI schedule operates on response acquisition and maintenance so that unnecessary responses typically are _____, if not eliminated.

reduced (lessened)

174 With respect to extinction, conditioning an organism under an FI schedule usually leads to stronger _____ to extinction.

resistance

Variable-interval Reinforcement

variable-interval

175 Fixed-ratio is to variable-ratio reinforcement as fixed-interval is to _____-_____ reinforcement.

time (time interval)

176 In variable-interval reinforcement, the schedule for reinforcement varies around some _____ value.

interval (time interval)

177 Ferster and Skinner (1957) reinforced a pigeon to peck at a disc in a Skinner box similar to one used for rats. The reinforcement was varied around a three-minute _____, ranging from a few seconds to six minutes.

variable-interval

178 This bird gave more than 30,000 responses over a fifteen-hour period, pausing to stop only once for fifteen seconds. A remarkably consistent response rate is maintained by the _____-_____ schedule.

consistent (steady)

179 As Figure 11 indicates, the VI schedule can maintain a very rapid and _____ response rate.

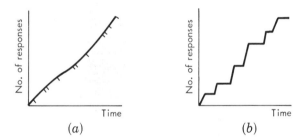

(a)   (b)

Figure 11. Smoothed cumulative response curves representing (a) acquisition and (b) extinction of an animal responding under variable-interval reinforcement. Hatch marks in a designate occurrence of reinforcement.

180 The rate of response under a VI schedule is a function of the range of the time intervals used. If intervals are short during early training, there is a high probability that conditioning will be _____ and steady.

rapid

181 Resistance to extinction is also very high under a VI schedule. The slope of the extinction curve in Figure 11 shows that response rate remains _____ for some time after reinforcement is terminated.

steady (high)

182 The obvious implication is that variable-interval reinforcement is effective for acquisition of a response and also, since resistance to extinction is high, for _____ a response.

maintaining (continuing, etc.)

You should
say "No."

183 Under an FI schedule, rats and pigeons seem to develop a "sense of time." Would you think this would occur under a VI schedule? _____.

vary (change)

184 Under an FI schedule the animal learns to anticipate when reinforcements will occur. Under a VI schedule such anticipation is not possible because time intervals between reinforcement _____.

variable (irregular,
inconsistent)

185 The effects of VI reinforcement on human behavior are illustrated in many ways. Fishermen never know when the fish will bite, but their behavior indicates a past history of _____ reinforcement.

reinforced

186 The variations in waiting for bites constitute the VI schedule for fishermen. The fact that they continue to fish suggests that fish have bitten in the past, i.e., fishermen have been _____ previously.

steady (consistent,
regular)

187 Some professors find it wiser to give "pop quizzes" rather than regularly scheduled quizzes in order to maintain a _____ rate of study from students.

response

188 Because variable-interval reinforcement promotes a higher _____ rate than FI reinforcement, it should be more effective in everyday motivational situations.

In summarizing information about schedules of reinforcement, one might well point out that both variable-ratio and variable-interval reinforcement tend to be more effective than continuous or fixed reinforcement of the same types in maintaining a behavior that has been initially conditioned. This statement, though not always true, generally holds.

Aversive Stimulation

Earlier in the unit, negative reinforcement was differentiated from positive reinforcement. Negative reinforcement refers to the strengthening of a response by the removal of a stimulus. Negative reinforcement is one type of aversive stimulation. Escape behavior is also considered a function of aversive stimulation.

There are two other major types of aversive stimulation. In *avoidance* behavior, the response serves to prevent the occurrence of a stimulus. *Punishment* refers to an aversive stimulus which suppresses or inhibits a behavior on subsequent occasions. Let us examine the concept of punishment first.

Punishment

189 When a child is spanked for crying, a dog is whipped for barking, or a husband is given a tongue lashing for drinking, the purpose of such "stimulation" is to try to ensure that the behavior begetting the punishment +++++.

190 A reinforcing stimulus tends to strengthen a behavior; it tends to increase the probability of its _____.

191 As aversive stimulation, punishment tends to cause a behavior to be suppressed, i.e., to increase the probability of its _____.

192 Punishment usually is intended to eliminate completely an undesired behavior. This is very hard to do once a behavior has been _____.

193 As with reinforcement, there are two major classes of punishment, primary and secondary. Administering electric shocks to a rat, or the "back of m' hand" to a human, are primary aversive stimuli. Threatening a person with gestures or words would constitute _____ punishment.

194 A punishment involving biological pain can be defined as a primary aversive stimulus; the threat of pain or the possibility of hurt would symbolize _____ reinforcement.

195 The presentation of a negative reinforcer can serve as a punishment; so can the withdrawal of a _____ reinforcer.

196 Solitary confinement is used in prisons as a punishment for misbehavior. Such confinement withholds the company of _____ from the prisoner.

197 A child who has been reinforced at home for attention-seeking behavior is ignored at school by the teacher and children. The child stops this behavior in school. Ignoring the child serves to eliminate +++++ in school, if not at home.

---

does not occur again (is inhibited, suppressed, or extinguished)

repetition (recurrence)

extinction (decrease, inhibition)

conditioned (learned)

secondary (conditioned)

secondary

positive

people (others)

attention-seeking behavior

198 Experimental evidence has been accumulated which indicates that a conditioned response may be suppressed in the presence of the aversive stimulus (or potential). However, a strongly conditioned response is probably never completely _____ (Skinner, 1953).

extinguished (elimi-
    nated, inhibited)

199 Punishment serves to suppress a response temporarily or in the _____ of the aversive stimulus.

presence

200 A husband who has been tongue-lashed for drinking learns to drink so that his wife does not notice it. This means that the wife's behavior has not _____ the husband's drinking entirely.

extinguished (elimi-
    nated, inhibited)

201 An adolescent who is strongly reinforced by his peers for swearing learns not to swear in front of his parents. But their punishment for swearing may serve only to _____ this behavior in their presence.

inhibit

202 There is a general covariation between strength of an aversive stimulus and behavior inhibition. That is, a strong electric shock usually serves to control a rat's undesired behavior better than a _____ shock.

weak (mild)

203 There is also covariation between (1) response inhibition and the (2) time interval between the response and administration of punishment. In general, the quicker the punishment is delivered after undesired behavior, the greater the probability of _____ of behavior.

inhibition

204 Some mothers delay punishment of their children "until father gets home." Other things being equal, this is less _____ than immediate punishment.

effective

205 Following principles already described, consistent punishment tends to inhibit a response much more quickly than intermittent or inconsistent punishment. In general, the more consistent the punishment, the greater the probability of _____ of behavior.

inhibition

206 Punishment as a form of aversive stimulation serves to _____ the response to which it is functionally related. However, it does not necessarily extinguish the response altogether.

inhibit (suppress)

Escape

Negative reinforcement refers to removing a stimulus in order to strengthen a response. This is precisely what is involved in escape behavior. In the Skinner box described earlier, the rat could escape electric shock by pressing the bar. Similarly, human beings come in from the rain, change from heavy to light clothing in the summer, or relieve their hunger by eating as efforts to escape aversive consequences of rain, heavy clothing, or food deprivation.

207 The relief which these behaviors bring constitutes reinforcement of the response which causes it. That is why escape behavior is often called ＿＿＿＿＿ reinforcement.

negative

208 Negative reinforcement typically leads to ＿＿＿＿ behavior.

escape

209 A below-average student may escape possible ridicule and scorn from classmates by not volunteering to respond to a teacher's questions. In this way, nonverbal behavior is strengthened by ＿＿＿＿＿ of ridicule.

absence

210 All of us daydream to a greater or lesser extent. Not infrequently, ＿＿＿＿＿ is a form of escape from everyday concerns. (Part V, Unit 3 presents an extended discussion of daydreaming as escape behavior.)

daydreaming

211 The schizophrenic finds solace by withdrawing from social contact and ordinary activities. Schizophrenic behavior is often referred to as an "＿＿＿＿＿ from reality."

escape

212 Escape behavior differs from punishment in that escape refers to the removal of an aversive stimulus, while punishment refers to the application of an ＿＿＿＿＿ ＿＿＿＿＿.

aversive stimulus
(S^a)

Avoidance

Although we often use escape and avoidance as synonyms, there is a technical difference between the two so far as conditioning goes. Escape refers to the removal of an existing stimulus or condition. Avoidance refers to the prevention of a condition, rather than active escape from a situation or removal of an aversive stimulus. Avoidance behavior can be described in the following manner:

$$S^d \cdots R \rightarrow (S^a)$$

where the parentheses refer to the idea that aversive stimulation does *not* occur.

R (driving slowly)
S^a (avoiding a ticket for speeding.)

213 The sight of a police car ordinarily is enough to cause drivers to keep within the speed limit. Denote this situation in the diagram:

$$S^d \text{ (police car)} \cdots R \, (_____) \rightarrow (S^a) \, (_____)$$

Brady (1957) has described how, under certain conditions, the attempt to avoid aversive stimulation may lead to ulcer formation. Two monkeys were placed side by side in identical transparent experimental chambers. Weak electric shock was introduced via electrodes attached to the animals. It could be terminated by the bar pressing of only one monkey (the "executive"), although both monkeys had levers to press. The executive monkey developed ulcers, whereas its partner, which also received shock when the executive monkey missed, did not.

avoid

214 In this study, the punishing aspects of shock itself were not responsible for ulcer development. Ulcers were related to avoidance of shock. Only the executive monkey —the one who had power to _____ shock—developed ulcers.

social

215 There are many other examples of avoidance conditioning in social situations. For example, avoidance provides a basis for apology. In our culture, apologies are offered in order to avoid possible unpleasant _____ consequences.

avoid

216 A student came into his class late. "I'm sorry," he muttered, as he hurried to his seat. In this way he was seeking to __ __ __ his professor's disapproval.

anxiety

217 Avoidance conditioning also seems to be an important basis for anxiety. Fear of unknown consequences is termed _____.

possible (anticipated, potential)

218 People who are chronic worriers tend to be those who anticipate possible but unknown aversive consequences which they feel they must avoid. These people avoid __ _____ aversive stimulation.

aversive

219 A hypochondriac is a person whose illness is not due to a biological fault or to tissue damage. He apparently gives reports of "feeling ill" in order to avoid possible _____ stimulation of people or situations. (Part V, Units 1 to 3 contain further discussions of anxiety and other means of avoiding or escaping aversive stimulation.)

220 The effects of aversive stimuli, then, tend to be the opposite of reinforcing stimuli. A reinforcement leads to the repetition or strengthening of a behavior. Aversive stimulation leads either to _____ of a behavior or to the strengthening of a behavior when a stimulus is removed.

decrease (inhibition)

221 Negative reinforcement and escape behavior both refer to the fact that a behavior is strengthened when a stimulus is _____.

removed

222 Avoidance conditioning differs from escape in that the former involves anticipation of an _____ stimulus rather than actual exposure to one.

aversive

223 Punishment is used primarily in an attempt to _____ a particular response.

eliminate (extinguish)

224 Punishment may cause response inhibition, but it probably does not completely _____ the behavior in question.

extinguish

225 Despite the fact that effects of punishment tend to be temporary, it is widely used to control behavior. Perhaps this is because its use is reinforcing to the _____ who administers it.

person (organism)

Response Differentiation and Chaining

The principles of learning discussed so far have emphasized antecedent and consequent conditions which affect behavior or the learning of behavior. In particular, properties of stimuli and reinforcement have been examined along with processes of respondent and operant conditioning. Relatively little emphasis has been placed on the learned behavior itself. This section is concerned with the shaping of behavior. Response differentiation is the technical term applied to the process of learning a particular behavior out of many others that might be learned under given conditions.

226 Ferster and Skinner (1957) have described how a pigeon can be trained to peck at a disc on the side of its cage. The procedure is similar to that of training a rat to press a lever in a Skinner box. Initially, there are many motor _____ observed when a pigeon is placed in the cage.

responses

227 The bird walks around the cage, moves its head up and down, ruffles its wings, and so forth. In other words, it demonstrates _____ responses.

228 The task is to teach the bird a specific response, pecking at a disc. This response is to be differentiated or shaped out of a variety of _____ already being demonstrated.

229 At first the pigeon receives food from a dispenser every time it goes near the disc. Food serves as a _____ for approach behavior.

230 Gradually the pigeon is reinforced only when its head is close to the disc. Finally, it receives food only when it pecks the _____ itself.

231 Through a series of successive approximations, then, the pigeon's behavior is shaped for _____ the disc.

232 At first, the behavior is variable, but the selective application of reinforcement serves to _____ the pecking response.

233 The experimenter successively reinforces appropriate turning behavior, then the pecking behavior after a turn has been made. Thus he _____ successive approximations of the pigeon's disc pecking.

234 Shaping behavior through gradual, selective reinforcement of behavior involves a series of successive

_____ .

235 Response differentiation occurs when a particular response, out of a variety demonstrated, is learned. Usually a series of successive approximations is selectively reinforced in the process of _____ _____ .

Response differentiation (R^D) is described symbolically (Keller, 1954):

$$\begin{array}{l} R^\Delta \\ R^D \longrightarrow S^r \\ R^\Delta \end{array}$$

From your knowledge of S^d and S^Δ, you should be able to figure out that R^Δ refers to a response which may occur in conjunction with the differentiated response (R^D) but it is not functionally related to the reinforcement (S^r).

Answer column (left margin):

many (a variety of)

responses

reinforcement

disc

pecking

shape (differentiate)

shapes (differentiates; even reinforces is acceptable)

approximations

response differentiation

236 The R^Δ is not reinforced; only the _____ response is reinforced.

differentiated

237 Symbolize the reinforcement of disc pecking, as distinct from head turning and wing ruffling, with food.

R^Δ (head turn)
R^D (_____) $\rightarrow$ S^r (_____)
R^Δ (wing ruffling)

R^D (disc peck)
S^r (food)

Perhaps at fairs or amusement parks you have seen chickens which have been taught to "play" toy pianos or perform similar tricks. It is through selective reinforcement of a particular response, involving successive approximations of the behavior, that such learning occurs.

238 Response differentiation is involved in the learning of practically all human skills. Learning to throw a basketball correctly, to play the piano, to operate a machine—all these involve _____ _____.[5]

response
differentiation

239 A good teacher of academic, athletic, industrial, or artistic skills learns to present stimuli clearly and to apply reinforcements selectively and at the most appropriate time in order to encourage the particular _____ to be learned.

response (behavior)

240 Shaping behavior (specifically, response differentiation) involves the selective (1) _____ of a desired behavior out of a series of successive (2) _____ of the response to be learned.

(1) reinforcement
(2) approximations

Learning usually involves a complex intertwining of stimulus discrimination and response differentiation. It is a rare instance when a single response or a stimulus-response connection is not related to something that has already occurred or does not lead to other behavior. A child learns to communicate with both spoken and written language in this way; a basketball coach teaches his team the fine points of the game this way; in fact, just about every human skill can be explained by the chaining of stimuli and responses. Particular stimuli are discriminated, and

[5] Two articles demonstrating the application of these principles to everyday behavior are: B. F. Skinner, "How to Teach Animals," *Scientific American*, 185: 26–29, 1951; and R. W. Lundin, "Musical Learning and Reinforcement Theory," *Music Educators Journal*, 46: 46-50, 1960.

particular responses are differentiated, and, as a matter of fact, these processes are so interconnected that one response often produces the stimulus for the next.

241 Chaining can be diagramed as follows:

$$S^\Delta \qquad R^\Delta \qquad S^\Delta \qquad R^\Delta$$
$$S^d \cdots R^D \rightarrow S^d \cdots R^D \rightarrow S^r$$
$$S^\Delta \qquad R^\Delta \qquad S^\Delta \qquad R^\Delta$$

This diagram is essentially a doubling of the $S^d \rightarrow R$ and $R \rightarrow S^r$ diagrams presented earlier in the unit. Spurious or unnecessary stimuli are denoted by **(1)** _____. Unnecessary responses are labeled **(2)** _____.

(1) S^Δ

(2) R^Δ

242 A simplified example of chaining can be ascribed to the processes involved in driving a car.

S^d (key in switch $\cdots$ R^D (turns key) $\rightarrow$
S^d ("feels" accelerator with foot) $\cdots$
R^D (pushes accelerator) $\rightarrow$
S^r (getting car moving)

The S^r (getting the car moving) is itself related to previous events (e.g., learning to value a car for going to work) and other chains leading to S^r (e.g., getting paid for getting to work). The process of chaining is extremely complex, as you can see, and not all of the S^d's and R^D's are included in the above example. The point we wish to make is that chaining provides a means for _____ how complex behavior is learned.

explaining

243 Chaining involves the combining of several S^d's and R^D's, subsequently leading to _____.

reinforcement (S^r)

SUMMARY

Two models have been presented in order to demonstrate how behavior is learned. Pavlov's model, called respondent or classical conditioning, emphasizes the association of a neutral stimulus with an unconditioned stimulus. If the previously neutral stimulus becomes capable of evoking the same behavioral response as the unconditioned stimulus, it is then called a conditioned stimulus. The learning of simple reflex behavior and, to some extent, emotional behavior that is mediated primarily by the autonomic nervous system, can be explained by use of the respondent-conditioning model. This model emphasizes associated antecedent stimuli which give rise to a common response.

The operant-conditioning model emphasizes behavior consequents, rather than response antecedents. What follows the response to be learned, rather than what precedes it, serves to shape much of our everyday voluntary behavior, i.e., behavior mediated primarily by the central nervous system.

Principles of reinforcement are of obvious importance to an understanding of learning and, especially, of operant conditioning. A positive reinforcement refers to a response consequent which increases the probability of response repetition. (Praise for knowledge of assignments tends to increase the probability of continued study.) A negative reinforcement is so defined when it strengthens an existing behavior upon its removal (for example, the threat of punishment serves to inhibit insubordination). Thus punishment refers to a response consequent which inhibits or suppresses a behavior. It is a form of aversive stimulation. Attempts at escape behavior seem to be a natural reaction to negative reinforcement. Avoidance behavior, or the attempt to prevent the occurrence of a stimulus, is another way of reacting to aversive stimulation.

Some interesting research has been conducted on different schedules of reinforcement. Regular, or continuous, reinforcement usually is the best schedule to follow in early stages of behavior acquisition or learning. However, variable-interval reinforcement (i.e., reinforcing behavior on an irregular time schedule) and variable-ratio reinforcement (successively supplying different amounts of reinforcement) tend to be effective for maintaining an acquired behavior. Fixed-interval and fixed-ratio reinforcement are generally less effective than intermittent reinforcement or maintaining a conditioned response.

Knowledge of reinforcement and aversive stimulation is of importance in the understanding of how behavioral conditioning occurs. Research in conditioning has been conducted on relatively discrete behavior, such as lever pressing to obtain primary reinforcements (e.g., food, water, or other basic drive satisfactions), or secondary reinforcements (e.g., money with which to purchase food).

Stimulus discrimination refers to the process of distinguishing a particular stimulus from among many other present. Response differentiation refers to the process of shaping a particular behavior or movement out of many others of a similar sort. Both processes are fundamental to learning. Principles of chaining—the complex intertwining of multiple stimulus discriminations and response differentiations—are necessary to explain how most everyday behavior is learned, according to principles of operant conditioning.

The respondent- and operant-conditioning models presented in this unit provide a convenient way to introduce principles of learning. Extended treatment of these models and other theories of conditioning and learning can be found in the references which follow.

REFERENCES

Deese, J.: *The Psychology of Learning*, McGraw-Hill Book Company, New York, 1958.

Delgado, J. M. R.: "Evaluation of Permanent Implantation of Electrodes within the Brain," *EEG Clinical Neurophysiology*, 6:637–644, 1955.

Ferster, C. M., and B. F. Skinner: *Schedules of Reinforcement*, Appleton-Century-Crofts, Inc., New York, 1957.

Hilgard, E. R.: *Theories of Learning*, 2d ed., Appleton-Century-Crofts, Inc., New York, 1956.

Holland, J., and B. F. Skinner: *The Analysis of Behavior*, McGraw-Hill Book Company, New York, 1961.

Keller, F. S.: *Learning: Reinforcement Theory*, Random House, Inc., New York, 1954.

Kimble, G. A.: *Hilgard and Marquis' Conditioning and Learning*, Appleton-Century-Crofts, Inc., New York, 1961.

Lawson, R.: *Learning and Behavior*, The Macmillan Company, New York, 1960.

Lundin, R. W.: *Personality: An Experimental Approach*, The Macmillan Company, New York, 1961.

Miller, N. E.: "Analytical Studies of Drive and Reward," *American Psychologist*, 16:739–754, 1961.

Mowrer, O. H.: "Two-factor Learning Theory Reconsidered, with Special Reference to Secondary Reinforcement and the Concept of Habit," *Psychological Review*, 63:114–128, 1956.

Mowrer, O. H.: *Learning Theory and Behavior*, John Wiley & Sons, Inc., New York, 1960.

Olds, J.: "Pleasure Centers in the Brain," *Scientific American*, 195:105–116, 1956.

Russell, R. W.: "Psychopharmacology," in P. R. Farnsworth (ed.), *Annual Review of Psychology*, 15:87–114, Annual Reviews Inc., Palo Alto, California, 1964.

Skinner, B. F.: *The Science of Human Behavior*, The Macmillan Company, New York, 1953.

Skinner, B. F.: "How to Teach Animals," *Scientific American*, 185:26–29, 1951.

SELF-REVIEW QUIZ

1 What is the most common synonym for respondent conditioning? For operant conditioning?
2 Pavlov dealt mainly with reflex behavior. He paired a neutral stimulus (a bell tone) with an unconditioned stimulus (meat or meat powder) to produce a _____ _____ (salivation) in a dog.

3 Most behavior which is respondently conditioned is mediated by the _____ nervous system.

4 Respondent conditioning is principally concerned with substitution of stimuli presented _____ the response.
(a) Consequent to
(b) At the same time as
(c) Antecedent to

5 Which choice above is most appropriate for operant conditioning?

6 (a) In learning experiments and in practical situations, what is the major criterion for extinction of a learned response? (b) What are two major methods used to extinguish respondently conditioned behavior?

7 A previously extinguished response suddenly recurs for no observable reason. What learning principle does this demonstrate?

8 (a) Represent the operant-conditioning model in notational system. (b) What is the variable in this model which is most significantly related to learning?

9 What are the two major criteria for evaluating the strength of food or water as reinforcements in a Skinner-box experiment?

10 Define negative reinforcement and give an example.

11 Water, food, and shelter are ordinarily conceived of as (a) _____ reinforcers; money, esteem, and power are ordinarily conceived of as (b) _____ reinforcers.

12 (a) Distinguish between fixed-interval and fixed-ratio reinforcement. (b) Between fixed-ratio and variable-ratio reinforcement.

13 Match the following:

(a) punishment	1. The response serves to prevent the occurrence of a stimulus.
(b) avoidance	2. The stimulus inhibits the response.
(c) escape	3. A stimulus is terminated to strengthen a response.

14 What kind of aversive stimulation was used in Brady's experiment with "executive monkeys"?

15 Shaping a particular response by reinforcing a series of successive approximations of the response is symbolized by R^D. What does this symbol mean?

16 Operant conditioning explains the learning of complex behavior by means of a series of S^{d}'s, R^{D}'s, and S^{r}'s. The process is termed _____.

part IV

The Development of Behavior

Leslie F. Malpass

In order to understand why a person behaves as he does at any given time, we find it useful to know something about the history of his predisposing conditions. This unit traces important developmental conditions which affect behavior. Information is presented about conception and prenatal development, birth and infancy, childhood, adolescence, and young adulthood. Particular emphasis is laid on the so-called formative years, between birth and later childhood.

Physical maturation is obviously important in setting limits on the behavior a child demonstrates. Perhaps of greater interest, however, are the socializing influences which determine behavior. Research has indicated that behavior patterns demonstrated in early childhood can be related, with a high degree of accuracy, to those in late adolescence (Neilon, 1948). "As the twig is bent" refers to the same idea. The influence of childhood behavior on later behavior deserves consideration. It is not presumed that behaviors demonstrated early in life cannot be changed; but since children tend to be exposed to similar social conditions in their homes in later childhood, most of them show continuities in behavior patterns.

This unit also presents information about the characteristic physical changes in adolescents and the problems they often face in gaining emancipation from parental control. The discussion of peer relationships and family relationships in adolescence leads to material about contemporary courtship and marriage customs and an analysis of the vocational considerations that face young adults today.

This unit relies on material from Parts II and III. It should provide a basis for better understanding of the theories of personality presented in Part V.

unit 1

Early Development

The prenatal period between conception and birth represents the period of greatest development proportionally in the entire life of the human being. In a little more than nine calendar months, a fantastically complex organism develops from a single cell, the fertilized ovum. Prenatal development is divided into three fairly distinct periods, culminating in birth. Some of the major characteristics of conception, of the germinal, embryonic, and fetal developmental periods, and of the newborn, are discussed in this unit.

Conception and Prenatal Development

conception

1 Human conception occurs when a male sex cell unites with a female sex cell. The uniting process, or _____, is the first step in the development of a new human being.

(1) sperm(atozoa)
(2) ovum

2 Sex cells produced by human males are called spermatozoa (singular, spermatozoon or sperm). Those produced by females are called ova (singular ovum, or egg). Men can produce **(1)** _____ in large numbers almost any time. Woman usually produce a single **(2)** _____ once a month.

ovaries

3 Ova are female sex cells produced by two small glands called ovaries. Typically, the left and right _____ produce ova in alternating twenty-eight-day menstrual cycles.

cycle (month)

4 Newly produced ova migrate from the ovaries to the uterus, via the Fallopian tubes, every twenty-eight days. Twenty-eight days, of course, constitute the ordinary menstrual _____.

Fallopian tubes

5 Fertilization usually occurs, if at all, in the F_____ t_____. Ordinarily it occurs in the middle of the menstrual cycle.

161

6 Most human females conceive before the ovum reaches the uterus. Ova migrate from the **(1)** _____ to the **(2)** _____ via the Fallopian tubes.

(1) ovaries
(2) uterus

7 Spermatozoa are male sex cells produced by two sex glands called testes. Spermatozoa may be produced by the _____ at almost any time.

testes

8 A new biological entity is conceived when a sperm unites with an egg. The fertilized _____ is called a zygote.

ovum

9 The fertilized ovum is called a **(1)** _____. Since most women produce only one ovum approximately every four weeks, conception can occur only about **(2)** ++++ in the human species.

(1) zygote
(2) once a month (every twenty-eight days)

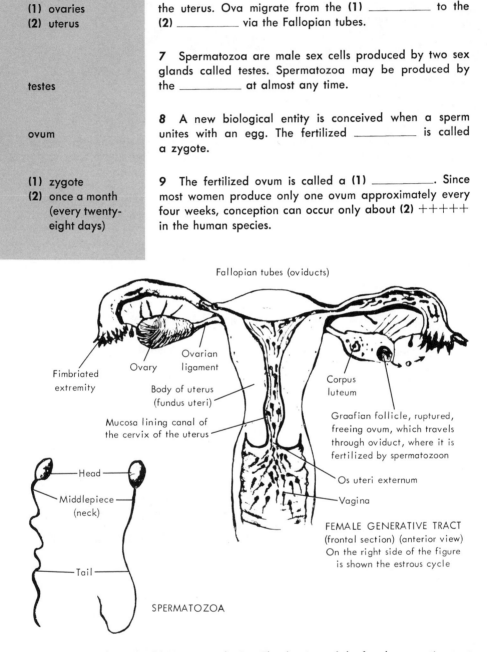

Fallopian tubes (oviducts)

Fimbriated extremity

Ovary

Ovarian ligament

Body of uterus (fundus uteri)

Mucosa lining canal of the cervix of the uterus

Corpus luteum

Graafian follicle, ruptured, freeing ovum, which travels through oviduct, where it is fertilized by spermatozoon

Os uteri externum

Vagina

FEMALE GENERATIVE TRACT
(frontal section) (anterior view)
On the right side of the figure is shown the estrous cycle

Head

Middlepiece (neck)

Tail

SPERMATOZOA

Figure 12. Mechanisms of human reproduction. The drawings of the female generative tract and spermatozoa permit detailed analysis of how reproduction occurs. (From *Blakiston's New Gould Medical Dictionary*, McGraw-Hill Book Company, 1949, used by permission.)

10 If a zygote splits in a particular way, two separate but practically identical zygotes result. If both of them develop to maturity, identical _____ are born.

twins

11 Identical twins, because they result from a particular type of splitting of the _____, cannot be of different sexes.

zygote

12 A zygote is an **(1)** _____ fertilized by **(2)** _____. An ovum ordinarily is produced once every **(3)** _____ _____.

(1) ovum
(2) sperm
(3) twenty-eight days (lunar month)

13 Sometimes two ova are produced at about the same time. If they are fertilized by two sperm, two _____ are conceived.

zygotes

14 When two ova are fertilized by two spermatozoa and the resulting zygotes develop to maturity, they are called fraternal twins. Because they develop from dissimilar zygotes, _____ _____ are no more genetically alike than ordinary brothers and/or sisters.

fraternal twins

15 Because they result from a unique splitting of a single fertilized ovum, identical twins have (almost) exactly the same _____ characteristics.

genetic (hereditary)

16 Two individuals, who were conceived from the union of two separate ova and spermatozoa at about the same time and who developed in the uterus together, are called _____ _____.

fraternal twins

17 If you knew two brothers of exactly the same age, one of whom had brown hair and eyes and the other had blond hair and blue eyes, you would know they were **(1)** _____ twins. They could not be **(2)** _____ twins.

(1) fraternal
(2) identical

18 The prenatal period is divided into three parts: (a) germinal stage—first two weeks, (b) embryonic stage—third to eighth week, (c) fetal stage—ninth week to birth. Any development occurring prior to birth occurs in the _____ period.

prenatal

19 The first two weeks of prenatal development are designated as the _____ stage.

germinal

20 The embryonic stage lasts from the third to the eighth week of prenatal development. The word embryo, means "to teem," or "to swell." Embryonic refers to the

growth (teeming)

rapid _____ of cells.

21 The third stage of prenatal development is the fetal period, from fetus, meaning "young one." This period

(1) ninth
(2) birth

extends from the **(1)** _____ week after conception until **(2)** _____.

22 The entire prenatal period is divided into three

(1) two weeks

stages. The germinal stage occupies the first **(1)** _____ _____ after conception; the embryonic stage oc-

(2) third to eighth
(3) ninth
   birth

cupies the **(2)** _____ to _____ weeks; and the fetal stage occurs between **(3)** _____ week and _____.

The Germinal Period

23 After conception has occurred in the Fallopian tube, the zygote divides and redivides, again and again, through the process of cell division. The collection of cells forming

(1) Fallopian
(2) germinal

the new organism remains in the **(1)** _____ tubes for about the first seven to ten days of the **(2)** _____ period.

24 Seven to ten days after conception, the small cluster of cells, called a blastocyst, begins to migrate from the

blastocyst

Fallopian tubes downward into the uterus. The _____ continues to develop in size and complexity through cell division.

25 When the blastocyst enters the uterus, it is composed of hundreds of cells, but it is only the size of a pinhead.

uterus

At this time it burrows into the lining of the _____ and becomes functionally attached to the mother.

26 It takes about two weeks from conception (the germi-

(1) blastocyst
(2) uterus

nal period) for the **(1)** _____ to attach itself to the lining of the **(2)** _____.

27 During the last part of the germinal period, the blastocyst becomes differentiated into three distinct layers of cells. The three cell layers are called the ectoderm (outer membrane), mesoderm (middle membrane), and endoderm (inner membrane). The outer layer of the blas-

ectoderm

tocyst is called the _____.

28 The ectoderm is the outer layer of the blastocyst. The middle layer of cells is called the **(1)** _____; and the inner layer of germinal cells is called the **(2)** _____.

(1) mesoderm
(2) endoderm

29 The ectoderm develops, ultimately, into the epidermis (outer skin), hair, teeth, sensory cells, and nervous system. From the outer layer of the blastocyst [i.e., **(1)** _____] develop(s) **(2)** _____ [tongue/teeth/toes].

(1) ectoderm
(2) teeth

30 The mesoderm subsequently develops into dermis (inner skin), muscles, skeleton, and the circulatory and excretory organs. From the middle layer of germinal cells, called the **(1)** _____, develops the **(2)** _____ [moustache/fingernails/skeleton].

(1) mesoderm
(2) skeleton

31 The Eustachian tubes, trachea, lungs, lining of the gastrointestinal tract, and the endocrine glands develop from the inner lining of the blastocyst, i.e., the endoderm. _____ glands develop from the endoderm.

Endocrine

32 The three germinal cell layers of the blastocyst are:
(1) _____ (outer layer)
(2) _____ (middle layer)
(3) _____ (inner layer)

(1) ectoderm
(2) mesoderm
(3) endoderm

Match the following:

33 mesoderm ___ (a) outer skin, hair, teeth, sensory cells, nervous system

(b)

34 endoderm ___ (b) inner skin, skeleton, muscles, circulatory, excretory systems

(c)

35 ectoderm ___ (c) Eustachian tubes, trachea, endocrine glands, lungs, gastrointestinal tract linings

(a)

36 *Review:* The germinal stage of prenatal development occupies about the first two weeks after conception. During this time the blastocyst migrates from the **(1)** _____ _____, where it was first formed, to the **(2)** _____, where it becomes attached to the mother.

(1) Fallopian tubes
(2) uterus

The Embryonic Period

The germinal period merges into the embryonic period during the second week after conception. During the embryonic period (third to eighth week after conception) the major biological characteristics begin to develop. Table 7 should be used as a reference for this section.

Table 7. Developmental Schedule for Embryonic Period

Body development	By the end of:
General shape: elongated, curved (⅕ in. long)	Four weeks
Primitive eye and ear cavities	
Arm and leg buds	
Umbilicus and umbilical cord	
Primitive tail	
Heart and cardiovascular system	
(Blood circulation—carries food to cells,	
wastes from cells via umbilical cord)	
Primitive nervous system (nerves and ganglia)	
Primitive organs of digestive system—	
stomach, pancreas, intestines, liver,	
gall bladder	
Primitive organs of respiration (lungs)	
Head and heart regions separated	Six weeks
Primitive olfactory (smell) cavity	
Ear buds	
Limb buds appear	
Upper arm, forearm, hand are differentiated	
Thigh, calf, foot are differentiated	
General size—1 in.	Eight weeks
Neck region distinct	
External ear	
Eyelids differentiated	
Limbs bent at elbows and knees	
Tail disappears	
Spontaneous movement	
Response to skin (tactile) stimulation	

37 By the end of the first four weeks of prenatal life, it is possible to discern the general shape of the body, i.e., it is _____ and _____; the primitive cavities for two of the sense organs (the _____ and _____), and the means of obtaining food from the mother, i.e., the _____ _____.

See Table 7

38 By the end of the germinal stage, the embryo has developed different systems for maintaining basic life processes. The heart and the _____ system; the brain, nerves, and ganglia which will make up the _____ system; the stomach, pancreas, and intestines, which are part of the _____ tract; and the lungs, which are part of the _____ system, are all present in primitive form.

See Table 7

39 In addition to the development of eye and ear cavities, the umbilical cord and the beginning of the circulatory, nervous, digestive, and respiratory systems, the human organism shows its allegiance to the animal kingdom in the first four prenatal weeks by developing a rudimentary _____ .

tail

40 By the end of the sixth prenatal week, limb buds (i.e., the beginnings of _____ and _____) and primitive organs for olfaction and hearing have appeared.

arms
legs

41 By the end of the eighth week after conception, the embryo has taken on distinctively human characteristics even though it is only about 1 inch long. The "tail" has disappeared; the ear is formed; protective coverings of the eye have begun to develop; and the head and trunk regions are separated by a _____ region.

neck

42 Spontaneous movements and response to skin stimulation are observable by the end of the eighth prenatal week. Stimulation of the skin is called _____ stimulation.

See Table 7

43 All important anatomical and physiological parts and systems have been differentiated by the end of the _____ period.

embryonic

44 The embryonic period ends, roughly, at the end of the _____ week of prenatal life, when it merges with the fetal period.

eighth

The Fetal Period

Some of the major developments that occur during the fetal period are given in Table 8. The schedule should be used as a reference for the next several items.

45 The fetal period begins about nine weeks after conception. It lasts until pregnancy is terminated in birth, at the end of about forty weeks. During the fetal stage (i.e., from the _____ to _____ month), the child develops rapidly.

third
ninth

46 By the end of the thirteenth week, external **(1)** _____ organs are discernible and fingernails and **(2)** _____ have begun to develop.

See Table 8

47 By the end of the twentieth week, glands to regulate external body temperature, i.e., **(1)** _____ glands, are operative, fingers can reflexively **(2)** _____ , and spontaneous gross body movements are first observed.

(1) sweat
(2) grasp

48 Breathing is possible at six months after conception, when the fetus is about _____ [6 inches/12 inches/18 inches/24 inches] long and weighs about _____ [½/1½/2] pounds.

See Table 8

49 Various reflex movements, presumably related to survival functions, are fully developed by the end of the seventh month. These include those used for ingesting food, i.e., the **(1)** _____ reflex, and those for holding onto things, i.e., the **(2)** _____ reflex.

(1) suctorial
(2) grasp

Table 8. Developmental Schedule for Fetal Period

Developmental events	By the end of:
All anatomical parts clearly differentiated Respiratory, digestive, nervous, circulatory systems, including glands, clearly differentiated	Twelfth week
Generally length is about 3 in. Fetal hair present Primitive nails on fingers, toes External sex organs discernible	Thirteenth week
Gross spontaneous body movements detectable by mother Many reflexive movements—fingers can "grasp" Sweat-gland secretions possible	Twentieth week
General length—12 in., weight 24 oz Respiratory movements (breathing) possible	Twenty-fourth week
General size—12 in., weight 2½ lb Fully developed reflex movements: "Startle" (general body) Suctorial (sucking) Grasp (hand) Babinski (toe fanning)	Twenty-eighth week
Capacity to use all sense organs General size—about 20 in. in length weight—about 7 lb Disappearance of fetal body hair	Fortieth week

50 Birth generally occurs about 280 days after conception. Counting from time of conception, fetuses who at birth are younger than 182 days [**(1)** _____ weeks], or older than 322 days [**(2)** _____ weeks] rarely survive. These figures indicate roughly, for the human species, the upper and lower limits for survival after development *in utero*.

(1) twenty-six weeks
(2) forty-six weeks

EARLY PREGNANCY

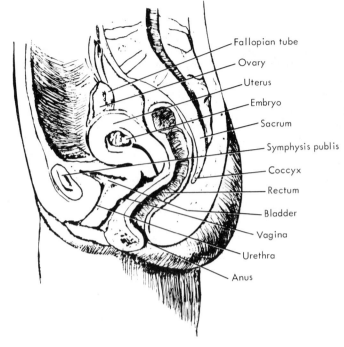

- Fallopian tube
- Ovary
- Uterus
- Embryo
- Sacrum
- Symphysis pubis
- Coccyx
- Rectum
- Bladder
- Vagina
- Urethra
- Anus

PREGNANT UTERUS AT TERM

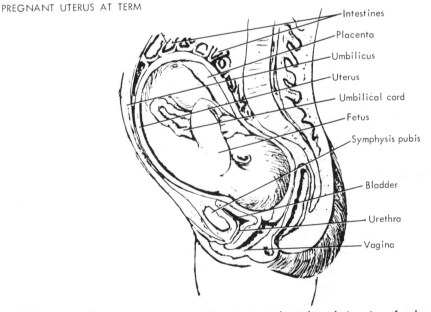

- Intestines
- Placenta
- Umbilicus
- Uterus
- Umbilical cord
- Fetus
- Symphysis pubis
- Bladder
- Urethra
- Vagina

Figure 13. Prenatal human development. The drawings show the relative size of unborn infants at about age two months and nine months, together with details of the female reproductive tract. (From *Blakiston's New Gould's Medical Dictionary*, McGraw-Hill Book Company, 1956, used by permission.)

Prenatal Influences on Development

51 The placenta is the sac which envelops the developing organism. It serves as a protective device for the _____.

fetus (embryo)
(These terms are sometimes used as synonyms, although technically they refer to different stages in development.)

52 The placenta serves as a sort of net or strainer through which nutritional and other types of substances from the mother's blood pass to the child. Infectious diseases are transmitted to the unborn child if they are caused by substances small enough to pass through the _____.

placenta

In addition to infectious diseases, several other conditions are known to influence abnormal prenatal development. These include maternal malnutrition, endocrine irregularities, blood incompatibility (Rh factor), and injury. People used to blame heredity for unfortunate results of these conditions.

53 Congenital deformities or defects can result from either hereditary factors or abnormal _____ development.

prenatal

54 The occurrence of congenital deformities or defects due to prenatal conditions is related to the time during pregnancy when the mother is affected. Particular defects are related to disturbance of prenatal growth at a particular _____.

time (period)

55 Ingalls (1950) reports studies on the effect of anoxia (lack of oxygen) on prenatal development in mice. Knowing when a particular structure was differentiated, he correctly predicted the occurrence of various developmental deviations (e.g., harelip, blindness) as a function of _____.

anoxia

56 Rubella (German measles) may cause deafness in the child if contracted by the mother in the second or third month of _____, because the inner ear develops between the seventh and tenth weeks.

pregnancy

57 Similarly, since the brain structures are being laid down between the third to twelfth weeks of prenatal life, mental defects may also occur if _____ is contracted during this time.

rubella (German measles)

58 If rubella is contracted by the mother during the first three months of pregnancy, the virus almost always is transmitted to the embryo across the placental barrier. This typically results in one or more of the following in the child: _____ _____, deafness, cataracts, heart disease.

mental deficiency

59 List four conditions which can result from rubella if contracted in the first three months of pregnancy. +++++.

See the two pre-ceding frames.

60 Syphilis, malaria, smallpox, chickenpox, and mumps are all infectious diseases. They are caused by agents small enough to pass through the _____.

placenta

61 Depending on the prenatal stage in which the mother contracted the disease and upon factors such as degree of toxicity in the mother, these diseases can result in _____ deformities or defects.

congenital

62 Maternal malnutrition, as well as anoxia and infectious disease, may affect the development of the fetus. Bowlby and others (1950) studied children born to mothers in occupied countries during World War II. They found relationships between _____ in mothers and birth weight and length of neonates (newborn).

malnutrition

63 C. A. Smith (1951) reported a relationship between the quality of the mother's diet during pregnancy and the number of premature births and stillborns. This lends credence to the idea that maternal _____ is related to development of children *in utero*.

malnutrition

64 The effects of the mother's smoking and drinking alcohol on unborn children have been studied. It is known that both smoking and drinking alcohol increase the fetal heart beat, but there is no conclusive evidence that either one in moderation causes developmental irregularities in the fetus. Most physicians, however, discourage expectant mothers from (1) _____ or drinking (2) _____.

(1) smoking
(2) alcohol

65 The human fetus can be conditioned to move at the "sound" of a buzzer. Several investigators have found that when pressure is applied to an expectant mother's abdomen at the same time that a buzzer is sounded, the child can be _____ to respond to the buzzer.

conditioned

66 Conditioned response studies of fetuses have been used as evidence that unborn children can learn. Since the cortex is functionally undeveloped at birth, this type of learning must be mediated by subc____ical structures.

subcortical

67 Many animal studies have demonstrated that postnatal development of offspring can be altered by subjecting pregnant animals to unusual conditions. Fowler (1962) subjected pregnant rats to irradiation and then traced out unusual _____ behavior in the offspring.

postnatal

68 Controlled studies of irradiation effects on humans are not possible, but children born to pregnant women who survived the Hiroshima holocaust tended to demonstrate various unusual physical and behavioral reactions to the effects of _____.

irradiation

69 Keely (1962) demonstrated that overcrowding of pregnant rats resulted in deviant offspring behavior. Controlled studies of _____ of humans are not available, of course.

overcrowding

70 Thompson et al. (1962) studied the effects of maternal emotional states on postnatal development of offspring. Pregnant rats subjected to fear-evoking stimuli gave birth to offspring either more or less _____ than those from a control group.

emotional (fearful)

71 The type of postnatal _____ behavior demonstrated was related to the period of pregnancy in which the mother was affected.

emotional

72 Again, controlled studies of effects of maternal emotion are not possible with humans. Sears, Maccoby, and Levin (1952), however, reported relationships between verbal reports of maternal emotional states and later _____ behavior.

maternal

73 Mothers who expressed pleasure at becoming pregnant tended to be more expressive in their affection for their children than those not expressing _____ at pregnancy.

pleasure

74 These latter studies, however, do not show how maternal _____ affects the developing fetus.

emotion

Studies of the effects of maternal infectious diseases, malnutrition, and endocrine imbalance on the unborn child indicate that prenatal conditions, as well as heredity, may influence postnatal development to a considerable extent.

Birth and the Neonate

Birth represents the culmination of prenatal development. At the end of pregnancy, signals are given to the mother that her body is no longer to be called upon to sustain the child's life in her body. Instead, the child will be ejected from the stable intrauterine environment, where its survival needs have been supplied by the mother, into the external environment. When this occurs, the complicated machinery of the child's body is ready to take over survival functions. Inhalation of oxygen and ingestion of food supply nutritive requirements. Internal mechanisms regulate respiratory, digestive, circulatory, and eliminatory functions. Sensory mechanisms are ready to respond to various types of stimuli which impinge on them. Birth, then, is a time of literal separation of child from mother. It is also the time when the child, as an independent organism, must be able to respond effectively to a new and constantly changing environment.

As Gesell, Piaget, and others have pointed out, the infant at birth is essentially a creature of reflex. He is endowed with certain kinds of primitive response mechanisms, which when necessary, perform survival functions. The neonate is "human" in the sense of demonstrating the usual anatomical and physiological characteristics of Homo sapiens. But his repertoire of activities is limited, and, at least during the first few weeks, 70 to 80 per cent of the time is spent in sleep (Buhler, 1930, Gesell, 1949).

The birth process and some important aspects of neonatal development are presented in this section.

The Birth Process

75 Pregnancy is terminated in birth. Birth ordinarily occurs about 280 days (ten lunar months) after conception. Pregnancy thus lasts about _____ weeks.

forty

76 Birth occurs when the mother and fetus are biologically "ready." That is, it occurs when the placenta is no longer capable of supplying nutriment to the (1) _____, and the fetus is maturationally able to (2) _____ outside the uterus.

(1) fetus
(2) survive (live)

Note: If you are familiar with the birth process, skip to frame 81.

77 The process of birth labor begins with a series of uterine contractions. At first the _____ are spaced some time apart, but gradually they occur closer together.

contractions

78 Firstborn children (called primipari) are usually born about seventeen hours after labor begins. Uterine contractions occur only about two minutes apart toward the end of _____.

79 When contractions occur about two minutes apart, the fetus has been pushed far down the birth canal by _____ _____. At this time the fluid-filled amniotic sac, in which the fetus has developed, ruptures.

80 As uterine contractions continue, the cervix (entrance to the uterus) dilates enough to accommodate passage of the fetus from the uterus. The fetus passes from the uterus through the dilated _____ and the vagina (birth canal) into the outside world.

81 Review: The birth process involves the following: The fetus migrates from the _____, through the _____, over a period of several hours. This movement is caused by uterine _____ and terminates in birth.

82 In the usual birth, the baby's head is presented first. In breech births, the child's buttocks are presented first and the head last. Thus _____ births may be dangerous to both mother and baby; but they seldom occur.

83 Sometimes, because of potential danger to mother or child, babies are removed from the uterus surgically, i.e., by Caesarian section. Caesarian section refers to _____ delivery.

84 Surgical delivery of a child is termed _____ section.

85 Breech births and Caesarian-section births are relatively rare. Modern obstetrics (the science of pregnancy and delivery) has made such births reasonably safe for both mothers and babies. Safety has resulted from an increased knowledge of _____.

86 During the last stages of birth the mother often is given an anesthetic to relieve pain. Many mothers prefer "natural childbirth" to receiving an _____.

87 There seems to be a relationship between the mother's fear of birth pain and the birth pain she reports (Smith, 1961). Doctors who advocate "natural childbirth" with no anesthetic prepare mothers for birth by trying to reduce their fear of _____.

---

labor

uterine contractions

cervix

If you could not complete these, reread frames 77 to 80.

breech

surgical

Caesarian

obstetrics

anesthetic

pain

Obstetricians recommend "natural childbirth" for mothers when it is felt that the mother can tolerate pain and cooperate better with the obstetrician during labor. Presumably, natural childbirth results in greater satisfaction for the mother and reduces the possibilities of injury to the child, although neither of these contentions has been unequivocally supported.

Neonatal Development

88 "Neo-" means new; "natal" means birth. Thus, the birth process terminates in the delivery of a _____.

neonate (newborn child)

89 The typical neonate is born fully equipped for life but is not, of course, breathing at birth. The obstetrician usually holds the neonate upside down and pats him on the back to start the _____ process.

breathing

90 The "birth cry" results from a sudden ingestion of air into the neonate's lungs. Does the birth cry represent (a) an experience of pain, or (b) a reflexive activation of the vocal cords by air entering the lungs? _____.

(b)

91 The newborn child is capable of only a few spontaneous reflexive-type behaviors. It has relatively little, if any, cortical control over behavior. Previous chapters have pointed out that _____ behaviors are controlled by the "old brain" rather than by the cortex.

reflexive

92 Breathing, sucking, swallowing, digesting, and elimination are all _____ behaviors in the neonate.

reflexive

93 Besides the reflexive behaviors presumably related to food intake (a neonate sucks when he is hungry, even when food is not presented), certain other reflex behaviors are present in the neonate. Most _____ demonstrate the plantar reflex (toe extending), grasp reflex, and startle (Moro) reflex. (Skip to frame 97 if you know about these reflexes.)

neonates

94 Reflexive extension of the toes when the bottom of the neonate's foot is stimulated is called the plantar reflex. Tickle the sole of a newborn child's foot, and you will observe the _____ reflex. This reflex is very rarely present in older children and adults.

plantar

95 In addition to the plantar reflex, most neonates demonstrate the grasp reflex. Approximately 75 per cent of newborn children can support their own weight by means of the _____ reflex.

grasp

96   A sudden loud sound typically produces the so-called Moro reflex in the neonate. This is a response characterized by an extension of both arms and legs and then their return to an enveloping position. The _____ reflex, like other reflexes present at birth, disappears after a few weeks.

Moro

97   Observation of some reflexes at birth and of other developmental occurrences prompted G. Stanley Hall (1904) to posit the "recapitulation theory" of development. This theory suggests that a child's development represents a _____ of his evolutionary development.

recapitulation

98   Hall suggested that such developmental facts as **(1)** appearance and then disappearance of the "prenatal tail," **(2)** the neonatal grasp reflex, and **(3)** the creeping-then-walking sequence observed in most children recapitulate man's gradual development from a four-legged to a two-legged animal. This is why Hall's theory is known as the _____ theory.

recapitulation

99   Hall's theory suggests that the grasp reflex is a throwback to an earlier evolutionary stage when the neonate had to "hang on for dear life" when the mother was frightened and leaped from tree branch to tree branch. If the neonate did not _____ the mother reflexively, it was doomed.

grasp

100   Most biologists who have intensively studied relationships between structures and functions of different species believe that man evolved from a "lower" species. However, they seem to feel that Hall's _____ _____ is not scientifically defensible.

recapitulation
theory

101   Another theory about newborn children that lacks scientific verification is Otto Rank's well-known concept of the "birth trauma" (trauma means wound or injury). Rank's theory suggests that the birth process produces a psychological _____.

trauma (wound, injury)

102   Rank (1929) suggested that the neonate must suffer psychological shock when he is ejected from the stable, warm, fluid environment of the uterus into the "blooming, buzzing confusion" of the outside world. The birth trauma represents _____ shock or injury.

psychological

103   Obstetricians, psychologists, and psychiatrists have not verified Rank's _____-_____ theory. It might be useful for you to stop and consider why such verification would be difficult, if not impossible.

birth-trauma

104 In addition to the reflexive movements already described, the neonate demonstrates responsiveness to all types of sensory stimulation. Light, sound, pressure, movement, odors, and sugar and certain acid solutions are able to evoke responses. These _____ stimuli do not, of course, bring forth the complex responses seen in older children.

sensory

105 The neonate does not "see" in the sense of being able to discriminate between various light stimuli. His eyes cannot converge on an object at first; sometimes they move in different directions at the same time. But when a light is flashed in the neonate's eyes, he closes them. By this we know the neonate is responsive to _____ stimuli.

light (visual)

106 The neonate responds to intensity of light stimuli by eye closure, but he does not discriminate between various types of visual stimuli. He does not use his eyes to _____, in the usual sense of visual discrimination.

see (discriminate)

107 Can the neonate discriminate visually between his mother and father?

No (not before at least two weeks after birth)

108 Just as the neonate cannot interpret visual stimuli as he does later on, neither does he "hear" in these terms. If the infant responds to sounds, obviously his hearing apparatus is operative. But the neonate does not know the difference between "pretty baby" and "ugly child" when spoken by his mother (i.e., as _____ stimuli).

sound (auditory)

109 Neonatal response to sound stimuli varies with volume and duration, but apparently not with pitch, within the human voice range. Loudness, that is, (1) _____, is correlated roughly with intensity of response. Also, sounds of short (2) _____ are likely to elicit more responses than those extending over time.

(1) volume

(2) duration

110 The neonate is capable of responding to odors as well as to visual and auditory stimuli. Olfactory stimulation by means of ammonia, for example, elicits a typical intense body movement. Thus, we know that the neonate responds to certain types of _____ stimulation.

olfactory

111 Sugar and some acid solutions typically elicit suctorial responses in the neonate. This indicates that the neonate's _____ buds are operative at birth.

taste

112 The neonate responds to sugar and certain acid solutions by sucking, but salt solutions tend to inhibit sucking responses which may be present. Response to salt, sugar, and acids indicates that the neonate can _____ between (at least some) gustatory stimuli at birth.

discriminate

113 Extreme and sudden temperature deviations elicit characteristic responses. "The burnt child dreads the fire" cannot be applied to the neonate (the newborn does not "know" what fire is). But the child does respond with energetic body movements to sudden _____ changes.

temperature
(thermal)

114 Pain response is suggested by the newborn's reactions to extreme temperature and intense pressure stimulation (such as pinching, if you wish to be so barbaric). It is difficult to determine the parameters, or limits, of_____ response in the neonate.

pain

115 *Review:* All the sensory modalities are operative at birth. The neonate's behavioral repertoire is essentially reflexive; little voluntary control of behavior is demonstrated by the _____.

neonate

Maturation

Maturation refers to the process of biological development which results in changes in structure and behavior. Sometimes behavior occurs without prior practice or experience, as in the flying of young birds or in unusual cases of "spontaneous walking" in human infants. In these instances, maturation of the appropriate body systems, rather than learning, accounts for the behavior. There are very few examples of human behavior, however, where maturation can be separated from the effects of practice.

In most developmental activities during infancy (e.g., walking, talking, toilet training), there is little profit in providing training before the maturation of relevant biological structures and processes. Maturation, then, is important to developing behavior. Four principles about maturation summarize a great deal of research from biology and behavioral sciences. They are:
1. Differentiation increases with development.
2. Integration increases with development.
3. Sequences in maturation are more predictable than rate of maturation.
4. Maturation sets limits on learning.

116 One of the major principles which seems to govern the maturation process in all living things is that *differentiation increases with development*. Cell division in the newly fertilized egg is an example of the way that _____ increases with development.

differentiation

117 As the fetus grows in the uterus, development occurs along the line from its head to its tail. This line is called the cephalo-caudal axis (head-tail axis). Growth along the _____-_____ axis is another example of how differentiation increases with development.

cephalo-caudal

118 When we speak of an axis we imply a direction. The cephalo-caudal axis means a _____ from head to tail.

direction

119 Infants can control their head movements before their arm movements. They can control their arms before they can use their legs for locomotion. This indicates that the _____-_____ trend in development continues after birth.

cephalo-caudal

120 As the infant develops, movements involving the whole body come before controlled action of specific body parts. This illustrates a tendency to develop along the mass-specific—movement axis. Like the cephalo-caudal trend, this developmental tendency also suggests that _____ increases with development.

differentiation

121 The fact that an infant "cries all over," instead of showing anger or sorrow by tear secretions in the eyes as adults do, suggests that the _____-_____ development tendency continues from the prenatal to the postnatal stages.

mass-specific

122 An infant typically grasps a spoon with his whole hand before he learns to use the thumb and index finger for spooning. This progression suggests, again, the tendency to develop according to a _____-_____ trend.

mass-specific

123 Human development also occurs along a proximo-distal axis. The proximo(near)distal(distant) axis refers to the development of body parts (1) _____ the center of the fetus before the development of body parts more (2) _____ from the center.

(1) near

(2) distant

124 The fact that the trunk of the body develops prior to the arms and fingers exemplifies the **(1)** _____ developmental tendency. That gross arm movements occur before fine finger movements illustrates the **(2)** _____-_____ trend in locomotion.

(1) proximodistal

(2) mass-specific

The three developmental trends mentioned strongly suggest that differentiation increases with development. In addition to the trends designated, Piaget (1954) has suggested an additional "social-development" tendency, the egocentric-socialization axis. Infants are at first concerned only with themselves and subsequently with others. At birth, infants seem to care for no one and nothing but themselves. Food and other requirements are supplied them so that "others exist for them." During the first six months of postnatal life, however, infants learn to perform various social acts, such as reaching toward and smiling at other people.

125 Piaget thus suggests that there is a developmental tendency from egocentrism to _____.

socialization

126 Although the egocentrism-socialization trend is not strictly a maturational tendency, according to our definition, it seems to be related to biological _____ in early childhood. Related concepts will be discussed in subsequent sections.

development

Four developmental tendencies were used to illustrate the general principle that differentiation increases with development. If you cannot remember these tendencies, review frames 117, 120, 123, and 125. If you can give examples to show you understand that these four developmental tendencies represent the principle that differentiation increases with development, you will have demonstrated familiarity with these concepts.

127 A second principle about maturation states that *integration increases with development.* (We are not referring to race relations, although the principle might be extrapolated to social conditions.) As maturation continues, better _____ of body movements occurs.

integration

128 In any motor act (sitting, standing, pressing door-bells or bar levers, driving cars, putting your arm around someone else), a complex series of muscle movements occurs. Such acts are usually performed very awkwardly at first, but coordination _____ as the acts are repeated.

increases (improves)

129 The development from uncoordinated to highly co-ordinated muscle movements as a function of maturation illustrates the idea that integration of body parts increases with _____.

development

130 Language development provides a good illustration of the second principle of maturation. A baby first gurgles and grunts without "saying" words. He learns to articulate the tongue-lip-respiratory tract and jaw movements as maturation permits. These integrating movements are func-tions of _____.

maturation

131 In infancy, expressive speech involves integration of the tongue, lips, respiratory tract, and jaws. Expressive speech is dependent on _____ of these body parts.

integration

132 Maturation is a necessary condition for expressive speech; social reinforcement is also extremely important in the development of _____ speech.

expressive

133 For example, a proud father looks at his baby, and the baby moves his lips and emits a sound like "mum-mum." The father smiles at Junior and says "Mum-mum-mummy, that's right." Junior again emits "mum-mum," and the proud father repeats his routine. The father serves as a _____ reinforcer for Junior's developing expressive speech.

social

134 The development of expressive speech illustrates the principle that integration of body parts in speech is in part a function of both maturation and _____.

social reinforce-
ment (learning)

135 *Review:* The two major principles about maturation stated so far are:
(1) _____
(2) _____

Check frames
116 and 127.

136 A third principle of maturation states: *Sequences in maturation are more predictable than rate of maturation.* Most infants first hitch themselves along bellywise, then creep, then stand, then toddle, then walk. But the age at which one child achieves each of these activities may be much different from that of another. This is why
(1) _____ of maturation is more predictable than
(2) _____ of maturation.

(1) sequence
(2) rate

137 Jane creeps at six months, stands alone at nine months, and walks at eleven months. John creeps at seven months, stands alone at eleven months, and walks at thirteen months. The sequences for this type of motor development are **(1)** _____ for both babies, but the **(2)** _____ are different. Incidentally, empirical data indicate that girls usually demonstrate earlier development than boys (Gesell and Ilg, 1949).

(1) similar (the same, alike)
(2) rates

138 McGraw (1935) observed two fraternal twins from birth. Johnny and Jimmy crept, stood alone, walked, ran, and climbed in the same order or **(1)** _____. But Johnny demonstrated most of these motor behaviors before Jimmy. Their developmental rates were **(2)** _____.

(1) sequence

(2) different

139 Individuals vary more in **(1)** _____ than in **(2)** _____ of motor development.

(1) rate
(2) sequence

Most children learn to walk at about the age of one year and to control elimination of waste at about the age of fifteen to eighteen months. This suggests that maturation of some characteristics occurs as a species function and that we may set up a rough time schedule to anticipate when children will reach certain levels of development.

140 Baby monkeys can walk almost from birth, but baby humans cannot walk for some months after birth. This suggests that rate or age of maturation of some functions is a characteristic of the _____.

species

141 *Review:* The fact that species variations occur in the maturation of similar activities does not obviate the third principle of maturation that has been stated, namely, +++++.

Check frame 136.

142 A fourth principle of maturation suggests that if control of skeletal-muscular functions in walking, using utensils, etc., is at first a function of maturation, then _____ *sets limits on learning.*

maturation

143 An infant cannot learn to control movements involved in directing a spoon toward and into the mouth until his skeleton and his nervous and muscular systems are sufficiently _____ to permit such learning.

matured (developed)

144 Which of the following best illustrates the idea that maturation sets limits on learning?

    a. John could not feed himself with a spoon at twenty-four months of age.

    b. John could not feed himself with a spoon at twelve months but could do so by twenty-four months.

    c. John could handle a spoon as well at twenty-four months as at thirty-six months.

145 *Review:* A child cannot learn to catch a ball until he is able to coordinate the body systems required to do so. This also illustrates that maturation $+++++$.

146 Cell division, the cephalo-caudal trend, proximo-distal trend, and mass-specific trend demonstrate that _____ increases with development.

147 The production of increasingly recognizable speech sounds as the body parts used in speaking mature illustrates the principle that _____ increases with development.

148 Variation in rate but not in sequence of development indicates that _____ of maturation is more predictable than rate.

Maturation in Infancy

For our purposes, infancy is defined as the developmental period spanned by birth and the second birthday. Table 9 denotes the monthly age at which significant anatomical, sensory motor, and language developments occur. Pratt's descriptive chapter on the neonate, Arnold Gesell's chapter on infant behavior, and Helen Thompson's excellent survey of physical growth, all of which are in Carmichael's *Manual of Child Psychology* (1954), provide detailed descriptions of the wealth of research which has contributed to the generalizations described in this unit. The reader is referred also to a series of articles by Irwin and his colleagues published in the *Journal of Speech and Hearing Disorders* between 1946 and 1952 for a comprehensive description of the development of children's speech.

149 Developmental schedules are used to compare the maturation level of a given child with that of a normative group. A representative sample of children of his age, sometimes broken down according to sex and other variables, comprises a _____ group.

Margin answers:

b

sets limits on learning

differentiation

integration

sequence

normative

Table 9. Developmental Schedule for Motor and Language Development in the First Two Years

Age in months	Motor skills	Language skills
1	Lifts chin when prone on belly; smiles; sheds tears	Crying sounds
2	Lifts chest when prone on belly; follows (eyes) moving person; tonic neck reflex	Babbles spontaneously
3	Unclenches hands, reaches (no contact); eye convergence	Coos at others
4	Sits with support; bilateral symmetrical movements; reaches (with contact); "knows" mother; follows (eyes) small moving objects	Laughs, turns head to voice
6	Sleeps all night; sits upright in chair; grasps with whole hand	Differentiated sounds (no language)
8	First teeth; sits alone; stands with help; hand preference; gives up clenched object; may be on solid food	Spontaneously combines two syllables
10	Stands alone momentarily; creeps; prehensile (forefinger) grasp; may attempt to feed self	Imitative sounds ("mummum"); Responds to simple command
12	Walks when led (perhaps alone); pulls self upright; manipulates spoon	One to three single words
14	Walks alone (toddles); some bowel control	Three to six single words (spontaneous use)
16	Increase in certainty, straightness of walking; imitative scribble; perhaps nocturnal bowel control	Five to ten single words (spontaneous use)
18	Runs without falling much; spontaneous scribble; some urinary control; fairly complete bowel control	Repeats requests; joins two words; starts use of verbs, adjectives, and adverbs; identifies body parts
20	Builds three-block tower; climbs stairs with help	Joins words in concepts; follows complex directions
24	High-level prehensile skill; fetches things on request; walks upstairs alone; complete urinary control (diurnal)	Uses descriptive adjectives and nouns and can join words in simple sentences

SOURCE: Adapted from Gesell and Ilg (1949) and Hurlock (1959).

150 Gesell and his coworkers (Gesell and Ilg, 1949) have devised developmental schedules to indicate ages at which most children they studied were sufficiently mature to demonstrate the onset of particular behavior. These _____ _____ provide rough predictions of the age of maturation for many forms of behavior in children.

151 Gesell and Ilg have described maturational development in terms of a "developmental spiral." This implies that the child takes two maturational steps forward and one backward. The backward step presumably reflects consolidation of previous maturational gains in the _____ _____.

152 The developmental spiral can be illustrated in many ways. For example, in studying covariation between increase in length of sleep periods and age in infancy, the upward gradient of the developmental spiral may be represented by _____ in the length of sleep periods.

153 (Refer to Table 9.) By six months of age, most children sleep $+++++$.

154 The downward gradient of the developmental spiral can be illustrated by the fact that, having accomplished all-night sleeping at six months, many infants wake up once or twice a night during the seventh or eighth months. (Whether Gesell and Ilg are correct in assuming this is a "consolidation of maturational gains" in the _____ _____ is of course debatable.)

155 A child grasps a spoon with his whole hand at about **(1)** _____ months of age; attempts to feed himself about **(2)** _____ months; and manipulates a spoon in self-feeding quite adequately about **(3)** _____ months of age.

156 For several weeks at twenty-four months of age, an infant refuses to feed himself without help. For Gesell and Ilg this would represent a _____ gradient of the developmental spiral.

157 Most children demonstrate the following sequence:
  (a) Sit with help: _____ months
  (b) Sit alone: _____ months
  (c) Stand with help: _____ months
  (d) Stand alone: _____ months

158 Most children can achieve fairly complete bowel control by _____ months.

Left margin answers:

developmental schedules

developmental spiral

increase

all night

developmental spiral

See Table 9

downward

See Table 9

See Table 9

159 Most infants are maturationally "ready" to begin urinary training by fifteen to eighteen months; typically, they achieve fairly complete daytime control of urination by _____ months of age.

See Table 9

160 Children usually toddle at about twelve to fourteen months, walk straight and with certainty by **(1)** _____ months, and run without falling at about **(2)** _____ months of age.

See Table 9

161 Gesell and Ilg (1949) indicate that hand preference, or handedness, may be related to the tonic neck reflex (t.n.r.). The t.n.r. refers to the tendency to extend the right arm and bend the left when the head is moved to face right. Converse arm movements are observed in the _____ _____ _____ when the head is moved to face left.

t.n.r. (tonic neck reflex)

162 The t.n.r. seems to be predictive of handedness. If a two-month-old infant consistently demonstrates left head turns and corresponding left arm extensions, it would be reasonable to predict _____ [right/left]-hand preference in later infancy.

left

163 A child is right-handed. The chances are that his t.n.r. was to the _____ in early infancy.

right

164 Reflexive head turning and arm extending in the same direction are basic t.n.r. characteristics, which occur by the **(1)** _____ month of postnatal life. They are related to hand preference, which is first observed at about the **(2)** _____ month.

(1) second

(2) eighth

Some evidence shows that there are centers for handedness in the subcortex or old brain. These may influence the expression of the t.n.r. reflex and later hand preference. However, there is good reason to believe that handedness occurs as a function of learning and practice as well as of possible biological predisposition (Hurlock, 1959).

165 It has been said that language is the cement which holds society together. Receptive language refers to the understanding of language used by someone else. Expressive language refers to the use of language by the behaver. Imitative sounds exemplify _____ language.

expressive

166 Imitative sounds first occur regularly at about ten months of age. "Mum-my" and "dad-dy" are examples of sounds enunciated by the mother and imitated by the child (and sometimes vice versa). When they are produced by the mother and repeated by the child, they are called _____ sounds. They illustrate expressive language.

imitative

167 Receptive language refers to the receipt and understanding of language. A child turns his head toward another person's voice at about four months. He responds to simple commands at eight months. He follows complex directions at twenty months. These are illustrations of _____ language.

receptive

168 A mother shows her thirty-month-old baby some pictures of a train, a cup, a gun, and a cat. She asks the infant to identify each as she points. The child looks at her and smiles as if to say, "Let's begin." The baby's response indicates that _____ language is operative.

receptive

169 A child uses "first words" typically at about twelve to fourteen months of age. Vocal speech is an example of _____ language development.

expressive

170 At eighteen months the infant can usually join two words together. At twenty-four months he can name many common objects. At thirty months he uses words in primitive sentences as _____ language.

expressive

171 Expressive language refers to (1) +++++. Receptive language refers to (2) +++++.

(1) spoken (expressed, etc.) language
(2) received (heard, understood, etc.) language

172 Both imitative sounds and spontaneously spoken sounds represent _____ language.

expressive

It is important to consider motor and language development for two reasons. First, these developmental processes exemplify some of the principles already mentioned. Second, they are important in and of themselves because they provide background material for understanding the more complex personal-social behavior that occurs in later childhood and adolescence. For the same reasons, it is well to become acquainted with the early development of emotional behavior.

Early Development of Emotional Behavior

Getting consensual agreement about the designation of fear, rage, or even affection in young infants is more difficult than is commonly believed (Sherman, 1927). Independent observers often disagree when they try to judge how an infant's behavior represents an emotion. Perhaps this disagreement is related to the fact that infants cannot speak; it is also related in part to the observers' knowledge of what preceded the infant's emotional response. In any event, careful evaluations of independent judgments of emotional behavior indicate that specific emotions cannot be reliably identified as early in life as many people might believe.

Table 10. Developmental Schedule for Differentiation of Emotions in Infancy

Emotional behavior observed first at:	By the age of:
General excitement and excitability	Birth
Distress and delight (general)	Three months
Fear; disgust; anger (elicited by, and/or directed toward, specific events)	Six months
Elation; affection (elicited by, and/or directed toward, specific events). Affection for adults contrasted with that for children	Twelve to fifteen months
Jealousy and joy (in the presence of specific events), as distinguished from general distress or delight	Eighteen to twenty months

SOURCE: Adapted from Bridges (1932).

173 The only "emotion" at birth, for which reliable agreement has been obtained, is general _____.

excitement

174 Even distress and delight, as judged emotions, do not become differentiated until about _____ months of age.

See Table 10

175 It is not until about six months of age that disgust, _____, and _____ are reliably differentiated.

See Table 10

176 Elation and affection, as emotional reactions, were differentiated from other emotional reactions at about the age of _____ months.

See Table 10

The foregoing data serve to emphasize that emotional behavior is difficult to designate accurately in early infancy. This does not mean that the child may not "feel" or even demonstrate the behaviors listed. It does reflect an inadequacy of interpretation of such behavior on the part of adults.

Social Stimulation in Early Infancy

Practically every high school student has heard that the past is prologue to the present. This generalization certainly seems to hold true for social behavior. Social behavior in the present is in large measure a function related to past social behavior. Religious leaders, educators, parents, and behavioral scientists have all reported that experiences in early childhood have their effects on behavior in later life. This section examines some studies made by biologists and psychologists who were interested in trying to pinpoint specific aspects of early socialization.

177 Scientists who specialize in the study of behavior patterns of different species of animals are called ethologists. Ethologists study _____ patterns.

178 Konrad Lorenz, an Austrian _____, became interested in the effects of experiences in very early life on later behavior. For convenience of observation, he selected greylag geese as experimental animals.

179 Lorenz discovered that if a gosling exerted persistent effort in following a moving object about thirteen to sixteen hours after birth, it tended to adopt the _____ _____ as a mother regardless of other nonparental characteristics it might possess (e.g., size, shape, texture).

180 Lorenz's goslings would adopt him as their mother if they followed him persistently (for ten minutes or more) between _____ and _____ hours after hatching. This period of time has been called the *critical period* for imprinting of goslings. A summary of experimental literature dealing with this concept has been provided by J. S. Scott (1962).

181 Lorenz used the term "imprinting" to describe the functional relationship between particular patterns of social behavior occurring during the _____ _____ in early life and later behavioral patterns.

behavior

ethologist

moving object (thing, etc.)

thirteen and sixteen

critical period

182 Goslings who mistook Lorenz for their mother demonstrate the process of _____ .

imprinting

183 In studying imprinting, and the critical period for it, Lorenz systematically investigated specific aspects of early experience in relation to +++++ .

later behavior

184 Laboratory attempts to define the critical period in imprinting for ducklings have been conducted by Eckhard Hess (1958), among others. He confirmed Lorenz's observations about the _____ _____ for imprinting ducklings and has observed the same phenomena for other species as well.

critical period

185 Hess found that a duckling put in a runway near a slow-moving mechanical duck between thirteen and sixteen hours after hatching would follow the toy duck thereafter as if it were a mother. Such ducklings presumably were _____ to a mechanical mother.

imprinted

186 Imprinting in ducklings can occur with nonliving "mothers" as well as with _____ mothers.

real (live, etc.)

187 Strength of imprinting is related to the postbirth age (critical period) of the imprinted animal. Hess demonstrated that imprint strength is also related to the amount of effort expended during the _____ _____ .

critical period

188 If one duckling follows a "mechanical mother" 100 feet in ten minutes and another follows his "mother" the same distance in twenty minutes, an operational measure of effort expended for imprinting ducks is given (Hess, 1958). If a difference in strength of imprinting is observed under these two conditions, one can conclude that +++++ is an imprinting variable.

effort expended
(movement
demonstrated)

189 Two variables that have been experimentally investigated in imprinting ducklings are the **(1)** _____ of imprinting and **(2)** the amount of _____ expended in following.

(1) age
(2) effort

190 Harlow (1958) has suggested a process something like imprinting of human infants. That is, infants may be imprinted for "contact comfort" (i.e., tactile-kinesthetic stimulation) by the age of ten to twelve months. He states that an infant should receive appropriate _____ _____ if he is to learn to receive and express affection appropriately later in life.

contact comfort
(tactile-kinesthetic
stimulation)

**contact-comfort
(tactile-kinesthetic)**

191 Harlow points out that the mother supplies contact comfort in addition to nutriment and general health care. So far, however, no one has been able to designate exactly what and how much is appropriate _____-_____ stimulation in infancy.

Casler (1961) has provided an excellent survey of the effects of lack of maternal care on infants younger than six months of age. Maternal care is a general term encompassing the concepts of physical care, contact comfort, and other kinds of stimulation provided by the mother. Some of these studies will be discussed in the next unit. The work of Lorenz, Hess, and Harlow has excited considerable interest in imprinting and the hypothesis of the critical period in development (Scott, 1962). These concepts have some significant implications for understanding social behavior in early infancy.

SUMMARY

It has been said that "as the twig is bent, so grows the tree." Knowledge about prenatal, paranatal, and postnatal development confirms this adage, at least in part. Certainly, some infectious diseases contracted by the mother, particularly in the first three months of pregnancy, can markedly affect the unborn child. This is true, also, of malnutrition during pregnancy.

Knowledge about developmental deviations is interesting, but for most people, the characteristics of normal development are of greater significance. Developmental schedules which describe typical development of children both before and after birth are useful to parents as well as to child specialists. It is important, too, to know something about principles of maturation, viz., that differentiation and integration of body parts increase with development, and that sequences of maturation are more predictable than rate of maturation.

Knowledge of these principles is important, in part, because maturation sets limits on learning. This is demonstrated in a variety of ways in child development: Learning to walk, talk, and handle utensils and to respond to toilet training are all dependent on the child's neuromuscular maturation. Some interesting research on imprinting suggests that, at least for some infrahuman animals, there are critical periods in infancy when certain behaviors are learned best. The full implications of these studies for humans are not yet completely understood. Material in the next unit is related in part to principles of early development and conditioning described in this unit.

REFERENCES

Bowlby, J.: *Maternal Care and Mental Health,* World Health Organization, Geneva, 1951.

Bridges, Katherine M. B.: "Emotional Development in Early Infancy," *Child Development,* 3:324–341, 1932.

Buhler, C.: *The First Year of Life,* The John Day Company, Inc., New York, 1930.

Carmichael, L.: *Manual of Child Psychology,* John Wiley & Sons, Inc., New York, 1954.

Casler, L.: "Maternal Deprivation: A Critical Review of the Literature," *Monographs of the Society for Research in Child Development,* 26:1–64, 1961.

Fowler, H., S. P. Hicks, C. J. D'Amato, and F. A. Beach: "Effects of Fetal Irradiation on Behavior of the Albino Rat," *Journal of Comparative and Physiological Psychology,* 55: 309–314, 1962.

Gesell, A., and F. Ilg: *Child Development,* Harper & Row, Publishers, Incorporated, New York, 1949.

Hall, G. S.: *Adolescence: Its Psychology and Its Relation to Physiology, Anthropology, Sex, Crime, Religion and Education,* Appleton-Century-Crofts, Inc., New York, 1904.

Harlow, H.: *Mother Love* (film), Carousel Films, from Columbia Broadcasting System "Conquest" series, New York, 1958.

Hess, E.: "Imprinting in Animals," *Scientific American,* 198:81–90, 1958.

Hurlock, E.: *Developmental Psychology,* McGraw-Hill Book Company, New York, 1959.

Ingalls, T.: "Congenital Deformities Not Inherited," *The New York Times,* Dec. 20, 1950.

Kagan, J., and H. A. Moss: *From Birth to Maturity,* John Wiley & Sons, Inc., New York, 1962.

Keeley, K.: "Prenatal Influence on Behavior of Offspring of Crowded Mice," *Science,* 135: 44, 1962.

Lorenz, K.: *King Solomon's Ring: New Light on Animal Ways,* Thomas Y. Crowell Company, New York, 1952.

McGraw, M.: *Growth: A Study of Johnny and Jimmy,* Appleton-Century-Crofts, Inc., New York, 1935.

Neilon, P.: "Shirley's Babies after Fifteen Years," *Journal of Genetic Psychology,* 73: 175–186, 1948.

Piaget, J.: *Construction of Reality in the Child,* Basic Books, Incorporated, Publishers, New York, 1954.

Rank, O.: *The Trauma of Birth,* Harcourt, Brace & World, Inc., New York, 1929.

Scott, J. S.: "Critical Periods in Behavioral Development," *Science,* 138:949–958, 1962.

Sears, R., E. Maccoby, and H. Levin: *Patterns of Child Rearing,* Harper & Row, Publishers, Incorporated, New York, 1957.

Sherman, M.: "The Differentiation of Emotional Responses in Infants," *Journal of Comparative Psychology,* I, 7:265–284; II, 7:333–351, 1927.

Smith, C. A.: *Physiology of the Newborn Infant,* 2d ed., Charles C. Thomas, Publisher, Springfield, Ill., 1951.

Smith, J. I.: Personal communication, based on studies at Tulane University Medical Center, 1961.

Thompson, W. R., J. Watson, and W. R. Charlesworth: "The Effect of Prenatal Stress on Offspring Behavior in Rats," *Psychological Monographs*, 76:1–26, 1962.

SELF-REVIEW QUIZ

1   What is the technical term used to describe the new biological entity resulting from the union of a human sperm with an ovum?

2   The first two weeks of prenatal development are termed the _____ stage.

3   About a week after conception the blastocyst becomes differentiated into three distinct layers of cells. Name each layer and indicate some major body parts which develop from each.

4   All important anatomical and physiological parts and systems are differentiated by the end of the eighth prenatal week. This is toward the end of the _____ stage of development.

5   The total time for pregnancy is about how many weeks?

6   Give at least three conditions which often affect the child if the mother contracts rubella during the first three months of pregnancy.

7   That aspect of medicine dealing with pregnancy and delivery is termed _____.

8   Name and define three reflex behaviors present at birth.

9   The cephalo-caudal, mass-specific, and proximodistal trends exemplify the maturational principle that _____ increases with development.

10   State the principle demonstrated by the fact that uncoordinated movements develop into highly coordinated ones.

11   Children learn to walk and talk at different ages, in part as a function of maturation. This exemplifies the principle that (a) _____ are more predictable than (b) _____ of development.

12   Lorenz, Hess, and others have studied the relationships between certain behavior occurring during the critical period and later behavior patterns. The relationships presumably are a function of a process called _____.

unit 2

Development in Childhood

Infancy

The last unit reviewed some prenatal and natal conditions which affect development and summarized specific maturational aspects of early infancy. This unit continues the analysis of childhood development, using Freud's concept of developmental determinism as a point of departure.

Freud suggested that all children pass through several distinct developmental stages. These developmental stages are related roughly to age levels. Consequently, Freud's theory of developmental determinism has often been termed the "ages-stages" theory.

This theory has provided a useful framework for explaining different levels of development in childhood and is widely used by many psychologists, social workers, physicians, and other child specialists. However, as the material in this unit indicates, contemporary knowledge about maturation and learning in childhood has pointed up the need for reformulating aspects of Freud's ages-stages theory.

developmental
determinism

1 Developmental determinism predicates that the process of development itself determines behavior. Freud's ages-stages theory is based on the concept of _____ _____.

body

2 Freud stated that all behavior in childhood is related to the pursuit of pleasure or the avoidance of pain. Different developmental stages are related to the pleasure achieved principally from the stimulation of particular parts of the _____, whose function is directly related to maturational age.

pleasure

3 A developmental stage presumably is related to _____ experienced from stimulation of particular parts of the body.

4 Freud called those parts of the body capable of arousing feelings of pleasure the erogenous zones. At different developmental stages, the mouth, the anus, and the genitals were stated by Freud to be pleasure-evoking or _____ zones.

erogenous

5 Erogenous zones are parts of the body which, when moderately stimulated, give rise to feelings of _____.

pleasure

6 The three psychosexual stages through which Freud presumed all children traverse are the oral, the anal, and the phallic stages. These stages will be used as points of departure for examining child development in the early years. The mouth region is related to the **(1)** _____ stage; the anal region, to the **(2)** _____ stage, and the genitals to the **(3)** _____ stage.

(1) oral
(2) anal
(3) phallic

7 The first year of life is designated by psychoanalysts as the oral stage because the _____ cavity is supposed to be the zone of primary pleasure for the infant (Freud, 1904).

oral (mouth)

8 According to classical psychoanalysis, pleasure in the first year of life arises chiefly from **(1)** _____ stimulation. The lips and mouth constitute the **(2)** _____ zone associated with the first developmental stage.

(1) oral
(2) erogenous

9 The oral stage is divided into two phases, called the oral-receptive and the oral-aggressive phases. Oral activities involving intake of food for body use or pleasure would be representative of the first, or oral-_____, phase.

receptive

10 Fixation at, or regression to, the oral-receptive stage might be indicated by an adult's dependence on smoking, or by fingernail biting. Both of these are activities which involve the _____ region.

oral (mouth)

11 Biting to represent displeasure would be representative of the oral-_____ stage.

aggressive

12 Both oral-receptive and oral-aggressive behavior are associated with the Freudian concept of _____ determinism.

developmental

13 Attacking other people verbally and derisive spitting on the part of an adult might suggest a regression to the oral-_____ stage, if one were given to psychoanalytic interpretation.

aggressive

**developmental
determinism
(ages-stages)**

14 Relationships between oral activity and other behaviors have been studied by child specialists other than Freudians. Conclusions from many of these studies do not support the psychoanalytic theory of _____ _____.

15 As you know by now, at birth the child is endowed with a suctorial reflex. Sucking activity is related to length of food deprivation in infants. Most normal neonates demonstrate a spontaneous sucking _____ between three to four hours after feeding.

reflex (response)

16 Stomach contractions are also related to food deprivation. In most neonates, these contractions are severe enough three to four hours after feeding to result in the _____ reflex, in restless behavior, and finally, in crying.

sucking

17 Child specialists have studied the source of food and types of food-presentation schedules as variables relating to infant behavior. Breast and bottle feeding are the most common _____ of food for infants.

sources

18 Timed schedules and self-demand feeding are the most common types of food _____.

presentation

19 Advocates of breast feeding claim that human milk is better for the child than cow's milk and that psychological benefits accrue to both child and mother from _____ feeding.

breast

20 Several studies have compared the behavior of breast-fed and bottle-fed children. None of the studies has shown that breast feeding is unequivocally superior to _____ feeding (Orlansky, 1949; Mussen, Conger, and Kagan, 1963).

bottle

21 The breast and bottle are different sources of nutriment and, possibly, of tactile-kinesthetic stimulation. The infant who is held closely and comfortably by the bottle-feeding mother can receive as much _____-_____ stimulation from the mother as can the breast-fed infant.

**tactile-
kinesthetic**

22 Feeding practices of American mothers have shown alternation between schedule and self-demand feeding. Schedule feeding occurs when the mother feeds the child at specified intervals. A mother who feeds her infant every four hours practices _____ feeding.

schedule

schedule

23 Many pediatricians (physicians specializing in child care) recommend schedule feeding. The purpose of _____ feeding is to get the child to adapt to a fixed-interval feeding schedule, presumably because it is beneficial to the child and convenient for the mother.

fixed-interval

24 Schedule feeding represents a kind of _____-_____ feeding schedule.

self-demand

25 Proponents of self-demand feeding contest the idea that schedule feeding is better for the infant. Such people claim that infants' food needs are so variable that feeding should be regulated by the baby's _____-_____ rather than by the mother's arbitrary schedule.

self-demand

26 When an infant's feeding is regulated by his own behavior, which suggests to the mother that he is hungry, rather than by an arbitrarily imposed schedule, _____-_____ feeding is being practiced.

schedule
self-demand

27 Several investigators have reviewed relationships between schedule and self-demand feeding and child behavior (Orlansky, 1949; Yarrow, 1961). There are no data which unequivocally favor _____ or _____-_____ feeding, although a great deal of "expostulatory evidence" has been presented by advocates of both methods.

Other investigators have studied the effects of early feeding experiences on later behavior. While some reports seem to support this psychoanalytic concept, other data run counter to this position (Casler, 1961; Yarrow, 1961). The problem of determining whether specific feeding practices in infancy are related to behavior in later life is an enormously complex one. While it is impossible to discuss summarily the classical psychoanalytic position in terms of "oral-stage" developmental determinism, studies of types and sources of nutriment in infancy do not unequivocally support the Freudian theory that certain types of oral activities, or interference with them, determine later behavior.

Sensory Deprivation and Maternal Separation

Margaret Ribble, a child psychiatrist, observed that infants need three types of sensory stimulation, in addition to nutritive-oral activity. The three types of sensory stimulation are tactile (touch), kinesthetic (movement), and auditory (hearing) (Ribble, 1943).

28 Ribble (1943) claimed that all infants require affectionate handling. This involves gentle pressure on the skin, or _____ stimulation.

tactile

29 Tactile stimulation involves direct contact between the mother and child. Ribble claims that kinesthetic stimulation is a second necessary stimulation. When a mother rocks her child, she is providing _____ stimulation.

kinesthetic

30 Gently holding an infant provides **(1)** _____ stimulation; causing the infant's body to move slightly by shifting him from time to time provides **(2)** _____ stimulation.

(1) tactile

(2) kinesthetic

31 In addition to tactile and kinesthetic stimulation, infants require auditory stimulation for healthy development (Ribble, 1943). When a mother talks to, coos at, or sings to her child, she is providing _____ stimulation.

auditory

32 Ribble's claims have excited much research about the effects of sensory stimulation or its deprivation in infancy. However, as was pointed out in the last unit, the question of exactly what and how much is required for appropriate _____, _____, and _____ stimulation of infants has never been answered precisely.

tactile
kinesthetic
auditory

33 Rene Spitz, another child psychiatrist, studied the effects of certain types of stimulus deprivation on infants (1949).[1] Spitz observed a group of infants raised in a hospital with a minimum of human handling. This minimum handling is analogous to stimulus _____.

deprivation

34 Spitz compared the hospital-ward group of infants who received minimum human handling with another group of infants reared in the hospital ward of a women's correctional institution. The latter children were reported to receive normal amounts of _____.

handling
   (stimulation)

35 Children reared in the hygienic hospital ward with minimum human handling demonstrated some rather severe behavioral reactions. Those reared in the prison hospital ward did not show such reactions. Spitz suggests that minimum _____ _____ may have disturbing effects on infant behavior.

human handling
   (sensory stimulation)

[1] Criticisms of the Spitz studies have been cogently described by S. Pinneau, "Infantile Disorders of Hospitalism and Anaclitic Depression," *Psychol. Bull.* 52: 429–452, 1955. Spitz's reply to these criticisms is found in the succeeding article of this volume.

36 Spitz described two major effects that might result from minimal stimulation of infants. One is called *marasmus,* the other *anaclitic depression.* Both conditions are presumed to result from minimal sensory stimulation in

_____ .

infancy

37 Marasmus is described as a physical debilitation, or wasting away, despite the availability of adequate nutriment and hygienic handling. Films of "emotionally starved" infants are used to attest to the condition of _____ (Spitz, 1949).

marasmus

38 The condition known as marasmus refers to $+++++$.

physical debilitation in spite of available food

39 Marasmus may be accompanied by anaclitic depression. Acute lack of responsiveness to environmental stimulation is the chief symptom of _____ _____ (Spitz, 1949).

anaclitic depression

40 When it is presumed that the infant is without organic disability, when it is known that he has been subject to minimum human handling, and when the child does not react to loud sounds, lights flashed in his eyes, and similar stimulation, Spitz would conclude that the infant is demonstrating _____ _____ .

anaclitic depression

41 *Review:* Ribble and Spitz have contributed remarkably to speculations about the effects of _____ _____ on infant behavior. While their studies were not well controlled and their results not empirically valid, they have stimulated other research, both animal and human, on the effects of early experiences on later behavior.

sensory stimulation (or human handling)

42 The effects of different kinds of stimulation and deprivation on infant behavior and later behavior have been studied by means of controlled experiments with animals. Studies of animals at Yale, Wisconsin, and other research centers indicate that the type and amount of tactile-kinesthetic (1) _____ or its converse, (2) _____ , affect infant and later behavior.

(1) stimulation
(2) deprivation

43 Beach (1954) has indicated that not only the type and amount of "gentling" (of which tactile-kinesthetic stimulation seems to be a basic component) but also the age at which _____ occurs, affect the behavior of young animals.

gentling

44 Levine (1961) and others reported that gentling of rats in the first twenty days of life may be related to improvement of learning-task scores. This means that rats given specified "doses" of human handling in early life got _____ [(a) lower scores than/(b) higher scores than/(c) the same scores as] rats not gentled, or those negatively conditioned for learning by electric shock.

(b)

45 Gentling refers to the conditioning of young or wild organisms by gentle handling. This is analogous to "tender loving care" for humans. Basic components of t.l.c. are thought to be gentle _____-_____ stimulation.

tactile-kinesthetic

46 Harlow and his research associates (1959) have studied the effects of tactile-kinesthetic stimulation in unique ways. They have reared baby rhesus monkeys with different kinds of "mothers." Some monkeys were reared by their biological mothers; others were reared by substitute inanimate _____.

mothers

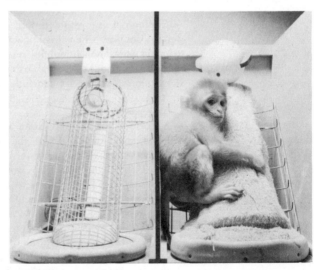

Figure 14. Love in infant monkeys is demonstrated toward terry-cloth "mothers," but not towards wire-mesh "mothers." (Photograph courtesy of Harry Harlow, used by permission.)

47 Harlow's monkey mothers presumably gave typical amounts of mother love to their children. One fundamental question the investigators asked was: What are the basic components of _____? (Heretofore, poets, writers, and philosophers have been brave enough to try to answer this question, but not scientists.)

love

48 The problem was to obtain infant reactions to the gentling, or love, supplied by different kinds of mothers. Three kinds of mothers were used: biological mothers, wire-mesh mothers, and terrycloth mothers. The inanimate mothers were about the same size as the biological mothers, and some were supplied with milk-giving nipples, but none of the _____ or _____ mothers moved spontaneously.

wire-mesh
terrycloth

49 The two kinds of inanimate mothers were basically different in terms of the amount of presumed tactile-kinesthetic "comfort" they provided the infant monkeys. Wire-mesh mothers were relatively hard and unyielding to infant body pressures; terrycloth mothers were relatively soft and yielding. Which resembles the biological mother more in this respect? _____ _____.

terrycloth mothers

50 Monkey infants reared on wire-mesh mothers demonstrated significantly more neurotic-fear behavior as infants than those reared on terrycloth mothers. Further, the differences in _____-_____ behavior tended to remain in adulthood.

neurotic-fear

In a later series of studies, Harlow and Harlow (1962) studied the effects of a variety of experimental conditions instituted in infancy on the later behavior of monkeys. These included being reared in isolation from other animals, raised with mothers, and raised with peers. The results of these studies are summarized in Table 11.

51 These data show that monkeys reared in total isolation, with an absolute minimum of handling for six months, are deviant in terms of all three behaviors studied, i.e., _____, _____, and _____.

play, defense, sex

52 The data also point out that, so far as the later demonstration of sex and play behaviors is concerned, monkeys reared with their own mothers alone but with no exposure to _____ demonstrate severely deviant sex and play behavior later on.

peers (other monkeys)

53 In fact, the Harlows' data indicate that monkeys reared with _____ but without their mothers demonstrate normal behavior in later life.

peers

54 Apparently stimulation from peers supplies whatever is necessary for normal monkey behavior in later life, at least as far as _____, _____, and _____ are concerned.

play, defense, sex

Table 11. The Effects of Social Deprivation on Play, Defense, and Sex Behavior*

Experimental condition	Present age	Behavior†				
		None	Low	Almost normal	Probably normal	Normal
Raised in total isolation:						
Cage-raised for 2 years	4 years	P,D,S				
Cage-raised for 6 months	14 months	D,S	P			
Cage-raised for 80 days	10½ months			P,D,S		
Partially raised in isolation:						
Cage-raised for 6 months	5–8 years		P,S	D		
Surrogate-raised for 6 months	3–5 years		P,S	D		
Raised with mother:						
Normal mother, no play with peers	1 year	S	P			D
Motherless mother, play in playpen	14 months			D	S	P
Normal mother, play in playpen	2 years					P,D,S
Raised with peers:						
Four raised in 1 cage, play in playroom	1 year				P	D,S
Surrogate-raised, play in playpen	2 years				S	P,D
Surrogate-raised, play in playroom	21 months					P,D,S

* In summary, the results of experiments are that the monkey's capacity to develop normally appears to be determined by the seventh month of life. Animals isolated for six months are aberrant in every respect. Play with peers seems to be even more necessary than mothering to the development of effective social relations.

† P = play, D = defense, S = sex.

SOURCE: H. and M. Harlow, "Social Deprivation in Monkeys," *Scientific American,* 207:142, 1962. Used by permission.

55 A study was made of infant chimpanzees reared under "institutional" conditions, i.e., without normal mothering. These chimpanzees did not demonstrate more physical defects or a higher mortality rate than others reared by their biological mothers. Apparently such ill effects are not a necessary consequence of "institutional _____."

mothering

56 These studies suggest that specific kinds of mothering can be supplied from different agents and that method of _____ is more important in shaping later behavior than the fact of blood relationship itself.

mothering

Some hypothesized effects on children of maternal deprivation have already been suggested by reference to the Spitz studies. Yarrow (1961) has reported the significant studies on maternal deprivation. They are summarized in Table 12.

Bowlby points out that many English children who were separated from their mothers during the London bombings and reared for extended periods in rather impersonal nurseries demonstrated more difficulties in the areas of learning, socialization, and emotional behavior than did children not separated from their parents. Bowlby also reported on children in occupied countries who were separated from their mothers (or substitute mothers, such as older siblings and other relatives) and reared impersonally in evacuation or concentration camps.

57 The children in these studies tended to show more ill effects in emotional, learning, and social behavior later in life than those not _____ from their mothers in such circumstances. (See also A. Freud, and D. T. Burlingham, 1944, and Maas, 1963.)

separated

58 Because of obvious problems, it is not possible to run controlled studies of the effects of maternal _____ on human children. Several interesting studies are available, however (Casler, 1961; Yarrow, 1961).

deprivation (separation)

These investigations indicate that maternal deprivation is not a single variable and that various approaches have been used to study its effects on child behavior.

59 These and other studies indicate that the amount, the quality, and the consistency of substitute mothering may influence the long-term _____ of the child (Yarrow, 1961).

development

Table 12. Research on Maternal Separation*

Investigator	Subjects	Age at time of study	Age at time of experience
Ainsworth & Boston (1952)	One case	Observation: 3 years Follow-up tests: 5 to 6½ years	13 months
Berg & Cohen (1959)	40 schizophrenic women in mental hospital 40 neurotic women	20–40 years	Birth to adulthood
Bowlby (1944)	44 juvenile thieves	5.7 to 17 years	Birth to adolescence
Bowlby (1953)	49 children in residential nurseries or hospitals	12–48 months	12–24 months
Bowlby, Ainsworth, Boston, & Rosenbluth (1956)	60 children with previous sanitarium experience 57 controls	6–14 years	Range: Birth to 4 months
Edelston (1943)	42 children hospitalized for illness	2½–15 years	Range from early infancy
Heinicke (1956)	Children in residential and day nurseries	15–31 months	12–30 months
Lewis (1954)	500 children in reception center	Under 5 to over 15 years	Birth to adolescence
Robertson & Bowlby (1952)	Unspecified number of children in hospitals	18–24 months	18–24 months
Roundinesco, David, & Nicolas (1952)	20 children placed in institution	12–17 months 3–51 weeks	12–17 months
Schaffer (1958)	76 infants in hospital for illness		3–51 weeks
Spitz & Wolf (1946)	123 children in a nursery	14 days to 18 months	5–7 months

* This summary of studies describes a number of investigations of maternal separation. Parents and children were separated for varying lengths of time. Original studies can be found by reference to the source of this table.

Techniques or type of data	Data on early experiences	Contaminating conditions
Rorschach CAT Stanford-Binet Weigl-Goldstein Sorting Test Goldstein-Scheerer Cube Test	Retrospective report	Hospitalization for tuberculosis
Case history	Limited retrospective data	Rejection
Case history Psychiatric diagnosis Clinical observation	Variable retrospective data Direct observation	Institutionalization Rejection Institutionalization Rejection Hospitalization for Illness
Intelligence test Clinical evaluation by teacher, psychologist, psychiatrist, social worker	General retrospective data	Rejection Hospitalization for tuberculosis
Clinical observation	Limited retrospective data	Illness Rejection
Standardized observation and doll play	Direct observation	None reported
Clinical assessment	Variable retrospective data	Institutionalization Rejection
Clinical observation	Direct observation	Hospitalization
Clinical observation	Direct observation	Institutionalization
Cattell Infant Test Standardized observation Home follow-up	Direct observation	Illness Hospitalization
Clinical observation	Direct observation	None reported

SOURCE: Leon I. Yarrow, "Maternal Deprivation," *Psychol. Bull.*, 58: 459–490, 1961. Used by permission.

60 For example, Maas (1963) studied a group of young adults who, during their early childhood, were separated almost completely from their parents for three years. They were exposed primarily to substitute _____ in institutions.

mothers (parents)

61 Apparently the surrogate mothering was appropriate in terms of amount, quality, and consistency because these children showed no ill effects from the early _____ later on in life.

separation

62 Several of the studies cited in Table 12 suggest that the closer the affectional relationship between mother and child prior to separation, the more severe will be the child's immediate reaction to _____.

separation

63 On the other hand, close preseparation relationships tend to make it easier for the child to establish close ties with surrogate parents and with others later in life. At least, this generalization seems to hold from available studies about _____ _____.

maternal separation
(deprivation)

More studies of direct relationships between parents and children are needed in order to make better generalizations about both the immediate and long-term effects of sensory deprivation and maternal separation on children's behavior.

Toilet Training

Table 9, p. 184, gives information about the ages at which most children in the United States can be expected to achieve bowel and urinary control. These are, respectively, about eighteen months and twenty-four months. However, wide variations in age of achievement are observed. Because of Freud's influence on pediatricians and other child specialists, it is well to contrast his ideas about the relationships between toilet training and personality with the results of empirical studies.

64 Freud's psychosexual theory (1904) suggests that between approximately twelve and twenty-four to thirty months the child receives primary pleasure from anal activities. Toilet training is related to control of anal activities and typically occurs during the _____ period.

anal

65 Training in cleanliness (toilet training) involves the substitution of voluntary control over elimination for a reflexive reaction to internal pressure. During the second year of life, the child is encouraged to _____ elimination of waste instead of behaving reflexively.

control

66 Freud claimed that the child first derives pleasure in the anal stage from the stimulation of mucous membranes involved in expelling waste. He called this phase the anal-expulsive phase. If a child later shows a tendency to "get rid of his feelings" indiscriminately, a Freudian would be interested in the possibility of fixation at or regression to the _____-_____ developmental stage.

anal-expulsive

67 According to Freud, expelling wastes is related to pleasure during the anal-expulsive phase. Indiscriminate _____ activities later in life represent either fixation at, or regression to, the anal stage.

expulsive

68 The anal-expulsive phase is related to tension associated with expelling waste. The second aspect of the anal stage is the anal-retentive phase. When the child receives pleasurable stimulation from retaining feces, he is demonstrating _____-_____ behavior (Freud).

anal-retentive

69 The child who learns to retain waste products in violation of parent pleading is called an anal-retentive child. Freud suggests that hoarding behavior, greed, and neurotic constipation in adulthood can be considered manifestations of an _____-_____ person.

anal-retentive

70 According to Freudians, a child may become fixated at the anal stage if he is overly indulged or extremely deprived during toilet training. A child who demonstrates parsimony (frugality), petulance (obstinacy), and/or pedantry (orderliness) would be demonstrating behavior characteristic of the _____ stage.

anal

(1) parsimony
(2) pedantry
(3) petulance

71 The so-called "anal character" demonstrates frugality [(1) _____], excessive orderliness [(2) _____], and/or obstinacy [(3) _____] (Freud).

72 The anal character is supposed to become compulsive in his concern over orderliness (e.g., cleanliness and punctuality). Freud defined excessive concern over _____ as pedantry.

orderliness

73 Compulsive orderliness would represent _____, according to Freud.

pedantry

74 Obstinacy may be a continuation of an infantile reaction against the parent's desire to have the child "give up" his body wastes during the anal stage (Freud). Petulance is another word for _____.

obstinacy

75 Excessive frugality, or _____, is related to the anal-retentive phase of the anal stage.

parsimony

76 Data from several studies (Orlansky, 1949) indicate that excessive severity in toilet training can evoke undesired responses from the child. Severely trained children often demonstrate compulsive and/or aggressive behavior later in life. However, these studies do not prove an invariant relationship between the anal stage of development and compulsive and _____ behavior.

aggressive

77 Anal stimulation obviously does not provide the only source of pleasure during the second year. During this time the child also learns to walk, to talk, and to become more socially responsive to others. Any or all of these behaviors may give rise to as much pleasure as _____ activity.

anal

78 *Review:* Many students of child development have rejected the Freudian idea that anal activity provides the *chief* source of _____ during the second year. It is difficult, if not impossible, to test the idea empirically.

pleasure

Beginning Socialization

Most children are able to talk and walk at about the age of twelve to fifteen months (see Table 9, Part IV, Unit 1). Like toilet training, such activities are learned when the child is maturationally ready and when appropriate social reinforcement is available.

79 Maudry and Nekula (1939) studied social relationships between 92 young children. Between six to fourteen months very little social interaction was observed. Between fourteen to eighteen months of age children became more socially responsive. From nineteen months on, children were primarily _____ in their activities.

social

80 Social responsiveness is defined in most child studies in terms of (1) more interest in people than in material things, (2) cooperativeness rather than aggression toward others in play, and (3) respect for the property of others. Social _____, so defined, typically occurs toward the end of the second year of life.

responsiveness

81 Criteria of social responsiveness in young children include: **(1)** more interest in _____ than in material things; **(2)** _____ rather than aggression; **(3)** respect for the _____ of others.

margin:
(1) people
(2) cooperation
(3) property

82 "Parallel play" is more common than "cooperative play" in one- and two-year-old children. When children play alongside others without much social interaction, they demonstrate _____ play.

margin: parallel

83 The fact that most two-year olds demonstrate parallel play does not refute the observation that they are also socially responsive. Most children are capable of being socially _____ from eighteen to nineteen months on.

margin: responsive

84 Parallel play refers to +++++.

margin: playing alongside others without social interaction

85 Parental behavior has a great deal to do with the elicitation of social responsiveness and/or parallel play in early life. Since the former is usually praised, one would expect such behavior to be _____ by the child.

margin: repeated (demonstrated)

86 A child's behavior can be rewarded in a variety of ways. Smiling, giving material things, and praising him are means of _____ social responsiveness.

margin: rewarding (reinforcing)

87 Children's social behavior can be punished in many ways, too. As you already know, punishment tends to _____, rather than strengthen, a behavior.

margin: decrease (depress, inhibit)

There are many specific ways in which parents seek to prevent or to extinguish particular social behaviors in their children. Most of the particular parental behaviors can be classified under three general headings: *rejection, overprotection,* and *overindulgence.* Ordinarily these are considered undesirable ways of reacting to child behavior, but they are used widely in our culture.

88 When a mother spanks her two-year-old she is demonstrating overt _____. She may also reject him by neglecting him.

margin: rejection

89 If the child has no other social reinforcers, such maternal behavior could very well lead to a decrease in the child's _____ responsiveness.

margin: social

90 Parents can demonstrate rejection of their children in several ways. Desertion is perhaps the most obvious. Corporal punishment, verbal threat, and threatening gestures are others. Neglect is still another way of demonstrating _____.

rejection

91 If a child's social behavior was inhibited because of parental rejection, we could say that the child was punished by _____.

rejection

92 A parent can decrease a child's social responsiveness by overprotection or overindulgence as well as by rejection. A mother who prevents normal independent behavior in her child demonstrates _____.

overprotection

93 By restricting his activities, including social contacts with other children, an overprotective mother may prevent normal _____ child behavior.

independent

94 A mother may restrict independent child behavior or she may "infantilize" her child. Both maternal behaviors represent maternal _____, according to David Levy, a child psychiatrist (1943).

overprotection

95 Infantilization refers to techniques used by the mother to keep her child at the infancy stage and thus dependent on her. _____ is a symptom of overprotection.

Infantilization

96 The overprotective mother often sees her child's independence and interest in others as a threat to her control over him. She can demonstrate _____ by minimizing possibilities for new experiences and by keeping him "her baby."

overprotection

97 Some mothers prevent independent behavior and social responses to others in their children by pampering or overindulging them. Giving a child "anything he wants" is a form of _____.

overindulgence

98 The overindulged child typically controls his mother's behavior. This is demonstrated by the fact that _____ children are given what they want when they want it by their mothers.

overindulged

99 The major differentiation between overindulged and overprotected children is in terms of who controls whom. The (1) _____ mother controls the child; the (2) _____ child controls the mother.

(1) overprotective
(2) overindulged

100 *Review:* It has been suggested that _____,
_____, and _____ are undesirable ways of
controlling a child's behavior. However, they are often
observed in American child-rearing practices.

rejection,
overprotection,
overindulgence

This section has described Freud's concept of developmental determinism. In particular, it illustrates the major
ideas about his first two stages of psychosexual development, which serve as a backdrop against which to describe
some important studies about feeding practices, sensory
stimulation and maternal deprivation, toilet training, and
beginning socialization. Freud's generalization about the
importance of the period of life covered by the so-called
oral and anal stages is confirmed by many studies, although some of his specific conclusions are not supported,
and areas of development not emphasized by Freud have
been found to be extremely important.

Older Childhood

The previous units described variables associated with
development in early childhood, particularly during the
first two years of life. As the child continues to develop
in later childhood, the facts of physical growth appear to be
correspondingly less important than data about socialization. This section, therefore, emphasizes the latter aspects
of development. Freud's concept of developmental determinism continues to be a useful point of departure for
discussion of studies relating to selected aspects of later
childhood.

101 The phallic stage occurs roughly between the third
and sixth years of life (Freud, 1949). During this time the
child presumably receives primary pleasure from stimulation of the genitals. Freud called this period the _____
stage.

phallic

102 During the phallic stage, the child is supposed to
demonstrate an instinctual attraction for the _____
[opposite/same] sex parent.

opposite

103 The instinctual attraction of the child for the opposite-sex parent is supposed to result in fear of the same-sex parent. The attraction and fear are presumed to bring
about severe conflict in the child. This severe _____
was termed the Oedipus complex.

conflict

104 Freud indicated that the Oedipus complex is resolved if/when the child represses ("unconsciously forgets") his desire for the opposite-sex parent because of fear of consequences from the _____-sex parent.

same

105 Unconscious forgetting, or _____, thus enables children to resolve the Oedipus complex.

repression

106 The Oedipus complex is supposed to be an inevitable consequence of child development (Freud). The name of the conflict comes from the Greek tragedy-legend about _____.

Oedipus

107 Repression is the means by which the Oedipus complex is resolved. Identification is the means by which the child substitutes desire for the opposite-sex parent for desire to be like the same-sex parent, in order to gain the same satisfactions. For Freudians, _____ means to learn unconsciously to behave like someone else.

identification

108 Repression and identification are mechanisms presumably used by the child to resolve conflict in the phallic stage. The child _____ his erotic desires for the opposite sex because of fear of the same-sex parent.

represses

109 Identification involves social imitation. The family provides the first models for such imitation. A preschool-age boy learns to wear trousers and a shirt, to accept short hair, and to be domineering in his dealing with others by imitating his father, i.e., through the process of _____.

imitation (identification)

110 When the preschool child imitates the father, he responds to stimuli in the same manner as his _____. (Repression and identification will be discussed further in Part V, Unit 3.)

father

111 The child continues to respond to stimuli as his parent does (i.e., he continues to identify with his parent), if these responses are reinforced. Parents are the chief reinforcers of _____ behavior in their children's early life.

identification

112 Mrs. Smith's four-year-old daughter walks like her mother, pretends to powder her nose as her mother does, and acts at her "tea parties" as she sees her mother act at bridge luncheons. Such social _____ is one aspect of identification.

imitation

113 Young children imitate peers as well as parents. When three-year-old Johnny throws mud at others because he has seen playmate Sammy doing it, he is demonstrating _____ identification.

peer

114 Peer identification apparently is not so important in the social learning of two- to three-year-olds as _____ identification. Can you see why this may be true? (Remember the principle of reinforcement given in Part III, Unit 2.)

parent

115 Anthropological studies indicate that social imitation occurs in all societies. The social roles which young children learn to play are primarily products of stimuli and _____ supplied by parents and peers.

reinforcements

116 A primitive New Guinea child learns to hunt and trap animals by going with and observing his father on hunting expeditions. The son _____ with the father by imitating his behavior, i.e., by responding to the stimuli and reinforcements as the father does.

identifies

117 Learning masculine behavior, such as aggression, may involve having the son _____ the father's social behavior. Some interesting studies of such behavior have been reported by P. S. Sears (1951).

imitate

118 One study hypothesized that, in our culture, fathers provide the significant stimuli and reinforcements for their son's learning to be aggressive. Groups of three- to five-year-old boys and girls from father-present and _____- absent homes were used as subjects.

father

119 Eleven boys and ten girls from father-present homes were compared with the same numbers of boys and girls from _____-_____ homes. Reasonable matching of groups was attempted (age, socioeconomic background, etc.). (Remember that absence of the father is presumably related to absence of "masculine" aggression in boys but not in girls.)

father-absent

120 Every child was led individually into a playroom and encouraged to play with dolls representing children and parents. Hidden observers recorded all instances of presumed gestural or verbal _____ demonstrated by the child in his doll play.

aggression

121 Girls from father-present and father-absent homes at each age level did not differ in the amount of aggression shown in doll play. However, the younger boys from father-absent homes demonstrated less _____ than boys from father-present homes. This was not true for the five-year-old boys.

aggression

identify

122 Results of this study support the idea that three- to four-year-old boys in our culture learn to _____ with their fathers in terms of imitating aggressive behavior.

imitate (identify with)

123 The presumption is that girls and older boys do not _____ their fathers so much in learning this type of social behavior (Sears, 1951).

A young child learns social responsiveness primarily through identification with his parents, i.e., according to the principles of stimulus discrimination and reinforcement. One might expect that generalization, as a principle of social learning, might also be demonstrated in his behavior. The principle of generalization suggests that a response attached to one stimulus will occur in the presence of a similar stimulus.

generalization

124 A woman who looks and acts like a child's mother elicits the same behavior from the child that his mother does. This represents the principle of _____.

generalization

125 A study of the generalization of social responsiveness in three- to five-year-old children was reported by Bishop (1951). Children were first observed in interaction with their mothers in two playroom situations. By having them individually interact in the playroom with an unfamiliar woman, _____ of children's responses was presumably tested.

In the same way as with their own mothers, i.e., belligerently

126 The children in this study were consistent in terms of aggressive, noncooperative, and resistive behavior with their own mothers. If you know that generalization did occur in this instance, how do you suppose the children behaved with the strange adult? +++++.

127 Bishop's study suggests that responses of young children to social stimulation and reinforcement in the home can be expected to be generalized to similar social stimuli outside the _____.

home

social responsiveness

128 If a child is reinforced for social responsiveness in his own home, one can reasonably predict, other things being equal, that _____ _____ will be demonstrated in similar situations outside his home.

To summarize this section, we may say that whether social responsiveness is generalized to people outside a child's home depends to a considerable extent on the amount and consistency of stimulation and reinforcement for such behavior in his home. Generalization of social responsiveness depends to some extent on identification with (i.e., social imitation of) responsive parent behavior.

Behavior Control and Home Atmosphere

Relationships between "home atmosphere" and child behavior have been reported in several studies. Generally, home atmosphere refers to the general types of social stimulation and reinforcement supplied by parents. The studies reported in this section refer primarily to social relationships between parents and children. There are relatively few studies of sibling interaction. This aspect of behavior control and home atmosphere will be presented in a succeeding section.

129 Radke (1946) studied the social behavior of forty-three boys and girls three to five years old enrolled in nursery school and kindergarten. Behavior was rated in terms of competitiveness, rivalry, affection shown others, talkativeness, popularity, and similar social behavior in children, which might be presumed to be related to _____ behavior.

parent

130 Children's behavior ratings were based on direct and indirect observations, e.g., play sessions, teacher ratings, interviews, and picture-story tests. Direct observation means that one sees for himself. The observation of play sessions is an example of _____ observation.

direct

131 Teacher ratings and interviews are two examples of indirect observation of child behavior. Tests requiring children to make up stories about pictures is another method of _____ observation.

indirect

132 There was a considerable degree of similarity for most children on the different behavior _____ supplied by teachers in the Radke study.

ratings

133 In this study, parent behavior was rated from information gained through interviews and questionnaires. Radke was primarily interested in the kinds of behavior control demonstrated by parents over children. No direct _____ of parent-child interaction was attempted.

observation

Parents were rated primarily in terms of (1) *type* of control used (democratic or autocratic), (2) *severity* of control (degree of control exerted), and (3) *source* of control (one or both parents). Child behavior could thus be related to these three types of parent control over child behavior. Radke's study of independent ratings of child behavior and parent behavior suggests that children from homes where "democratic" control is exerted tend to be rated as more successful in interpersonal relationships than those from "autocratic" homes.

type

134 The terms autocratic and democratic refer to _____ of parent control.

democratic

135 In this study, the tendencies to be more tolerant of child desires, to participate more actively with the child in activities, and to demonstrate less active supervision of the child were represented as "_____ control."

autocratic

136 Children from democratic homes were rated as more sensitive to praise or blame from others, more considerate of others, less quarrelsome, and more competitive than children from _____ homes.

(1) false
(2) true
(3) true
(4) false

137 (Answer true or false from previous frame.) Children from "autocratic homes" tended to be rated as: **(1)** more competitive _____; **(2)** less sensitive to praise or blame _____; **(3)** more quarrelsome _____; **(4)** more considerate of others _____.

type

138 Radke's ratings of parent control as "democratic-autocratic" referred to the type of control exerted over child behavior. Democratic control was correlated with the preferred _____ of child behavior.

parents

139 Source of parent control referred to whether one or both parents exerted principal control over child behavior. Children from homes where both _____ shared control were independently rated as "better adjusted."

shared

140 In other words, children who were likely to be rated as better adjusted by teachers and others outside the home came from homes where parents _____ control of child behavior.

source

141 In Radke's study, type of control refers to democratic or autocratic parent reinforcements of child behavior. Single-parent versus shared control of child behavior refers to _____ of control, rather than to type of control.

shared

142 Children who received better behavior ratings tended to come from homes where control was _____.

severity

143 Severity of parent control over child behavior was studied in terms of rated degrees of punishment applied by parents. "Severe" and "mild" punishment and "strongly permissive" (very little parent control) were terms used to describe _____ of parent control.

severe-punishment

144 Homes in which corporal punishment was typically and frequently used to control child behavior were called severe-punishment homes. Children who were independently rated as more unpopular, less sensitive to others, and less competitive than other children tended to come from _____-_____ homes.

more (in each case)

145 Children from "mild-punishment" homes were independently rated as _____ popular; _____ sensitive to others; _____ competitive than children from severe-punishment homes.

(1) popular
(2) considerate
(3) competitive

146 From this study, one might conclude that children from homes where mild rather than severe punishment is typical are more likely to be **(1)** _____ with peers, **(2)** _____ of others, and **(3)** _____ in social striving.

(1) shared
(2) mild

147 Children from democratic homes, where both parents **(1)** _____ the discipline and where punishment was **(2)** _____, tended to be rated as better adjusted in nursery school or kindergarten than those from autocratic homes.

indirect

148 Radke's study of type, source, and severity of parental control over child behavior was based on interviews. Therefore it depended on _____ observation of parent behavior with their children.

(3)

149 In addition to using interviews and questionnaires to obtain information about parent control, Radke talked to and watched the children in school, used picture-story tests, and obtained teacher ratings of children. These represent _____ [(1) direct/(2) indirect/(3) both types of] evidence about child behavior.

parent control

150 This study suggests that relationships exist between the type, source, and severity of _____ _____ and child behavior.

151 Relatively few well-designed studies of home atmospheres have been conducted. Those cited already, by Sears and Radke, are notable examples. Baldwin, Kallhorn, and Breese (1949), of the Fels Research Institute at Antioch College, also provided pertinent data for inferences about relationships between _____ _____ and child behavior.

home atmosphere

152 Behavior of children in the Fels Institute study was evaluated from information supplied by the parents and teachers and from observations of the children in school (i.e., both _____ and _____ observation).

indirect
direct

Baldwin, Kallhorn, and Breese designed thirty scales to rate parent behavior in the home. These thirty ratings comprise the Fels Parent Behavior Rating Scales (Table 13). The thirty items comprising Fels Parent Behavior Rating Scales are grouped into nine groups or clusters. Each of the nine clusters is presumed to measure some common aspect of parent behavior.

153 Two general types of home atmosphere, democratic and controlled, were studied by Baldwin and his colleagues. These social-behavior classifications are similar to those described by Radke (democratic and autocratic). Baldwin's "controlled" homes were similar to Radke's _____ homes.

autocratic

154 Homes in which parents (1) arbitrarily made decisions about child behavior, (2) administered discipline without discussion, and (3) did not tend to answer their children's questions reflecting curiosity would most likely be classified as _____ [democratic/controlled] homes.

controlled

155 Homes rated to represent (1) a high degree of permissiveness of child behavior, (2) free and open discussion between children and parents about discipline, and (3) a high level of parent interest in answering children's questions were designated _____.

democratic

156 Democratic and controlled homes were differentiated by Baldwin in terms of parent permissiveness versus control; amount of parent-child discussion about (1) _____; and response of parents to children's (2) _____.

(1) discipline
(2) questions

Table 13. Fels Parent Behavior Rating Scales*

Warmth	Child-centeredness	Child-subordinating _____	Child-centered
	Approval	Disapproving _____	Approving
	Acceptance	Rejecting _____	Devoted
	Affectionateness	Hostile _____	Affectionate
	Intensity of contact	Inert _____	Vigorous
Possessiveness	Babying	Withholding help _____	Overhelping
	Protectiveness	Exposing _____	Sheltering
	Solicitousness	Nonchalant _____	Anxious
Democracy	Justification of policy	Arbitrary _____	Rational
	Democracy of policy	Dictatorial _____	Democratic
Intellectuality	Acceleration	Retardatory _____	Acceleratory
	Readiness of explanation	Thwarting curiosity _____	Satisfying curiosity
	Understanding	Obtuse _____	Keen
Restrictiveness	Restrictiveness of regulations	Freeing _____	Restrictive
	Coerciveness of suggestions	Suggesting Optionally _____	Mandatory
Severity	Readiness of enforcement	Lax _____	Vigilant
	Severity of penalties	Mild _____	Severe
Interference	Readiness of criticism	Uncritical _____	Critical
	Quantity of suggestions	Nonsuggesting _____	Suggesting
Adjustment	Adjustment	Maladjusted _____	Well-adjusted
	Discord in the home	Harmonious _____	Conflictful
	Effectiveness of policy	Unsuccessful _____	Successful
	Disciplinary friction	Concordant _____	Contentious
Activeness	Activeness of the home	Inactive _____	Active
	Coordination of the home	Chaotic _____	Coordinated
	Sociability of the home	Reclusive _____	Expansive
	Duration of contact	Brief _____	Expansive contact
	Clarity of policy	Vague _____	Clear
	Emotionality	Objective _____	Emotional

* This scale has been carefully designed and validated. Reasonably high reliability for behavior ratings between scores was found. A complete description of the scales can be found in A. F. Baldwin, J. Kallhorn, and F. H. Breese, "Patterns of Child Behavior," *Psychological Monographs*, vol. 58, no. 3, 1945. Used by permission.

157 In a parent-controlled or autocratic home one might expect relatively little overt aggression (disobedience or quarreling) from children. Baldwin's findings support this assumption. In general, the Fels study showed that the higher the degree of parent **(1)** _____, the less the direct **(2)** _____ shown by children.

(1) control
(2) aggression
(disobedience)

158 Children from homes rated high in control tended to be quiet, well behaved, and socially nonaggressive children. They also demonstrated less rated originality, creativeness, and spontaneous verbal expression than children from _____ homes.

democratic

159 This study suggests that excessive parent control is likely to inhibit rated originality, _____, and spontaneous verbalization.

creativity

160 Children from homes rated high in democracy tended to be more aggressive, competitive, socially outgoing—and disobedient. In general, the more active the _____ practiced by parents, the more pronounced were these behaviors as demonstrated by their children.

democracy

161 Democracy and control by parents was related to aggression, social outgoingness, and _____ in children (Baldwin, 1949).

disobedience

162 Interestingly enough, Baldwin reported a positive correlation between democracy and control practiced by parents. That is, most democratic parents utilized sufficient _____ to prevent chaotic child behavior.

control

163 Major findings of this study suggest that the child is socially reinforced for competitive and aggressive behavior, for expressing his opinions about discipline, and for independent behavior in the _____ home.

democratic

164 Children from indulgent homes were contrasted with those from democratic homes by Baldwin (1945). It was reported that children who were rated less competitive, less sociable, and less original tended to be from _____ homes.

indulgent

165 In general, Baldwin's results indicate that children from _____ home atmospheres tend to show more acceptable social behavior.

democratic

(1) more inde-
pendent
(2) more aggressive
(3) more vocal
about discipline
(more dis-
obedient)

child

child

marital

adjustment

the opposite sex
(esp., the oppo-
site-sex parent)

166 Review: This suggests that children from democratic homes are more likely to be: **(1)** _____ _____, **(2)** _____ _____, **(3)** _____ _____.

167 The Sears, Radke, and Baldwin studies suggest that parent adjustment may be related to _____ adjustment.

168 MacFarlane, Allen, and Honzik (1954) have reported that, of all family variables studied in a longitudinal investigation of many children, marital adjustment was most highly correlated with _____ adjustment.

169 In this study, economic-status and parent-personality factors were not as highly related to child behavior as _____ adjustment.

170 MacFarlane's study suggests that parents who demonstrate high levels of rated marital adjustment can be expected to have children with high rated levels of _____. (These findings have support from studies by Terman, a psychologist, and Burgess, a sociologist.)

The studies of children given here suggest that the types of social reinforcements provided by parents, and the consistency with which they are supplied, are more important in shaping child behavior than is a universal "instinctual" or psychosexual attraction toward the opposite-sex parent. While there has been no attempt to disprove the Freudian hypothesis that the phallic stage is a universal determinant of child behavior, studies by Sears, Radke, and Baldwin (among others that could be cited) suggest that social learning provides more appropriate reasons for most child behavior than does psychosexual development.

Freud described the childhood years from (roughly) six to puberty as the latency stage. During these years children are supposed to repress sexual interest because of the resolution of the Oedipus complex. If you are not able to recall what the Oedipus complex represents, refer to frames 103 to 105.

171 For Freud, repression meant "pushing painful thoughts into the unconscious." Resolution of the Oedipus complex would mean repression of interest in +++++.

172 In learning theory, latency refers to the interval occurring between stimulus and response. For Freud, the period of repressed sexual activity between age six and puberty is termed the _____ period.

latency

173 For our purposes, the terms latency period and older-childhood years refer to the same general age level, i.e., between ++++.

six years and
puberty

174 During the latency period there is supposed to be an increase in interest in activity with the same-sex peers which corresponds with a _____ in interest in heterosexual activity (Freud, 1949).

decrease

175 However, anthropologists have found that in many primitive tribes there is a sharp increase in heterosexual activity between six years and puberty. This does not support the Freudian conception of the _____ period.

latency

176 Kinsey's studies (1949, 1953) indicate that the sex activity of six- to ten-year-olds in American society is far greater than most adults realize. That is, at this age there seems to be less repression of _____ than Freud believed.

sex

177 These studies also fail to support Freud's ideas about _____ of sex activity in later childhood.

repression

178 The Freudian concept of psychosexual determinism has not been confirmed by anthropological and sociological evidence. There *is* evidence to support the idea that children in the _____ period continue to identify with their parents as well as with their peers.

latency (older
childhood)

Although few behavioral scientists believe that the psychosexual age actually determines the psychosocial stage, they agree that the mechanism used by children at earlier ages to imitate social behavior (i.e., identification) continues to be used in later childhood.

Studies of Siblings

179 Some interesting studies of behavior characteristics among firstborn and younger siblings have been reported. More than 80 per cent of American children have _____.

siblings

180 It is evident that a child does not live in the same family when he is the only child as he does when younger _____ are born.

siblings (sisters
or brothers)

changes

181 That is, when a younger sibling is born, the family constituency changes, and the role of the older child _____ (if for no other reason than that the new child makes him a big brother, or sister).

182 Some studies, e.g., by Kawin (1934) and Bonney (1942), suggest that one can expect most older children to demonstrate less self-confidence, less competitiveness, less leadership ability, and less persistence than their younger

siblings

_____.

(1) competitive
(2) persistent

183 In other words, younger children tend to be more confident, **(1)** more _____, and **(2)** more _____ than firstborn children.

stimulation

184 Studies of firstborn and younger children suggest that the firstborn receive different types of social _____ than younger siblings.

Some possible reasons for different types of social stimulation for firstborn versus younger children have been described by Mussen, Conger, and Kagan (1963, p. 405). They suggest that the firstborn child *may* be:
1. Less adequately stimulated because of the relative inexperience of parents.
2. Expected to accomplish more at a faster rate than younger children.
3. Expected to assume responsibility earlier than younger siblings.
4. In addition, firstborn are usually alone in having to give up the status of "only child."

responsibility

185 Younger siblings are born to parents with greater experience, who typically have learned to expect less of their children in terms of early accomplishment and _____.

firstborn

186 Whether the reasons cited above are the most accurate or important in accounting for differences between firstborn and younger children, they suggest a basis for believing that different types and amounts of social stimulation are given to _____ and younger siblings.

only

187 The behavior characteristics of the only child have been the subject of studies by Fenton, Goodenough, R. B. Guilford, and others (Hurlock, 1959, chap. 6). Results reported are contradictory; there is no predictable behavior pattern for _____ children.

188 Only children have been reported to be both more *and* less popular with peers, more *and* less tractable and cooperative, and more *and* less inclined to emotional disturbance. Such contradictory findings do not permit description of typical _____-child behavior characteristics.

only

189 Some differences between only children and their peers have been reported for pop_____ity, co_____tiveness, and emo_____ality, but the differences are too small to permit generalizations.

popularity
cooperativeness
emotionality

190 Most studies of only children fail to control for socioeconomic variables. Since a high per cent of only children come from homes rated as middle-class or upper _____ status, this consideration may be of more importance than the fact of "onliness" itself.

socioeconomic

191 Socioeconomic variables probably influence family size (Bossard and Sanger, 1952). Only children are more likely to come from _____ [upper/working]-class families.

upper

192 Bossard indicates that discipline in large families is more likely to be enforced by siblings than by parents. This, of course, does not prove that only children are more effectively disciplined than children from _____ families.

large

193 Studies of older children from large and small families have failed to demonstrate that size of family by itself is basically important in determining behavior characteristics. Child behavior and family _____ are not strongly related.

size

In this section we have pointed out that behavior in later childhood is not necessarily a function of (1) psychosexual development per se, of (2) ordinal position in the family per se, or of (3) family size per se.

Older children are larger, more active, and more mobile than younger children. They have more and more frequent contacts with other adults (e.g., teachers) and with peers than do younger children. Body size, activity, and mobility may account better for differences observed in the behavior of older and younger children than the Freudian concept of psychosexual "ages and stages."

Peer Influences

194 In general, the older the child, the more mobility he demonstrates. Increased _____ usually permits more social contacts. Consequently, the older child has opportunities to identify with more people than the younger child has.

195 The older child, because of increased mobility, usually has more opportunities to play with other children than does the younger child. In later childhood, peers, as well as parents, become models with which to _____.

196 Obviously, older children react against their peers as well as identifying with them. But identification with _____ is an important socializing influence in later childhood.

197 One of the significant facts of the later childhood years is that children begin school. Most children start school at about age _____.

198 This throws them into contact with many other children of their own age. It also represents the first significant separation from their _____.

199 In a sense, since she has custody of the child for several hours per day and thus demonstrates many maternal functions, the teacher becomes a substitute _____ for the child.

200 Just as the teacher becomes, in a sense, a substitute mother for the child, other children become _____ siblings. (This is an oversimplification of social relationships in school but serves to make a point.)

201 For most American children, school is not only a major source of new information but also a means for providing social stimuli and reinforcements. Both _____ and other _____ are important socializing influences.

202 In spite of the importance of the school and age peers as socializing agents, the child's primary identifications between six to ten years seem to be those he makes within his own _____.

mobility

identify

peers

six

mothers (family, etc.)

mother

substitute

teachers
children

family

Discipline as Behavior Control

203 Control of children's behavior (discipline) has been of concern to parents since families began. Any and all types of behavior _____ have been termed discipline, but there has been little systematic study of the discipline of children.

204 Discipline as a form of behavior control typically refers to the process of getting children to do what parents or others want them to do. Discipline, then, can be defined as a process of learning responses _____ by others.

205 From a parent's viewpoint, a process of supplying rewards and punishments which affect the acquisition, continuance, or discontinuance of behavior in the child can be referred to as _____.

206 Viewed in this light, discipline is not synonomous with punishment. Discipline also can be viewed in terms of its effects on the continuance of behavior. It can be rewarding or punishing, depending on whether it teaches the child to (1) _____ or (2) _____ a behavior.

207 A mother wants her child to acquire a new behavior ("Comb your hair this way."). She can (1) _____ the child's combing in the desired way, attempt to (2) _____ undesired ways of combing hair, or do both.

208 If the intention of the parent is to get the child to discontinue some behavior, the parent could either withhold (1) _____ or use aversive stimulation or (2) _____ as forms of discipline.

209 Aversive stimulation as discipline for children usually takes one of several forms. Verbal threat, active (or physical) punishment, and deprivation of something presumably desired by the child are the three major forms of _____ _____ commonly employed by parents to extinguish undesired behavior.

210 Lewis Carroll once wrote this doggerel:
Speak harshly to your little boy
And beat him when he sneezes;
He only does it to annoy
Because he knows it teases.
The advice to speak harshly and beat refers to the application of _____ _____ as a form of discipline.

Margin notes:
control
desired (wanted)
discipline
(1) acquire (continue) (2) inhibit (discontinue)
(1) reinforce (reward) (2) inhibit (punish)
(1) rewards (2) punishment
aversive stimulation (punishment—in popular usage of the term)
aversive stimulation (or, physical and verbal punishment)

211 Lewis Carroll's doggerel designates two major types of aversive stimulation, _____ and _____. Deprivation is another type.

212 Corporal punishment is only one form of _____.

213 Verbal punishment includes threat, criticism, and reproof. A father says to his son, "If you do that again, I'll whale the daylights out of you." He is using _____ as a form of verbal punishment.

214 When a mother says, "Clean up the living room, or no dessert tonight," she, too, is using _____ as a disciplinary technique.

215 Threat is only one form of verbal punishment. Criticism and reproof are others. George's teacher says, "Your ears are dirty, and your tie needs straightening." She is using both _____ and _____ as forms of verbal punishment.

216 *Review:* Verbal punishment is so defined when verbal behavior on the part of the parent leads to inhibition or discontinuance of an undesired child behavior. Three common forms of verbal punishment are _____, _____, and _____.

217 Parents typically use both verbal and physical means to demonstrate their unhappiness about child behavior. _____ and _____ punishments constitute two major forms of discipline leading to extinction of behavior.

218 The other major form of behavior control used by most parents in our society is _____ the child of something he wants.

219 If a parent, instead of threatening to withhold dessert from the child, actually does so in an attempt to get him to stop "messing up the living room," she is using _____ as a form of punishment.

220 Not infrequently parents use threat of deprivation as a means of trying to exert behavior control. Many parents use the +++++ of allowance or of food to control child behavior.

Left margin answers:

verbal
active (physical)

discipline (aversive stimulation, behavior control)

threat

threat

criticism
reproof

threat
criticism
reproof

Verbal
physical (active or corporal)

depriving

deprivation

threat of
deprivation

221 When a father says, "Don't let me see anything below C on your report card next time, or you won't get your allowance," he is using threat of deprivation in his attempt to _____ behavior.

control

222 When behavior control by positive as well as negative reinforcement is used to define discipline, a new perspective is added to the common concept of discipline. Many people think only of corporal _____ when they think of discipline.

punishment

Most parents would agree that corporal punishment inhibits undesirable behavior, at least temporarily or in their presence. There are some questions about other effects of corporal punishment, however. These include the distinct possibilities of (1) parents generalizing the form of this discipline and (2) the child generalizing his reaction to punishment. Once the parent uses corporal punishment, typically he finds it an easy way to control his child's behavior. Having spanked the child for gross misbehavior, he finds it easier to use spanking to control less serious behavior.

223 The illustration given above suggests that spanking becomes _____ as a form of behavior control for the parents.

generalized

224 A mother spanks her five-year-old for running across the street without looking. The child stops this behavior, and mother spanks him for many other things for which she previously had not spanked. This demonstrates the principle of _____ in behavior control.

generalization

225 Parents learn to spank children, then, because of the results that corporal punishment brings. They should be aware, though, that children may also learn to generalize from corporal _____.

punishment

226 The child may learn to view the parent in a generally negative manner rather than in a positive way if excessive or consistent punishment is used by the parent. That is, the parent may become a generalized _____ reinforcer for the child.

negative

227 Use of excessive corporal punishment may lead to the parent becoming a _____ _____ reinforcer for the child, rather than being a teacher who helps the child discriminate between what is acceptable and what is not.

generalized
negative

inhibits
(suppresses)

suppression
(inhibition)

punishment

punish (discipline)

discipline

parent

suffering
(disturbance)

corporal (active,
physical)

(1) punishment
(2) deprivation

228 Corporal punishment may serve only to cause the child to suppress a behavior in the presence of the parent. In this case, it merely _____ the child's response.

229 A mother puts soap in her child's mouth for saying something she does not like. She is hoping that the child will not say the words again under any circumstances, but she may be ensuring only that he suppresses the words in her presence. In this case, punishment leads to _____ of the response in the presence of the mother. (As used here, suppression refers to volitional withholding of a response. It will be discussed further in Part V, Unit 3.)

230 Another possibility in either excessive or indiscriminate use of physical punishment with children is that such punishment often results in excessive hostility or timidity in the child. Sometimes a child's undesired behavior is proportional to the strength of _____ the parent has used in the past.

231 Indiscriminate or excessive punishment is often generalized. Many people also feel it is unfair (if not inhuman) for an adult to _____ a child, much smaller than he, by striking him.

232 There is no doubt that many parents who use corporal punishment as _____ do achieve their desired results in child behavior. Not infrequently, however, they report undesired results in terms of their own behavior.

233 A mother reported that she had stopped her ten-year-old from showing "outrageous" table manners by spanking him, but that it made her feel so bad that "it wasn't worth it." In this case the _____ suffered more than the child, perhaps.

234 "Beat in haste, repent at leisure," represents the idea that indiscriminate corporal punishment may lead to _____ for the parent, as well as for the child.

235 For the reasons given, most authorities in child care view _____ punishment with ambivalence. It may lead to desired extinction or inhibition of behavior, but it also may yield other undesired results to both parent and child.

236 *Review:* In attempting to extinguish undesired behavior in a child, a parent typically uses three major types of aversive stimulation: verbal and corporal (1) _____ and (2) _____ of something desired.

verbal	**237** Criticism, reproof, demanding an apology, and threat are forms of _____ punishment.
active	**238** Spanking a child represents _____ punishment.
deprivation	**239** Withholding affection or material objects (toys, food) are forms of _____.
reinforcement	**240** In addition to aversive stimulation of the types mentioned, positive _____ may be used to discipline children.
(1) verbal (2) material (3) nonreinforcement	**241** Positive reinforcement may consist of either verbal or material rewards or of nonreinforcement of an undesired behavior. (1) Praising a child exemplifies _____ reward. (2) Giving him candy for "helping mother" exemplifies _____ reward. (3) Ignoring undesired "show-off" behavior represents _____ of behavior.
verbal material	**242** Eight-year-old Peter shines the family car with his father and earns effusive thanks and an ice-cream soda. Father thus uses both _____ and _____ rewards in an effort to control (discipline) future cooperative behavior.
nonreinforcement	**243** Nine-year-old Jeff begins to talk to his mother while the parents are talking to one another. Mother ignores Jeff in order to teach him to talk when adults are *not* speaking. Ignoring Jeff in this instance represents _____ of an undesired response.
bribery	**244** Once bribery of children is instituted, it is usually difficult to discontinue. Not infrequently parents will substitute the promise of a reward in return for an immediate change in their child's behavior. This represents _____.
Bribery	**245** For example, a child learns to go to bed because of the bribe, rather than because rest is the good and appropriate thing for him to do. _____ brings mixed blessings, then, as a reinforcer.
affection	**246** Carl Rogers once said, "Bribery is the prostitution of affection." This suggests that parents may offer bribes (i.e., promises or things) as a substitute for their _____.
consequence	**247** The consequences of the child's behavior themselves can often be used as a most effective reinforcer. What the child himself gets, rather than what the parent gives, as a _____ of the child's behavior may be considered either as positive reinforcement or aversive stimulation, depending on whether the child continues or discontinues the behavior.

248 It is our view that *responsible self-direction* should be the ultimate aim of discipline with children. By this, we mean that children should learn to be socially _____ but in a self-directing manner.

responsible

249 If a child learns to be responsible in his behavior without having to rely on others to govern his conduct, we should say that he has achieved the purpose of discipline, that is, _____ _____-_____.

responsible self-direction

Parents can teach responsible self-direction by a judicious utilization of both positive reinforcements and aversive stimuli. But no formula is available to tell parents what and what not to do in any given situation. Parents and teachers must decide for themselves what they want from children and how they can best obtain it. If responsible self-direction is desired, permitting children to enjoy—or suffer—the consequences of their behavior seems to be the most effective way of exerting discipline, but for most parents, it cannot be the only method used.

Knowing what behavior is desired, determining the types of consequents appropriate to obtain it, and then being consistent in supplying appropriate reinforcements and/or punishments constitute the elements for effective discipline.

SUMMARY

Probably the most influential single theory for explaining development in childhood was supplied by Freud. His concepts of developmental determinism are widely espoused by clinicians and by some pediatricians. Freud suggested that, at different ages, different parts of the body provide primary foci for the pursuit of pleasure or avoidance of pain. Thus, oral stimulation is of primary importance during the first year; anal stimulation has greater significance during, roughly, the second year; and so on.

Freud's concepts provided the basis for many research studies dealing with the effects of tactile-kinesthetic stimulation in infancy, with feeding practices, and with toilet training, as possible sources of behavior problems. Some of the research with infrahuman animals, like that conducted by Harlow with infant monkeys, is highly imaginative. Such studies have interesting implications for human development.

Controlled research with children is difficult to accomplish. Some important studies have been reported about peer influences and the effects of different kinds of behavior controls exerted by parents. The studies indicate that, for our culture in general, appropriate child behavior is most likely to be conditioned by parents who share in the practice of democratic rather than indulgent or overcontrolling discipline. Principles of learning theory can be applied to the analysis of child behavior. Research suggests that they offer more promise as valid explanatory constructs than does the Freudian concept of developmental determinism.

REFERENCES

Baldwin, A., J. Kallhorn, and F. H. Breese: "Patterns of Parent Behavior," *Psychological Monographs*, vol. 58, no. 3, 1945.

Baldwin, A., J. Kallhorn, and F. H. Breese: "The Appraisal of Parent Behavior," *Psychological Monographs*, vol. 63, no. 299, 1949.

Beach, F., and J. Jaynes: "Effects of Early Experience upon the Behavior of Animals," *Psychological Bulletin*, 51:239–263, 1954.

Bishop, B.: "Mother-Child Interaction and the Social Behavior of Children," *Psychological Monographs*, vol. 65, no. 328, 1951.

Bonney, M. E.: "A Study of Social Status on the Second Grade Level," *Journal of Genetic Psychology*, 60:271–305, 1942.

Bossard, J., and M. Sanger: "The Large Family," *American Sociological Review*, 17:3–9, 1952.

Bowlby, J., et al.: "The Effects of Mother-Child Separation: A Follow-up Study," *British Journal of Medical Psychology*, 29: 211–247, 1956.

Bowlby, J.: "Separation Anxiety," *International Journal of Psychoanalysis*, 49:81–113, 1960.

Casler, L.: "Maternal Deprivation: A Critical Review of the Literature," *Monographs of the Society for Research in Child Development*, 26:1–64, 1961.

Davenport, R., E. Menzel, and C. Rogers: "Maternal Care during Infancy: Its Effect on Weight Gain and Mortality in the Chimpanzee," *American Journal of Orthopsychiatry*, 31:803–809, 1961.

Freud, A., and D. Burlingham: *Infants without Families*, International Universities Press, Inc., New York, 1944.

Freud, S.: *An Outline of Psychoanalysis*, W. W. Norton & Company, Inc., New York, 1949. (Original papers, 1904.)

Harlow, H., and R. Zimmerman: "Affectional Responses in Infant Monkeys," *Science*, 130: 421–432, 1959.

Harlow, H., and M. Harlow: "Social Deprivation in Monkeys," *Scientific American*, 207, 5:136–146, 1962.

Kawin, E.: *Children of Preschool Age*, The University of Chicago Press, Chicago, 1934.

Kinsey, A. C., et al.: *Sexual Behavior in the Human Female*, W. B. Saunders Company, Philadelphia, 1953.

Levine, S.: "Stimulation in Infancy," *Scientific American*, 202:80–86, 1960.

Levy, David: *Maternal Overprotection*, Columbia University Press, New York, 1943.

Maas, H. S.: *The Young Adult Adjustment of Twenty Wartime Residential Nursery Children*, Child Welfare League of America, 1963.

MacFarlane, J., L. Allen, and M. Honzik: "A Developmental Study of Normal Children," *University of California Publications on Child Development*, no. 2, 1954.

Maudry, M., and M. Nekula: "Social Relations between Children of the Same Age," *Journal of Genetic Psychology*, 54: 193–215, 1939.

Mussen, P., J. Conger, and J. Kagan: *Childhood Development and Personality*, 2d ed., Harper & Row, Publishers, Incorporated, New York, 1963.

Orlansky, H.: "Infant Care and Personality," *Psychological Bulletin*, 96:1–49, 1949.

Radke, M.: *The Relation of Parental Authority to Children's Behavior and Attitudes*, The University of Minnesota Press, Minneapolis, 1946.

Ribble, M.: *The Rights of Infants*, Columbia University Press, New York, 1943.

Sears, P. S.: "Doll Play Aggression in Young Children," *Psychological Monographs*, vol. 65, no. 6, 1951.

Sears, R., E. Maccoby, and H. Levin: *Patterns of Child Rearing*, Harper & Row, Publishers, Incorporated, New York, 1957.

Spitz, R.: "The Role of Ecological Factors in Emotional Development in Infancy," *Child Development*, 20:145–156, 1949.

Spitz, R.: *Somatic Consequences of Emotional Deprivation* (Film), NYU Film Library, New York, 1949.

Yarrow, L.: "Maternal Deprivation: Toward an Empirical and Conceptual Re-evaluation," *Psychological Bulletin*, 58:459–490, 1961.

SELF-REVIEW QUIZ

1 Give Freud's concept of developmental determinism.

2 In adolescence or adulthood, fingernail biting to reduce tension presumably is related to the _____ stage. The tendency to be abusive to others could represent regression to the _____ stage (Freud).

3 Does the majority of studies presented in the text support Freud's theory of developmental determinism?

4 Describe and evaluate two types of disorders which Spitz claimed were due to poor infant care.

5 What are three major ways, presumably undesirable, by which many parents control the behavior of young children?

6 Freud termed the process by which the child unconsciously imitates his parent's behavior, and thus attempts to be like him/her, the process of _____.

7 Radke and Baldwin reported studies about relationships between home atmosphere and child behavior. In these studies what was meant by "home atmos-

phere"? Cite three types of home atmospheres de-scribed in these studies.

8   What is the latency period (Freud)? Do studies bear out Freud's contentions about children's activities dur-ing this period?

9   Do younger or older siblings in American families tend to be more persistent, competitive, and confident?

10   "Only" children tend to come from middle-class families. Is "onliness" or class status more important in terms of the characteristics demonstrated by these children?

11   Parents use two major types of punishment to control (discipline) their children. (a) Threat, reproof, and criticism exemplify _____ punishment. (b) Spank-ing exemplifies _____ punishment.

12   According to the text, what should be the principle goal of discipline?

unit 3

Adolescence and Early Adulthood

The transition from childhood to adulthood is not always easy. In Western culture, adolescence has been thought of typically as a period of turbulence, when problems abound and the worst is sure to happen. Not infrequently parents blame the maturational aspects of adolescence for behavior they deplore. Physical changes by themselves cannot account for psychosocial problems. Endocrinological changes do not determine choice of peers or the ways in which parents react to adolescents' choice of friends. They do, however, mark the onset of adolescence and may well be related to behavior problems. But they are not responsible per se for parent-child conflict, dating difficulties, change in religious behavior, and the like, which may occur during adolescence.

Physical Changes in Adolescence

1 Adolescence has been called the "in-between" developmental stage. This refers, of course, to the idea that adolescence occurs in between $+++++$.

childhood and adulthood

2 Adolescence comes from the Latin word *adolescere,* meaning "to grow" or "to grow to maturity." Ordinarily, the beginning of _____ is marked by the signs of puberty, or sexual maturity.

adolescence

3 Adolescence, then, refers to the time of life between _____ (or, onset of sexual maturity) and adulthood.

puberty

4 Freud suggested that at puberty the child's basic interests and sources of erotic satisfaction become centered in heterosexual behavior. Freud termed the final psycho_____ stage the genital stage.

sexual

5 In the genital stage the person presumably is impelled toward heterosexual behaviors because of changes in endocrine functions which lead to _____ maturity.

sexual

235

6 Sexual maturity is typically associated with the resolution of the latency stage, during which Freud says that the child is attracted to members of the same sex. The genital stage is characterized by attraction to members of the _____ sex.

opposite

7 The Freudian conception of adolescence (i.e., resolution of the **(1)** _____ stage and entrance into the **(2)** _____ stage) places major emphasis on sexual maturity. In this instance, Freud's view of adolescence is somewhat similar to some other descriptions of adolescence.

(1) latency
(2) genital

8 Dramatists, poets, and some psychologists have described adolescence as a period of "storm and stress" due to physical maturation. The onset of puberty was supposed to be the cause of psychological _____.

conflict (stress, etc.)

9 Freudian psychologists and those who emphasize the storm-and-stress theory are similar in their emphases on relationships between **(1)** _____ maturation and **(2)** _____ factors. They differ, however, in their explanations of such relationships.

(1) sexual
(2) psychological

10 While proponents of the storm-and-stress theory emphasize sexual _____ as the important contributor to psychological problems in adolescence, many cultural anthropologists and social psychologists disagree with them.

maturation

11 The anthropologists Margaret Mead (1949) and Ruth Benedict (1934) have reported that the physical changes that occur during puberty do not necessarily result in psychological problems or _____.

conflict (stress, etc.)

12 In many primitive societies (e.g., Mead's studies of New Guinea and Samoan tribes) puberty is *not* stress-producing. This is also true for many persons in our own society. The sexual changes which occur during puberty do not *necessarily* cause conflict or _____.

stress

13 It seems reasonable to assume that whether an adolescent demonstrates conflict or stress during adolescence depends not only on **(1)** _____ changes at adolescence but also on social **(2)** _____ before and during adolescence.

(1) sexual
(2) conditioning (learning)

Sexual changes and social conditioning both contribute to the behavior of the adolescent. Both nature and nurture provide stimuli and reinforcements to the child at puberty. However, neither by itself is able to supply all the reasons why adolescents behave as they do.

14 Most students of human behavior agree that puberal changes occur which *can* cause storm and stress if effective _____ conditioning has not preceded and/or does not accompany sexual maturity.

social

15 Puberty (from the Latin *pubertas*, "age of manhood") technically refers to the first phase of adolescence and is related to hormonal changes which regulate _____ behavior.

sex

16 Hormonal changes lead to development of both primary and secondary sex characteristics. Those sex characteristics referring to reproduction itself are called _____ sex characteristics.

primary

17 Sex characteristics which refer to body changes associated with, but not actually involved in, reproduction are designated _____ sex characteristics.

secondary

Part II, Unit 2 described the glandular system and its major functions. Table 14 describes some major functions of the anterior pituitary gland and the gonads as they relate to sex development. However, it is important to remember that the entire glandular system works as a unit.

(anterior) pituitary

18 The production of hormones which stimulate physical growth is a function of the _____ gland.

pituitary gonads

19 The production of androgens and estrogens (male and female hormones) is a function of the _____ gland and _____. Several kinds of androgens and estrogens have been isolated.

sex

20 Specific ovarian hormones are related to ovulation and other secondary _____ characteristics in girls (see Table 14).

testicular (androgen)

21 Lowering of voice pitch, growth of pubic hair, and other secondary sex characteristics in boys are related to specific _____ hormones.

menarche (menstruation)

22 The onset of menarche (menstruation) is used as the most common sign of puberty in girls. There is wide variation in the age of achieving _____.

menarche (menstruation)

23 In our culture, the age range ten to fourteen years is typical for achieving _____ among girls.

Table 14. Glandular Aspects of Sex Development and Function

Glands	Gland product (most frequently a hormone)	Function
Pituitary (Anterior lobe)	Growth hormones	Stimulate growth, gonad activity, fusing of epiphyses
	Gonadotropic hormones Androgen (male hormone present in both male and female)	Growth of prostate, seminal vesicles, penis, etc.
	Estrogen (female hormone present in both sexes)	Produces secondary sex characteristics
	Progestogen	Inhibits action of pituitary
		Stimulates growth of breasts,* mammary glands, uterus, Fallopian tubes, vagina
Gonads Ovaries	Theelin	
	Follicular hormone	Stimulates secretion of estrogen
	Germ cells	Causes ovulation*
	Corpus luteum	Broadening of hips*
	Estrogens (ovarian hormones)	Growth of pubic hair* Changed musculature*
Testes	Androgens (testicular hormones)	Lowering of voice pitch*
	Spermatozoa	Broadening of shoulders*

SOURCE: H. W. Bernard, *Adolescent Development in American Culture,* Harcourt, Brace & World, Inc., New York, 1957, p. 148. Used by permission.
* Denotes secondary sex characteristic.

24 Heredity, nutrition, specific diseases, and even general health have been related to the onset of _____ in girls.

menarche (puberty)

25 In boys, no outward observable physiological change designates sexual maturity. The appearance of pigmented pubic _____ serves as a convenient sign.

hair

26 A more accurate method of determining fertility in boys is urinalysis for creatine and androgen, two hormones. Creatine is found in sexually immature boys. Sexually mature boys produce _____.

androgen

estrogen

X rays of bone
development

sex

sexual

secondary

shoulders

voice

sexes

hips

breast

mammary

27 Correspondingly, estrogen is produced by sexually mature girls. Presence of _____ is a more accurate way of assessing fertility than knowledge of menarche per se.

28 It has been found that predictions of age of menarche can be made from X-ray photographs of bone development during the preadolescent growth spurt (Harding, 1952). In fact, this method, $++++$, is the most accurate way of predicting onset age of menarche.

29 *Review:* The presence of estrogens and androgens indicate maturity of female and male reproductive apparatus. Menarche in girls and nocturnal emission in boys are consequences of the appearance of primary _____ characteristics.

30 Typically, boys achieve _____ maturity about one to two years later than girls.

31 In addition to the appearance of primary sex characteristics, puberty is also marked by _____ sex characteristics.

32 Secondary sex characteristics which appear at puberty are marked with an asterisk on Table 14. Appearance of pubic hair is usually accompanied by broadening of the hips in girls, and broadening of _____ in boys.

33 Enlargement of the larynx ("voice box") results in a deepening of a boy's _____ at puberty.

34 At puberty, the pores of the skin become larger, and this enlargement gives the skin a coarser look. Because of a temporary maladjustment in the sebaceous glands, acne is often observed in both _____.

35 Approximately two years prior to menarche, girls' hips typically increase in width and roundness. This change in appearance of _____ is due in part to growth of the pelvic bones and in part to early adolescent fatty deposits in the hip region.

36 In addition to showing characteristic hip development, girls at puberty typically demonstrate marked _____ development associated with activity in the mammary glands.

37 Following menarche, the breasts become larger because of the development of the _____ glands.

38 *Review:* The two secondary sex characteristics which girls and boys both demonstrate are the development of **(1)** _____ and _____ hair and **(2)** changes in the skin, i.e., _____.

(1) pubic and axillary
(2) acne

39 In addition to the appearance of primary and secondary sex characteristics, puberty is typified by other physical changes. The most obvious physical _____ occur in body proportions, in height, and in weight.

changes

40 During puberty the various body parts all become larger but not at the same rate. Because of this, puberty is characterized by changes in legs-hips-trunk-shoulder _____.

proportions

41 The legs grow proportionally more than the t_____, and the hips and shoulders widen. These changes in body proportions are characteristic of both boys and girls.

trunk

42 Increase in height during puberty is reflected in relatively rapid lengthening of the legs and trunk. This spurt in _____ is related to action of the pituitary gland.

height

43 As you already know, the anterior pituitary releases g_____ hormones in the early stages of puberty.

growth

44 When the gonadotrophic (gonad-stimulating) hormone is released, it also affects the _____ hormones, so that a gradual retardation of height increase occurs.

growth

45 An inadequate supply of the pituitary growth hormone results in dwarfism. An oversecretion of the hormone would result in _____.

giantism

46 Gross deviations in height, such as dwarfism or giantism, are directly related to activity of the anterior _____ hormones.

pituitary

47 The circus giant is the result of an _____ of the growth hormone.

oversecretion

48 The circus dwarf is the result of an _____ of the growth hormone.

undersecretion

49 Changes in body proportions and height are related to changes in weight during puberty. About 50 per cent of all adolescents go through a "puberal-fat" stage. This _____-_____ stage seems related in part to hormonal changes and in part to increased food intake which accompanies rapid growth.

puberal-fat

50 Typically, the puberal fat disappears after puberty. A sex difference in age of appearance of weight changes shows girls demonstrating earlier _____-gain spurts than boys.

weight

51 For girls, the greatest gain in weight is just before and just after the onset of m_____.

menarche

52 For boys, weight gain typically occurs about one to two years later than for _____.

girls

In summary, the Freudian concept of psychosexual determinism and other traditional concepts of adolescence emphasize sexual maturation that begins with puberty. Puberty is a stage of development which is dependent on hormonal changes produced primarily by the pituitary gland and the gonads. The appearance of primary and secondary sexual characteristics is a function of certain endocrinological changes. The growth spurt typical of adolescence is also related to these physiological changes. However, sexual maturation and growth by themselves hardly account for the variety of behavioral change which characterizes contemporary adolescents. Peer socialization, changing family relationships, increased education, and other personal and sociocultural considerations help to determine behavior during adolescence.

Social Behavior

This section deals primarily with social behavior in adolescence: relationships with peers and those within the family. These areas of social behavior are selected because of their widespread relevance.

53 Freud (1949) suggested that most children begin to show marked interest in the same-sex peers during preadolescence (the latency period). This interest in _____ relationships continues to develop in most adolescents during and after puberty.

peer

54 Peers often supplant parents as models of behavior in adolescence. In part, this seems to be a function of maturation, in part, a function of social _____ or learning.

conditioning

55 Some of the physical changes which occur during adolescence may serve as internal stimuli and reinforcers to behavior. Certainly, observable changes in height, weight, and secondary sex characteristics in one adolescent seem to serve as social _____ and _____ to some of his peers.

56 The importance of the peer group in adolescence is pointed up by the fact that most adolescents will risk parent disapproval to win or maintain _____ approval (Coleman, 1961).

57 Psychoanalysts interpret this fact to mean that the adolescent identifies with the peer group more than with his parents. Instead of explaining in terms of social stimulation and reinforcement, Freudians use the concept of _____.

58 Psychoanalysis explains peer socialization in adolescence more in terms of identification than by using concepts of social stimulation and _____.

59 Several studies have shown that, as the American adolescent gets older, there is a shift from identification with "the crowd" to _____ with a small, select group.

60 In other words, in early adolescence the child is more influenced in his behavior by what "most kids" do. He responds to the _____ group as a kind of general social reinforcer.

61 As he gets older, the adolescent is reinforced more by the particular _____ and/or clique with which he identifies.

62 As a general social reinforcer, the adolescent "crowd" is composed of adolescents similar in socioeconomic background and interests. The cli_____ requires more personalized social relationships.

63 This may be the reason why crowds are usually less important than _____ as social reinforcers for older adolescents.

64 Apparently, availability of contact by itself is not a sufficient reason for _____ formation.

65 In other words, adolescents do not form these small, intimate groups simply because they live near each other or have available _____ at school.

---

stimuli
reinforcements

peer

identification

reinforcement

identification

peer

group

clique

cliques

clique

contact

66 Among the most important correlates of clique membership is socioeconomic status. Hollingshead (1944) and other sociologists have found that the vast majority of "best friends" are composed of peers with highly similar _____ backgrounds.

socioeconomic

67 Keislar (1955) reports that the unpopular adolescent in school typically comes from a lower _____ group than the majority of his classmates.

socioeconomic

68 Rated unpopularity seems to be related to lack of knowledge about social skills which adolescents from _____ socioeconomic strata demonstrate.

higher (other)

69 Adolescent cliques form because of reasons other than proximity or available contact. Factors such as mental ability, social maturity, interests, age, and socioeconomic status are all related to _____ formation.

clique

70 Socioeconomic considerations seem to play an important part in influencing social maturity of adolescents. In early adolescence, physical maturity is correlated with _____ _____ (Hurlock, 1959).

social maturity

71 Younger adolescents who are physically mature are likely to be judged socially mature. Social maturity seems more related to _____ maturity in early adolescence than in late adolescence.

physical

72 Tyron (1939) reported that at age twelve most girls admired other girls who were quiet and conforming. At fifteen, however, the same girls said they admired girls who were active, attractive to boys, and showed ability to be entertaining. The change in ratings of the activity dimension are in part a function of change in _____.

age

73 Boys at ages twelve and fifteen consistently reported admiration for others who showed daring and leadership in physical activities. They differed in their evaluation of personal appearance. Older boys rated personal _____ higher than younger ones.

appearance

74 In the Tyron study, competence in physical activities did not change in terms of rated social value between ages twelve and fifteen. Presumably +++++ is not subject to as much variation with age of boys as is interest in personal appearance.

competence in
physical activities

75 _Review:_ Social behavior in adolescence is affected by socioeconomic status, age, and physical maturity. Mental age has also been related to clique membership in _____.

adolescence

Figure 15. A college clique. School clubs, fraternities, and sororities promote the formation of cliques. Several clique characteristics described in the text can be observed in the fraternity group pictured here.

clique

mental ages

76 Mental age and socioeconomic status are related to each other, and socioeconomic status is related to _____ membership.

77 It should not be surprising that boys with similar mental ages tend to form cliques more easily than those with dissimilar _____ _____.

78 Bud and Bob are the same age and attend the same school. Bud demonstrates normal mental ability and is from a working-class family. Bob's IQ is well above average. His father is in the upper-income bracket. Based on available knowledge only, there is _____ [(1) a high probability/(2) a low probability/(3) an equal chance] that they would be in the same school clique.

79 Adolescents are acutely aware of their acceptance by the peer group. How peers behave toward them is used as the criterion for peer _____ by most adolescents.

80 Ausubel and Schiff (1955) found that the social reinforcements supplied by peers are used by adolescents in general ways to predict social _____.

Specific criteria used to predict social acceptance by adolescent peers include (1) membership in cliques; (2) rating their behavior as "popular," and (3) invitations received to attend social events.

81 An adolescent is likely to rate himself high in peer acceptance if he/she (1) belongs to a _____, (2) believes himself to be _____, and (3) receives invitations to _____ _____.

82 There is a relationship between self-rated social _____ and ability to predict status in a peer group (Ausubel and Schiff, 1955).

83 On the whole, girls seem better able than boys to predict their social acceptance in the _____ group.

84 Ability to predict one's social acceptance develops more slowly than ability to _____ the social status of others.

85 The adolescent who does not report himself as socially accepted by his peer group may substitute other activities for peer-group behaviors. For example, the unpopular adolescent may become absorbed in a hobby, or in daydreaming, as a _____ for social activities with his peers.

86 It is possible, of course, that previous conditioning for hobbies, daydreaming, or other substitutes for peer activities may result in (rather than be a reaction to) lack of _____ acceptance.

Margin answers: (2); acceptance; acceptance; (1) clique (2) popular (3) social events; acceptance; peer; predict; substitute; peer

peer acceptance

87 The cause-effect relationships between _____ _____ and substitute activities are not well defined.

88 There is some evidence (Gough, 1952) for the belief that the more accepted an adolescent rates himself, the more active he is in group activities. Social acceptance

activity

and _____ in adolescent groups thus appear to be related.

89 *Review:* Peer socialization in general and social acceptance in particular seem to follow the principles of

accepted

social learning. If an adolescent wants to be _____ by his peers, he must be able to discriminate acceptable peer-group behavior and then demonstrate it.

Peer socialization, then, is obviously important for most adolescents. It is highly stressed in the American culture and not infrequently results in the supplanting of parental values by those of the peer group. In our society, different behaviors are differently valued and reinforced by peers at different age levels. Social acceptance seems to follow principles of social learning at all developmental stages, including adolescence.

Religious Behavior

Values, ethics, morality, and religion sometimes pose very difficult questions for adolescents. Some of the questions will be dealt with in greater detail in Part VI. However, some very interesting studies of religious behavior in adolescence deserve mention here. For example, there is some evidence to suggest that college students of this generation show more interest in religion than did those of a generation ago (Pressey and Jones, 1955).

religious affiliation

90 Still other evidence indicates that few college students change their religious affiliation. When changes in _____ _____ do occur, they are likely to be toward more liberal faiths (Allport et al., 1958).

change

91 If religious beliefs change, religious behavior tends to _____ also.

92 Time spent in prayer, church attendance, and participation in church groups tends to decrease in later adolescence. Religious behavior is, in part, a function of

belief

religious _____.

93 Religion is unrelated to membership in high school "leading crowds," if Coleman's study (1961) is representative. It is not necessary to profess a particular _____ affiliation to belong to such a high school group.

religious

94 In fact, religious affiliation plays a smaller role than family or social status in determining membership in an adolescent _____.

crowd (group)

95 In all but one of several high school groups studied (Coleman, 1961), there was almost no tendency for adolescents to designate their friends on a _____ basis.

religious

96 Other studies indicate that knowledge of moral principles, rules of conduct, or Biblical information are not sufficient to ensure ethical _____ on the part of adolescents.

behavior (conduct)

97 Several studies cited in Seidman's book (1962) point to little or no relationship between knowledge of right and wrong and actual cheating, lying, altruism, and loyalty. These behaviors were not related to _____ belief, either.

religious

Vocational Problems and Possibilities

Young people today face a work world of unprecedented opportunity. Technological changes in agriculture, business, and industry require higher skills than ever before. Correspondingly, the demands for farm help and unskilled labor are proportionately less than in the past. Technological "blessings" are not entirely unmixed. Somewhere between 600,000 to 800,000 young people between sixteen to twenty-one years of age were out of school but unemployed during the 1962 school year (U.S. Department of Labor, 1963). This number is equal to the populations of San Francisco, St. Louis, or Boston. A tremendous number of young people will be vying for jobs by 1970.

98 Figure 16 shows that by 1970 the largest group of employable youths will have a _____ _____ education.

high school

99 There will be a larger combined total of youths with *less* than a high school education than of those with a _____ education, however.

college

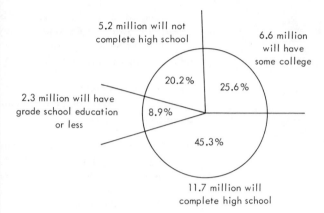

Figure 16. Characteristics of youth entering the labor force, 1960 to 1970. (*Manpower Challenge of the 60's*, U. S. Department of Labor, 1963, used by permission.)

25

100 About _____ per cent of young people will have completed college by 1970.

101 The President's Committee on Youth Employment (1963) stated that the demand for farm workers will decrease about 20 per cent between 1960 and 1970. Fewer _____ jobs will be available in the future.

farm (agricultural)

102 Only about one out of ten farm boys in 1963 could expect to make a living from _____ by 1970.

farming (agriculture)

103 The demand for unskilled labor will remain at about the same level in 1970; i.e., there will be approximately +++++ jobs for unskilled workers.

the same number of

104 Proportionately, however, this means that there will be fewer unskilled jobs in 1970 for the available _____ force.

work (labor)

105 It is encouraging to know that 20 per cent more sales-managerial jobs and 40 per cent more technical-professional jobs will be available by 1970. These occupations probably will require more than a high school _____.

education

It is a commonplace that job income is related to educational preparation. That is, the more education one has, other things being equal, the more income he can expect. This relationship is demonstrated clearly in Figure 16 above.

106 In 1960, men with less than an elementary education earned on the average between $_____ and $_____.

2,000
3,000

8,000

elementary school

college

107 On the other hand, men with college degrees earned, on the average, approximately $_____.

108 Men with college degrees earned about twice as much, on the average, as men with _____ _____ education.

109 The average man with one to three years of college earned somewhat more than the average high school graduate. Strictly on an income basis, some _____ work is better than none at all.

Figure 17 relates income to education. It does not isolate variables such as socioeconomic status, family background, race, and other considerations, some of which are presented in other parts of this book. We should point out here that the unemployment rate is about twice as high for Negroes as for whites. What is very highly encouraging is that local, state, and Federal leaders are taking steps to deal with problems of potential unemployment among older adolescents and adults.

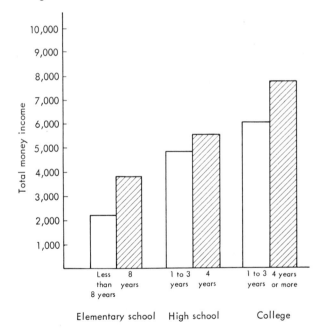

Figure 17. Median income of U. S. men by educational level. (Bureau of the Census, *Current Population Reports*, Series P–60, no. 39, 1961, used by permission.)

110 In order to deal with problems of youth, many states and large cities have appointed youth-planning commissions. Among other duties, these commissions study and make recommendations about unempl_____.

unemployment

Federal

111 Sometimes state and local agencies articulate with Federal agencies which lend assistance for vocational-education and -training programs. The National Defense Education Act is sponsored by the _____ government, for example, but funds are disbursed through local sources.

unions
management

112 Unions and industrial management also have set up committees to study youth-employment problems. Many training and apprenticeship programs have been initiated by both _____ and _____.

school

113 Many schools have set up offices which are dealing with the vocational problems of adolescents who are both in and out of _____.

nonachievers

114 For example, schools are now trying to identify "nonachievers" early in their school career and then set up remedial programs for these _____.

115 Remedial academic programs are not appropriate for some adolescents. For various reasons, some youths are not oriented (and cannot be, even under existing remedial programs) to academic work. For such people more functional job-oriented _____ are required.

programs (courses)

vocational

116 Most high schools and colleges improve their guidance and counseling services so that they can be of greater service to students needing _____ guidance as well as personal help.

Various local, state, and Federal agencies are endeavoring to deal more systematically with the vocational problems which the population explosion and improved technology have brought. Converging lines of evidence strongly suggest that education provides a viable means for helping youths to prepare effectively for the work life that lies ahead of them.

Dating Behavior

similar to (like)

117 Dating activities provide good examples of some principles which were discussed earlier. For example, several studies have shown that both younger and older adolescents prefer dating people who are _____ _____ themselves.

socioeconomic

118 Girls, particularly, are more likely to demonstrate dating preferences for boys from their own _____ stratum who show similar religious and recreational interests.

recreational

119 For college men there is a lower correlation between dating preferences and similarity with the girls' socioeconomic status, religious, and _____ interests.

dating

120 One study (Ehrmann, 1955) suggests that there is a trend to dating with less regard to similar socioeconomic and religious backgrounds among older adolescents. This trend in _____ practices is demonstrated more by college men.

competitive

121 Competitive dating ("playing the field") is more common proportionately among younger than among older adolescents. Continuous, single dating ("going steady") is more common than _____ dating among high school seniors than among freshmen.

parental control

122 Competitive dating is possibly related to parental control over the dating practices of younger adolescents. Continuous single dating may reflect a weakening of _____ _____ over dating practices of older adolescents.

opposite

123 Going steady carries with it the disadvantage of possible restriction of social contact with different members of the _____ sex.

adolescent

124 Among older adolescents, going steady also increases the probability of premarital sexual relations and early marriage. It appears to be one of the factors responsible for the high divorce rate among those who marry during the _____ years (Hurlock, 1959).

There are, of course, other considerations in determining whether an adolescent will "go steady" or "play the field." To be aware of the relative advantages and disadvantages of continuous, single dating and competitive dating might be considered a sign of social maturity.

Dating in adolescence usually brings many problems for parents. These problems often develop into friction between parent and adolescent. One of the most common problems centers around the latchkey. "Latchkey problems" refer not only to the time that an adolescent is supposed to be in the house at night and who is to retain the key. The term has been generalized to include other questions, such as whom the adolescent is dating, where the girl and boy go, and related considerations.

125 Latchkey problems is a euphemism used to describe many points of concern about _____ which involve parents and their adolescent children.

dating

126 There are more and sharper conflicts between girls and mothers than between sons and fathers or mothers (Coleman, 1961). Also, there are very few social class differences in number and severity of "_____" conflicts.

latchkey

127 The fact that there are more conflicts between mothers and girls than between fathers and their adolescents is hardly surprising since, in our culture, the _____ has the larger number of contacts with adolescents.

mother

128 This is not to say that fathers demonstrate no concern about their adolescents. Fathers in our culture seem to be particularly concerned about their daughters' dating behavior. This is reflected in a reported increase in _____-_____ conflict when the daughter is about seventeen.

father-daughter

129 Powell (1955) found the greatest number of "latchkey" conflicts for both boys and girls and their mothers occur between fourteen and seventeen years. These are the ages when most parents attempt greater _____ over the dating practices of their children.

control

As one might expect, there are no unequivocal rules about parent-adolescent problems which tell either group what to do. Interpersonal variables are extremely complex. Again, however, it is suggested that the principles of learning theory can be applied to the solution of such problems.

130 If a parent and an adolescent can discriminate a common goal (e.g., can agree beforehand on the time to be home), this agreement can serve to reduce possible conflict. The "time-in" behavior of the adolescent determines the type of consequent supplied by the _____.

parent

131 It would seem advisable that adolescents and parents agree ahead of time on the types of consequences that would follow the observance or nonobservance of the agreement. Agreeing on the _____ itself is often a problem.

consequence

132 *Review:* The latchkey problem has been used in part to illustrate the idea that, for most individuals in our culture, adolescence is a time of gradual emancipation from parental control. Adolescent independence is a term used by some writers to describe this process of _____ _____ from parental control.

133 In the previous unit it was stated that most parents either overtly or covertly want their children to demonstrate responsible self-direction as adults. Gradual emancipation in adolescence can help them to achieve +++++.

134 Most parents report ambivalence about the way their adolescents demonstrate their desire for independence. This _____ about independence may contribute to the problems of gradual emancipation from their control.

135 Some groups and societies have formal rites by which the transition from the status of a child to that of an adult is accomplished. These *rites de passage* serve the purpose of emancipation from childhood dependency to adult _____.

136 For most American adolescents, there are no such rites (the ceremonies for Jewish adolescent boys are an exception). Parents, the church, the school, peers, and the law all may provide different guidelines about when dependency is to be relinquished and _____-_____ is to be assumed.

137 Because of inconsistencies in the ways different social reinforcers affect adolescents, the transition from dependence to _____ is often difficult for them in America.

138 Inconsistencies in social conditioning of adolescents not infrequently occur within the family of the _____.

139 *Review:* There are many ways in which parents can *add* to the problem of gradual emancipation of the adolescent and thus hinder responsible _____-_____. You probably can cite some of these from your own experience or from that of your friends.

In America and Europe, boys tend to demonstrate fewer problems than girls in achieving independence. Ausubel (1955) reports that boys have fewer problems than girls in achieving independence. You might want to

gradual emancipation

responsible self-direction

ambivalence

independence

self-direction

independence (self-direction)

adolescent

self-direction

speculate about why this is so. There are no formulated, simple answers to the problems of adolescent emancipation from parental control. Understanding by both adolescents and their parents of the goals of both groups is obviously required.

Courtship and Marriage

The beginning of adolescence is denoted by physiological changes—the onset of puberty. The end of adolescence is usually denoted by other kinds of events. Legally, an adolescent becomes an adult in the United States when he becomes twenty-one years old and achieves voting privileges (although in many states he is treated as an adult if convicted of a criminal act before that age). From an economic standpoint, an adolescent is usually recognized as an adult when he becomes vocationally self-sufficient, regardless of whether he or she elects to continue to live at home.

Most parents, implicitly or explicitly, begin to treat their children more like adults when they recognize that their adolescent is courting—or being courted. Courtship customs and their significance vary among groups, but among various criteria representing transition from adolescence to adulthood, courtship is treated as a significant milestone on the way to social maturity.

courtship

140 Courtship is characterized chiefly by intent to marry. Customs in courtship vary among different culture groups and even within a culture group. In some societies parents arrange the _____ without regard for the prospective marriage partners.

control

141 Studies of American courtship patterns reveal changes in the degree of control a parent exerts over courting customs. Today parents exert less _____ over courtship than previously (Coleman, 1961).

control

142 Parents are less successful in controlling courtship patterns than previously, but many still try to do so. Persuasion and threat of withdrawal of support are two means parents use to _____ courtship customs.

threat of withdrawal of support

143 Most parents still use persuasion and the ++++ to get their children to court the persons whom they (the parents) desire.

144 Adolescents today demonstrate relatively more independence in selecting courtship partners than they did in the past. They tend to be more _____ of parental control in courtship.

independent

145 Young people today receive more education in general and more information about marriage in particular than did previous generations. Knowledge itself undoubtedly contributes to a more liberal attitude toward _____.

courtship

146 Access to more information (e.g., from schooling and mass media) by today's young adults is accompanied by a tendency to seek premarital advice more than in previous generations. This is another indicator of change in _____ customs in America.

courtship

147 Landis (1951) reported that over 55 per cent of young adult women in today's generation actively sought premarital advice. Only 25 per cent of their mothers had sought _____ _____.

premarital advice

148 Advice seeking during courtship does not ensure the obtaining of appropriate knowledge. It does suggest that young adults probably are exposed to more information about marriage than were previous generations and, as has been said, _____ usually has a liberalizing effect on behavior.

information (knowledge)

149 Engaged couples ordinarily come from the same socioeconomic, religious, national, and racial backgrounds, but "mixed marriages" are on the increase. _____ _____ demonstrate a tendency to break with traditional marriage patterns (Bossard and Boll, 1957).

Mixed marriages

150 Mixed marriages occur more frequently between partners representing different religious, national, and socioeconomic groups than between different racial groups. The number of _____ mixed marriages is actually very small in proportion to other types of mixed marriages.

racial

By far the greatest tendency is to court and marry within one's own culture group. Several studies have shown that, in courtship and marriage, the adage, "Birds of a feather flock together" is more true than its converse, "Opposites attract." College graduates tend to marry college graduates; men of Spanish descent tend to marry women of Spanish descent; Catholics tend to marry Catholics. Socioeconomic status, education, national origin, and religious affiliation are reasonably good predictors of the general characteristics of the person one will marry. As stated previously, however, the trend in America is to cross these traditional boundaries for marital partners. This tendency reflects more liberal courtship and marriage behavior than existed in previous generations.

Sex is one consideration that most people immediately think of when dealing with questions about marriage. The importance of this behavior, both for species survival and personal satisfaction, can hardly be overestimated; but there is, likewise, no necessity to overdramatize it.

number
frequency

151 The number and frequency of sexual outlets for married men and women have been described elsewhere and need not concern us here. Kinsey and others have written several books which indicate the relationship of the _____ and _____ of sexual outlets and thus have provided indexes of "normal" behavior in our culture.[1]

peak

152 The peak of sexual activity in most men is passed prior to, or very early in, their marriage. The _____ of sexual activity in most women is not reached until the late twenties, usually several years after marriage (Kinsey, 1953).

sexual activity

153 Landis (1951) indicated that differences between men and women in peak age _____ _____ are related, for many men and women, to reported satisfaction in marriage.

desire

154 The frequency of reported desire for sexual activity in women and men has been reported in several studies. Reported _____ is related to the menstrual cycle in women.

cycle

155 Ovarian hormones regulate the menstrual _____. The hormones determine when the ovum is released by the ovaries and when menstruation will occur.

ovum

156 The _____ is usually released from the ovaries about fourteen days after the start of menstruation. Release of the ovum is called ovulation.

[1] It should be noted that some scientists feel that Kinsey's data must be taken with several grains of salt since he depended on personal reports of his respondents for the source of his information.

sex desire

cycle

stability (duration)

shorter

separated

divorce
separation

divorce
separation

children

greater (higher)

157   Reported sex desire is related to time of ovulation and menstruation in women. Peaks of reported _____ _____ thus occur about twice per month for many women, although wide variations occur among individual women.

158   Men do not demonstrate the same bimodal curve of reported desire as women. This may be because men do not undergo a biological rhythm similar to the menstrual _____ in women.

Marital Stability

159   Marriage customs, like courtship customs, have changed somewhat in terms of stability. Divorce and separation rates are two criteria used to assess _____ of marriage.

160   At the turn of the twentieth century, approximately 5 per cent of marriages ended in divorce. In 1960 more than 25 per cent of marriages ended in divorce. The rise in divorce rate indicates a _____ duration of marriage.

161   The rise in divorce rate has been accompanied by a rise in rate of legal separation and desertion. Approximately two million married people are _____ each year in the United States.

162   It seems safe to infer that divorce and separation represent dissatisfaction with marriage. However, rise in _____ and _____ rates does not necessarily mean rise in marital unhappiness.

163   That is, there may have been just as high a proportion of unhappy marriages in the past, but social custom or other factors may have limited _____ and _____.

164   As variables, (1) size of family, (2) socioeconomic status, (3) religion, and (4) age are related to divorce. Regarding (1), divorces are twice as common in childless marriages as in marriages with _____ (Jacobson, 1950).

165   Jacobson's study showed an inverse relationship between family size and divorce rate. In other words, the smaller the family, the _____ the probability of divorce.

166 Mr. and Mrs. Abel have four children. Mr. and Mrs. Kant have no children. Other things being equal, which of these couples has a higher probability of divorce or separation? +++++.

Mr. and Mrs. Kant

167 Size of family is only one characteristic related to unsuccessful marriage. Socioeconomic status is another. If there are more divorces and separations among the working class than among the professional-managerial class, marriage stability and _____ status are thus inversely related.

socioeconomic

168 Mr. X is a laborer making $1.05 per hour. Dr. Y is a physician making $20,000 per year. If socioeconomic status is inversely related to divorce rate, which man has a higher probability of being divorced? _____.

Mr. X

169 Size of family and socioeconomic status are related to duration of marriage. You already know that similarity of religious belief between marriage partners is also related to _____ of marriage.

stability (duration)

170 Mixed religious marriages are typically subject to pressures from the families of both husband and wife. This may be why such marriages end in divorce or separation more _____ than do non-mixed religious marriages.

frequently

171 Mixed religious marriages have a higher probability of failure than non-mixed religious marriages, but many _____ _____ marriages succeed admirably, and there is a trend toward them (Bossard and Ball, 1957).

mixed religious

172 Age, family size, socioeconomic status, and religious considerations are positively correlated with separation or divorce. In general, statistics indicate that the younger the marriage age, the _____ the likelihood of divorce or separation (Jacobson, 1950).

greater

173 The age–divorce-rate generalization just given applies particularly to marriages contracted between ages fifteen to thirty. The highest divorce and separation rates occur in the _____ groups.

younger

174 *Review:* Four considerations related to marital disintegration are: (1) family _____, (2) _____ status, (3) _____ affiliation, and (4) _____ at marriage. Perhaps you can think of other factors related to marriage stability.

(1) size
(2) socioeconomic
(3) religious
(4) age

SUMMARY

Adolescence has been described as a time of "storm and stress." Though not necessarily true, this description is often accurate. The onset of puberty, with the attendant development of primary and secondary sex characteristics, is usually accompanied by changes in social behavior and interests. In turn, these may lead to problems for both parents and children.

Not infrequently, parents in the United States are unwilling to give their adolescents the independence and autonomy their children desire. Their opposition often results in family conflict. Conflict may be intensified when the adolescent peer group exerts a relatively continuous influence on the individual by rewarding behavior it considers desirable, regardless of the older generation's approval.

Coupled with the tendency to seek autonomy from parent control, there is some evidence to suggest that older adolescents spend less time in religious activities than they did earlier in life. However, interest in questions about religion continues to be high for college students, even though their active support of religious institutions tends to diminish. Studies of adolescent social behavior suggest that peer socialization in general and social acceptance in particular seem to follow the principles of social learning.

The importance of effective vocational planning during adolescence is emphasized by the relatively high unemployment figures for out-of-school young people between sixteen and twenty-one years of age. Several recent studies indicate that there will be a decrease in the proportion of agricultural and unskilled labor jobs in the near future. Young people with higher educational achievements will receive preference for available sales, managerial, technical, and professional job opportunities.

Problems of vocational selection and placement often occur at about the same time that young people progress from adolescent dating experiences to courtship and marriage. Questions relating to social relationships and sexual compatibility are among the most important problems encountered in the early years of marriage. How they are resolved may determine the degree of satisfaction experienced by each of the marriage partners and the stability of the marriage itself.

Peer socialization, vocational planning, and marital relationships are extremely complex issues. Perhaps because of their complexity, behavioral scientists have not yet come up with hard and fast analyses of, and answers to, the problems that they raise.

REFERENCES

Allport, Gordon W., J. M. Gillespie, and J. Young: "The Religion of the Postwar College Student," *Journal of Psychology*, 25:3–33, 1948.

Ausubel, D., and H. M. Schiff: "Determinants of Individual Differences in Socio-empathetic Ability among Adolescents," *Journal of Social Psychology*, 41:39–56, 1955.

Benedict, R.: *Patterns of Culture*, Houghton Mifflin Company, Boston, 1941.

Bernard, H. W.: *Adolescent Development in America*, Harcourt, Brace & World, Inc., New York, 1957.

Bossard, J., H. S. Ball, and E. S. Ball: *One Marriage — Two Faiths*, The Ronald Press Company, Nw York, 1957.

Coleman, J. S.: *The Adolescent Society*, The Free Press of Glencoe, New York, 1961.

Ehrmann, W. W.: "The Influence of Comparative Social Class Comparison upon Premarital Heterosexual Behavior," *Marriage and Family Living*, 17: 48–53, 1955.

Eister, A. W.: "Some Aspects of Institutional Behavior with Reference to Churches," *American Sociological Review*, 17:64–69, 1952.

Gough, H. G.: "On Making a Good Impression," *Journal of Educational Research*, 46:33–42, 1952.

Harding, V. V.: "A Method of Evaluating Osseous Development from Birth to 14 Years," *Child Development*, 23:181–184, 247–271, 1952.

Hollingshead, A.: *Elmtown's Youth*, John Wiley & Sons, Inc., New York, 1949.

Hurlock, E. B.: *Developmental Psychology*, 2d ed., McGraw-Hill Book Company, New York, 1959.

Jacobson, P. A.: "Differentials in Divorce by Duration of Marriage and Size of Family," *American Sociological Review*, 15:235–244, 1950.

Kagan, J., and F. Moss: *From Birth to Maturity*, John Wiley & Sons, Inc., New York, 1962.

Keislar, E. R.: "Peer Group Ratings of High School Pupils," *Journal of Experimental Education*, 23:275–278, 1955.

Landis, P. H.: "Marriage Preparation in 2 Generations," *Marriage and Family Living*, 13: 155–56, 1951.

Mead, M.: *Male and Female*, William Morrow and Company, Inc., New York, 1949.

Monahan, B.: "Does Age at Marriage Matter in Divorce?" *Social Forces*, 32:81–87, 1953.

Powell, Marvin: "Age and Sex Differences in Degree of Conflict," *Psychological Monographs*, vol. 69, no. 2, 1955.

Pressey, S. L., and A. W. Jones: "1923–1953: 20–60 Year Age Changes in Moral Codes, Anxieties, and Interests, as Shown by the 'X-O' Tests," *Journal of Psychology*, 39:485–502, 1955.

Seidman, J.: *The Adolescent: A Book of Readings*, rev. ed., Holt, Rinehart and Winston, Inc., New York, 1962.

Shuttleworth, F.: "The Adolescent Period: A Graphic Atlas," *Monographs of the Society for Research in Child Development*, vol. 14, no. 1, 1949.

Tyron, C. M.: "Evaluation of Adolescent Personality by Adolescents," *Monographs of the Society for Research in Child Development*, vol. 4, no. 4, 1939.

SELF-REVIEW QUIZ

1 (a) The term _____ means "to grow to maturity"; (b) the term _____ refers to sexual maturity.

2 (a) Primary sex characteristics have to do with _____. (b) Secondary sex characteristics refer to +++++.

3 What are the names of the male and female hormones, the presence of which indicates sexual maturity?

4 In early adolescence, the peer group often supplants the parents as a source of significant social relationships. (a) Use Freud's term to describe the process by which allegiance to a group is formed. (b) Use learning-theory terms to describe why this process occurs.

5 Crowd and clique memberships are affected by several variables. Name three.

6 Which appears to be the least important determinant in adolescent group membership? (a) Family background, (b) socioeconomic status, (c) religious affiliation.

7 What do studies show about relationships between knowledge of right and wrong and actual cheating, lying, altruism, and loyalty.

8 By 1970, the largest proportion of employable youth will have a _____ education.

9 What kind of relationship exists between amount of education and median job income?

10 With reference to dating practice, "playing the field" refers to _____ dating; "going steady" refers to _____ dating.

11 The unit refers to problems related to "time in" at night and to dating problems in general, as (a) _____ problems. The ages at which such problems exist most frequently are between the years (b) _____ and _____.

12 Intent to marry is signified in our culture by _____ customs.

13 So far as tendency to court and to marry within or without one's culture group is concerned, which phrase is more apt for society in the United States?
(a) "Opposites attract."
(b) "Birds of a feather flock together."

14 Name three variables that have been correlated with divorce rates.

part V

Concepts of
Personality

Paul R. Givens

Many explanations have been offered for man's behavior. Those presented in this unit have been particularly influential. Modern literature, drama, poetry, and even the language of the common man have been strongly affected by the forceful and penetrating insights about behavior contributed by Freud and other personality theorists presented in Part V.

The major concepts of psychoanalysis are presented in Unit 1. These viewpoints can be contrasted with those of self-psychology in Unit 2. The educated person should become acquainted with these different viewpoints, not only because they provide intellectual stimulation, but also because they represent some of the most influential explanations for human behavior which are currently available. Unit 3 includes a description of adjustment mechanisms which all of us use in everyday life.

unit 1

Freudian Psychoanalysis

This unit gives a general introduction to personality theory and emphasizes the fundamental concepts of Sigmund Freud. Personality is viewed as the unique, characteristic, and organized responses which a person acquires through the interaction of heredity and environment.

Sigmund Freud, whose contribution to contemporary thinking in both academic and popular circles is considerable, was born in Moravia in 1856 and died in London in 1939. Originally he was trained in neurology but later turned to an analysis of hysteria. His emphasis was on the unconscious, and while others had pointed to the importance of unconscious strivings, Freud systematically worked through a detailed statement of the intricacies of unconscious motivation. Though others who followed him have suggested at times extensive modifications of Freud's concepts, many of his basic concepts have stood the test of careful scrutiny. The modern psychologist would contend, however, that Freud's views should be stated in more behaviorally definable terms so that they could be more easily tested in the laboratory.

The beginning student will want to read translations of Freud's works. *Psychopathology of Everyday Life* is recommended. The student should consult the bibliography at the end of this chapter for other references. C. S. Hall's little book, *A Primer of Freudian Psychology*, is a good secondary source, which deals with what Freud has to say about the motivation of everyday behavior.

Several aspects of Freud's theory are given only passing recognition here. Freud was a meticulous searcher into his own thoughts and feelings. His self-analysis of dreams and other phenomena brought to him many insights. Furthermore, he used the technique of free association to unveil some of the hidden secrets of unconscious thought.

A student is at a great disadvantage today if he has not read some of Freud's works. You should know a great deal about this man who has greatly influenced modern thinking about human behavior.

General Concepts about Personality

1 It is sometimes said that heredity determines what a person is able to do; environmental influences determine what an individual actually does. Human behavior, therefore, involves the interaction of **(1)** _____ and **(2)** _____.

(1) heredity
(2) environment

2 Human behavior results from the _____ of heredity and environmental learning.

interaction

3 The interaction of heredity and environment suggests that the behavior of the individual is determined by *learned* and *unlearned* influences. A pupillary reflex is a(n) **(1)** _____ response and a dislike for red hats is a(n) **(2)** _____ response.

(1) unlearned
(2) learned

4 Unlearned factors combine with _____ factors to determine an individual's responses to his environment.

learned (acquired)

5 The total set of responses which are characteristic of an individual is often referred to as the individual's *personality*. Although this is not a complete definition, it emphasizes that the term personality involves behavior which is _____ of the individual.

characteristic

6 The total set of responses which consistently occur in the individual's behavior is a brief (but as yet incomplete) definition of _____.

personality

7 Since we want to describe behavior which is characteristic of a person, we must conclude that personality involves the responses which _____ the person.

characterize

8 Another key idea of psychologists in defining personality is the concept that an individual tends to *organize* his responses in a *unique* way. In order to make our definition more complete, therefore, we must recognize that individuals differ from one another in that each person is _____ in his manner of organizing responses.

unique

9 To suggest that Bill and John will not respond to the same situation in the same way is to say that each of them is unique in his organization of responses. Bill will not _____ his responses in the same way as John.

organize

10 By organization of responses we mean that we interpret stimuli in terms of our past experiences and our present hopes, fears, and other expectancies and that these determine how the responses will be _____.

organized

11 Simply knowing that a picture of a woman is presented to you is not sufficient to predict your response to the picture. If the picture is of your mother, you will give one kind of organized response; if it is that of a stranger, you will _____ your responses in a different way.

organize

12 In review, we have said that personality involves characteristic responses. To say "John usually acts this way," is to indicate that there are certain responses which _____ John's behavior.

characterize

13 Unique responses are also emphasized. To say, "John can dance like no other person," is to say that his personality is also composed of _____ responses.

unique

14 To say, "You can't always tell how John will react to a girl," is to suggest that John is capable of _____ his responses to his environment in such a way that simply knowing that he is with a girl is not sufficient to predict his response.

organizing

15 The three key words which are necessary for the definition of personality are: **(1)** _____ responses, **(2)** _____ responses, and **(3)** _____ responses.

characteristic
organized
unique

16 The term personality is used in everyday speech to refer to social attractiveness. In referring to Mary as "having a good personality," we are saying that Mary is socially _____.

attractive

17 _____ _____ is not used by psychologists and other behavioral scientists as a criterion for the definition of personality. The term is more likely to be used by the ordinary person in describing personality.

social attractiveness

18 It is difficult to study all the factors which affect an individual's way of _____ his responses, because much of his behavior is covert (within the individual) rather than overt (open to public observation).

organizing

19 The behavior which we are most likely to be able to observe and measure is _____ behavior. For example, we can see an individual scratch his head, talk to others, or throw a ball.

overt

20 Let's go over this again. Covert means _____;
overt means _____.

within
without

21 While overt behavior is often available for measurement, the behavioral scientist is often able to make intelligent guesses about the nature of the inner, or _____,
responses.

covert

22 The inner, or _____, responses are often referred
to as the "real" personality, which is made up of organized beliefs, values, expectancies, and similar phenomena.

covert

23 The inner or covert responses make up the _____
personality.

real

24 Thus, we find it difficult to measure the characteristics
of the _____ personality.

real

25 Sometimes personality theorists refer to a person's
real personality as being that part of him which is covert
and thus difficult to _____.

measure

26 While the direct measurement of _____ behavior is difficult, it is still possible to infer certain characteristics of an individual's private world.

covert

27 The effect of the individual's organized covert world
can be observed and _____.

measured

28 Just as the physical scientist may observe the effects
of an electron without having seen one, so the behavioral
scientist may describe man's _____ behavior by observing and measuring his overt behavior.

covert

29 As the behavioral scientist makes inferences regarding the inner (_____) organization of individuals,
he arrives at general concepts which are designed to
explain individual and group behavior.

covert

30 Such concepts are referred to as explanatory concepts. Personality theorists attempt to construct _____
_____ which are reliable.

explanatory
concepts

31 When I suggest that John will strike George if George
knocks his bike over, I am proposing a "frustration-leads-
to-aggression" concept as an explanation for John's behavior. This kind of concept is called an _____ concept.

explanatory

Behavioral scientists attempt to develop a small number of concepts to explain a large range of human responses. The benefits of comprehensive concepts are obvious; they permit the inclusion of many particular behavior descriptions and increase effective communication.

Tension Reduction

Tension reduction is a concept which has had wide acceptance in the behavioral sciences. This explanatory concept suggests that behavior is continued if it results in tension reduction for the organism.

32 Learned behavior, i.e., behavior which changes as a result of experience, occurs, according to some personality theorists, because such behavior results in the reduction of

tension
_____ .

33 Most personality theorists believe that learning accounts for a great number of man's responses. This is not to say that man has no built-in unlearned responses. Reflexes, which are relatively simple, unlearned responses

reflex
to stimuli, are built-in responses. A _____ , however, is not an instinct.

34 An instinct is defined as a complex unlearned pattern of responses. Since it is "built into" the organism, it is not

learned
_____ .

35 The difference between a reflex and an instinct is that a reflex is a simple, unlearned response, whereas an

complex
instinct is a _____ , unlearned pattern of responses.

36 If I flash a light in the eyes of a dog, the pupils

reflex
will dilate; this is a _____ . The fact that a dog may go through very involved procedures to care for its young

instinct
would be considered an _____ .

37 Another feature of instincts is that they are less stereotyped than reflexes. We say then that instincts differ

more
from reflexes in that they are _____ [more/less]

less
complex and _____ [more/less] stereotyped.

38 Variability in instinctive behavior results in instincts

reflexes
having greater adaptive aspects than _____ .

39 Instinctive behavior is _____ [more/less] vari-

more
able than reflexes.

40 Write "yes" beside those characteristics which define instincts.

_____ complex
_____ stereotyped behavior
_____ learned
_____ adaptive
_____ simple
_____ varied behavior
_____ unlearned
_____ nonadaptive

complex
varied behavior
unlearned
adaptive

41 Since most modern personality theories emphasize learning, they are not based on the concept of unlearned responses such as _____ and _____.

reflexes
instincts (either
order)

42 Some theories use the concept of need. A human need refers to a lack or deficit within the individual. A hunger need is a condition wherein the individual lacks _____.

food (nourishment)

43 Human needs may be biogenic or learned. If they are biogenic, they arise from something the body lacks. A need for nourishment is a _____ need.

biogenic

44 A learned need is one which the individual has acquired by experience. For example, the need for status is a _____ need.

learned

45 The tension-reduction theory says that whenever an individual has a need for something, he becomes tense. This tension is often referred to as a drive. A drive for status signifies that the organism _____ status and is striving for it.

needs (lacks)

46 In the above example, the act of striving for the status represents the _____.

drive

47 The tension-reduction concept implies that the individual who has a need will strive to reduce the _____ caused by the need.

tension (drive)

48 The tension-reduction concept states that the tension, which is the _____, will persist until behavior of the individual reduces it.

drive

49 A person having a need for status will respond in a number of ways until he has _____ the tension resulting from the need. The behavior resulting from the drive is often referred to as instrumental behavior.

reduced (eliminated)

50 We say therefore that any behavior resulting in tension reduction is called _____ behavior.

instrumental

51 Instrumental behavior is usually directed toward a goal. Thus, a hungry person will seek the _____ of food.

goal

52 The order of events in a tension-reduction diagram is as follows: A need (or **(1)** _____) → drive (a state of **(2)** _____) → instrumental behavior → goal.

(1) lack (deficit)
(2) tension

53 Let us go over an example of this. Suppose John lacks companionship, which he has learned to require. We say that John has a _____ for companionship.

need

54 John's lack of companionship results in tension (drive), and he therefore seeks admission to a club. Seeking admission to the club is the **(1)** _____ _____; admission to the club is his **(2)** _____.

(1) instrumental
    behavior
(2) goal

55 This kind of diagram (need → drive → instrumental behavior → goal) is helpful in understanding behavior as explained in terms of _____ _____.

tension reduction

56 Tension reduction is one kind of explanatory _____ used in personality theory.

concept

57 Whenever behavior is directed toward a particular goal, we say the organism is motivated. Motivation, therefore, requires that the behavior be _____-directed.

goal

58 The term which describes goal-directed behavior resulting from a state of tension is _____.

motivation

We shall return later to a consideration of some personality theories based primarily on the concept of tension reduction. Many personality theorists (e.g., Allport, 1955; May, 1953) argue that much of man's behavior cannot be adequately accounted for by the concept of tension reduction. They argue that there are other very important explanatory concepts in personality theory. One alternative is the principle of goal direction.

Goal Direction

59 Many people prefer to feel that they are striving for goals, rather than responding to inner tensions. Therefore, _____ direction is an important explanatory concept in personality theory.

goal

(1) tension
reduction
(2) goal direction

60 The two explanatory concepts we have mentioned are **(1)** _____ _____ and **(2)** _____ _____.

goal

61 While the tension-reduction concept holds that deprivation tends to strengthen drives, it is found that prolonged deprivation may actually weaken _____-seeking behavior.

goal

62 The significant concept determining whether or not a person will continue to strive for a goal is the perceived probability of success; then he will continue to strive toward a _____.

increases
(strengthens)

63 If goal achievement is realized, it is sometimes found that the effect has been a strengthening of an expectancy rather than a reduction of tension. The effect of reaching a goal, therefore, _____ effort rather than decreases it. For example, a person may acquire a bachelor's degree in college and consequently be motivated to achieve a higher degree.

tension-reduction

decreases

64 The notion of increase of effort resulting from goal achievement seems contradictory to the _____-_____ concept, which holds that goal achievement _____ [increases/decreases] motivation.

equilibrium

65 Although the tension-reduction concept holds that the ultimate result of goal achievement is restoration of equilibrium, goal achievement often seems to disturb _____.

goals
equilibrium

66 Human behavior seems often to be directed toward the attainment of _____ rather than the restoration of _____.

functional autonomy

67 Gordon Allport, an American personality theorist, notes that man often continues to strive for goals long after they have ceased to reduce biological tensions. He refers to this as *functional autonomy of drives*. The tendency of certain motives to become independent of the biological needs from which they originated is called _____ _____ of drives.

autonomous
(independent)

68 It has been found, for example, that rats will continue to dig through sand after they no longer have to do so in order to get food. The fact that they persist in their digging illustrates that the rat's behavior has become functionally _____ of the original drive which instigated it (Earl, 1957).

69 The concept of goal direction involves not only goals of which we are aware, i.e., conscious goals, but goals of which we are not aware, i.e., _____ goals.

unconscious

70 Our behavior may result from both _____ and _____ goals.

conscious
unconscious

71 Many personality theorists (especially the psycho-analysts) emphasize the importance of unconscious motivation. A child may continually irritate his younger brother but be unaware of the basis of his behavior because the goal is _____

unconscious
(unknown)

72 Goal direction implies that the expectations of the individual are very important in determining his behavior. These may result in the development of (1) _____ or (2) _____ goals.

(1) conscious
(2) unconscious

73 Several personality theorists feel that there are certain universal _____ toward which all men strive. The idea of a particular goal that guides man's destiny is called a teleological viewpoint.

goals

74 Teleology is the idea that everything in nature can be explained in terms of purpose. The idea that all men are destined to feel inferior is a _____ viewpoint.

teleological

75 Explaining man's behavior in terms of past events is often referred to as causality, whereas accounting for man's behavior in terms of where he is headed (i.e., his goals) is a _____ explanation.

teleological

76 If Johnny's cheating on a test is due to past experience in which he was rewarded for cheating, this would be a _____ [causal/teleological] explanation of his behavior.

causal

77 If I say that Johnny's cheating is due to his desire to raise his grade-point average, then this would be a _____ explanation of his behavior.

teleological

78 Several personality theorists (e.g., Allport, 1955; May, 1953) emphasize teleological as well as _____ explanations of human behavior.

causal

79 It becomes apparent that tension-reduction theorists are more apt to emphasize causality, while goal-direction theorists may consider _____ as well as causality.

teleology

80 If we were to hold strictly to causality, we would say that Johnny is a bully because he has learned to use bullying as a way of reducing _____.

tension

81 To hold that Johnny's behavior resulted from goal-directed purposive motivation is to suggest a _____ explanation.

teleological

In summary, we have said that personality theories are developed to explain man's behavior. Some theories are based primarily on the explanatory concept of tension reduction; others are founded on that of goal direction.

Tension reduction stresses the idea that reduction of tension is the motivating force in all behavior (see frames 47, 48). However, the concept of goal direction stresses the idea that man's behavior is greatly influenced by the goals he establishes and strives for (see frames 65, 66).

Self-direction

A third explanatory concept in personality theory involves the idea of self-direction. In order to understand this principle, we must understand the use of the term "self."

Self-direction is based on the general premise that much of man's behavior can be predicted by knowing the feelings and thoughts the individual has about himself. A man may be greatly distressed if he disagrees with this evaluation but may feel little irritation at being called a failure if he perceives himself as a failure and accepts this judgment as true.

82 The term self is used in this way as being similar to an object; i.e., we have an attitude toward the _____ as an object.

self

83 We may view the self in somewhat the same manner in which we view our car or our house. We have attitudes toward the self; thus we say it is viewed as an _____.

object

84 The self may also be thought of as a process. We may think of the self as a group of events such as thinking and feeling. We may think of the self as object or as _____.

process

85 If we say, "He has a high opinion of himself," we are speaking of the self as **(1)** _____; if we suggest that his self will react to his failure in school, we are speaking of the self as **(2)** _____.

(1) object

(2) process

When we view the self as a process, we are thinking of it as a doer; whereas the self as an object involves all the reactions we have toward what we think, say, and do.[1]

Various writers use the term in different ways; sometimes they speak of the self as process, sometimes as object.

86 Self theorists submit that the individual's unique reactions to his surroundings are determined by his concept of _____.

self

87 For example, Johnny may be quite humiliated and embarrassed upon receiving much attention at a party, because he has a self-image which includes the feeling, "I am not worthy of the attention of others." Thus, his self-_____ determines his reaction.

image

88 Self theorists would further insist that the individual's self-image influences the reactions of the individual to an extent that knowledge of _____-_____ is essential if an individual's behavior is to be understood.

self-image

89 In summary, we have said that theories of personality may be classified in terms of three general explanatory concepts: **(1)** _____ _____, **(2)** _____ _____, **(3)** _____-_____.

(1) tension
 reduction
(2) goal direction
(3) self-direction

While a particular approach to personality may include aspects of all three of these concepts, generally each theory emphasizes one and minimizes the others. All personality theorists do not agree on a single explanatory concept of human behavior. Such disagreement is to be expected among personality theorists because there is much to be learned about the intricate workings of the human personality.

During the last fifty years, much has been discovered about human behavior, of course, and the personality theories we shall be considering throughout this unit are efforts to make sense out of the information we now have and that which we still need.

[1] This distinction is made by C. Hall and G. Lindzey, 1957.

Freudian Psychoanalysis

The first personality theory we shall consider is Freudian psychoanalysis. It originated with Sigmund Freud (1856 to 1939). Freud's personality theory has greatly influenced the thinking of modern Americans, novelists and playwrights as well as specialists in the "helping professions" of medicine, psychology, and social work.

Although the complete works of Freud are available, the beginning student is encouraged to read *The Basic Writings of Sigmund Freud* or *An Outline of Psychoanalysis*, both of which are available in paperback form.

Figure 18. Sigmund Freud (Collection Viollet, Paris). (G. Kisker, *The Disorganized Personality*, p. 64, McGraw-Hill Book Company, 1964.)

**Freudian
psychoanalysis**

90 We refer to Freud's theory as _____ _____ because there are other revisions of psychoanalysis which followed Freud's original writings.

91 Sigmund Freud was trained in medicine and, thus, many of his concepts evolved from clinical experience, i.e., the experience of talking to _____ in his office.

patients (people)

92 Further, Freudian theory was developed primarily from _____ experience in talking with abnormal patients.

clinical

93 Freud, however, developed some penetrating insights into human behavior which apply to all individuals, whether they are normal or _____.

abnormal

94 Freud did not only develop a personality theory. He also instigated a method of treating mental illness which also carries the name psychoanalysis. In our thinking in this book, we are concerned with psychoanalysis as a _____ theory rather than as a method of treatment.

personality

Conflict and the Components of Personality

Freud emphasized that the human personality is motivated by tension caused by conflict. This suggests immediately that his theory would fit under the general principles of tension reduction. Further, Freud felt that nothing occurs by chance; everything is determined by the organism interacting with the environment. In the process of interacting, conflicts may arise between the fundamental urges of the organism and the restrictions of the environment.

95 In order to understand human behavior, we must know how the (1) _____ and the (2) _____ interact to cause conflict.

**(1) organism
(2) environment**

96 Personality conflict can be explained, Freud proposed, once we know about the components of personality. He suggests that there are three basic aspects of personality: the id, the ego, and the superego. These components of (1) _____ are intricately involved in creating (2) _____ within the individual.

**(1) personality
(2) conflict**

97 The id is a term used to describe all the uncivilized animal-like impulses the individual experiences. "The urge to kill," for example, would be an impulse of the _____.

id

98 While we often refer to id impulses in the third person (as "it" making one do something), Freud did not mean to suggest that the _____ was a thing or a "little man" within us.

id

99 The id consists of all biopsychological impulses present at birth. Id _____ are always seeking expression.

impulses

100 The id obeys the pleasure principle, i.e., id impulses are seeking to obtain _____ and avoid pain.

pleasure

101 (1) _____ avoidance and (2) _____ seeking are typical behavior of infants. Therefore, Freud suggests that infants' behavior results primarily from (3) _____ impulses.

(1) pain
(2) pleasure
(3) id

102 Freud proposed that in order for the id to avoid pain and experience pleasure, it uses two processes: *reflex action* and *primary process*. These processes are for the purpose of avoiding _____ and experiencing _____.

pain
pleasure

103 Sneezing and coughing would be examples of _____ action.

reflex

104 The primary process refers to attempts to release energy (reduce tension) by forming an image of that which will reduce tension. A thirsty person imagining a glass of water illustrates the _____ _____ which aims to reduce tension.

primary process

105 Freud felt that nocturnal dreams are experiences wherein the organism is attempting to realize wish fulfillment and thus reduce (1) _____. Nocturnal dreams, therefore, illustrate the (2) _____ _____ at work.

(1) tension
(2) primary process

106 The processes which carry out the purposes of the id are called _____ action and _____ process.

reflex
primary

107 Give some examples of reflex action and primary process. +++++.

If you cannot, refer to frames 102 to 105.

108 Freud notes, therefore, that the individual has a set of raw, untamed impulses which make up the (1) _____, and that they follow the (2) _____ principle.

(1) id
(2) pleasure

109 Since the individual cannot survive simply by following id impulses, it becomes necessary for him to react realistically to his surroundings. The set of tendencies to do this is called the ego. The ego, therefore, is more _____ than the id.

realistic

110   While the infant's behavior consists primarily of id reactions, he soon learns that certain objects help him to get pleasure while others mean pain. These learnings and the reactions resulting from them make up the _____.

111   The id is said to obey the _____ principle.

112   The ego is learned and obeys the reality principle; i.e., tension reduction will be delayed in order to release it more fully at a later time. When a child screams for his ice cream, we say he is obeying the _____ principle.

113   When the child agrees to wait until lunch for his ice cream, we say he is obeying the _____ _____.

114   Stagner (1961, p. 315) writes, "Through perception we become aware both of objects which promise pleasure and of threats and potential punishments. If the perceptual system is working satisfactorily, these are balanced judgmentally, and a decision is reached as to whether the amount of pleasure to be gotten is worth the pain involved." He is describing Freud's concept of the _____.

115   Freud held that the ego obeys the reality principle by means of the *secondary process*. This term refers to the workings of the individual's intelligence in conducting realistic behavior. The secondary process may be defined simply as _____ thinking.

116   If a person feels hungry, he may have an impulse to rob a store. This illustrates an _____ impulse.

117   If a person decides to work for money to buy food, he is probably obeying the _____ principle.

118   The plan to work for money in order to buy food illustrates the _____ process.

119   Freud suggested that id impulses are often inhibited by the _____ because of fear of punishment. That is, the ego "has the power" to punish unacceptable impulses from the id.

120   Freud reasoned, however, that fear of punishment is not the only reason for inhibition of _____ impulses. Rather, the individual inhibits unacceptable impulses because of inner standards of "goodness" and "badness." He proposed, therefore, a superego.

---

ego

pleasure

pleasure

reality principle

ego

realistic

id

reality

secondary

ego

id

121 The superego is made up in part of what we popularly call "conscience." It is our concept of what is "right" and "wrong," "good" or "bad." The superego tends to inhibit impulses of the _____.

id

122 The id and the superego are often antagonistic; therefore the superego tends to _____ the id impulses.

inhibit

123 What we consider as good or bad behavior is determined by our _____.

conscience
(superego)

124 Freud points out that since the id "knows no morality," i.e., it is amoral, it must be controlled. The sense of right and wrong which constitutes part of the superego is _____ from experiences with other individuals.

learned

125 The superego regulates id impulses and is _____ [moral/amoral]. The superego also represents our concept of our ideal selves. This is sometimes referred to as the ego ideal.

moral

126 The concept of ourselves at our very best is the _____ _____.

ego ideal

127 The superego, therefore, is made up of two parts: (1) _____, (2) _____ _____.

(1) conscience
(2) ego ideal

128 That behavior which parents teach us is wrong makes up our _____.

conscience

129 That behavior for which they reward us becomes the _____ _____.

ego ideal

130 We tend to accept those values which our parents and others hold. Thus we say that we introject, i.e., accept as our own, the morality of others. Consequently, since we _____ the morality of others, we may feel guilty for behavior which violates the principle of this morality.

introject

131 We learn to view our behavior as good or bad as we observe other significant persons in our lives and determine what for us is _____.

morality (good and bad behavior)

132 One of the main functions of the superego is to strive for perfection. In order to do this, the _____ must inhibit id impulses and persuade the ego to substitute moralistic goals for _____ goals.

superego

realistic

133 It may be said, then, that the superego strives for _____.

perfection

realistic

134 The ego demands _____ responses.

pleasure
pain

135 The id strives for _____ and the avoidance of _____.

These three components of personality (the id, the ego, and the superego) are presumed to work in unison under the organization of the ego.

Freudian psychoanalysis places much emphasis on conflict as motivation for behavior. Intrapersonal conflict involves the interaction of the id, ego, and superego. Furthermore, it also involves the restrictions of the environment.

Concepts of Motivation

Now that we have some idea of Freud's view of the components of personality, we shall examine his concepts of man's basic motivation. What are the driving forces of man? To answer this question is to deal with the concept of motivation. Though Freud went through several revisions of his theory, he finally suggested that man inherits life instincts and death instincts. Freud did not make a long list of motives; rather, he settled for two major kinds of instincts.

While many contemporary behavioral scientists feel that the concept of instinct is an unacceptable way of explaining behavior, we must understand the way Freud used the term, lest some confusion results in interpreting his notions regarding instinct. The German word *trieb,* which Freud used to describe the two basic motives, should probably be translated as "drive" rather than "instinct."

life
death

136 Taking these translation difficulties into account, we may understand that Freud felt that the _____ instincts and _____ instincts were categories into which our important motives could be classified.

death

137 The life instincts include those urges which have to do with the survival of the organism; the destructive urges of man make up the _____ instinct.

libido

138 Life instincts derive their energy from the libido, a word used to denote all the mental energy available to the individual. The total life energy of the individual makes up the _____.

libido	**139** A significant concept of psychoanalysis is the idea that every person has only a limited store of _____, or mental energy.
psychoanalytic	**140** The strength of this energy and the way it is used constitutes an essential feature of Freudian _____ theory.
sex (sexual)	**141** Freud felt that a large amount of libidinal energy is invested in the sex urge. This would suggest that the way in which _____ energy is used determines much of man's personality.
sex	**142** The term "sex" is used by Freudian psychoanalysis in a very broad sense. It applies to several forms of cutaneous satisfactions. Freud did not use the term _____ to refer only to genital behavior.
life libido	**143** The sex urge is an aspect of the _____ instinct which uses much _____ energy. It is present in infants and children as well as in adults.
cutaneous	**144** As Freud used the term, sex includes all kinds of cutaneous satisfactions. Thus, sexual experience in children would include sucking behavior, reaction to stroking of the skin, and similar _____ satisfactions.
sexual	**145** Areas of sexual stimulation are at first diffuse in the newborn. However, as the child gets older, the areas of _____ stimulation become more localized.
localized	**146** As the person develops, the regions of sexual stimulation become more _____ rather than diffuse.
cathexis	**147** In order to understand how the libidinal energy manages to influence personality growth, we must understand Freud's concept of cathexis. Cathexis is the investment of libidinal energy in an *idea, memory, object,* or *activity.* Thus, if I love someone, Freud would hold that this person is an object _____ for me.
memories ideas activities	**148** It is important to note that we may have not only a cathexis for objects but also for _____, _____, and _____.
object (memory idea, activity)	**149** The libidinal energy is very transient, so that it can be placed on an _____ and then withdrawn.
person	**150** The very young child places much of the energy on himself as a love object, but later may place much libidinal energy on another _____.

151 There are several different directions in which libidinal energy may move. For instance, it may move toward self (narcissism), toward others (object love), or toward unreal fantasies (introversion). Libidinal energy, therefore, is not constantly fixed on a particular object or idea, but is capable of _____.

moving (changing)

152 The movement of libidinal energy toward self is called _____.

narcissism

153 Sometimes our energies become fixed on infantile love objects. Freud referred to this as fixation. Energy directed toward self is _____, that directed toward infantile love objects is fixation.

narcissism

154 An example of directing energy toward an infantile love object might be found in an adult sucking his thumb. This is called _____ of energy.

fixation

155 An adult may find himself to be quite inadequate because his libidinal energies are _____ at an infantile level.

fixated

156 When libidinal energy does become fixed, the libidinal energies often are directed into socially acceptable channels. Freud referred to this as sublimation. If the individual does not direct the energy toward the self in the form of _____, or toward unreal fantasies, then he may sublimate the energies.

narcissism

157 If a woman has strong desires to place libidinal energies on a child of her own but is unable to marry, she may _____ her energies by babysitting for other women's children.

sublimate

158 Let us review some of the names given to the ways in which libidinal energy is distributed. Match the following:

(a)—1

(b)—3
(c)—2

(a) sublimation   1. directing toward socially accepted behavior
(b) fixation   2. self-love
(c) narcissism   3. remaining on an infantile level

159 Earlier, the concept of cathexis was introduced. You will recall that Freud defines the investment of energy in an idea, memory, object, or activity as _____. We should also note that energy is also used in a more negative way by the ego to restrain the id from acting impulsively. This use of energy is called anticathexis.

cathexis

anticathexis

160 The use of energy in a negative way to restrain the ego from acting impulsively is called _____.

Freud discussed extensively the various ways in which the ego defends against id impulses and referred to these as defense mechanisms. We shall discuss a few defense mechanisms in a succeeding unit.

You will recall that Freud spoke of the life and death instincts. Freud did not have a great deal to say about the latter instincts because he thought they worked quite subtly.

death

161 The individual, according to Freud, expresses death tendencies in many ways. An excessive desire for sleep, a tendency to bite one's fingernails, or willful neglect of personal health, have been referred to as illustrations of the _____ instinct in man.

death

162 In referring to the death instinct, Freud wrote that "the goal of all life is death." All men, therefore, have a wish to die. This led to his principle of the _____ instinct (C. Hall and G. Lindzey, 1957, p. 40).

(1) life

(2) death

163 An interesting Freudian concept is that aggression in men is an instance of self-destructive tendencies directed outwardly toward others. It can be seen, therefore, that love for objects or people is part of the **(1)** _____ instincts, while aggression is a manifestation of the **(2)** _____ instincts.

We have noted in the frames of this section that Freud had much to say about human motivation. He proposed that every person has a limited store of mental energy, called libidinal energy. This energy may be directed toward self (narcissism), remain on an infantile level (fixation) or be expressed in socially approved behavior (sublimation). Investment of this energy can be made in ideas, memories, or objects, and this is called cathexis.

The totality of man's striving is viewed by Freud as involving an attempt to show constructive responses (life instinct) or destructive responses (death instinct).

Conscious and Unconscious Processes

In order to understand more fully the workings of the personality as outlined by Freudian psychoanalysis, we must examine more closely the relationship of *conscious, preconscious,* and *unconscious* behavior. Freud was an emphatic believer in the significance of unconscious influences on personality development.

unaware (not conscious of)

164 We have said earlier in this program that to be "conscious" is to be aware of our behavior and surroundings, whereas to be "unconscious" indicates that we are _____ of our behavior and surroundings.

(1) conscious
(2) preconscious
(3) unconscious

165 Psychoanalysts usually refer to three levels of awareness: (1) _____, (2) _____, and (3) _____.

unconscious

166 Freud attributed the greatest significance to the _____ level of awareness.

Figure 19. A possible result of unconscious reactions and impulses. Unconscious desires for self-destruction often cause traffic accidents.

167 The word conscious refers to our mental content (thoughts and feelings) of which we are aware. For instance, if I decide to kick a stone, I may be completely aware of my actions. Consciousness, therefore, is not a mystical state, but simply refers to degrees of _____.

awareness

168 While we speak of "the" conscious or "the" unconscious, actually these are not things located anywhere; rather, they are terms describing the degree of awareness of our _____ and _____ and surroundings.

thoughts
feelings

169 Preconscious thoughts are those which can quite easily become conscious because there is little resistance (anticathexis) to their becoming known to the individual. Remembering your house number may involve bringing the number from the _____ to the _____ level.

preconscious
conscious

170 Bringing a thought from the preconscious to the conscious level simply means increasing our _____ of it.

awareness

171 It is easier to become aware of what we are thinking if the thoughts have an association with language. It is difficult to remember early childhood experiences because they occurred before the development of _____.

language

172 In order to bring an experience to the _____ level, we must be able to label it with words or perhaps images.

conscious

173 If you are unable to think of an experience, then you cannot symbolize it. It is necessary, therefore, to be able to _____ an experience in order to be aware of it and recall it.

symbolize

174 The individual must at least be able to symbolize an experience, i.e., give meaning to it, before he will be able to _____ it.

recall (remember)

175 If it is extremely difficult or impossible to bring a thought to the conscious level, then it is said to be _____ rather than preconscious.

unconscious

176 A person may be irritable in a particular situation but is not aware of the cause of his irritability. Perhaps he is anxious because he is in the presence of intellectually superior individuals. He cannot verbalize this feeling at the present because he is not conscious of it. After some reflection on the occasion, the individual may be able to _____ his feelings.

symbolize

177 Freud further claimed that energy is expended in the inhibition of a thought. The use of energy for this purpose is called anti_____.

cathexis

178 An example: If a boy tries to remember the name of an old girl friend, there is a cathexis for remembering her name. However, if the girl friend discarded him for another, there may be an _____, or inhibiting force, which causes him to forget her name.

anticathexis

179 The opposing forces of a cathexis and anticathexis set up what Freud called endopsychic conflicts. These are conflicts _____ [within/without] the individual rather than between the individual and his environment.

within

180 From our earlier discussion of id, ego, and superego relationships, we can see that there are many conflicts between the id and the _____, and between the ego and the _____. Freud indicates that the superego and the id do not usually come directly in conflict with each other.

ego
superego

181 Conflicts within the personality often cause the individual to keep certain _____ out of consciousness.

responses (thoughts, feelings)

182 The process by which the individual excludes from consciousness certain thoughts which cause anxiety is called repression. This is a way of refusing to recognize unwelcome _____.

thoughts

183 A large part of the individual's unconscious is made up of those thoughts which have been _____ from the conscious.

repressed

184 When unwelcome thoughts are _____, Freud contended that they still have a great influence on the individual's thoughts and actions.

repressed

185 For example, one may feel hatred toward his mother, but he _____ the thought because he has been taught not to feel this way. However, he may punish her in subtle ways—by being late for meals, forgetting to pick up clothes, and so forth.

represses

Consciousness is defined here as those thoughts and feelings which are within awareness. Unconsciousness indicates a state wherein the individual is unable to symbolize his thoughts and feelings. These terms are simply convenient ways of describing our levels of awareness, and they are therefore useful in understanding repression. Repression is the process of keeping out of consciousness those thoughts and feelings which are threatening to the individual when brought to awareness.

In this section it has been emphasized that there are degrees of consciousness. Repression is a process we shall discuss later in more detail. It is sometimes easily detectable in the behavior of others. Can you think of a situation wherein you have observed evidence of it in others?

Anxiety

Freud noted that individuals have a kind of built-in "alarm system" which tells them when there is danger of unwelcome ideas reaching conscious expression. This is called anxiety. Anxiety is tension resulting in physiological changes (e.g., increased heartbeat, increased breathing, etc.) and feelings of dread and inadequacy. Having unconscious feelings of guilt, for example, may result in anxiety.

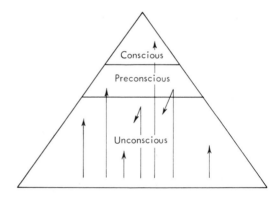

Figure 20. A schematic representation of the degrees of consciousness and the repression of unacceptable impulses. (G. Kisker, *The Disorganized Personality*, p. 145, McGraw-Hill Book Company, 1964.)

186 Anxiety involves physiological tension, but it also involves changes in the thoughts of the individual (see Knapp, 1963). When a person shows anxiety, there are both _____ changes and changes in what the individual _____.

physiological
thinks

187 When we are very anxious about something, we feel actual muscle (1) _____ but also a tendency to (2) _____ about things related to our problems.

(1) tension
(2) think

physiological

188 In anxiety, therefore, we have _____ changes (e.g., the heart beats faster, muscles become tense) as well as changes in what we think about.

189 Freud classified three kinds of anxiety, each according to its source: reality anxiety, neurotic anxiety, and moral anxiety. These are not qualitatively different but rather are classified according to the _____ of the anxiety.

source

190 Reality anxiety results from the perception of an actual or anticipated physical danger to the person. The tension and other feelings resulting from the danger of getting run down by a train is _____ _____.

reality anxiety

191 Freud felt that reality anxiety may be either inborn or result from learned responses to certain situations. Freud felt, therefore, that such anxiety is due to either _____ or _____ influences.

hereditary (inborn)
environmental
(learned)

192 A person may be taught ways of dealing with actual physical danger. For instance, the army trains soldiers to develop certain habits in reaction to the tension of _____ _____.

reality anxiety

193 Freud felt that there is another source of anxiety, which is a feeling of danger when the instincts are seeking expression. This he called neurotic anxiety. It is a fear which occurs when there is a possibility that the anticathexis of the ego will fail to prevent expression of _____.

instincts

194 For example, a person may have strong hostile id impulses which are attempting to break through the restraints, or **(1)** _____, of the ego. The tension he feels as a result of this is **(2)** _____ anxiety.

(1) anticathexis
(2) neurotic

195 Sometimes neurotic anxiety is expressed in the form of phobia, which is a highly persistent irrational fear. If a person was extremely afraid of mice, water, or moustaches, he would be demonstrating a _____.

phobia

196 A phobia is a fear which is out of proportion to any actual danger involved. The resulting tension is an example of _____ _____.

neurotic anxiety

197 Freud suggested the interesting hypothesis that a feared object may actually be desired or may symbolize something desired. The threatened breakthrough of the desire causes the highly persistent irrational fear called a _____.

phobia

198 Neurotic anxiety presumably requires much work on the part of the _____. For this reason, it is more trouble than _____ anxiety, for which the individual is usually better prepared.

ego
reality

199 An example of a phobia having a basis in desire may be found in a situation wherein a boy has a phobia reaction to dances. Whenever he goes to a dance, he experiences difficult breathing and must leave the situation. The dance may symbolize closeness to girls, which he desires. The phobia reaction, which is a highly persistent _____ fear, protects him from his desires.

irrational

200 Neurotic anxiety involves essentially the "fight" between the instincts of the _____ and the restraining forces of the _____. This fight is characteristic of normal people as well as of mental patients. Most of us have developed some neurotic anxiety as a result of being punished for being impulsive.

id
ego

201 To summarize what we have said, we have mentioned two of the three kinds of anxiety which Freud spoke of. These are: (1) _____ anxiety and (2) _____ anxiety.

reality
neurotic

202 Reality anxiety involves fear of actual or real _____; neurotic anxiety involves fear that _____ impulses will be expressed.

danger
id

203 Freud describes a third kind of anxiety, moral anxiety, which results from the superego censoring the individual's overt or covert behavior. The censoring of behavior is done by the two parts of the superego: the (1) _____, and (2) the _____ _____.

(1) conscience
(2) ego ideal

204 If a person feels ashamed because he has stolen something, the tension and personal unhappiness is termed _____ anxiety.

moral

205 Furthermore, moral anxiety may result simply from thinking of stealing, because the _____ acts to punish certain kinds of responses, whether they be overt or covert.

superego

206 While we speak of the _____ punishing someone, we are not referring to a "thing." This term indicates a class of behavioral responses.

superego

Feelings of dread and inadequacy accompanied by feelings of physiological tension are the essential features of anxiety. Anxiety, according to Freud, may take three forms: reality anxiety, neurotic anxiety, and moral anxiety. Reality anxiety is a fear of actual danger; neurotic anxiety is a tension resulting from fear that certain id impulses will be expressed. Moral anxiety stems from the censoring of the conscience and the ego ideal.

Some Criticisms of Freudian Psychoanalytic Theory

Freudian psychoanalysis has been criticized because the concepts are often very vague and difficult to define. This criticism implies that Freudian concepts can with difficulty be put to experimental tests. Freud's critics find it difficult to measure functions such as cathexis or anticathexis, conscious, unconscious, id, and superego. Therefore they consider Freudian concepts very vague.

207 Another criticism of Freudian _____ is that Freud based his findings on observations which were made under uncontrolled conditions, i.e., from memory of clinic visits rather than from orderly research on individuals.

psychoanalysis

208 Freud's critics submit that his observations must be verified under _____ conditions in order to attain objectivity.

controlled

209 Some critics would contend that Freud should have conducted more laboratory experiments to test the validity of his concepts. Such experiments could have been repeated by others. In this manner Freud's concepts would have been based on controlled _____.

observations

210 Freud's critics also note that his findings are based primarily on the observation of abnormal individuals. This perhaps caused him to have a more _____ [optimistic/pessimistic] outlook on the nature of man and invited him to observe more pathos in man than actually occurs.

pessimistic

211 A fourth criticism is that Freud emphasized hereditary influences on man and failed to recognize sufficiently the _____ conditions which affect the development of personality.

environmental

212 You will recall that Freud emphasized two basic instincts in man: the _____ instinct and the _____ instinct.

life
death

213 Freud felt that these two basic instincts of man were
_____ rather than learned.

inherited (innate)

In this section the criticisms of Freud's theory have been briefly mentioned. The four major criticisms are: **(1)** His concepts are too vague; **(2)** his observations were not made under controlled conditions; **(3)** his observations were made primarily on abnormal individuals; **(4)** he gave perhaps disproportionate emphasis to hereditary rather than environmental influences on behavior.

SUMMARY

In this unit the student is introduced to the thinking of Sigmund Freud. The influence of his views on western thought is seen in numerous ways. For instance, modern methods of discipline reflect Freudian psychoanalytic concepts. All personality theorists of any note have been criticized, and Freud has not been without his critics. Freud's major contribution to modern psychological thought might well be found in the stimulation he gave to the search for the unknown quantities of human behavior.

Throughout the unit it is noted that Freud holds that life and death instincts are the prime motivations of behavior. From the instinctual energies arise conflicts among the id, the ego, and the superego—the basic components of personality. These conflicts are sometimes not within man's awareness and are therefore unconscious. Freud submits that these unconscious conflicts are important determiners of behavior. Repression is a consequence of conflicts and leads to anxiety. Man's awkward attempts to deal with the pain of anxiety are apparent in his behavior.

Freudian psychoanalysis is fundamentally a causal theory of behavior, and thus it stands in contrast to some of the concepts which will be discussed in the next unit.

REFERENCES

Allport, G. W.: _Becoming: Basic Considerations for a Psychology of Personality_, Yale University Press, New Haven, Conn., 1955.

Blum, G. S.: _Psychoanalytic Theories of Personality_, McGraw-Hill Book Company, New York, 1953.

Earl, Robert W.: "Motivation, Performance and Extinction," _Journal of Comparative and Physiological Psychology_, 50: 248–251, 1957.

Freud, S.: _The Ego and the Id_, The Hogarth Press, Ltd., London, 1927.

Freud, S.: "The Psychopathology of Everyday Life," in *The Basic Writings of Sigmund Freud,* Random House, Inc., New York, 1938.

Freud, S.: An *Outline of Psychoanalysis,* W. W. Norton and Company, Inc., New York, 1949.

Hall, C. S.: *A Primer of Freudian Psychology,* The World Publishing Company, Cleveland, 1954.

Hall, C. S., and G. Lindzey: "Psychoanalytic Theory and Its Applications in the Social Sciences," in G. Lindzey (ed.), *Handbook of Social Psychology,* I, 143–180, Addison-Wesley Publishing Company, Inc., Reading, Mass., 1954.

Hall, C. S., and G. Lindzey: *Theories of Personality,* John Wiley & Sons, Inc., New York, 1957.

Jones, E.: *The Life and Work of Sigmund Freud,* Basic Books, Inc., Publishers, New York, vol. I, 1953; vol. II, 1955.

Knapp, P. H.: *Expressions of the Emotions of Man,* International Universities Press, Inc., New York, 1963.

May, R.: *Man's Search for Himself,* W. W. Norton & Company, Inc., New York, 1953.

McClelland, D.: *Personality,* Holt, Rinehart and Winston, Inc., New York, 1951.

Monroe, R.: *Schools of Psychoanalytic Thought,* Holt, Rinehart and Winston, Inc., New York, 1955.

Sawrey, N., and C. Telford: *Dynamics of Mental Health,* Allyn and Bacon, Inc., Boston, 1963.

Sears, R. B.: *Survey of Objective Studies of Psychoanalytic Concepts,* Social Science Research Council, New York, 1943.

Stagner, R.: *Psychology of Personality,* McGraw-Hill Book Company, New York, 1961.

SELF-REVIEW QUIZ

1 Which of the following is not considered by the author to be an essential element in defining personality: (a) uniqueness, (b) organization, (c) characteristic behavior, (d) social attractiveness?

2 A complex unlearned pattern of responses is called _____.

3 The concept that everything in nature can be explained in terms of purpose is called _____.

4 Explaining man's behavior in terms of past events is called _____.

5 The tendency of certain motives to become independent of biological needs is referred to as: (a) goal direction, (b) functional autonomy of drives, (c) tension reduction, (d) teleology.

6 List the three explanatory concepts about personality given in this unit.

7 Freud's three components of personality are _____, _____, and _____.

8 The superego is made up of two parts, the _____ and the _____.

9 What are the two basic instincts in man about which Freud wrote?

10 Cite the three levels of awareness to which psychoanalysts refer.

11 Freud referred to three types of anxiety. They are _____, _____, and _____ anxiety.

12 Give four criticisms of Freudian psychoanalysis.

unit 2

Goal Direction and Self-direction

Previous units have presented principles of learning which have great significance for the understanding of human behavior. Our fundamental view of man's nature affects the kind of learning theory we find most acceptable. For this reason it is important to examine carefully the significant concepts of personality as a system of interacting elements.

The question of whether man's behavior should be explained in terms of mechanical determinism or teleology is an old one. Behavioral scientists from various disciplines have wrestled with the seeming contradictions found in these two approaches to the study of man. Some have "solved" the puzzle through rigid adherence to a mechanical view of man; others stress the ability of man to organize his behavior in unique ways so that concepts of self and "distinctly human goals" become necessary in explaining human behavior.

The following unit is an attempt to program some of the important concepts of self- and goal direction which have emerged in personality theory. Special attention is given to Carl Roger's views concerning man's tendency to actualize himself. Rogers has done some pioneer thinking in this area and draws heavily on his experience as a psychotherapist. Henry Murray's distinctions between man's various needs have also found some acceptance among personality theorists. These are discussed briefly.

The emphasis throughout the unit is on contrasting goal-directed and self-directed views, and the tension-reduction view. Although these overlap considerably, the contrast is well worth considering.

Goal Direction

In the beginning of this part, personality concepts were classified into three major groups: (1) those emphasizing tension reduction; (2) those accenting goal direction;

(3) those giving major importance to self-direction. Freud's concepts would fit the tension-reduction category. It was also stated that, rather than feeling that they are responding only to inner biological tension, many individuals prefer to believe that they are also seeking goals.

reduction

1 Goal achievement may result in tension _____.

equilibrium

2 It is quite often true, however, that goal achievement increases tension. Rather than restoring the individual's equilibrium, it may actually disturb his _____.

equilibrium

3 When a student chooses to attend college, he may actually be seeking a situation which will disturb his _____ rather than maintain it.

tense (dissatisfied)

4 Individuals seem to search for goals and often feel _____ if they do not realize them.

Henry Murray (1938), a Harvard professor and clinician, proposed a list of goals toward which man seems to strive. Perhaps, through a brief study of Murray's list, we can better understand the study of personality through analysis of goals. Murray lists twenty needs which he feels are basic to man. We shall consider only a couple of them as examples of how personality can be viewed in terms of goal-seeking behavior. Murray defines the term "need" somewhat differently from the way we defined it earlier. Murray feels that the term is a "convenient fiction or hypothetical concept which stands for a force." (Murray, 1938, p. 123.)

goal

5 That is, Murray suggests that a need leads the organism to respond to certain external stimuli and may be directed toward a particular _____.

affiliation

6 One of the needs Murray postulates is the need for affiliation. Murray felt that man needs to greet, join, and live with others. This is the _____ need, which is universal among men.

affiliation

7 The _____ need accounts for the high motivation of individuals to join organizations or to feel rejected if they are not allowed entrance to a desired group.

8 Another need proposed by Murray is achievement. In the American occupational structure, for example, we encourage people to strive for the "top position." Thus, in our culture we note not only affiliation needs, but needs for _____.

9 Some interesting research is being conducted to determine whether these _____ are universal or are peculiar to certain individuals under certain circumstances.

10 These needs for _____ and _____ have been studied by showing individuals a set of pictures and asking them to tell stories about the pictures.

11 The Thematic Apperception Test consists of composing stories in response to pictures. Both _____ and _____ needs have been studied in this way.

12 The _____ _____ Test is useful in studying these and other needs of man. It consists of twenty pictures which are used to stimulate stories. It is usually referred to as the TAT.

13 Using this method, a researcher asks an individual to indicate a story suggested by the picture. Furthermore, he asks him to tell what has happened previously and how it will come out. For example, if the themes of the individual's stories include accounts of individuals struggling to succeed we may infer that he has a strong _____ need.

Another way in which the achievement motive can be measured is illustrated by research conducted by McClelland et al. (1953). These researchers asked male college students to write five-minute stories in response to four pictures exposed for twenty seconds in a group situation. Answer sheets were provided containing the following questions:
1. What is happening?
2. What has led up to this situation?
3. What is being thought?
4. What will happen?

Two of these pictures were from the TAT, and two others were especially designed for this study. The pictures consisted of the following: two men working at a machine; a boy sitting at a desk with a book in front of him; a father and son talking; a young boy possibly dreaming of

Sidebar answers:
achievement

needs

achievement
affiliation

achievement
affiliation

Thematic
Apperception

achievement

the future. The experimenters gave instructions to the subjects so as to create conditions of failure, success, etc., and noted the effect of these instructions on the kinds of stories the individuals would give in response to the pictures. Through analyses of the stories, the individual received an achievement-motive score according to the number of achievement-related responses he gave to the pictures. This then was related to such variables as cultural background and performance on problem-solving tasks.

achievement
(If you miss this,
refer to the above
paragraph.)

14 Presumably, a person's achievement score would be high in proportion to the number of responses related to
_____.

achievement

15 Actually, the scoring of the achievement motive is more complex than is suggested here. In any event, the score is useful in studying the influence of factors such as cultural background on the _____ motive.

research
(experimentation)

16 It is out of Murray's concepts of the achievement motive that experimentation of this kind has developed. This is an illustration of a theory generating _____.

goal
tension

17 While we consider aspects of Murray's theory as belonging under the heading of goal direction, actually some aspects of his theory are based on the notion of tension reduction. Murray felt that both _____ direction and _____ reduction are important explanatory principles.

Murray has classified human motivation according to *process activity, modal needs,* and *effect needs.* These three dimensions of motivation will be defined since they reflect a rather unique classification of human motivation (Murray, 1938, p. 127f.).

process

18 Process activity refers to unorganized and non-directed activities such as daydreaming or frantic, confused behavior under conditions of intense rage or fear. Unorganized thoughts, speech, etc., which seem directionless, are called by Murray _____ activity.

process activity

19 If I should sit and reminisce about "the good old days," I would be engaging in behavior which Murray calls _____ _____.

less

20 The more ordered my thinking, the _____ likely it would be to be classified as process activity.

21 Modal needs refer to doing something for the pleasure of doing it well. Modal needs are rewarded only when something is done _____.

well

22 The rewards which come from creating an excellent theme in an English course are an example of the rewarding consequences of _____ needs.

modal

23 Effect needs are those which lead to a particular end result or goal. Thus, effect needs and modal needs involve _____-directed behavior.

goal

24 The goal of _____ behavior is excellence or perfection; the goal of _____ needs is achievement of a desired state of some kind.

modal
effect

25 If you aspire to become a good mathematics student, working for the achievement of this goal reflects the _____ needs of man.

effect

26 In summary, Murray's distinction between process activity, modal needs, and effect needs is that:
  (1) process activity is +++++;
  (2) modal needs are +++++;
  (3) effect needs are +++++.

(1) random, unorganized activity;
(2) activity enjoyed when well done;
(3) activity directed toward a particular goal

27 Henry Murray has provided, therefore, a classification of goals which is important to Americans and has thus helped us to understand personality in terms of _____ direction.

goal

This brief section on goal direction is designed to help you realize that this is an important point of departure for better understanding of personality. The distinction we are making, however, between goal direction, tension reduction, and self-direction is only for convenience. There is a great deal of overlap in the concepts of self-direction and goal direction.

Sources of Goals

Human goals seem to stem from four basic sources:
1. Biological tension

2. Symbolic value
3. Teaching of parents and others
4. Functional autonomy

If you can remember these, well and good; if not, you can refer to them during the next 15 frames.

28 Let us consider each of these briefly. If I am hungry, I may decide to do something to get food. Thus I set up a goal because of _____ tension.

physiological
(biological)

29 I may decide to take a premedical course in college in order to become a physician. In doing so my goal is established because it symbolizes many ultimate _____ such as status or money.

goals

30 I take the course not for immediate tension reduction, but because it _____ future satisfaction.

symbolizes

31 Immediate goals may be important because they _____ ultimate goal fulfillment.

symbolize

32 Other goals may become part of our thinking and feeling because we have accepted the belief of parents and other significant individuals that the _____ are worthwhile.

goals

33 Our parents probably exert considerable influence in our selection of _____.

goals

34 We have said that goals may arise from _____ tension.

physiological
(biological)

35 Goals are also set up because of their _____ value.

symbolic

36 We are influenced greatly in our choice of goals by _____.

parents (other individuals significant to us)

37 We also perhaps engage in goal-directed behavior simply for the gratifications resulting from goal-seeking activity. This tendency to seek goals for the sheer pleasure of goal seeking reminds us of Murray's concept of _____ needs and Allport's concept of functional autonomy of drives.

modal

38 If I begin to save money for the purpose of buying the necessities of life and later save it because money saving is an activity I thoroughly enjoy, Allport would say that my drive to save money is now _____ autonomous.

functionally

39 To say that my money-saving drive is functionally autonomous is to say that it is _____ of original goals.

independent

40 When engaging in activities becomes a goal in itself, i.e., when an individual does something because he enjoys it, such engagement is explained in terms of _____ _____.

functional
autonomy

41 These concepts of _____ direction place emphasis on the question, "What does the person want?" rather than on "What is driving the person?"

goal

Definition of the Self

In our analysis of personality concepts thus far, we have referred to two major concepts: (1) concept of tension reduction; (2) concept of goal direction. We conclude this unit with an analysis of self-direction.

42 What do we mean by the term self? This is a difficult question to answer; however, all of us know that certain experiences have greater self-reference than others. If I say, "I feel sad," this statement has a self-reference; if I say that the lady who lives down the street feels sad, the statement probably involves little _____-_____.

self-reference

43 We speak of a person thinking, feeling, and so forth. What is the "person"? The person or the self can be defined as the unity of our feelings and thoughts about our behavior and experience. In this sense the _____ is an object about which we think and feel.

self

44 When the term is used in this way, a person has thoughts and feelings about his behavior and experiences much as he would have about an _____.

object

45 If a person says, "I am ashamed of how I acted," he is expressing a dissatisfaction with the _____.

self

46 The word self is often used to refer to a process, as well as to an object. Used in this way, _____ is the organizing activities of the total personality.

self

47 The term self, when used to indicate process, includes the notion that self is the _____ activities of the personality.

organizing

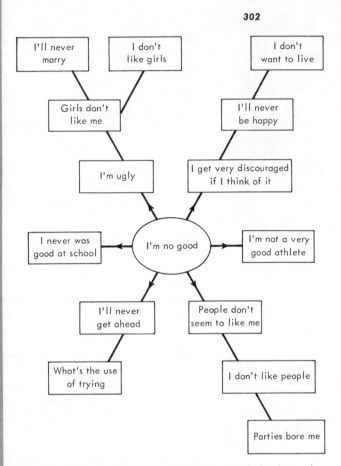

Figure 21. A basic self-concept of "I'm No Good" leads to other attitudes which support it. (Henry Clay Smith, *Personality Adjustment*, p. 186, McGraw-Hill Book Company, New York, 1961.)

48 You might recognize a similarity between this concept of self and the concept of the ego, which was considered in the section on _____ psychoanalysis.

Freudian

49 When we say that John will react to a stimulus according to the influences of his past experiences, the organization of these experiences is the self when used as a _____.

process

50 When ego and self are used as identical terms, the self is conceived of as a _____.

process

51 When the self is referred to in an objective sense (e.g., in speaking of one's attitude toward his behavior and experience) the term is used as a reference to an _____, as when we say, "I am proud of myself."

object

52 The term self may be used to mean both object and process. We may have thoughts and feelings about our behavior and experience, and these thoughts and feelings may cause us to react in certain ways. Thus, the self may be viewed as both _____ and _____.

object
process

53 We shall define the self as the unity of thoughts and feelings about our behavior and experience which affects the organization of our responses. This definition of the self views it as both _____ and _____.

object
process

54 For example, we may think of our behavior and experience in a certain situation as being inferior to others. This feeling may result in our deciding not to attempt a new skill. In this instance, the term self is used as an _____ of feelings and thoughts as well as a _____ which affects the direction of behavior (Hall and Lindzey, 1957).

object
process

Theorists who emphasize self-direction point out that the individual has certain thoughts and feelings which determine the course of his behavior. Thus, you cannot always predict the response an individual will give by knowing only the objective stimulus. You must know the meaning the stimulus has for the person, and this is determined by self-concepts.

Development of the Self

How does one develop a self? According to our definition, an infant has no self. Self is apparently not part of our genetic makeup. It seems necessary that we learn to distinguish the self from nonself. For an excellent discussion, see G. Allport (1961).

55 It would appear that the newborn infant has no concept of the fact that he is an object separate from other objects. Gaining this notion seems to be the beginning of a _____.

self

56 As the baby grows, he seems gradually to gain a self. He senses that his body is different from the crib or from his mother's body. The self emerges as the infant responds to his _____.

surroundings
(environment)

learning

57 A concept of self, therefore, is due to _____ [learning/instinct].

58 Learning the "I" or "me" is the beginning of a lifetime of self-referring experiences. The self is the product of becoming aware of the "_____" and its contrast with events and persons which are "not I."

"I" (me)

59 The earliest stages of development of the self involve distinguishing between one's own body and +++++ in the environment.

other objects and events

60 When an infant lies in his crib and gazes at his hands, he probably is as yet unable to distinguish the _____ and _____.

"I"
"not I"
(self and nonself)

61 As the child develops language, his sense of personal identity becomes greater. Identifying his body and his possessions, as contrasted with other persons and objects, are functions of _____.

language

62 A child is given a name, and this helps him gain a more vivid identification of _____.

self

63 At about two years of age, the child's self-awareness seems suddenly to emerge. This event seems to be due to an increase in ability to perceive and use _____.

language

64 The two-year-old learns that he can control to some extent the people and objects about him. This sense of _____ which the two-year-old feels reflects an increased self-_____.

control
awareness

65 The two-year-old often becomes quite inquisitive as he becomes more aware of self as contrasted with _____. This inquisitiveness and newly discovered ability to control others often results in negative behavior.

nonself (surroundings, others)

66 We can see much development in a child from the time he is unaware of the differences between himself and his surroundings to the stage in which he realizes that he can _____ his surroundings.

control

67 By the time they are two years of age, many children develop negative attitudes. One explanation for this is the increase in _____-awareness.

self

68 As the individual develops further, he gains a sense of identification with other people and objects. This is referred to as an extension of self. Feeling a closeness to his surroundings, the child will _____ the self to include other people and other objects.

extend

extended

extends

self-concepts

self-concept
self

(1) self
(2) self-concept

(1) awareness
(2) evaluation

self

(1) aware

(2) self-concept

Self-concepts

self
self-concept

self-concepts

reactions

69 When a person refers to "my fraternity" or "my ball team," he is suggesting that he has _____ the self to include these things.

70 As the individual _____ himself to include individuals and objects outside of himself, he begins to find that sometimes his behavior is approved by others and that at other times it is disapproved.

71 In this way he develops self-concepts, i.e., concepts of himself as being a "good" person, "bad" person, or other type of person. The way in which others react to you determines the kind of _____-_____ you will develop.

72 We shall distinguish between the terms "self" and "self-concepts." For instance, I am aware of sitting here, and this awareness is the self; but I might also be aware that I am a clumsy person, and this is a self-concept. If I am aware that I am cooperative, this would reflect my _____-_____; if I am aware that I am holding a pencil, this reflects the _____.

73 An awareness of the "I" or "me" is the (1) _____, while the evaluation of the "I" or "me" is the (2) _____-_____.

74 The term self implies (1) _____; the term self-concept implies (2) _____.

75 Recognition of one's feelings, thoughts, actions, etc., is the _____.

76 The infant appears to be (1) _____ of his surroundings, but as yet probably has not developed a (2) _____-_____.

77 _____-_____ appear to be acquired from one's social environment (Allport, 1961).

78 We have made a distinction between _____ and _____-_____, but many authors do not do so (Allport, 1961, 110–138; Chein, 1944).

79 We have seen that an individual is not born with a sense of self but rather develops this from experience. As he extends himself, others become important to him and they help determine his _____-_____.

80 Our self-concepts emerge out of our own experiences and the _____ of others to us.

(1) personal experiences (2) reactions of others to us	**81** We develop our self-concepts out of two types of experiences: **(1)** +++++ and **(2)** +++++.
self-concepts	**82** The significant individuals in our lives are, of course, parents, teachers, and others who greatly affect the kinds of _____-_____ we develop.
parents, teachers and others who greatly affect us	**83** Examples of significant others are +++++; that is, those who greatly affect the kinds of self-concepts we develop.
parents	**84** Significant others are those **(1)** whose opinions and attitudes we respect and respond to; **(2)** who hold positions of authority and are able to exercise some control over us. Thus, included in our list of significant others most likely would be our _____.
opinions we re- spond to control	**85** The significant others for us are those whose +++++ and those who exercise _____ over us.
authority (prestige)	**86** An example: Suppose that you were swimming, and a swimming instructor told you that you were an excellent swimmer. His opinion might affect your self-concept in this area because he holds a position of _____ in the field of swimming.
respect	**87** Notice that these self-concepts emerge not only in reference to authorities, but to anyone whom we _____ and respond to.
significant individ- uals in your life	**88** Example: If your parents continue to tell you that you are worthless, then you are apt to hold this concept of yourself because they are (usually) +++++.

In this section we have said that self develops out of experience with the environment, which includes significant other persons. A distinction has been made here between self as awareness and self-concept which implies evaluation of the "I" or "me."

The Ideal Self

Something else which greatly affects our behavior is referred to as the ideal self. As the term implies, this is the behavior and experience to which you aspire. For many people, going to church is working toward becoming their ideal self.

89 The ideal self is the kind of person one feels he should be. You can readily see that this corresponds to Freud's concept of the _____.

superego (more specifically, ego ideal)

90 The _____ self grows out of the demands made upon the person during his formative years; however, the individual may soon take on these expectations and make them part of himself.

ideal

91 For example, parents may demand that a child be courteous to adults. As the child grows older, he may incorporate standards of courtesy into his own ideal self, so that now his motive for being courteous is not to please his parents but to live up to his _____ _____.

ideal self

92 If there is a discrepancy between the individual's behavior and his expectations of how he ought to behave, how would you expect a person to respond? +++++.

(1) anger against others
(2) guilt
(3) anger toward self (Any of these reactions might be found. Do you see why?)

93 An example: If I feel that it is bad to feel hostile toward another person, this suggests that if I become hostile, I'll feel _____.

guilty (or perhaps angry toward self)

94 If a person is not living up to his expectations for himself, he may blame others and express anger toward them. This tendency to _____ _____ for one's own troubles is a fairly common reaction.

blame others

95 You'll notice that merely having hostile thoughts may lead to _____.

guilt

96 You may feel guilty and repress the hostile feelings or thoughts because they are not consistent with the _____ _____.

ideal self

97 For Freud, the concept of repression represents a defense against feelings which may suggest that one is not living up to his ideal self. In the previous example, _____ of hostile feelings occurs because you've learned that it is "bad" to feel this way.

repression

98 There are many other so-called defenses which the person may use to guard against impulses that tell him that he is not living up to his _____ _____. Some of these will be presented in the next unit.

ideal self

99 There is also a set of beliefs and feelings which a person wants others to have toward him. This is referred to as the *social self*. While our self consists of our private knowledge of the thoughts and feelings which typify us, the social self is concerned with +++++.

how others view us

100 Our total behavior which we display to others for their approval is referred to as the _____ _____.

social self

101 Let's review some of this material. When we say that the child is suddenly aware of his body as being separate from other objects, we say he is developing a _____.

self

102 If a person says that he is a sinful person, this is an expression of a _____-_____.

self-concept

103 The behavior and thoughts which a person holds as being "himself at his best" constitute the _____ self.

ideal

104 Whenever Mary compliments the boss's wife, she may be displaying her _____ self.

social

It was mentioned earlier that sometimes there is a difference between the self-concept and the ideal self. Such a discrepancy may cause the person much anxiety. Ideally there should not be a great discrepancy between the self-concept and the ideal self.

Measurement of the Self

Measurement of the self is considered by self theorists to be important in explaining human behavior (Rogers and Dymond, 1959; Kilpatrick and Cantril, 1960). One method used in the study of self is called the Q technique. The Q technique consists of sorting cards which have statements on them along a continuum from those most characteristic to those least characteristic of the person (Stephenson, 1953).

105 If I read a statement which I think is very characteristic of me, I place it on one end of the distribution. If it is very unlike me, I place it on the opposite end of the distribution. This procedure is part of the _____ technique.

Q

106 If I distribute the statements according to how I feel and thus evaluate my thoughts and behavior, the result would be a measure of my _____-_____.

self-concept

107 The (1) _____ technique, therefore, is a method of measuring a person's (2) _____-_____.

(1) Q
(2) self-concept

108 I may have a hundred cards in front of me, which I am sorting into eleven stacks. In using the _____ _____, I'll place a card in the last stack on the right if I feel that the statement on this card is very descriptive of me.

Q technique

109 Briefly, the Q technique is described as a procedure whereby ++++.

an individual sorts
statements along
a continuum de-
pending upon
whether they de-
scribe him or do
not describe him

110 The Q technique can be used for various other kinds of sortings. I might sort the cards in a way which would describe the kind of person I would like to be. Thus I would be getting a measure of my _____ self.

ideal

111 One of the advantages of the Q technique is that it permits evaluation of different aspects of the self. For example, a person may distribute the cards in terms of his _____-concepts and then again in view of his concepts of himself as he would like to be (i.e., his _____ _____).

self
ideal self

112 Sometimes there is a marked discrepancy between a person's self-concept, as measured by the Q sort, and his _____ self.

ideal

113 Another way of studying the relationship of self-concepts to the _____ _____ is by investigating the kinds of aspirations individuals hold for themselves.

ideal self

114 I might ask you to throw darts at a target, observe your score, and then have you estimate your score on the next trial. Your level of aspiration is measured by your _____ of your next score.

estimate

115 If you estimated that your next score would be much higher than your present score, we would say that you had a high level of _____.

aspiration

116 It has been found that the level of aspiration an individual shows will fluctuate from one task to another. It seems, then, that this characteristic is not a _____ trait.

constant (consistent)

117 While one's levels of _____ do not seem to remain constant on different tasks the individual performs, their observation is an interesting way of studying some of the factors affecting the expectations a person has for himself.

aspiration

It has been found that a person's aspiration level will be affected by the group with which he is being compared. For example, it was found in one investigation that Negroes, when informed that they were doing as well as whites on a task, lowered their level of aspiration (Preston and Bayton, 1941).

118 This study suggests that the level of aspiration is affected by the _____ with which individuals are being compared.

group

119 *Review:* There are at least two ways in which we can study self-concept and ideal self. They are: (1) by means of the _____ and (2) by study of _____.

(1) Q technique
(2) levels of
aspiration

120 One of the real limitations of studying individual behavior by means of the Q technique or level-of-aspiration studies is the tendency of individuals to distort reports of their thoughts about themselves. Unconsciously a person might _____ his conscious report of what he is thinking.

distort

121 For example, if you assert, "I am very cooperative," this statement may be a distortion of the truth perhaps because unconscious factors cause you to be hostile. On the conscious level you state that you are _____, but on the _____ level you are motivated by hostile impulses.

cooperative
unconscious

In spite of the possibility of distortion in self-report, highly provocative theories of self-psychology have their bases in the concepts of self, social self, self-concept, and ideal self. These theories of self-psychology have stimulated much research (Combs and Snygg, 1959; Mead, 1934).

The Self-psychology of Carl Rogers

Carl Rogers, a contemporary psychologist, has developed a theory of self-psychology which has as its basic concept the assertion that man has a tendency to actualize himself, i.e., to maintain and improve himself. This tendency, according to Rogers, is inherent in the very nature of man. While man does not always actualize himself, the tendency to do so is present (Rogers, 1951).

The tendency to actualize can be described as the tendency of the organism to:

1. Reduce biogenic drives
2. Become more independent of its surroundings
3. Make optimum use of abilities
4. Create
5. Grow to a higher level of effectiveness

You will probably want to refer to this list as you read the next twenty frames.

Figure 22. Carl R. Rogers interviewing a client. Used by permission of Carl R. Rogers.

biogenic

122 This list suggests first that the tendency to reduce biogenic drives means the motivation of the organism is toward reduction of tension caused by certain _____ needs.

tension (or drive, or need)

123 Some theorists believe that _____ reduction resulting from meeting the biological requirements of man is the central concept of motivation.

124 Secondly, the organism develops in a direction from dependence on external forces (especially other people) to independence or autonomy. The little child who attempts to crawl illustrates the movement from **(1)** _____ upon others to **(2)** _____.

(1) dependence
(2) independence

125 As we mature, normally we become less dependent and more _____ of our surroundings.

independent

126 Of course man never becomes completely _____ of other people or his physical surroundings.

independent

127 A third aspect of the tendency to actualize oneself is making optimum use of one's abilities. When a person improves his tennis-playing skills, he may be striving to make greater use of his _____.

abilities

128 The tendency to make greater use of one's abilities applies to physical skills as well as to social and intellectual skills. Very seldom, if ever, do we make maximum use of our _____.

abilities

129 When we do approach optimum use of our abilities, we are demonstrating the tendency to _____.

actualize

130 A fourth point is that man strives to see relationships in his environment and to produce novel ideas. This is called the tendency to _____.

create

131 To create refers to seeing relationships among things, objects, and ideas and producing _____ ideas and products.

novel

132 Not satisfied with simply adjusting to his surroundings, man tends to **(1)** _____ new ideas and products, and this tendency is included in the concept of **(2)** _____.

(1) create

(2) actualization

133 The deliberate attempt to discover a new medical drug may be the result of the _____ tendency of man.

actualizing

134 Finally, the tendency to _____ is reflected in a person's efforts to advance from one level of effectiveness to a higher level of effectiveness.

actualize

135 When a man strives to improve his ability to deal with his surroundings, he is attempting to advance to a higher level of _____.

effectiveness

136 When a child persists in his effort to walk, he is showing what seems to be a tendency to move from one level of _____ to a higher one.

effectiveness

137 A normal person will continually seek to move from one level of effectiveness to a _____ level. If he is frustrated, this process will not continue.

higher

138 *Review:* Let us summarize these aspects of the tendency of man to actualize the organism:
  (1) He reduces _____ drives;
  (2) he becomes _____ of his surroundings;
  (3) he makes optimum use of his _____;
  (4) he is _____;
  (5) he grows from one level of _____ to a higher one.

(1) biogenic
(2) independent
(3) abilities
(4) creative
(5) effectiveness

Rogers placed major emphasis on the concept of self. He concluded that as a person develops, he becomes aware of certain thoughts and feelings that identify him as being different from others. Rogers used the term self in a rather broad sense, which includes both awareness and evaluation of one's behavior. This is not the same as the usage of the term in our previous discussion of self.

139 When I say, "I did not enjoy the concert," I am referring to the self which is not simply my (1) _____ of my experience but my (2) _____ of the experience. Thus Rogers uses the term self in a general sense. It is not unusual to find terms used differently by various personality theorists.

(1) awareness
(2) evaluation

140 Rogers uses the concept of the ideal self to mean the self-concept the individual would most like to possess. The person an individual would like to become is the _____ _____. Rogers uses this term in the same way as it was used in our earlier discussion of ego-ideal.

ideal self

actualize

141 Rogers proposes another major aspect of man, the tendency to actualize the self. This general tendency is part of man's overall inclination to _____ himself.

maintain and improve the self

142 Knowing the general tendency of man to actualize himself, you may say that self-actualization means that man tends to +++++.

An example of self-maintenance and -improvement is found in the persistence a child shows in the acquisition of a new skill. Rogers feels that this tendency to maintain and improve the self affects the way in which we interpret our experiences. If our experiences are consistent with our concepts of the self, then we perceive them accurately.

perceive (view)

143 For instance, if I view myself as a good tennis player and have the experience of winning a tennis match, then I am able to _____ or symbolize this experience quite accurately (Combs and Snygg, 1959).

144 The term "accurate perception" refers to the fact that the experiences are not denied or distorted, but rather given _____ interpretation.

accurate

perceiving

145 By accurately _____ the experiences, we do not need to be defensive about them.

146 Conversely, if one has experiences which run contrary to his own concept of self, then these experiences are denied or distorted. If I view myself as a good tennis player, I may not be able to accept the experience of being defeated. Such an experience, which is in contrast to my concept of the self, may be _____ or _____.

denied
distorted

147 Anxiety may result when there is an inconsistency between experiences expected by the self and those experienced in reality. Rogers notes that a person becomes defensive against those experiences which are not consistent with the self, and this defensive process is called the _____ or distortion of experience.

denial

148 There is a tendency to preserve the self-concepts we have developed; consequently we often _____ ourselves against anything which threatens to change them.

defend

(1) defensive
(2) perceived

(1) self
(2) anxiety

(1) maintain
(2) enhance

anxiety

deny
distort

rationalization

inconsistent

experiences

149 Distortion of experience and denial of experience are **(1)** _____ maneuvers to keep experiences from being accurately **(2)** _____.

150 If experiences which are inconsistent with the self were accurately symbolized in awareness, then the individual would show anxiety. Anxiety occurs because the individual is striving to maintain and enhance his concept of **(1)** _____; any experiences which run counter to this tendency cause **(2)** _____.

151 Both so-called normal and neurotic individuals show, in their everyday behavior, tendencies to **(1)** _____ and **(2)** _____ themselves.

152 If experiences are inconsistent with self, then they are not perceived accurately. To do so is to cause _____.

153 When inconsistent experiences occur, we develop certain defensive efforts to _____ or _____ the experiences. For example, we may rationalize our experience or behavior. Rationalization means giving a reasonable explanation for behavior which is not very reasonable.

Psychological defenses will be discussed in more detail in a later unit; however, a couple of examples will be given here. Let us assume that although I conceive of myself as a man of sound judgment, I lose money because of an impulsive investment in an unreliable stock. The mistake may be rationalized by suggesting that it was not my fault.

154 In the instance given above, the _____, "It was not my fault," was a distortion of behavior which was inconsistent with my self-concept, "I am a man of sound judgment."

155 Another example: Assume that a girl includes in her self-concepts the idea that she is very beautiful. If a significant person tells her "You're ugly," she may deny or distort the experience. In this situation, the experience (being told she is ugly) is denied or distorted because it is _____ with her own self-concept ("I am very beautiful.")

156 Rogers feels that successful counseling or psychotherapy results in the individual's reorganizing his self so that his self-concepts become more consistent with his _____.

**denied
distorted**

157 If there are changes in the self, then a greater number of experiences will be accepted by the self rather than being _____ or _____ by the self.

In Rogers's view, as defensive behavior becomes no longer necessary, the individual is freer to experience greater self-actualization. If the individual is busy defending himself, then he will not actualize himself (Rogers, 1951, p. 192).

Rogers's theory, which is supported to a fair degree by clinical observations and objective research, holds that all of us have within us the potential for greater self-actualization (Rogers, 1951; Rogers and Dymond, 1959).

How Is a Theory Judged?

158 The extent to which any personality theory is of value depends upon the following:
   a. The theory must account for a large number of facts, i.e., it must be *comprehensive*.
   b. It must lead to *accurate predictions*.
   c. The propositions of the theory must be *logically consistent*.
   d. The theory must set up *postulates which can be tested*.

Let us examine these further. First, if a theory is to be of value, it must be comprehensive, i.e., it must account for a large number of available _____.

facts

159 If the theory accounts for only a few facts, then it is not sufficiently _____.

comprehensive

160 For example, if a theory leads to the proposition that frustration results in aggression, then it should account for behavioral _____ which we gather from a variety of situations, e.g., clinic, laboratory, etc.

facts

161 In addition to this quality of _____, a theory should lead to accurate predictions.

comprehensiveness

162 Given certain situations, a theory attempts to _____ the responses of individuals.

predict

163 Suppose a theory stated that aggression results from frustration under certain conditions. If we establish these conditions and elicit frustration, then we would _____ from the theory that aggression would result.

predict

164 A third necessary characteristic of a worthwhile personality theory is that it must follow a set of rules; i.e., it must be logically _____.

consistent (If you missed this, return to frame 158.)

165 If a theorist defines a term in a certain way at one time, he must define it in the same way at another time. Furthermore, the concepts established by the theory must _____ follow from the assumptions.

logically

166 Using our example that frustration leads to aggression, let us examine a logically consistent example. Suppose that we said:
All men experience frustration.
Frustration always causes aggression.
All men experience aggression.
The conclusion that "All men experience aggression" meets our criterion of being _____ _____ with the first two statements.

logically consistent

167 It would *not* be logically consistent to say:
All men who experience frustration become aggressive.
John is aggressive.
John has been frustrated.
You will note from this that there may be many other reasons for aggression in addition to frustration. Thus, our conclusion is not _____ _____ with our premises.

logically consistent

168 We have said that a theory must be (1) _____, lead to accurate (2) _____ and be (3) _____ _____.

(1) complete
(2) predictions
(3) logically consistent

169 A theory of personality leads to observations of human behavior. A valuable theory must derive concepts which can be tested by _____.

observations (experimentation)

170 In the example being used here, ways must be found to measure _____ and _____.

frustration
aggression

171 If the concepts cannot be stated so that they can be measured in a reliable way, then _____ the concepts is impossible.

testing

172 It seems easier to test the effect of food deprivation on the activity level of man than to test the relationship of libidinal-energy level to human activity. The former is probably easier because it can be more easily +++++.

defined and tested

173 We have examined four criteria for judging the worth of a personality theory. The theory must provide:

(1) comprehensiveness

(2) accurate predictions

(3) logical consistency

(4) postulates which can be tested

(1) _____ ,

(2) _____ ,

(3) _____ _____ ,

(4) +++++.

SUMMARY

In this unit we have considered two approaches to personality: goal direction and self-direction.

While these two are similar, Murray and others would emphasize that we are motivated by our goals, whereas Rogers would suggest that man's striving for self-actualization is a motivating factor of central importance.

The views of goal direction and self-direction involve notions of teleological as well as causal explanations of human behavior. Several modern personality theorists feel that man is not only "pushed" by his inner tensions but also "pulled" by his goals.

The fundamental differences between the tension-reduction emphasis and the accent on self-actualization are important in the understanding of human behavior. The former emphasizes human motivation as developing mainly from conflict and tension caused by unfulfilled needs; the latter points to man's actualizing tendencies as being the center of human motivation.

There are also significant differences between the goal-directed and self-directed theorists on the one hand, and Freudian psychoanalysts on the other. The former theorists would give high status to the conscious or ego functions, while Freud emphasizes unconscious motivation.

The reader may subscribe to either the goal-fulfillment or self-fulfillment concepts. It is important, however, that he judge the significance of these concepts (or any set of theoretical concepts) in terms of comprehensiveness, accuracy of prediction, logical consistency, and testability.

REFERENCES

Allport, G.: *Pattern and Growth in Personality*, Holt, Rinehart and Winston, Inc., New York, 1961.

Chein, I.: "The Awareness of Self and the Structure of Ego," *Psychological Review*, 51:304–314, 1944.

Combs, A., and D. Snygg: *Individual Behavior*, Harper & Row, Publishers, Incorporated, New York, 1959.

Hall, C. S., and G. Lindzey: *Theories of Personality*, John Wiley & Sons, Inc., New York 1957.

Kilpatrick, F. P., and H. Cantril: "Self-anchoring Scaling: A Measure of the Individual's Unique Reality Worlds," *Journal of Individual Psychology*, 16:158–170, 1960.

McClelland, D., J. Atkinson, R. Clark, and E. Lowell: *The Achievement Motive*, Appleton-Century-Crofts, Inc., New York, 1953.

Mead, G. H.: *Mind, Self and Society from the Standpoint of a Social Behaviorist*, The University of Chicago Press, Chicago, 1934.

Moustakas, C. E. (ed.): *The Self: Exploration in Personal Growth*, Harper & Row, Publishers, Incorporated, New York, 1956.

Murray, H.: *Exploration in Personality*, Oxford University Press, New York, 1938.

Preston, M., and J. Boyton: "Differential Effect of a Social Variable upon Three Levels of Aspiration," *Journal of Experimental Psychology*, 29: 351–369, 1941.

Rogers, C. R.: *A Theory of Therapy, Personality and Interpersonal Relationships as Developed in the Client-centered Framework* (mimeographed).

Rogers, C. R.: *Client-centered Therapy: Its Current Practice, Interpretation and Theory*, Houghton Mifflin Company, Boston, 1951.

Rogers, C. R.: *On Becoming a Person*, Houghton Mifflin Company, Boston, 1961.

Rogers, C. R., and R. Dymond: "Psychotherapy and Personal Relationship as Developed in the Client-centered Framework," in S. Koch (ed.), *Psychology: A Study of a Science*, vol. III, *Formulations of the Person and the Social Context*, McGraw-Hill Book Company, New York, 1959, pp. 184–256.

Stagner, R.: *Psychology of Personality*, McGraw-Hill Book Company, New York, 1961.

Stephenson, W.: *The Study of Behavior*, The University of Chicago Press, Chicago, 1953.

SELF-REVIEW QUIZ

1 Which of the following concepts would Freudian psychoanalysis be most apt to accept? (a) self-direction, (b) tension reduction, (c) neither of these, (d) both of these.

2 Drives which are independent of original goals are called _____.

3 When ego and self are used as identical terms, the self is conceived as a(n) (a) process, (b) object, (c) either of these, (d) neither of these.

4 The term "self" implies awareness of one's behavior; the term "self-concept" implies (a) knowledge, (b)

body image, (c) evaluation, (d) self-condemnation.

5 The technique of personality measurement involving the sorting of cards is called (a) Q technique, (b) sorting technique, (c) multiphasic technique, (d) none of these.

6 List the three kinds of activity which resulted from Murray's classification of goals.

7 Human goals stem from at least four basic sources. They are:

(a) _____ (c) _____

(b) _____ (d) _____

8 Self-concepts emerge from two types of experiences. These are:

(a) _____ (b) _____

9 The tendency of man to actualize himself involves several kinds of activities. Give at least four.

10 What criteria should we use in judging the worth of a personality theory?

unit 3

Mechanisms of Adjustment

The human being is the most flexible of all organisms in making effective reactions to environmental changes. This flexibility is due to his superior ability in the manipulation of symbols. Man can reason on a highly abstract level, and thus he is able to profit from past experiences as well as to anticipate the consequences of his behavior.

If man's behavior were regulated exclusively by conscious volition, his adjustment to problems would perhaps be minimal. But man's behavior, as Freud emphasized, seems to be guided also by unconscious forces—motivations of which he is unaware. As he develops, man seems to learn subtly but assuredly certain ways of dealing with the anxiety-creating experiences of his life. This learning appears to be largely unconscious, so that by the time he reaches adulthood, certain habitual ways of adjusting to problems have been established.

All of us need to know more about the illogical and evasive ways in which we meet—or fail to meet—the problems in life which require personal adjustments. This unit is designed to help you become more familiar with some of the more common mechanisms with which we make these adjustments.

The Nature of Adjustment

drive

1 In our earlier discussions we said that man's behavior is in response to a state of tension, which is called a _____ state.

instrumental

2 Whenever a person's drive level is high, he shows responses to this condition, and his responses are referred to as _____ behavior, since the responses are instrumental in reducing the drive level.

physiological (biogenic)

3 Instrumental behavior involves responses to changes in our environment, both internal and external. We are stimulated by _____ as well as learned drives.

321

4 Physiological drives (e.g., hunger) and learned drives (e.g., drive for status) are not always reduced. We often set up goals for the purpose of reducing _____.

tension

"How about society trying to get adjusted to me?"

Figure 23. Some people have real difficulty in their personal adjustment.

5 Whenever goal-directed behavior is blocked, the person is frustrated and must make adjustive responses. Adjustive responses are necessary in relation to both _____ and _____ drives.

*physiological
learned*

6 Both human and nonhuman organisms show _____ responses to changes in both internal and external conditions.

adjustive

7 By internal conditions we refer to _____ changes and also to changes in the thoughts and feelings of the individual.

physiological

external
(environmental)

reality

environment

(1) real
(2) fantasy (not
real)

reality testing

reality

testing

self-concepts

adjustment

e.g., The Japanese
commit hari-kiri
for the honor of
giving a life for
the state.

---

8 Showing adjustive responses to the condition of being unable to go outside because of a snowstorm is an example of adjusting to _____ changes.

9 In the earlier unit on Freudian psychoanalysis we mentioned the functions of the ego. It will be recalled that ego functions refer to man's efforts to deal with _____.

10 Ego functions involve bringing yourself face to face with your own thoughts and the demands of your _____.

11 The newborn child does not know the realities of his environment; therefore he has to acquire an ego. To say that his ego must be developed is to say that he needs to know what is **(1)** _____ and what is **(2)** _____.

12 A sense of reality is obviously learned through experience. We test our environment to determine what is real and what is not real. The child will learn that fire is hot by touching a hot stove or perhaps by having someone tell him that it is hot. In Freudian terms, touching a stove is _____ _____.

13 Reality testing is one function of the individual which helps him survive. In the language of psychoanalysis, the ego aids the individual in his physical survival. As he grows, the person becomes able to anticipate and thereby to avoid possible dangers. This is made possible by the experience of testing _____.

14 A child might not want to put a coat on before going out in the cold weather. Thus, sometimes children do not learn from reality _____.

15 As we build ego responses through experiences, we take on certain self-concepts. As you will recall from an earlier chapter, _____-_____ determine how we perceive our world.

16 Significant changes in our environment require adjustive responses. These are called adjustment mechanisms. If I am cold, I may get a blanket to cover myself. This is an _____ mechanism designed to promote physical comfort.

17 We not only show adjustment mechanisms in response to threats to physical survival; we react in terms of our self-concepts. Sometimes these even lead to physical destruction. Can you give an example of this? +++++.

18 This example suggests that self-concepts are important in determining or motivating adjustment mechanisms. A young person may actually endanger his life by driving a car recklessly in order to demonstrate his bravery to his associates. This is an example of a self-concept motivating an _____ _____.

adjustment mechanism

19 When adjustment mechanisms are viewed in relation to self-concepts, it might be said that behavior will persist which is reinforced (is consistent with the self-concept) and will be extinguished if it is inconsistent with the _____-_____. Can you think of examples wherein self-concepts determined the reinforcement of a response?

self-concept

20 We are saying that _____-_____ act as reinforcers of responses.

self-concepts

21 Since it appears that sometimes we act as our own reinforcers, it follows that when we experience pain (anxiety), we will activate adjustive mechanisms which will +++++.

reduce or do away with the pain

22 Sometimes these mechanisms are self-deceiving; at other times they are not. Whenever the person feels unconsciously a need to defend against anxiety, the mechanisms are _____-_____.

self-deceiving

23 Whenever a person does something which is inconsistent with the self-concept, anxiety is created and may result in defensive behavior. An adjustment becomes necessary, and the self-deceiving way in which the adjustment is made is the _____ _____.

adjustment mechanism

24 Freud noted that these mechanisms are used to defend the ego, i.e., to maintain a consistency regarding what is real. In order to maintain a sense of consistency it becomes necessary to distort reality or deny experiences. What, then, are the two main kinds of adjustment mechanisms? **(1)** +++++; **(2)** +++++.

(1) denial of reality (experiences)
(2) distortion of reality

25 What kinds of things happen to us, or within us, to cause us to deny or distort reality?
  a. Threats from the outside world
  b. Inner promptings of the id
  c. Self-condemnation of the superego
Which of these do you feel is the most painful? +++++.

This, of course, not only varies from person to person, but from situation to situation.

26 You may learn from experience that a particular person is more brilliant than you, and his very presence may be a threat to you. If the reality of this is too painful to bear, the ego will trigger mechanisms of adjustment. This is an example of threat +++++.

from the outside world

27 You might feel, because of your past experience, that it is wrong to kiss a person of the opposite sex. The very thought of kissing such a person may cause anxiety because of the painful promptings of the _____.

id

28 It is possible that you will nonetheless follow through with the urge to kiss. Here the ego has relaxed and allowed a "dangerous" impulse to find expression. This is an example of the third source of anxiety. Do you recall it? +++++.

self-condemnation of the superego

29 List again the three sources of anxiety with which the ego must deal.
(1) _____
(2) _____
(3) _____

Refer to frame 25

30 You can find illustrations within your own behavior wherein facing reality is so painful that you must either distort reality or deny it. Using the illustrations above (or one drawn from your own experience), show how these threats might be handled. Let's look at the effect of motivation level on the way we approach our problems. We have said that we may get to the point when _____ or _____ of reality becomes necessary. But there are certain levels of motivation which result in dealing realistically with problems.

denial
distortion

31 In the first stage, referred to above as _____ _____, our motivation level is so weak that we may be satisfied with simple *images* of our goal.

wish fulfillment

32 As the motivation level increases (as the need becomes greater), there is a "push toward reality." Thus we become more aware of our needs and of what is necessary to meet them; there is an increase in _____ [realistic/wish-fulfilling] responses.

realistic

33 As motivation becomes more intense (as frustration increases), we then show _____ behavior which is directed more toward +++++ than toward attainment of the goal.

defensive
relief from anxiety

The following episode illustrates the three stages we go through in dealing with personal problems.

Let us suppose that as a man is driving through a desert, his car breaks down miles from the nearest water. At first he may not be particularly thirsty, and he imagines he will be picked up by some passing motorist. As the hours under the hot sun go by, his thirst increases, and he begins to imagine delicious cool drinks, thick milk shakes, or ice cubes tinkling in a glass. As more hours pass, his thirst becomes more acute, and the unrealistic images give way to an intense preoccupation with his thirst and the absence of any sign of water in the desert. He may now begin to think up various schemes for getting water out of his car

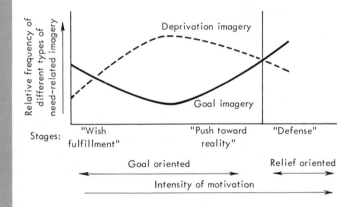

Figure 24. The hypothetical effect of increased motive intensity on thought processes. (David McClelland, *Personality*, The Dryden Press, Inc., New York, 1951.)

or to search in the surrounding territory for a spring, but he no longer spends much time in idle dreams of cooling drinks. Instead, he is active, anxious, and very conscious of his thirst. If we assume that many hours pass by, his thirst increasing in intensity all the time, his anxiety may become so acute and so painful that the bounds of reality begin to break down and he may begin to have hallucinations or see mirages of water in the distance or think that he actually hears the tinkle of ice cubes in a glass. Eventually he may, as it were, lose consciousness of his thirst altogether and become delirious, existing in a fantasy world in which his needs are being gratified (McClelland, 1951, p. 496).

1. wish-fulfillment
   (goal-oriented)
2. push toward
   reality (goal-
   oriented)
3. defense (relief
   from tension)

34 Fit the above-mentioned stages with the actual behavior of the man:

Behavior	Stage
(a) He imagines he will be picked up by a motorist.	1. _____
(b) He begins to think of schemes for getting water.	2. _____
(c) He sees mirages of water.	3. _____

tension (anxiety)

35 In everyday living we may become very defensive when our motivation becomes intense. The goal then becomes relief of _____.

What happens to cause a person to be motivated to reduce anxiety? Consider the following possibilities:
1. His goal-directed behavior is blocked; he is frustrated.
2. There is a conflict between motives.
3. There has been an increase in intensity of a motive.
If a person wants to be accepted by an engineering college and receives an F in a mathematics course, he may feel that this experience has blocked his goal-directed behavior.

anxiety

36 This experience described may be so painful as to lead to defensive behavior and efforts to reduce _____.

blocked

37 The above is an example of goal-directed behavior being _____.

defensive behavior

38 A person may be torn, for example, between the motive to love his mother and the motive to hate her. The resulting painful anxiety may lead to _____ _____.

(1) blocking of
    goal-directed
    behavior
(2) conflict of
    motives

39 We have said that two major reasons for a person being primarily motivated to reduce anxiety are:
(1) +++++
(2) +++++

motive (see
    frame 36)

40 The third possible explanation for a person becoming motivated to reduce anxiety is that there has been an increase in the intensity of a _____. Apparently the stronger a motive becomes, the more painful will be the result if it is frustrated. Very simply stated, if we want something very much, not getting it is more painful than not receiving something we have only a mild desire for.

Now that we have discussed in general terms the way man attacks problems and how he responds to situations which call for ego- or self-defensive, anxiety-reducing responses, we shall examine in the next parts of the unit specific mechanisms of adjustment.

We shall consider the defenses of repression, rationalization, identification, displacement, reaction formation, fixation, regression, and fantasy. It should be emphasized that these are typical responses to anxiety and are found in varying degrees among all men.

Repression

41 Freud felt that the basic mechanism of adjustment in the face of threat is repression. By _____, he meant dismissal from consciousness of a thought or feeling which is too painful to experience or recall.

repression

42 I may fail to recall a dental appointment. In so doing I am _____ a potentially painful memory.

repressing

43 While Freud says that the _____ represses the thought, others would rather interpret repression in more behavioral terms. Some feel that repression should be discussed in terms of the inhibition of a response in the presence of a painful stimulus. When the punishing stimulus is no longer present, the response is reinstated (Estes, 1944).

ego

44 Although we often *deliberately* suppress a thought or feeling, this is not repression. Repression is an automatic, unconscious process. If we consciously avoid thinking of something, this is _____.

suppression

45 When we consciously admit ideas or feelings to awareness, _____ occurs.

suppression

46 Since we do not recall all our experiences, we *selectively* remember those which have a positive association. This phenomenon of _____ recall has been demonstrated in many studies.

selective

A Study of Repression

One of the interesting classical experimental demonstrations of repression is a study conducted by Rosensweig (1941). College students were asked to solve some jigsaw puzzles which were labeled "intelligence tests." The students were motivated to work diligently at the tasks but were informed that if the tasks were not completed within the time limit, they would be removed. Two groups made up the study. The students were allowed to complete some of the puzzles; others were removed before they were completed.

When asked to recall the puzzles, the students recalled a significantly greater number of completed puzzles. This suggests that those tasks which were positively reinforced showed less repression than those which had a punishing effect (Rosensweig, 1941).

forget (deny, repress)

47 Failure to recall the uncompleted task might be interpreted to indicate the thought, "I am not very bright, because I didn't complete this task." If this thought is too painful to face, the person tends to _____ the tasks.

repression

48 College students were asked to describe all the experiences they could remember from a Christmas vacation. The experiences they recalled were predominantly pleasant ones (68 per cent). After a lapse of six weeks, the students' memories were primarily of pleasant vacation experiences. Again, this seems to be evidence of _____ of unpleasant experiences (Meltzer, 1930).

motivation

49 Several personality theorists, especially Freud, suggest that we often make "slips of the tongue" which reveal our true motivation. Our motives have been repressed but find expression occasionally in a disguised form. We do not, therefore, always know the _____ underlying our behavior.

slip of the tongue

50 Freud (1938) cites an instance wherein a female patient referred to a lady friend as one who had "thrown" a hat together instead of "sewn" the hat together. This is an example of a +++++.

repression

51 *Review:* Through the process of _____ we are able to exclude from awareness ideas and feelings which are painful.

punishing

52 In the language of learning theory, we express a response if it is not clearly defined because it then lacks the punishing qualities usually ascribed to it. The reason it can be expressed is that it is no longer _____.

53 Clinical experience has brought out some rather extreme forms of selective forgetting. Extreme cases of repression are referred to as dissociative reactions. In these cases, the individual may forget large segments of his behavior and become dissociated from reality. We have a dramatic demonstration of repression at work in cases of

dissociative reactions

_____ _____.

There are three major types of dissociative reactions:
1. Amnesia: loss of memory.
2. Dual or multiple personality; behaviorally, the individual takes on two or more different personalities.
3. Somnambulism: sleepwalking.

amnesic

54 When a person forgets his name, where he lives, etc., he is said to be _____.

forgets

55 The amnesia victim can usually retain motor habits of walking, talking, etc., but _____ more ego-related material.

recalled

56 Sometimes the "forgotten" experiences of the person can be recalled under conditions of hypnosis or special drugs. This suggests that the material is retained but not _____ during amnesia.

57 Although reported cases of dual or multiple personality are rare, they are quite dramatic. Cases have been reported wherein the individual acts sedate at times and at other times shows gay, frivolous behavior. These two

dual personality

"characters" constitute the _____ _____.

58 Cases have been reported wherein the individual will act quite sedate at times and then show the behavior of an extraverted person. While the person is in one character, he is amnesic for (has repressed) the other character. This switching on and off of personalities is not conscious

unconscious

but rather _____.

59 Somnambulism appears to be another dramatic demonstration of unconscious expressions of behavior which

repressed

for some reason or another have been _____.

60 According to Freud, dreams often reveal the function of repression as a mechanism of adjustment. In relating the content of a dream, we may think of it as a meaningless, silly experience; but to Freud a dream is full of meaning. Essentially, Freud felt that the dream is wish fulfillment. A dream is an attempt to reduce tension which cannot be

waking (conscious)

released in a _____ state.

61 To dream of injuring your mother may, according to Freud, reflect an unconscious hostility toward her which is too painful to accept in a waking state. The dream therefore is an enactment of a _____.

wish

62 We can see in Freud's concept of dreams as being _____ _____ an identification of Freud with the tension-reduction theorists.

wish fulfillment

63 We repress those things which do not reduce tension (or which generate tension), and in the relaxed state of sleep we show responses which are painful to emit in the _____ state.

waking

64 But we also have dreams in which we go over experiences which have been very painful in the waking state. In a "nightmare" the person seems to be releasing tension which he is unable to release in a waking state. Thus the dream again serves as a _____-reducing experience.

tension

65 In a dream we may be motivated by (1) _____ motives which cause us (2) _____ as they do in a waking state.

(1) repressed
(2) anxiety (or tension)

Freud and also many of his students suggest that the themes of dreams indicate certain underlying concerns which have been repressed. Alfred Adler, one of Freud's most famous students, contends that a dream of falling indicates that the dreamer is losing his sense of worth. It also suggests, according to Adler, that the person feels that he is above others in his status.

Repression is the process of dismissing from consciousness thoughts and feelings which are too painful to experience or recall. Examples of repression can be found in dream interpretation, selective memory, and certain mental disorders, such as amnesia or dual personality.

Rationalization

One of the most obvious mechanisms we use in adjusting to frustration or conflict is called rationalization. Many times we invent "good" reasons for our behavior to replace "real" reasons. We logically justify what we are doing or have done, and this justification seems to alleviate some of our anxiety.

reality	**66** Rationalization illustrates well that many of the mechanisms of adjustment involve denial of _____.
rationalization	**67** A student failed a test "because the questions were not fair"; Father cheated a bit on the income-tax return because "everybody does it." Although these may be conscious acts, they may be instances whereby an individual reduces his anxiety through _____.
unconscious	**68** Beliefs which appear to be logical to the person may not appear logical to others. Rationalizations are usually given as _____ explanations of behavior.
rationalization	**69** One of Aesop's familiar fables involves a fox who, unable to reach some grapes, proclaimed that they were sour. This is a kind of _____ which holds that those things we can't reach are not worthy of our effort.
"I didn't really like her anyway."	**70** Man often reacts in the same way as the fox. The boy who has been rejected by the girl he has been attempting to court may respond with a "sour-grapes" reaction. What might he say? +++++.

Sometimes we find we are glad that we didn't reach a goal we once strived to attain. If we are deceiving ourselves and others, this form of rationalization is referred to as "sweet lemon." For example, we may strive to be a military officer, but rationalize our failure to make the grade by saying that we're better off being an enlisted man since we get to know people of all walks of life.

sweet-lemon	**71** The above illustrates the _____-_____ form of rationalization.
deceive (also defend)	**72** It is important to note that sour-grapes and sweet-lemon forms of rationalization involve efforts to _____ the self.

Rationalization may be carried out by groups as well as by individuals. Members of a social club may insist that their enthusiastic effort to help the poor is based on humanitarian motives. Actually, it may be due to motives such as gaining publicity or feeling superior.

73 Rationalization, as a defensive effort to maintain self-respect, is probably one of the least unconscious of the mechanisms. It may involve more of an effort to deceive others than to deceive yourself. The person often finds himself "in a corner," as it were, and must publicly proclaim his motives as being acceptable. So we see in rationalization an effort to **(1)** _____ others as well as **(2)** one's _____.

(1) deceive
(2) self

74 Whenever there is incongruity between our behavior and our attitudes, it appears that we tend to reduce the incongruity (the cognitive dissonance) by changing our attitudes. For instance, we may rationalize our not taking exercises regularly by becoming skeptical of the value of exercise. In doing so we are adjusting our **(1)** _____ so that it is more **(2)** _____ with our behavior.

(1) attitude
(2) congruous
(consistent)

75 A series of experiments by Festinger (1957) and others suggests a theory of cognitive dissonance, which holds that a person may change his attitude toward an unpleasant task in an effort to rationalize his behavior. For example, an employee may come to like a job wherein he is compelled to perform all sorts of unpleasant chores. He _____ the situation through a change in attitude (Festinger, 1957).

rationalizes

76 Do you recognize that this is a possible explanation for the persistence of behavior which has no or few apparent rewards? Thus, the concept of _____ _____ may be of use in describing behavior which otherwise seems "mystical" or "unexplainable" (Festinger, 1957).

cognitive dissonance

Identification

We may identify with another person and become emotionally involved with him. As was pointed out in the unit on child development, usually the child identifies with his parents, so that what affects the parent in many ways affects also the child.

There are at least a pair of principles which determine whether or not we shall identify with others. First, we identify with those who are in close proximity to us. Second, we identify with those who are similar to us. One of the deterrents to international understanding is the fact that we tend to identify with individuals who live near us and not with those who live far from us.

77 In addition to the principle of proximity in determining identification, similarity also affects our degree of identification. We are, for example, apt to identify with individuals who are _____ to us in age, sex, race, and so forth.

similar

78 These two factors, _____ and _____, do not account for all identifications. We also identify with persons and events which enhance our feelings of self-worth.

proximity
similarity

79 We have all observed a boy identifying with the football hero. In so doing, he wants people to associate him with the hero or at least to feel that he is so associated. In this way, the young boy enhances his feelings of _____-_____.

self-worth

80 An individual may distort reality in order to gain, at least for the moment, freedom from feelings of inadequacy. When identification is based on this motivation, we can see that the person is defending against _____ caused by feelings of inadequacy.

anxiety

81 As a defensive response, we identify with others in order to gain feelings of _____.

adequacy

82 Identification can be carried out consciously or unconsciously. When it is unconscious, the individual deceives himself as he does in projection and other mechanisms of adjustment. Like all adjustment mechanisms involving defense of the ego, identification involves self-_____.

deception

83 Identification is not synonymous with imitation. In imitation we copy the behavior of others, but in identification we actually believe that we possess the characteristics of the model. Imitation is _____ [more/less] complex than identification. The self is _____ [more/less] involved in identification.

less
more

84 We said earlier that we may project our own characteristics to others in a nondefensive as well as in a defensive response. This may lead to identification with others and may be either _____ or _____.

defensive
nondefensive

85 Anna Freud, daughter of Sigmund Freud, has pointed out that one of man's most interesting tendencies is called "identification with the aggressor." When an individual adopts the behavior and attitudes of individuals who threaten him, he _____ with the aggressor (A. Freud, 1946).

identifies

86 It is important to note that identifying with the
_____ is not a conscious mechanism; it functions unconsciously.

aggressor

87 The little child, after returning from the dentist, may practice "dentistry" on his playmates. It seems that through this mechanism, the child takes on some of the characteristics and feelings of the aggressor and perceives less of a difference between himself and the aggressor. Thus the aggressor is _____ likely to threaten him.

less

Sarnoff (1962) proposes that the following situations must exist in order to evoke identification with the aggressor:
1. An aggressor who is determined to vent his hostile feelings upon another individual
2. A victim who is socially dependent upon the aggressor and who thus makes a convenient target for the aggressor's hostility
3. A social situation in which the victim cannot completely escape the hostility that the aggressor may wish to impose upon him

88 The first requirement for this type of identification is a(n) _____.

aggressor

89 Assuming an aggressor, we then need a _____ who is dependent on the aggressor.

victim

90 The third requirement is that there shall be a social situation from which the victim cannot _____.

escape

91 While this is found in parent-child relationships, it might also be found in adult-adult relationships. Can you think of an example involving adult-adult relationships? +++++.

aggression of a
majority group
toward a minority
group

92 It is interesting that some Jews become antisemitic, thus identifying with the antisemitic aggressor. The antisemitic situation in some parts of the United States meets all the above criteria for the evocation of identification with the _____.

aggressor

In a situation which meets the above criteria, individuals who identify with the aggressor are thought to be those whose parents were rejecting, frustrating, and hostile

(Sarnoff, 1962, p. 183). One investigator studied the personality differences between Jews who identified with the aggressor and those who did not. A questionnaire was used to measure the degree of identification, and two groups of high and low identifiers were established for one hundred Jewish college students. The characteristics found are given in Table 15.

Table 15. A Study of Identification

High identification (N = 45)	Low identification (N = 55)
Attitude toward parents	
1. Tendency toward hatred	1. Acceptance of parents
2. Reject parents	2. Feel that parents accept them
Attitude toward self	
1. Reject self	1. Secure
2. Chronic fears	2. Not easily frightened
3. Passive	3. Independent

SOURCE: Constructed from I. Sarnoff, *Jewish Identification with the Aggressor Related to Attitudes toward Self and Parent,* 1962, p. 183.

93 Study the information above. It is noted that the Jewish college students who show the greatest identification with the aggressor are those who feel _____ _____.

less secure (more frightened)

94 Rather than strike out against the aggressive majority, the identifiers tend to react _____ [passively/ aggressively] in response to aggression.

passively

95 Those showing low identification are more apt to resist aggressors. These students' attitudes toward parents promote _____ [greater/less] self-acceptance than those from the high-identification group.

greater

96 *Review:* Identification with the aggressor seems to be one way in which man defends himself in situations wherein there is a (1) _____, a (2) _____, and a (3) _____ from which it is impossible to escape completely.

(1) aggressor
(2) victim
(3) social situation

97 Through identification with the aggressor, the individual may be attempting to possess the power of the aggressor. In this way, the aggressor appears less threatening to the victim. The goal of identification with the aggressor seems to be to reduce +++++.

anxiety (get rid of the threatening feelings)

Identification as a mechanism of adjustment has benefits to the person which help him overcome problem situations. While some instances of identification involve self-deception, identification is often a momentary method of escaping from the realities of everyday living. We identify, for example, with the hero of a novel or movie. This may be a transient but refreshing engagement in fantasy—a healthy escape from reality.

Projection

The word "projection" derives from the word *projectus,* meaning to "cast forward." In behavioral science the word is usually used to refer to the tendency to ascribe to others one's own motivations, thoughts, and feelings. Like other adjustment mechanisms, it is largely unconscious.

Projection may be used as a way of protecting oneself from threatening feelings (anxiety) or it may be nondefensive. We tend to see our own behavior in others, and this might well be a correct perception of similarities between our behavior and the behavior of others.

projection

98   In the sense of the illustration given above, _____ is nondefensive.

99   Furthermore, we may attribute our traits to others out of sheer lack of information regarding what others are like. Ethnocentrism (tendency for a group to see all behavior in terms of its own standards) is an example of projection of our traits to others simply because of +++++.

ignorance of others
(lack of informa-
tion)

100   If I spend my childhood in a Pennsylvania coalmining area, I may quite correctly rate my associates as being very much like me. This may be a normal outgrowth of my experience and therefore may not be _____ projection.

defensive

101   Having spent a lifetime in a Pennsylvania coalmining area, I may attribute my characteristics to individuals who live in Spain. This may be an error because I have had different _____ than have Spaniards.

experiences

The tendency to see our traits in others has been demonstrated in research. It has been shown that people who rate themselves as being happy tend to see happiness in the pictures of others. It has been found that college students tend to project both favorable and unfavorable traits to one another (Golding, 1954; Sears, 1936).

102 While projection of some kind seems to go on in both defensive and nondefensive ways, we are primarily concerned here with projection as an unconscious defensive maneuver. The young child who, after hitting the child next door with a rock, proclaims, "I didn't do it; it was my hand," seeks to preserve his own feelings of "goodness" by projecting in a _____ way.

103 Examples of defensive projection are found in racial and other types of prejudices. It is sometimes suggested that gentiles who are prejudiced against Jews are _____ negative attitudes which have been repressed in relation to other aspects of the person's life.

104 The gentile, for example, may feel hostile toward his parents, but his guilt forces him to idealize the parent and his social group and thus seek other targets for his hostility. Thus, antisemitic feelings represent defensive projection of _____.

How can one determine whether or not the adjustment mechanism of projection is unconsciously operative? A couple of clues to it might be found if:
1. The person is attributing undesirable traits to others.
2. There is vigorous denial that the accuser possesses the traits (Jourard, 1963).

105 In attributing _____ traits to others, we often reveal projection as a defensive process.

106 We begin to suspect that projection is being used as an adjustment mechanism whenever the individual strongly _____ that he possesses the traits he attributes to others.

We sometimes speak of "rationalized projection" to point out that rationalization and projection are often combined in a single mechanism of adjustment. A person who is caught stealing may defend himself by saying,

---

Margin answers:

defensive

projecting

hostility (toward parents)

undesirable

denies

"Everyone else is doing it." Here the person seems to be converting his anxiety into a rational justification for his behavior.

(1) rationalized projection
(2) defensive

107 This is an example of (1) _____ _____. That man in his efforts to effect an adjustment will often engage in self-deception is illustrated by (2) _____ behavior.

Projection seems to begin early in life. A study involving eight-year-old children reveals this. Each child was given one desirable and one undesirable toy. Each child was asked to give one of the toys to another child. Subsequently, each child was asked to indicate which toy another would have given to him. The children who were forced to give up a toy indicated more frequently than the other children that their friends would have given them the undesirable toy (Sears, 1936).

greediness (selfishness)

108 The child tends to project his _____ to other children.

109 Viewed in a different way, projective behavior may be thought of as involving indiscriminate responses to a situation. The person may indiscriminately accuse others of impulses which he possesses. This _____ response to a situation seems to reduce anxiety for the moment.

indiscriminate

110 The purpose of the indiscriminate response seems to be to avoid whatever aversive stimuli are causing _____ (Lundin, 1961).

anxiety (feelings of worthlessness)

111 An experiment which has some relation to projection involved shocking rats every 100 seconds for an hour. This, of course, elicited aggression from the rats even after the shock ceased. Furthermore, if two rats were shocked together, each would become hostile toward the other, although the shock was no longer given. This appears to be an example of _____ response, similar to those shown in projection (O'Kelley and Steckle, 1939).

indiscriminate

112 Projection in a more exaggerated sense, involving extremely self-deceptive factors, is found in mentally disturbed individuals. The person completely _____ his undesirable characteristics and projects them to other persons or other situations.

denies

113 The paranoid individual may accuse others of hostile feelings toward him, but actually he unconsciously feels +++++.

hostile toward them

114 The homosexual may perceive that others are attempting to seduce him. Distinguish again between defensive and nondefensive projection. +++++.

You should review
the last several
frames if you
have difficulty in
doing this.

115 The fact that we project our feelings, thoughts, and motivations into our perceptions of our environment makes it possible for psychologists to diagnose behavior by means of projective techniques. For example, one of the projective tests consists of ink blots (Rorschach test) which the individual views and indicates whatever the blots remind him of. Through _____ _____, psychologists can often detect motivations of which the individual is not conscious.

projective tech-
niques (tests)

116 Not all projective techniques are tests in the sense in which we usually use the term. Attitudes are measured by means of projective techniques. For example, a child's attitude toward Negroes may be measured by such techniques as presenting him with a picture of Negro children playing and asking him whether or not he would like to join them. Through his responses, he is projecting his _____.

attitudes (biases,
prejudices, fears,
etc.)

We may project desirable as well as undesirable traits to others. Consider the lover who can see no wrong in the person he loves. This type of projection may also be defensive.

Ascribing favorable traits to others may be motivated by deep feelings of inadequacy or by an effort to distort reality. We can conclude, therefore, that projection of positive traits may also be defensive.

Displacement

In attempting to adjust our behavior to the behavior of other individuals, we often have difficulty in dealing with hostility. We noted earlier that we tend to repress impulses which are unwelcome to consciousness.

In some situations, hostile impulses may be very threatening to us, especially when we feel hostile toward someone whom we also love or fear. We have difficulty in directly expressing hostility toward those who instigated the hostility because we may also love or fear the person.

117 Instances wherein we feel hostile toward ourselves create **(1)** _____ which is difficult to tolerate. We also have aggressive feelings toward things or situations which we cannot **(2)** _____.

(1) anxiety (tension)

(2) control (tolerate)

118 We often have difficulty in repressing hostile impulses because to do so is to prevent tension reduction. While some repression may take place, many times we resort to a mechanism of adjustment called *displacement*. The process of directing aggression or hostility toward a person or object other than the original instigator of the aggression or hostility is termed _____.

displacement

119 A student, feeling that a professor has been unfair in the grading of an essay examination, may express hostile remarks to his parents as he returns from school. Realizing that direct aggression toward the professor may be punishing, the student directs hostility, instead, toward his _____.

parents

On a larger scale, displacement is illustrated in the prejudiced behavior of a majority group toward a minority group. A group of investigators (Dollard et al., 1939) performed an interesting study with a group of boys who were attending a summer camp. It became apparent that these boys were going to miss bank night at the movies because they were taking some long, dull tests as part of a testing program.

The experimenters had the boys rate Mexicans and Japanese on a brief attitude scale before and after the testing. More negative attitudes were expressed after than before the testing.

displaced

120 This study suggests that the boys _____ aggression from the test situation to the minority groups.

a minority group (which had nothing to do with the conditioning which created the hostility)

121 This study demonstrated that hostility may be directed away from the situation which instigated the hostility and toward +++++.

MR. BIGGOTT

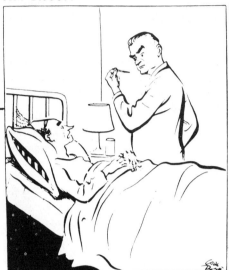

"In case I should need a transfusion, doctor, I want to make certain I don't get anything but blue, sixth-generation American blood!"

MR. BIGGOTT

Mr. Biggott: "Was it necessary, Reverend, to emphasize the Lord's — er — Jewish background in your sermon?"

MR. BIGGOTT

"Good heavens! It's not restricted!"

Figure 25. It has been found that some highly prejudiced individuals fail to get the point of these cartoons. (C. T. Morgan, *Introductory Psychology*, p. 359, McGraw-Hill Book Company, New York, 1956. Used by permission.)

122 Some investigators (e.g., Dollard, 1939) believe that frustration leads to aggression. It is rather easy to find illustrations of this in our personal lives as well as in groups, both national and international. Can you think of an example on a national level? +++++.

e.g., Nazi persecution of Jews
e.g., persecution of Negroes in parts of America

123 Frustrated by economic decline and other circumstances, the German people responded to Hitler's campaign of hatred. Thus, frustration led to _____ (see Fromm, 1941).

aggression (hostility)

124 Experiencing personal and national frustration, the German people _____ their frustration toward the Jews.

displaced

125 The mechanism of displacement involves generalization, which was referred to in previous units. A man may become angry with his wife, but feeling an inability to express his anger, he may _____ his hostile response to other aspects of his environment (perhaps toward the dog).

generalize

126 Our feeling that "all the world is lovely" after receiving a piece of good news may also represent _____.

generalization

127 If we generalize our hostility from our frustrations at home to those at school, we may express anger toward +++++.

others there (classmates, professors, etc.)

128 Some interesting studies with rats have shown that they will become aggressive toward a doll placed in a cage after they have been previously conditioned to express aggression toward other rats. The aggressive behavior toward the other rats seems to _____ to stimuli having similar characteristics (Miller, 1948).

generalize (become displaced)

129 Psychologists and psychiatrists who practice psychotherapy with individuals having adjustment problems often report that the hostility which the patient feels toward someone else is directed toward the therapist. If this displacement of hostility is rewarded, it is apt to continue; if punished, it will _____.

discontinue (be extinguished, etc.)

130 For example, a patient may feel hostility toward his father. The therapist, having some stimuli in common with father, may evoke hostile responses similar to those directed toward the father. This displacement of hostility may be accounted for by the principle of _____.

generalization

The mechanism of displacement becomes unnecessary when the individual is no longer in a frustrating situation. Thus, theoretically, all forms of hostility, both on a personal and group level, would cease if individuals were no longer frustrated.

Reaction Formation

Sometimes man's behavior is a contradiction of his motives. Sometimes repression of an impulse is accompanied by a tendency to show behavior directly opposite to the repressed impulse. This is called reaction formation.

reaction formation

131 Overt behavior is sometimes deceiving because of the function of the adjustment mechanism called _____ _____.

hostility (disdain, etc.)

132 If you are an extremely polite and friendly person, and you are using reaction formation in your overall adjustment, your true feelings may be _____.

behavior which is the opposite to that being repressed

133 Reaction formation is defined as $+++++$.

reaction formation

134 There are many illustrations of reaction formation, e.g., the paragon of virtue who really wants to sin, but reacts against his desire by his virtuous living; or the mother who "fights off" feelings of hostility toward the child by expressing unusual concern for him. As the student learns of the mechanism of _____ _____, he may become quite cynical of human behavior.

denying (reacting against)

135 Shakespeare's pronouncement, "The lady doth protest too much, methinks," suggests that she really is _____ her true motives. However, since the diagnosis of motives is a very complex undertaking, we should be careful not to conclude that anyone showing exaggerated behavior is engaging in reaction formation as an adjustment mechanism.

anxiety

136 Reaction formation may be very effective in that it removes the individual from situations which intensify his _____.

deceiving

137 Like other mechanisms of defensive adjustment, reaction formation is basically self-_____.

Some behaviorists regard reaction formation as an example of excessive conditioning in avoidance behavior (Mowrer, 1940). Mowrer placed rats in a cage and gave them shock which could be turned off by pressing a panel at one end of the cage. For some of the rats, the panel was electrically charged so that they would also be shocked when they pressed it. As the shock increased, some of the animals moved to the end of the cage opposite the panel.

138 What relevance might this study have for understanding reaction formation in humans? It might be interpreted that the rat was avoiding temptation by moving _____ [closer/further away from] the lever.

further away from

139 The avoidance behavior of the rats in the above experiment might illustrate suppression of a response. According to this interpretation, the true motive was to _____ [avoid/press] the lever.

press

140 When reaction formation is used, Freudians contend that the individual does one or both of the following:
  a. Expends energy (anticathexis) necessary to keep the motive expressed
  b. Maintains a perception of himself as responding to motives opposite to his true ones (Sarnoff, 1962)
The individual strives not only to keep the repressed motive imperative, but to maintain a self-concept of a person who responds to motives _____ to the repressed ones.

opposite

141 By responding to motives opposite to the true ones, the individual is aiding in his efforts to maintain a distorted self-_____.

concept

142 By ascribing to ourselves the virtuous behavior which may be the opposite of our true feelings, we are dealing with our anxieties in a different manner from those who use projection.
  (1) If a person is basically hostile and resorts to reaction formation, he may +++++.
  (2) If a person is basically hostile and uses projection, he may +++++.

(1) be very outgoing and affectionate
(2) ascribe hostility to others

Intellectualization

In discussing problems with troubled persons, psychotherapists have uncovered intellectualization, an adjustment mechanism which has unique characteristics. We have seen in projection and other mechanisms that the individual distorts the symbols associated with the undesirable impulses. In projection, for example, this is illustrated by denying impulses and ascribing them to others.

143 Through intellectualization, the impulses are admitted to consciousness, but the symbols associated with them have become highly distorted. An essential difference between this mechanism and other mechanisms is that in intellectualization the unacceptable impulses are permitted entrance to _____.

awareness
(consciousness)

144 Once the impulses are admitted to consciousness, the individual impersonalizes the impulses by describing them in intellectual terms. When the impulses are isolated from the symbols (words, ideas, images) which are truly associated with them in the unconscious we attribute this isolation to _____.

intellectualization

(See the two previous frames)

145 Intellectualization, as an adjustment mechanism, means ++++.

146 Intellectualization is called by psychoanalysts the mechanism of isolation. We can understand the term "isolation" in this sense, since the true symbols of the threatening impulses become _____ from those consciously expressed.

isolated

147 Which of the following reflects intellectualization?
a. I have rather strong feelings of animosity toward my mother.
b. I hate my mother.

a

148 By discussing threatening topics such as sex in impersonal intellectual terms, the individual sometimes evades facing impulses which are _____.

threatening (anxiety-producing)

149 As an individual gains insight into his feelings, defensive adjustment _____ may no longer be necessary.

mechanisms

150 In talking with individuals about their problems, a psychoanalyst may find that the individual's use of intellectualization may _____ his effort to gain insight into his true feelings.

deter (block)

151 One of the purposes of psychotherapy is to help an individual gain insight into his true feelings. As the individual gains insight, he would have _____ [greater/less] need for intellectualization.

less

152 By isolating the true meaning from the expressed meaning, we sometimes are able to read, talk, and think about topics which otherwise cause us much anxiety. This may lead to insights which will help us subsequently to deal more directly with the topics. Thus, intellectualization has a _____ as well as a defensive function.

helpful (growth)

153 In communicating feelings to others, a person using intellectualization will isolate the _____ meaning of words from the expressed meaning.

true

154 Isolating true meanings from _____ meanings is the basic process of intellectualization.

expressed

155 While intellectualization may have beneficial aspects, it must be emphasized that as a defensive-adjustment mechanism it has the troublesome characteristic of other mechanisms, i.e., it involves self-_____.

deception

Individuals may develop the habit of using only certain words to describe their experiences and of avoiding others. Carl Jung, a psychoanalyst who found some of Freud's views unacceptable, studied the reaction of people to words and found this to be a good indicator of their emotional problems. By means of the word-association technique, Jung found evidence of the mechanism of intellectualization. The fact that a person may have difficulty thinking of a word to associate with the stimulus word "tongue" may mean that this particular word arouses threatening associations.

word association

156 The technique of _____ _____ reveals many such associations which might well illustrate the need for intellectualization as a defensive-adjustment mechanism.

Like other defense mechanisms, intellectualization is often an adjunct to repression. By formulating his experiences in such a way as to avoid certain unpleasant feelings, the individual is defending against awareness of undesirable impulses.

Fixation and Regression

Fixation and regression are similar adjustment mechanisms which we shall consider together. Fixation means that, with regard to certain behavior, the individual's personality growth has become fixated at a certain level of development; i.e., the individual has demonstrated lack of growth beyond a certain stage. The mechanism of fixation requires some understanding of personality development.

157 Since fixation is a Freudian concept, we shall refer briefly to Freud's stages of psychosexual development. The unit on *Development in Children* stated that Freud postulated that man proceeds through the oral, anal, phallic, and genital stages of psycho_____ development.

sexual

158 Psychoanalysts explain some of the more severe neurotic and psychotic reactions as involving fixation at a particular stage of development. Individuals showing fixation of behavior simply show repetitive behavior which is often typical of the person at a(n) _____ age.

younger (earlier)

It has been rather dramatically demonstrated with rats that fixation may result when the animal is exposed to frustration. Note the following experiment (Maier, 1949):

A rat is placed on a stand and conditioned to jump from a small stand to one of two cards. If he jumps to the right card, he is rewarded with food, but if he chooses the incorrect card, he experiences pain by hitting his head and falling below. If the experimenter does not consistently reward his jumping to either of the cards, the animal refuses to jump. However, if he is prodded by a blast of air, the animal will resume his jumping to the cards but will show *fixation* of response by jumping only to one side or the other regardless of which of the two cards are in view.

fixation

159 This study seems to illustrate that _____ of response occurs as a result of frustration.

160 The experiment also suggests that as frustration (and consequent anxiety) becomes great, the organism's behavior becomes more _____ [flexible/rigid].

rigid

161 A man may have difficulty in relating effectively to women because he relates in the same way that he related to his mother at a very early age. His development in this respect has been arrested. In what way might he relate to women which would illustrate fixation of response? $+++++$.

e.g., being overly dependent upon them for attention

development

162 While we use the term "fixation" to mean the arrested _____ of behavior, the term "regression" refers to a return to behavior which is less mature than that which the individual is currently able to perform.

regression

163 The five-year-old child who reverts to thumb sucking, bed wetting, and baby talk after the birth of a little brother provides an illustration of _____.

Regression in children under laboratory conditions has been demonstrated in research (Barker, Dembo, and Lewin, 1941). These investigators placed two- to five-year-old children in a play situation designed to elicit frustration. After playing with desirable toys, the children were interrupted and were forced to return to less desirable toys. The children were allowed to see but not to play with the desired toys.

The behavior of the children was observed, and the level of play following the frustration was judged to be 1½ years below the level of their previous play. The play of the children was less complex, less constructive, and less well organized than before frustration. The evidence of regression here is found in the earlier age level of the play (reduced complexity of the play, etc.).

less

164 It seems that through regressive reactions the individual is able to return symbolically to an earlier stage of development wherein he was more secure. Regression means a return to behavior which is _____ mature than the individual is able to exhibit.

165 Although children often demonstrate regression, it can also be found in adults. Sarnoff (1962) gives an example of a young bride who before marriage was a sophisticated woman of the world. Finding the demands of married life created much anxiety, she showed regressive responses which took the form of "baby talk." This illustrates that regression is found not only among children but also among _____.

adults

maturity

166 The adult, in the face of threat, may withdraw to a lower level of maturity wherein his failures are less apparent. On a lower level of _____ he feels more secure.

167 By reverting to a more infantile level of adjustment the regressing person seems to excuse his behavior. This revised concept of himself as a helpless person will presumably result in other individuals expecting _____ [more/less] of him.

less

168 The regressing individual may or may not be aware of his defensive mechanism of adjustment. Thus regression may be found at both the _____ and _____ levels.

conscious
unconscious

169 Whether expressed with much or little personal awareness, regression is like other defensive adjustment mechanisms; i.e., it is fundamentally an effort to sidestep life's problems. The fundamental difference between fixation and regression is that fixation is **(1)** _____ development of behavior; regression is returning to an **(2)** _____ level of development.

(1) arrested

(2) earlier

170 We may observe that a child under one year of age tends to place objects in his mouth. In observing an adult gaining satisfaction through oral stimulation, we may conclude that his behavior is an example of either _____ or _____ .

fixation
regression

A study with rats suggests that perhaps regression is a returning to an early learned response which was effective in the solution of the problem at hand. Something similar to regression may be demonstrated in the following experiment (Martin, 1940):

Rats were trained to go to the right or left in a T-maze to acquire food. The number of times the rats were rewarded in this way varied among three groups. The situation was then reversed, so that the rat which had previously been rewarded for turning left now received a reward for turning right.

In the process of learning the second task, an electrical shock was given at the choice point. The results suggest that something like regression occurred in the face of this stress, since many of the rats showed the early learned response when shocked. It is interesting to note also that the rats receiving the most practice on the original learning showed the highest number of regressive responses after the shock.

171 Aspects of the above experiment demonstrated what appears to be regressive behavior. Reverting to a form of behavior characteristic of an earlier period of life is called _____ .

regression

172 As new insights are gained, fixation and repression may well be explained with more confidence as the fixation of, or reverting to, an early learned response which has been highly effective in _____ _____.

reducing tension
(anxiety)

173 Freudians suggest that fixation and regression are retreats of the libido to infantile modes of gratification. Regardless of the description, they seem to be generally _____ [healthy/unhealthy] reactions to stress.

unhealthy

In summary, the two ways of describing fixation and regression which we have discussed are:
1. Reverting to early learned responses which have been highly rewarded
2. Retreat of the libido to infantile modes of gratification

Fantasy

A mechanism of adjustment with which we are all familiar is withdrawal from reality by means of fantasy. This is a means of escaping the demands of reality and of participating in a dream world wherein satisfactions can be gained which are not experienced in reality.

174 Fantasy may be used as a defensive-adjustment mechanism, but we also experience much fantasy (via daydreams) which would not be considered defensive. Fantasy which is involved in our everyday solution of immediate or transient problems would not be considered _____ fantasy.

defensive

175 Fantasy which involves the solution of rather immediate problems is very useful to the individual. If I were to imagine the solution of an arithmetic problem after much covert rehearsal, this would be a nondefensive use of _____.

fantasy

176 As a seemingly universal activity of man (Singer and McCraven, 1961), fantasy may or may not be _____.

defensive

177 It is when one engages in fantasy for the purpose of _____ fulfillment or defense that it may take on unhealthy characteristics.

wish

178 The requirements for the development of unhealthy fantasy are that it be engaged in habitually for **(1)** _____ _____ and **(2)** _____.

(1) wish fulfillment
(2) defense

179 Daydreaming is a frequently used form of fantasy. Daydreaming seems to follow general themes with such frequency that it has been classified according to dominant themes. A familiar form of daydreaming is the "conquering-hero" type, wherein the individual sees himself possessing objects and powers which give the dreamer prestige. If we dream of being extremely wealthy and in possession of kingly powers, this is the
_____-_____ type of daydream.

180 The conquering-hero type of daydream may be described as a dream wherein the person possesses objects and powers which give him _____.

181 The daydreams of children (especially older children) include playing a hero role in saving someone from disaster. Daydreams of children in early childhood are more apt to involve possessing specific objects or engaging in specific amusements (Shaffer and Shoben, 1956). In noting the daydreams of both younger and older children, one sees clearly that the motive underlying their daydreams is _____ fulfillment.

182 Another form of daydream which involves an element of self-pity is the suffering-hero daydream. The young child whose fantasy is leaving home after being punished only to have his parents come penitently after him is engaging in a _____-_____ type of daydream.

183 Adults as well as children participate in conquering-hero-type daydreams, but their behavior may be more subtle than that of children. But like children, the adult daydream includes much self-_____.

184 Feeling unconsciously that others do not appreciate him, the adult develops physical disabilities which seem to have no organic bases. This may be an exaggerated form of the _____-_____ type of daydream.

185 At first thought it would seem that the conquering-hero daydream is unrewarding. Closer inspection of the motives involved suggests that the individual is gaining much _____.

186 Since sympathy seems to be a reward similar to praise, the conquering-hero daydream may be _____ by others.

---

conquering-hero

prestige

wish

suffering-hero

pity

suffering-hero

sympathy (pity, etc.)

rewarded
(reinforced)

187 In learning-theory terms, should the reward be withdrawn, the conquering-hero daydream would be _____.

extinguished

188 Another type of daydream observed in man is one wherein the individual dreams of the death of someone who is a deterrent to the dreamer's advancement or happiness. This is called a _____ daydream.

death

189 A death daydream in a child might include the fantasied act of killing a younger brother because the younger brother is a _____ to the child's happiness.

deterrent (obstacle)

190 We not only create daydreams as mechanisms of adjustment but also borrow them from novels, movies, etc. There is a vast amount of this fantasy in "escape" entertainment of all kinds. The daydreams are ready-made by the authors, and therefore they are referred to as _____ fantasies.

borrowed

191 In borrowed fantasies much identification is involved. This is another example of the involvement of two mechanisms of adjustment in one adjustment situation— the mechanisms of _____ and _____.

identification
fantasy

The motive underlying man's engagement in borrowed fantasies seems to be his need to feel adequate. Feelings of inferiority result in borrowed fantasies, but all forms of fantasy serve to create feelings of adequacy.

Flight into Reality

An interesting mechanism which you will recognize is the tendency to immerse oneself in activities in order to avoid facing problems. This is called flight into reality and is probably quite common to our culture.

192 The person who has "buried himself in his work" may be using _____ _____ _____ as a defensive mechanism.

flight into reality

193 The single woman whose occupation requires all her time and energy may be unconsciously avoiding the problem of relating to men. She is _____ the problem she needs to solve.

avoiding

194 Flight into reality is the tendency to immerse one-self in activities so as to avoid _____ _____.

facing problems

195 Like many other mechanisms, flight into reality is basically a self-_____ mechanism.

deceiving

It should be noted that flight into reality is not used consciously. Furthermore, in our culture we may reward this mechanism by admiring the person for his industriousness. Flight into reality is possibly one of the least apparent of the mechanisms we have discussed.

Defense and Feelings of Inadequacy

We have reviewed several mechanisms of adjustment which individuals often use in an effort to reduce anxiety. Often these mechanisms involve defensive behavior which has its roots in feelings of inadequacy. When an individual is being defensive, he often feels inadequate.

196 Whenever a person feels inadequate, he becomes anxious. Anxiety tends to be followed by _____ behavior.

defensive

197 It may be of value to discuss here some of the symptoms of feelings of inadequacy which have been proposed by several authors (Shaffer and Shoben, 1956). Feelings of inadequacy cause many behavioral changes because they instigate _____.

anxiety

198 One symptom of feelings of inadequacy is sensitivity to criticism. A defensive person becomes overly reactive to any type of _____.

criticism

199 Feelings of inadequacy also may cause a person to apply all criticism to himself. For example, such a person may generalize that two people talking together are criticizing him. Thus, the individual may _____ the reaction to other individuals.

generalize

200 Feelings of inadequacy may also cause the person to be withdrawn. Rather than actively invite and welcome interaction with others, they tend to cause him to _____.

withdraw

201 Another symptom of inadequacy is overresponsiveness to praise. The ego-enhancement effect is so great that the person will actually invite _____.

praise

202 Feelings of inadequacy often result in an inability to compete well with others. Without some assurance of winning, the individual may refuse to _____.

compete

203 A tendency to derogate others is also symptomatic of feelings of inadequacy. Finding fault with other individuals and situations is rather typical of individuals who feel inadequate. One's own sense of status is enhanced when he _____ _____.

derogates (disparages, downgrades) others

204 Which of the following statements are most likely to emanate from one who feels inadequate?
  a. "I can't wait to get into that soccer game!"
  b. "If you don't like the way I typed that letter, maybe you want me to quit."
  c. "Since Mr. Jones told me I was the best secretary he has ever had, I've been so thrilled that I haven't been able to get a thing done today."
  d. "Although I failed the course, I still contend that Professor Jones is a fine teacher."
  e. "I'd rather spend most of my time alone."
  f. "There's nothing I like better than to get a group together and go bowling."

b
c
e

205 What specific symptoms are illustrated in the statements that reflect inadequacy?

b. sensitivity to criticism
c. overreaction to flattery
e. withdrawal

206 Since at times and in varying degrees we all experience feelings of inadequacy, defensive mechanisms of adjustment are common to all of us. Rather than being found only in "abnormal" people, defensive-adjustment mechanisms are observed at times in _____ people.

normal

Values of Defensive Behavior

207 There are some values in defensive mechanisms. They help us to meet anxiety-creating situations immediately and allow us time to gather strength to meet them more directly at a later time. Defensive mechanisms of adjustment have many undesirable effects, but they also have some _____.

values (desirable effects)

208 One value of _____ _____ is that they help the person meet the immediate problem so that he can meet it more directly at a later time.

defensive mechanisms

209 In mechanisms of adjustment which are only somewhat defensive—or perhaps not defensive at all—the individual is able to escape the routine of life and perhaps develop new resources for problem solving. An interlude into fantasy, for example, may be refreshing and helpful to a person. He may return to reality with new _____ for problem solving.

resources (abilities)

210 Basically, however, defensive mechanisms tend to be self-_____.

deceiving

211 Defensive-adjustment mechanisms are developed to defend against _____.

anxiety

212 The ultimately nonadjustive feature of the mechanisms is found in the fact that they usually work to circumvent problems rather than to _____ _____ _____.

face them directly

SUMMARY

We can say that defensive-adjustment mechanisms are unconsciously developed for the purpose of:
1. Defending against anxiety
2. Deceiving the self
3. Circumventing problems

In thinking about mechanisms of adjustment, one should be careful not to think of them as things. The term mechanism refers to ways of behaving.

Adjustment mechanisms are probably universal and serve important functions in maintaining personality integration. Whenever man feels a need to deceive himself and others, defensive mechanisms of adjustment result. Although the use of such mechanisms results in tension reduction—or the avoidance of tension—ultimately they interfere with the development of mental health.

REFERENCES

Barker, R. G., T. Dembo, and K. Lewin: "Frustration and Regression: An Experiment with Young Children," *University of Iowa Studies in Child Welfare*, vol. 18, no. 386, 1941.

Dollard, J., L. Doob, N. Miller, O. Mowrer, and R. Sears: *Frustration and Aggression*, Yale University Press, New Haven, Conn., 1939.

Estes, W. K.: "An Experimental Study of Punishment," *Psychological Monographs*, vol. 57, no. 263, 1944.

Festinger, L.: *A Theory of Cognitive Dissonance*, Harper & Row, Publishers, Incorporated, New York, 1957.

Freud, A.: *The Ego and the Mechanisms of Defence*, International Universities Press, Inc., New York, 1946.

Freud, S.: "The Psychopathology of Everyday Life," in *The Basic Writings of Sigmund Freud,* Random House, Inc., New York, 1938.

Fromm, E.: *Escape from Freedom,* Holt, Rinehart and Winston, Inc., New York, 1941.

Golding, H. J.: "On the Avowal and Projection of Happiness," *Journal of Personality,* 23: 30–47, 1954.

Jourard, S.: *Personal Adjustment,* The Macmillan Company, New York, 1963.

Lundin, R. W.: *Personality: An Experimental Approach,* The Macmillan Company, New York, 1961.

McClelland, D.: *Personality,* Holt, Rinehart and Winston, Inc., New York, 1951, p. 496.

Maier, N. R. F.: *Frustration: The Study of Behavior Without a Goal,* McGraw-Hill Book Company, New York, 1949.

Martin, R. F.: "Native Traits and Regression in Rats," *Journal of Comparative Psychology,* 30:1–16, 1940.

Meltzer, H.: "Individual Differences in Forgetting Pleasant and Unpleasant Experiences," *Journal of Educational Psychology,* 21:399–409, 1930.

Miller, N. E.: "Theory and Experiment Relating Psychoanalytic Displacement to Stimulus-Response Generalization,"

Journal of Abnormal and Social Psychology, 43:155–178, 1948.

Mowrer, O. H.: "An Experimental Analogue of 'Repression' with Incidental Observations on 'Reaction Formation,'" *Journal of Abnormal and Social Psychology,* 35:56–87, 1940.

Munroe, R.: *Schools of Psychoanalytic Thought,* Holt, Rinehart and Winston, Inc., New York, 1955.

O'Kelley, L., and L. Steckle: "A Note on Long Enduring Emotional Responses in the Rat," *Journal of Psychology,* 8:125–131, 1939.

Rosensweig, S.: "Need-persistive and Ego-defensive Reactions to Frustration as Demonstrated by an Experiment on Repression," *Psychological Review,* 48:347–349, 1941.

Sarnoff, I.: *Personality,* John Wiley & Sons, Inc., New York, 1962.

Sawrey, J., and C. Telford: *Dynamics of Mental Health,* Allyn and Bacon, Inc., Boston, 1963.

Sears, R.: "Experimental Studies of Projection: I—Attribution of Traits," *Journal of Social Psychology,* 7:151–163, 1936.

Shaffer, L., and E. J. Shoben: *The Psychology of Adjustment,* Houghton Mifflin Company, Boston, 1956.

Singer, J., and V. McCraven: "Some Characteristics of Adult Daydreaming," *Journal of Psychology,* 51:151–164, 1961.

SELF-REVIEW QUIZ

1 Give three purposes underlying the development of defensive-adjustment mechanisms.

2 What are two main kinds of adjustment mechanisms?

3 Give three primary sources of anxiety.

4 Cite two primary reasons why people are motivated to reduce anxiety.

5 Psychoanalytic interpretations of dreams are based on two basic assumptions. What are they?

6 In the study of Jews who were high and low aggressors, the high-identification group was characterized by several personality and behavioral variables. Give at least four of them.

7 What are some clues that a person is unconsciously using the adjustment mechanism of projection?

8 What specific symptoms reflect feelings of inadequacy?

9 What are some values of defensive behavior?

10 Match the following:

_____ (a) Substituting good reasons for real reasons.

_____ (b) The child pretends that he is giving another child a hypodermic injection.

_____ (c) Ascribing to others one's own thoughts and feelings.

_____ (d) I'm angry with my boss so I kick the dog.

_____ (e) Behavior opposite to that being repressed.

_____ (f) Arrested development.

_____ (g) Defensive retreat to infantile behavior.

_____ (h) A type of daydream.

_____ (i) Becoming defensively immersed in one's vocation.

_____ (j) Mechanism of isolation.

1. Regression
2. Identification with the aggressor
3. Displacement
4. Suffering hero
5. Rationalization
6. Fixation
7. Intellectualization
8. Projection
9. Flight into reality
10. Reaction formation

part VI

Mind, Body, and Behavior

Max O. Hocutt

In this part we shall be concerned with a philosophical problem which has great importance for the understanding of human behavior. The question is whether men have minds, and if so, in what sense. The answers to this question we shall consider are psychophysical dualism, interactionism, parallelism, epiphenomenalism, hylomorphism, and functionalism.

Psychophysical dualism, the current commonsense philosophy, consists of the proposition that a man is composed of two distinct substances, mind and body. One difficulty of psychophysical dualism is explaining how these two substances are related. Interactionism and parallelism are different accounts of the relation of mind and body. Epiphenomenalism, hylomorphism, and functionalism are all materialistic philosophies which deny the existence of minds in the sense of separate substances. Epiphenomenalism is the theory that thinking is an activity of the brain. Hylomorphists view men as organized bits of matter which are able to reason, not because they have minds, but because of the complexity of their bodily organization. Functionalism is the theory that there are no minds but only mental functions—which are functions of the body.

Etymologically speaking, psychology means science of mind. It is natural, therefore, that psychologists are interested in and influenced by different philosophies of mind. Different psychologists approach the study of man differently and often disagree about how to interpret their findings. Such differences frequently reflect different philosophies. Thus, one can find functionalists, epiphenomenalists, hylomorphists, and psychophysical dualists among behavioral scientists.

In the last section of this part, we shall attempt to exhibit the philosophies implicit in the approaches of two schools of contemporary psychology. The two schools are ones with which the reader will have become familiar in preceding units. One of these is behaviorism, an approach which is related to Dewey's functionalism. Behaviorists aim to discover the conditions productive of behavior. They eschew any discussion of nonobservables such as "minds." Concepts of behaviorism were presented in the previous chapters on learning and are championed by such contemporary psychologists as B. F. Skinner and Kenneth Spence. The other approach, here termed self-psychology, is represented in this book by the units on personality. It has been defended by Carl Rogers and Gordon Allport, among others, and is related in a broad sense to the psychoanalytic theory of Freud and his followers. Self-psychologists suggest that they are psychophysical dualists by the ways in which they talk about the self as if it were something over and above the body, but there is some possibility of disagreement about this interpretation of their philosophy.

Psychophysical Dualism

1 The commonsense theory of the human individual is that he is composed of two parts, body and soul (or mind). We may be said to exercise with our **(1)** _____ but think with our **(2)** _____.

(1) bodies
(2) minds

2 In accordance with the division of man into two parts, mind and body, the activities of man have been divided into two kinds, physical and mental. The commonsense theory is that we engage in **(1)** _____ activities with our minds and in **(2)** _____ activities with our bodies.

(1) mental
(2) physical

3 The philosophy of common sense is that a man is composed of two parts, _____ and _____.

mind
body

4 Because he is composed of two parts, according to common sense, man's activities are either _____ or _____ activities.

physical
mental

5 Philosophies which classify everything under two categories are known as dualisms (from the term "dual," meaning "two"). Common sense is a form of _____.

dualism

6 The commonsense philosophy is a form of _____. Why? +++++.

dualism
because it recognizes two categories

7 The term dualism is not fully descriptive of the commonsense philosophy, since it does not specify what the two categories of common sense are. But if we prefix the term mind-body to the term dualism we shall have a term which fully describes the commonsense philosophy. The theory that man is composed of two parts and that everything in the universe falls under one of two categories which are related to these two parts will be known technically as _____-_____ _____.

mind-body dualism

8 The view that man has a body which is different from his soul was introduced into Western thought by the fifth-century B.C. Greek philosopher, Plato. The philosophy of the common man has, thus, been handed down for at least **(1)** _____ centuries and is owed to the philosopher **(2)** _____.

(1) twenty-five
(2) Plato

9 A common name for mind-body dualism is derived from Greek words. The name is "psychophysical dualism," from the Greek *psyché,* meaning "soul" (or mind) and the Greek *physis,* meaning "body" (or nature). The word "psychology" (which, etymologically speaking, means "science of mind") is clearly formed from the word **(1)** _____; the word "physiology" (meaning "science of body") is formed from **(2)** _____.

(1) *psyché*
(2) *physis*

10 The Greek term for soul (or mind) is **(1)** _____; the term for body (or nature) is **(2)** _____.

(1) *psyché*
(2) *physis*

11 If you wish to impress your friends, you will say, "The philosophy of the man on the street is _____ _____. (Use the Greek-derived name of this philosophy.)

psychophysical
dualism

12 According to psychophysical dualism, the soul and the body are different. Does this mean that they are also separate? _____ (The top of a table and its legs are different, but instead of being separate, they are very firmly joined together.)

No

The soul and the body are not separate during life. Plato maintained, however, that they become separated at death. Now the fact that two aspects (or parts) of a thing are different and distinct does not prove they are separable. The print on this page is different from the page. But it cannot be separated from the page, so as to leave two things, print and page.

13 Does the fact that man's soul differs from his body necessarily mean that it is separable from his body? _____.

No

14 If Plato is right, it is only during life that the soul is joined to the body. At death it becomes _____ from the body.

separated

15 If you destroy this page, you will destroy the print on it as well. According to Plato, if you destroy a man's body, you do not affect his soul. What makes for the difference in the two situations? +++++.

The soul is separable from the body; the print is not separable from the page.

16 Plato believed that the soul is immortal. To live forever is to be _____.

immortal

17 If human beings live forever, they are _____.

immortal

18 If the soul cannot be separated from the body, then it cannot be immortal. (T or F)

True

19 Why do you suppose the soul has to be separable (and not merely different) from the body in order for man to be immortal? +++++.

because the body dies, and if the soul were not separable from it, it would die also

20 What must be true regarding the relation of the soul to the body if the doctrine of immortality is true? +++++.

The soul must be separable from the body.

21 What is the Greek-derived name of the common-sense philosophy? _____ _____.

psychophysical dualism

22 Though we owe the first written expression of psychophysical dualism to Plato, the philosopher who must be given credit for giving it its first very clear formulation is the seventeenth-century thinker, Descartes. It was the accomplishment of _____ to define clearly mind and matter from a psychophysical-dualist point of view.

Descartes

23 The defining property of mind (or soul), according to Descartes, is that it *thinks*. What distinguishes bodies is that they are *extended* (i.e., take up space). In other words, if Descartes is right, minds are (1) _____ things, and bodies are (2) _____ things.

(1) thinking
(2) extended

24 As Descartes would define them, minds are (1) _____ things, and bodies are (2) _____ things.

(1) thinking
(2) extended

25 Descartes distinguished between the mind and its activities. The mind is a thing (or as he would term it, a "substance") and its activity is that of thinking. Thus, in Descartes's view, the mind is a **(1)** _____ which **(2)** _____.

(1) thing (substance)
(2) thinks

26 Whatever engages in activities is a thing. If Descartes is right, the mind thinks. It is therefore a _____.

thing (substance)

27 Descartes regarded the mind as a different sort of *thing* from the body because it engages in different kinds of _____ (specifically, thinking).

activities

28 Descartes emphasized that mind and matter are radically different substances which abide by different laws and have nothing in common. If he was right, can anything that is extended think? _____ Can anything that thinks be extended? _____.

No
No

29 On Descartes's view, the same thing can both think and be extended. (T or F)

false

30 Do you agree with Descartes on this matter? _____.

If you are a psychophysical dualist, your answer should be "yes."

31 When you say that a man both thinks and is extended, what you really mean, if Descartes is right, is that a man has a **(1)** _____ which thinks and a **(2)** _____ which takes up space.

(1) mind
(2) body

32 When people mean "the mind" they very often say "the brain." From the point of view of psychophysical dualism, this is a mistake. Why? +++++.

because the brain
is material

Interactionism and Parallelism

33 Interactionism is the theory that mind and body affect each other, or interact. Thus, if you believe that mental events cause physical events and that physical events cause mental events, you are an _____.

interactionist

34 The theory that mind and body affect each other is known as _____.

interactionism

35 Most psychophysical dualists are interactionists. That is to say, most persons who believe mind and body are two different things also believe that +++++.

mind and body
interact

It also illustrates
how physical
events (viz., drink-
ing alcohol) cause
mental events
(viz., feeling silly).

36 An interactionist would say that the following example illustrates how physical events affect the mind: If you
are hit a very hard blow on the head, you are likely to
become unconscious. What principle would the interactionist say the following exemplifies? If you drink large
quantities of alcohol, then you are likely to feel silly.
$+++++$.

37 An interactionist uses examples of physical events
which are usually followed by mental events to show that
body affects mind. He uses similar examples to illustrate
the reverse principle. The fact that when you feel embarrassed your face often flushes suggests that (1) _____
events cause (2) _____ events.

(1) mental
(2) physical

that mental events
(fright) cause
physical events
(trembling hands)

38 When you are frightened, your hands tremble. This
illustrates what? $+++++$.

interactionism

39 The theory that mind affects body and that body
affects mind is termed _____.

by showing exam-
ples of mental
events followed
by physical events
and of physical
events followed
by mental events

40 Suppose someone challenged you to show that interactionism is true. How would you go about doing it?
$+++++$.

41 It is possible to draw a simple diagram of interactionism.

$$ME_1 \rightarrow ME_2 \rightarrow ME_3 \rightarrow ME_N$$
$$\updownarrow \quad \updownarrow \quad \updownarrow \quad \updownarrow$$
$$PE_1 \rightarrow PE_2 \rightarrow PE_3 \rightarrow PE_N$$

The chain of ME's stands for mental events; the chain of
PE's stands for physical events. The $\updownarrow$ stands for _____
between mind and body.

interaction

ME = mental
events
PE = physical
events
$\updownarrow$ = interaction

42 Explain the elements of the following diagram of
interactionism.

$$ME_1 \rightarrow ME_2 \rightarrow ME_3 \rightarrow ME_N$$
$$\updownarrow \quad \updownarrow \quad \updownarrow \quad \updownarrow$$
$$PE_1 \rightarrow PE_2 \rightarrow PE_3 \rightarrow PE_N$$

$ME =$ _____ $PE =$ _____ $\updownarrow =$ _____.

43 Most psychophysical dualists are also interactionists, but some are not. These are known as "parallelists." The theory that mind and body do not interact, but are merely parallel to each other, is _____.

parallelism

44 What is the name of the theory that denies mind and body affect each other? _____.

parallelism

45 See the diagram of interactionism in frame 42. A diagram of parallelism would be the same diagram with what element left out? +++++.

the two-headed ↕ arrows

46 See the preceding frame. Draw a diagram of parallelism.

$PE_1 \rightarrow PE_2 \rightarrow$
$PE_3 \rightarrow PE_N$
$ME_1 \rightarrow ME_2 \rightarrow$
$ME_3 \rightarrow ME_N$

47 Two events that usually occur closely together in time are said to have high correlation. Whenever I push loose objects, they usually move. Pushing is an event usually followed by some object moving. There is, thus, high _____ between pushing and moving.

correlation

48 When you pour hydrochloric acid on cloth, the cloth usually disintegrates. This is an example of high _____ between events.

correlation

49 The fact that certain physical events (such as reading a book) are accompanied by certain mental events (such as knowledge), and the fact that certain mental events (such as being excited) are usually followed by certain physical events (such as increased random activity) are examples of high _____ between mental and physical events.

correlation

50 The evidence the interactionist gives for his theory consists of examples of high _____ between mental and physical events.

correlation

51 High correlation is often regarded as *evidence* for causation. (If, whenever you strike a gong with a hammer it makes a sound, then you have reason to believe that striking gongs with hammers causes them to ring.) This is an example of high correlation between two events. It is _____ that one event caused the other.

evidence

52 We have evidence for a belief when we have some ground (or some reason) for the belief. If two events frequently occur together, that is, if two events have high correlation, then we have some reason to believe they may be causally related. That is to say, high positive correlation is _____ for causation. Note: Sometimes, as the following frames imply, it is not very good evidence, but it is still relevant evidence.

evidence

53 High correlation between two events is *not* the same thing as causation, but it is _____ for causation.

evidence

54 Whenever I feel happy, I smile. This is an example of **(1)** _____ between being happy and smiling. It is **(2)** _____ that being happy causes smiling.

(1) correlation
(2) evidence

High correlation is evidence for causation, but it is not *proof* of causation. There may be correlated events which are causally unrelated. For example, every morning at 8 a.m., Mr. Pumper, the filling-station operator, opens his station. At the same time, Dr. Absentminded Professor starts his class.

55 **(1)** Is there high correlation between these two events? _____. **(2)** Do they cause each other? _____.

(1) Yes
(2) No

56 I read the newspaper every night at 7 p.m. after dinner. When the Joneses have finished their evening meal at 7 p.m., they watch television. **(1)** Do these events have high correlation? _____. **(2)** Are they causally related? _____.

(1) Yes
(2) No

57 May there be correlated events which do not cause each other? _____.

Yes

58 People who have cavities in their teeth are also frequently overweight. But decayed teeth and excessive fat do not cause each other. (Both may be the result of some third thing, such as eating too much candy.) What does this example illustrate? +++++.

that there may be a correlation between events without a causal relation between them

59 Does the fact that mental and physical events closely parallel each other necessarily imply that they interact with each other? _____.

No

No

True. Events may be
positively corre-
lated to a high
degree without
being causally
related.

parallel (correlated)

parallelist

(1) do
(2) do not

(1) parallel
(correlated)
(2) interact

(1) parallel
(correlated)
(2) interact

They would fail to
"keep time"; i.e.,
the operation of
the body would
be upset.

60 Does the fact that a person becomes unconscious when he is struck on the temple with a heavy object prove beyond the shadow of a doubt that hitting a person *causes* him to lose consciousness? _____.

61 It may be false that mind and body interact even though they closely parallel each other. (T or F)

62 Parallelism is the theory which denies that high correlation between mental and physical events is proof of interaction. The first philosopher to propose that mind and body can be _____ without interacting was the Dutch philosopher, Geulincx.[1]

63 Geulincx was a _____, that is, one who denies that mind and body interact.

64 Geulincx's doctrine of parallelism was illustrated by the analogy of two clocks which are wound, synchronized, and set to running. Both clocks tick at the same time. The two clocks (1) _____ [do/do not] have high positive correlation; the two clocks (2) _____ [do/do not] affect one another.

65 Parallelism asserts that mind and body are (1) _____, but do not (2) _____.

66 The simultaneous ticking of two clocks is a good illustration of the doctrine of parallelism because the ticking of the clocks is (1) _____ though they do not (2) _____.

67 If we carry the clock analogy further, we can see that there would be serious difficulties in supposing that two clocks interact. If the works of two clocks were to get mixed up, then neither would keep good time. If mind could affect matter, then what would happen to the "clock works" of the body? +++++.

[1] The credit for parallelism is often mistakenly given to Leibnitz. There is considerable doubt, however, whether Leibnitz can even be called a dualist, much less a parallelist.

68 Geulincx believed that interactionism is inconsistent with a law of physics known as the law of *conservation of energy*. According to his interpretation of this law, the energy in nature is constant. Yet if mind affects matter, then it introduces additional energy into nature. Therefore, he reasoned, if interactionism is true, the law of _____ _____ _____ is false.

conservation of
energy

69 The name of the law of physics which seems to state that the amount of energy in nature is a constant is the law of _____ _____ _____.

conservation of
energy

70 If mind affects matter, then does the amount of energy in nature remain constant or does it fluctuate? _____.

It fluctuates.

71 According to Geulincx, if the law of conservation of energy is true, then interactionism is (T or F)?

false

72 Geulincx looked upon mind and matter as analogous to two clocks. They are wound up in the beginning and synchronized. Their "ticktocks" occur at the same time; that is, they have high (1) _____; but they have no effect on each other; that is, they do not (2) _____.

(1) correlation
(2) interact

73 If a part of one clock got mixed up in the other clock, it would upset the works. This would be like introducing additional energy into nature and thus upsetting the law of _____ _____ _____.

conservation of
energy

In summary, psychophysical dualism is the commonsense philosophy that man is made of two parts, mind and body, and that his activities accordingly fall into two classes, physical and mental. Plato, believing in immortality, asserted that these two parts are separable. Descartes defined minds as thinking things and bodies as extended things.

One problem for psychophysical dualism is explaining how and whether minds and bodies can affect each other consistent with the law of conservation of energy. Geulincx denied that they can and held a doctrine known as parallelism, according to which mental and physical events are correlated but do not interact. Interactionism, however, is the more usual viewpoint of psychophysical dualists.

Materialism

Epiphenomenalism

74 If we deny that there are any such things as minds, we have a philosophy known as materialism. In other words, the theory that there are only material bodies is

materialism

_____.

75 Many philosophers and scientists have found reason to doubt that the human being is anything but a physical body. Their point of view is known as _____.

materialism

76 According to a popular usage of the word, a materialist is one who has no interest in the "finer things of life." There is no necessary connection between materialism in this popular sense and materialism in the present sense. In our sense, materialism is which? _____.
  a. The theory that the only real things are extended things
  b. The attitude toward life which consists in placing greatest value on material possessions

It is a, not b.

  c. Both

Perhaps you are wondering, "Why would a materialist deny anything so obvious as that minds are real?" One answer is that no one has ever *observed* a mind. No one has ever felt, seen, or heard a mind. Only the body can be observed.

77 According to the materialist, anything that cannot be

observed

_____ does not exist.

78 Can you observe the mind with any of your senses?

No

_____.

it cannot be observed (is unverifiable)

79 The materialist asserts that the mind is unreal because +++++.

One argument for materialism is the lack of any observational evidence for the existence of minds. Another is that to the question "Where is the mind?" we can only answer "Nowhere." The mind does not occupy space; therefore, says the materialist, it is unreal.

(1) it cannot be observed (2) it does not occupy space	**80** Thus materialism is the view that mind is unreal because of two reasons. These are (1) +++++ and (2) +++++.
	81 No doubt you have by now thought of an obvious objection to materialism: "If there is no such thing as a mind, then what do we think with?" This assumes that, in order to be able to think, we must have _____.
minds	
We must have minds to think.	**82** An obvious objection to materialism is the following: +++++.
	83 There are several varieties of materialism. One is epiphenomenalism. Epiphenomenalism tries to answer the question "What do we think with?" by saying that we think with the brain. According to _____, then, the substance which accounts for mental functioning is the brain.
epiphenomenalism	
material (because it has extension)	**84** A brain is a _____ [material/mental] thing.
(1) epiphenom- enalism (2) materialism	**85** The theory that thoughts are epiphenomena of the brain is (1) _____. It is a species of a more general theory which asserts that there are only material substances and which is termed (2) _____.
depends on the brain	**86** Epiphenomenalism is based on some well-known facts regarding the dependence of thought on the brain. A blow on the head may cause unconsciousness, and brain damage may lead to extensive deterioration of thought processes. This is evidence that thought +++++.
sensation	**87** Recent researches have demonstrated that sensations can be generated by direct stimulation of the brain. This suggests that _____ depends on the brain.
do not	**88** Conscious thought is apparently dependent upon the brain. This suggests that you _____ [do/do not] need to suppose the existence of a mind in order to account for thinking.
He would say that you think with your brain.	**89** How would an epiphenomenalist answer the objection that you have to have a mind in order to think? +++++.
obviously not	**90** If there are no minds, is there any problem of explaining how mind and body interact? _____.

91 Explaining how minds and bodies interact consistently with what we know about the physical world is a difficulty for psychophysical dualism. Does materialism have this difficulty? _____. Justify your answer. +++++.

92 The epiphenomenalist admits that there are thoughts. What he denies is that these thoughts require a **(1)** _____. Instead, they are a derivative of the **(2)** _____.

93 A diagram of epiphenomenalism would be the following:

$$PE_1 \rightarrow PE_2 \rightarrow PE_3 \rightarrow PE_N$$
$$\downarrow \quad \downarrow \quad \downarrow \quad \downarrow$$
$$ME_1 \quad ME_2 \quad ME_3 \quad ME_N$$

How does this differ from the diagram of interactionism? +++++.

94 Epiphenomenalists deny that there are any: **(1)** thoughts, **(2)** minds, **(3)** both. _____.

95 Draw a diagram of epiphenomenalism.

96 Epiphenomenalism says that thoughts, or "mental events," depend on the _____.

Hylomorphism

97 Epiphenomenalism is one type of materialism. Another is hylomorphism. You can see that the Greek words hylé and morphé are the roots out of which the word _____ is constructed.

98 The word hylomorphism is constructed out of hylé, meaning matter, and morphé, meaning form. Obviously, then, the philosophy that everything is made of matter and form is known as _____.

99 If hylé means matter and morphé means form, then hylomorphism means that everything is composed of _____ and _____.

Refer to the following explanation for frames 100 to 103.
    Hylomorphism is frequently and mistakenly confused with psychophysical dualism.
    According to psychophysical dualism, the mind and the body are two separable things. According to hylomorphism, however, form and matter are two inseparable aspects of the same thing.

100 (1) You can *distinguish* between the form of a door and the material of a door. (T or F)
(2) You can *separate* the form of a door from its material, leaving you with two things, a form and some matter. (T or F)

(1) true
(2) false

101 Form and matter cannot be _____ from one another.

separated

102 If two *things* are joined together, they can be separated from each other. Since form and matter cannot be separated from each other, they do not together constitute two things, but only _____.

one

103 The difference between hylomorphism and psychophysical dualism is this: (1) According to dualism, mind and body _____ [can/cannot] be separated; (2) according to hylomorphism, form and matter _____ [can/cannot] be separated.

(1) can
(2) cannot

104 Instead of saying that hylomorphism is the theory that everything is composed of "form and matter," it would be better to say that hylomorphism is the theory that everything is "matter which has a certain form." Which of the following two equations best represents the theory of the hylomorphist?
(1) A thing = form plus matter.
(2) A thing = formed matter.

(2) A thing =
formed matter.

105 A round ball of clay is (1) roundness joined together with clay, or (2) rounded clay? _____ _____.

(2) rounded clay

106 Which is true?
(1) Hylomorphism is the philosophy that everything is composed of two parts, form and matter.
(2) Hylomorphism is the philosophy that everything is formed matter.

(2)

107 If hylomorphism is true, then form is one thing, matter is another thing, and every object in the world is form joined together with matter. (T or F)

False

108 If, according to hylomorphism, a thing is formed matter rather than matter plus form, then is a thing a unity (i.e., *one* thing) or a duality (i.e., *two* things)?

a unity

109 The philosopher Plato had a pupil who became as famous as his master. That pupil was Aristotle. Hylomorphism is the philosophy of the student of Plato who was named _____.

Aristotle

110   The Greek who originated psychophysical dualism was (1) _____. His pupil, and the originator of the philosophy known as hylomorphism, was (2) _____.

(1) Plato
(2) Aristotle

111   Aristotle's belief was that what we term man's "mind" or "soul" is the form of his body. It is not a thing over and above the body, but the way in which the body is organized. Consider the following statements: (a) When a man dies, his body disintegrates; (b) when a man dies, his soul leaves his body. If Aristotle is correct, these are but two different ways of expressing the same fact. The "departure" of the soul consists in the fact that the body loses its _____.

form (organization)

112   The body, at death, decays. It is not destroyed but merely disintegrates. That is, it loses its _____.

organization (form)

113   A human being is an organism; that is, his parts are organized in certain ways. This organization constitutes the _____ of the human being.

form

114   According to Aristotle, it is by virtue of possessing a certain *form* that a thing is able to *function* in certain ways. Take the wood of a tree. It cannot (1) _____ as a chair until it acquires the (2) _____ of a chair.

(1) function
(2) form

115   The way a thing is organized is its (1) _____; the way it operates is its (2) _____.

(1) form
(2) function

116   Life consists in growing, taking nourishment, reproducing, and decaying. That is, life consists of certain ways of _____.

functioning

117   If Aristotle is right, in order for a thing to be able to function in a certain way, it must have a certain _____.

form

118   The same chemicals that constitute a man may be found in bottles on shelves in laboratories. Yet they are not alive. What sort of explanation would Aristotle give of this puzzling fact? +++++.

He would say they are not alive because they have not been put together in the right way; that is, they lack the proper form.

119   According to Aristotle, living things function in the ways which constitute life because they are _____ in the way which makes life possible.

formed

<table>
<tr><td>

(1) form

(2) function

form is necessary
  for functioning,
  i.e., if the form
  is destroyed, so
  is the function.

true

true

He meant **(2)**; he
  definitely did not
  mean **(1)**.

psychophysical
  dualist

functioning

formed

(a) 1
(b) 3
(c) 2

</td><td>

120 Aristotle defined the soul as the "principle of life."
By this he meant that the soul is the **(1)** _____
which the body has, by virtue of which it is able to
(2) _____ in the ways we call "being alive."

121 If the organization of an organism begins to break
down, then the organism begins to die. Aristotle would
account for this fact by saying that $+++++$.

122 If the soul is the principle of life, then every living
thing has a soul. (T or F)

123 According to Aristotle's view every living thing has
a soul. (T or F)

124 When Aristotle said that every living thing has a
soul, he meant **(1)** that there is a *thing* inside every living
thing which is different from its body and which is called
its soul; **(2)** that every living thing is organized in the way
which makes life possible. _____

125 See the preceding frame. If Aristotle had meant **(1)**,
then he would have been a _____ _____ rather
than a hylomorphist.

126 Aristotle believed that all living things have souls.
But he believed that the human being has a special kind
of soul. All living things reproduce, grow, and take
nourishment, but, he said, only human beings reason.
That is, reasoning is a way of _____ which is peculiar
to the human being.

127 If all differences in function are attributable to dif-
ferences in form, then the basis for man's special capacity
to reason is the fact that he is _____ in a special way.

128 Match the following:

    (a) psychophysical   1. Man thinks because there is
         dualism   a mind inside his body
                              somewhere.

    (b) epiphenom-   2. Man thinks because his body
         enalism   is organized in a complex
                              way which makes thinking
                              possible.

    (c) hylomorphism   3. Man thinks because he has a
                                  very large brain.

</td></tr>
</table>

129 If Aristotle is right, life is possible because man is formed in a certain way. Death, therefore, occurs when this form is _____.

destroyed

130 Aristotle's philosophy is known as _____.

hylomorphism

131 Aristotle denied that the soul is a separate *thing*. (T or F)

true

132 Define hylomorphism. +++++.

the theory that
  everything is
  formed matter
  and that man's
  soul (or mind) is
  the form of his
  body.

133 Is hylomorphism closer to materialism or to psychophysical dualism? +++++.

It is closer to
  materialism.

Functionalism

134 Hylomorphism and epiphenomenalism are both types of _____.

materialism

135 A third form of materialism is functionalism. You can guess easily enough that the theory that the mind is a function rather than a thing is _____.

functionalism

136 The philosophy of the human individual which asserts that there is no mental substance (or thing) but only a mental function is called _____.

functionalism

137 Match the following:
  (a) dualism   1. Mind is form.
  (b) hylomorphism   2. Mind is function.
  (c) functionalism   3. Mind is substance.

(a) 3
(b) 1
(c) 2

138 The function of a thing is what it does. The function of a vacuum cleaner is +++++.

to vacuum (to clean)

139 The function of a thing is +++++.

what it does

140 The functionalist says that mind is a _____ of the body.

function

141 The hylomorphist says mind is a (1) _____. The functionalist says mind is a (2) _____. The psychophysical dualist says mind is a (3) _____.

(1) form
(2) function
(3) thing (or
    substance)

(1) does not
(2) does

142 Functionalism **(1)** _____ [does/does not] deny that there are "minds." Functionalism **(2)** _____ [does/does not] deny that minds are things.

143 It may be objected against functionalism that there can be no mental functioning unless there is something to function. If this objection is to save psychophysical dualism, the thing which thinks must be a _____.

mind (not a brain)

(1) functions
(2) mind

144 Rats can solve mazes and learn very complicated routes to their food. We should ordinarily regard these as "mental" activities, yet we do not ordinarily attribute minds to rats. This suggests that it may be possible to have mental **(1)** _____ without also having a thing called a **(2)** _____.

do not

145 Pets have feelings; they are affectionate; they become sad. Yet we do not usually honor our pets by saying they have minds. This suggests that mental functions _____ [do/do not] require the existence of minds separable from the body.

true

146 In general, we can account for how dogs, rats, monkeys, and other animals learn without supposing that they have minds which are distinct from and separable from their bodies. (T or F)

true

147 Man appears to learn and remember according to much the same learning principles (operant and respondent) as do nonhuman animals. (T or F)

No

148 When we discuss operant and respondent learning, do we need to mention the mind at all? _____.

Some say "No."

149 When we explain how man learns and remembers, do we need to mention the mind at all? _____.

do not

150 If the functionalist is right, we _____ [do/do not] need to suppose there is a mental *thing* (or mind) over and above man's mental *functions* in order to account for the fact that he does perform mental acts.

John Dewey

151 The man who is given credit for originating functionalism is the twentieth-century American philosopher and educator, John Dewey. The man who popularized the idea that mind is not a thing but only a function of the body was _____.

152 Functionalism is the theory that $+++++$.

there is no mental
substance (or
mind) but only a
mental function

Dewey once said that mind is *adjectival* rather than *substantival*. What he meant is that certain ways of functioning can be classified as mental but that these are ways in which the body functions rather than ways in which a mind functions.

153 Grammatically speaking, we call the term "mental" an **(1)** _____. The term "mind" is a **(2)** _____.

(1) adjective
(2) substantive

154 When Dewey said that mind is adjectival rather than substantival, he meant which of the following: **(1)** that there is no such thing as mental functioning, or **(2)** that there is mental functioning but that this mental functioning is functioning of the body rather than of "mind."

He meant **(2)**.

155 Dewey denied which of the following: **(1)** that there are any thoughts; **(2)** that there is any thinking thing utterly distinct and separable from the body.

He denied **(2)**.

Dewey was one of America's greatest philosophers of education. His philosophy of mind may be illustrated by his most famous educational maxim: "Learn by doing." Doing, or practice, helps us to build up habitual responses.

156 It is clear that, for Dewey, learning consists of building up _____ _____.

habitual responses

157 According to Dewey's view, I know that $2 + 2 = 4$ when I can fill in the number 4 in the uncompleted equation "$2 + 2 =$ " and when I can count up to four. The knowledge that $2 + 2 = 4$ consists, if he is right, in the ability to _____ in certain ways.

function (respond,
behave, etc.)

158 To know arithmetic is, according to Dewey's view, to be able to **(1)** manipulate symbols, count things, and calculate; **(2)** have ideas in one's mind. _____.

(1); not (2)

To know that $2 + 2 = 4$ is, according to the psychophysical dualist's view, to have an idea "in the mind."

Dewey repudiated this account of knowledge. (Where is "in the mind"? There is no such place.) He believed that some other account of knowledge must be given.

function (respond, i.e., count, calculate, etc.)

159 Dewey's own account is that I have knowledge that $2 + 2 = 4$ when I can _____ in certain ways.

160 Are the following matched correctly? _____.
   (a) psychophysical dualism
   (b) functionalism

   1. To know arithmetic is to be able to count, calculate, etc.
   2. To know arithmetic is to have ideas of arithmetic in one's mind.

No

161 Are the following matched correctly?
   (a) psychophysical dualism
   (b) functionalism

   1. Mental functioning is functioning of the mind.
   2. Mental functioning is functioning of the body.

Yes

162 For Dewey, all knowledge is knowing how to do certain things. Thus the difference between a good baseball player and a good mathematician, if Dewey is right, is which of the following?
   a. The mathematician has some ideas of mathematics in his mind; the baseball player has no ideas about baseball.
   b. The baseball player has a skill but no knowledge, whereas the mathematician has knowledge which is not a skill.
   c. The baseball player is skilled at batting, catching, etc.; the mathematician is skilled at computing, manipulating symbols, etc.

c

In summary, materialists deny that there are minds on the ground that minds are not observable. Materialists do not necessarily deny the existence of mental activity; they merely deny that there are any nonmaterial things engaging in such activity.

According to epiphenomenalism, mental events are epiphenomena of the brain. Thoughts occur, but they have no power to affect the body. (This is the epiphenomenalist solution of the problem of interaction.)

Hylomorphism, formulated first by Aristotle, is the theory that there are only material things formed in certain ways and functioning in certain ways by virtue of their forms.

Man is a physical being, but one with a distinctive and complex organization which enables him to reason. His mind, if Aristotle is right, is this organization.

Functionalism is simply the theory that what we call the mind consists solely in those functions we call mental—such as reasoning, learning, feeling, etc.

Behaviorism and Self-psychology

In this section we shall show how the preceding philosophies have influenced modern psychologists in particular and behavioral scientists in general. You have been presented in this text with two major approaches to the study of the human being. One of these approaches emphasizes the behavior of the human being and concerns itself with the antecedent conditions productive of this behavior. This approach is here labeled "behaviorism." The other approach is concerned more with internal determinants of behavior. Its proponents disapprove of what they think is the attempt of behaviorists to "reduce" the human being to a material organism responding mechanically to stimuli. This approach we shall term "self-psychology." In this book, behaviorism is represented in Part III, Units 1 and 2, and self-psychology is represented in Part V, Units 1 and 2.

behaviorism

163 A view very similar to Dewey's functionalism has influenced many modern behavioral scientists. This view was termed behaviorism by its originator, John B. Watson, who was an associate of Dewey's at the University of Chicago. Obviously, the view that the only proper concern of psychology is the behavior of the human being is _____.

behavior

164 Etymologically speaking, the term psychology means science of the mind. However, the behaviorist Watson maintained that psychology would never become a science until it ceased to concern itself with the mind and began to study _____ instead.

function

165 The connection between Watson's behaviorism and Dewey's functionalism is obvious. To behave in a certain way is to _____ in a certain way.

(1) Watson
(2) behaviorism

166 The thesis that the only proper subject of psychology is behavior was proposed by (1) _____ and is entitled (2) _____.

167 Science requires verifiability. Watson said that if psychology is to become a science, it must reject the notion of a mind because the existence of mind is _____.

unverifiable

168 The orientation of many contemporary psychologists is behavioral rather than mental. They concern themselves exclusively with responses and the stimuli which produce responses. This orientation clearly involves accepting Watson's _____.

behaviorism

In earlier portions of this text you learned two principles which govern learning. One is the principle of respondent (or reflex) learning: Repeatedly pair the unconditioned stimulus with a neutral stimulus and the neutral stimulus will eventually elicit the same response as does the unconditioned stimulus.

169 Does the principle of respondent learning mention the mind? _____.

No

170 Pavlov, using a dog, performed the first experiments in reflex conditioning. He blew food powder in the dog's mouth after ringing a bell. Soon the bell alone would elicit salivation. This showed which of the following?
   a. That when the bell was rung, the dog immediately thought of getting food and so salivated.
   b. That the bell elicited the salivation response just as did the food powder.

It showed *b*. We do not know what the dog thought, or if he thought anything.

171 The principle of respondent conditioning (sometimes also called the law of association or the law of contiguity) asserts that (*a*) an organism which has had a reflex conditioned has associated two stimuli together in its mind; (*b*) an organism which has had a reflex conditioned has had two stimuli presented together repeatedly, so that one comes to elicit the same response as the other elicited before conditioning.

It asserts *b*. No mention is made of the mind.

172 Clearly, the principle of respondent conditioning is a _____ [behavioristic/psychophysical-dualistic] account of learning.

behavioristic

According to many psychologists, emotional learning follows the law of respondent learning. For example, take a stirring piece of music. Repeatedly pair this music with a flag. Eventually, the flag will elicit the same emotion as does the music. Thus is patriotism born.

173 The above statement may be called a behavioristic account of emotional learning because it mentions only (1) _____ and its causes without mentioning the (2) _____.

(1) behavior
(2) mind

174 What is an emotion? If you were a behaviorist, you would say which?
   a. The emotion of anger is a feeling in the mind.
   b. The emotion of anger is a certain response of the autonomic nervous system and associated organs together with a tendency to destroy or remove the stimulus eliciting this response.

You would say b.

A second important principle of contemporary behavioristic psychology is the principle of operant conditioning (the law of effect). It states that the consequences of a response will affect the probability with which the response will be emitted in the future. For example, give a dog food for lying down when you command him to do so, and it is more likely that he will lie down in the future when you give the command. This law may be diagrammed as follows:

$$S^d \rightarrow R \rightarrow S^r$$
(stimulus $\rightarrow$ response $\rightarrow$ reinforcement)

Under the old dualistic psychology, operant behavior was regarded as behavior caused by the "will." The "will" (a part of the mind) was thought of as the independent variable.

175 What is the independent variable in the law of operant conditioning?

reinforcement

176 There are three variables in the diagram of operant conditioning (see above). They are (1) _____, (2) _____, and (3) _____.

(1) stimulus
(2) response
(3) reinforcement

Suppose the teacher presents the pupil with the uncompleted formula "2 + 2 = ." The pupil may say "four." If he does, the teacher will give him an A. It is now more likely that, in the future, the pupil will say that two plus two equals four.

177 The unfinished formula is termed the (1) _____. The pupil's saying "four" is the (2) _____. The A grade is the (3) _____.

(1) stimulus
(2) response
(3) reinforcement

No

178 See the preceding paragraph. This is a roughly accurate account of how students learn arithmetic. Is there any mention of the mind? _____.

operant
respondent

179 Behaviorists believe that all human learning can be accounted for without the mind. They have been partially successful in making good this claim by using principles of _____ and _____ learning.

observable

180 Watson claimed behavior is a more suitable object of scientific investigation than is the mind because behavior is publicly _____.

Yes

181 Learning, from the point of view of the behaviorist, consists of the acquisition of a response under the presentation of stimuli. Is this similar to Dewey's view of learning? _____.

operant

182 This is a programmed text. It attempts to teach by presenting verbal stimuli which require verbal responses. By telling you when you are correct, it reinforces the desired response. This is obviously an application of the principle of _____ conditioning.

behavioristic

183 See the preceding frame. The method of teaching used in this book is based on a _____ [behavioristic/dualistic] psychology.

behaviorism

184 The claim of behaviorists is that no behavior requires for its explanation the assumption of the existence of a nonobservable mind. If you could find a form of behavior which could not be understood without taking into account the concept of mind, you would have refuted _____.

(1) mind
(2) behavior

185 Suppose you could point to some of man's actions which were not adequately explained without the assumption of mind. You have proved that behaviorism is false because the behaviorist says you do not need a **(1)** _____ in order to explain **(2)** _____.

self-psychology

186 Another school of contemporary psychology may, with rough accuracy, be termed self-psychology. The contention that behaviorists have overlooked an all-important variable in their approach to human behavior, the self, is a claim of _____-_____.

According to behaviorists, there are three terms in the formula of any human action that is not a reflex. These are: stimulus → response → reinforcement. According to self-psychologists, one important variable has been omitted from the above formula. The formula should read:

stimulus → self → response → reinforcement

187 The additional term in the second formula is _____.

self

188 Self-psychologists often accuse behaviorists of leaving out what important variable in their study of the human being? _____.

self

189 Self-psychologists often claim that there are at least three types of behavior for which behaviorists cannot account. These are: (1) unique, (2) self-actualizing, and (3) value behavior. Doing something in a way no one else does is (1) _____ behavior; striving to achieve some personal goal is (2) _____ behavior; acting morally is (3) _____ behavior.

(1) unique
(2) self-actualizing
(3) value

190 If I play the trumpet as no one else does, my playing is an example of _____ behavior.

unique

191 A young man who works hard to become a great composer is engaging in _____ behavior.

self-actualizing

192 Trying to be a worthwhile member of the community is an example of _____ behavior.

value

193 Three kinds of behavior claimed by the self-psychologist not to follow the "stimulus → response → reinforcement" pattern are: (1) _____, (2) _____, and (3) _____.

(1) self-actualizing
(2) unique
(3) value

194 According to the self-psychologist, what concept do we require to account for unique, self-actualizing, and value behaviors?

the self

195 Two different persons will respond differently to the same stimulus. If self-psychologists are right, that is because they have +++++.

different selves

196 The self of self-psychologists is not to be identified with the body. This makes it clear that the self-psychologist is using the term "self" much as the psychophysical dualist uses the term _____.

mind (or soul)

**psychophysical
dualism**

197 The philosophy of man held by the self-psychologist appears to be a version of _____ [psychophysical dualism/epiphenomenalism/hylomorphism/functionalism].[2]

198 The self in self-psychology seems to be another name for what the psychophysical dualist calls the

soul (or mind)

_____.

Like self-psychology, Freudian psychology is opposed to behaviorism. Indeed, the Freudian and self-psychological points of view are very similar. Freud's name for what self-psychologists call the self is the ego. Freud, however, thought the ego was only part of the mind. According to Freud, the mind has two other parts.

**id
superego**

199 If you will recall prior material about Freud, you will remember that these are the _____ and the

_____.

Self-psychologists often distinguish between the ideal self and the actual self, the actual self being what one is and the ideal self being what one hopes to be. Freud distinguished between the superego and the ego, the superego being one's ideals and the ego being one's sense of reality.

**(1) superego
(2) ego**

200 Apparently, Freud's term for ideal self was (1) _____, and his term for actual self was (2) _____.

Freud divided the mind into parts. In one division, it has three parts, the ego, the superego, and the id. In another, it is divided up into the conscious mind and the subconscious mind.

[2] The student should be warned at this point that, from the point of view of some self-psychologists, he is about to be led up the garden path. Many self-psychologists vehemently deny being psychophysical dualists. In my opinion this is somewhat like claiming to be a teetotaler on the grounds that one drinks only Coca Cola—when one calls Scotch whisky "Coca Cola." My arguments are historical and structural. Historically, contemporary self-psychology is based on Husserlian phenomenology, which may be traced through Kant to Descartes and is incomprehensible apart from this Cartesian tradition. Structurally, the self-psychologists attribute functions, powers, and other traits to the self. Whatever has functions or traits, however, is a thing. If, then, the self is not identical with the body or any part of it, it is an immaterial thing.

201 Now only a thing can have parts; thus Freud obviously treated the mind as a _____.³

thing

202 If Freud treated the mind as a thing different from the body, he was a _____ _____.

psychophysical
dualist

203 Since both Freud and the self-psychologists seem to speak of the mind or self as a thing different from the body, they are _____ _____.

psychophysical
dualists

SUMMARY

It is an important question for the understanding of human behavior whether we must attribute minds to men, or whether their behavior can be explained solely in terms of their bodily structures and physical environments.

Psychophysical dualism is the view that certain special human activities (mental activities) require, for their explanation, the supposition that there are nonmaterial things called minds which are somehow connected with men's bodies. But psychophysical dualism faces the difficulty of explaining just what this connection is, whether it is one of interaction or merely of parallelism.

Materialism, on the other hand, encounters no such problem. "We think with the brain," says the epiphenomenalist. "All so-called mental functions are merely functions of the body," seconds the functionalist. "Yes, and they are functions of which men are capable because they have rather special and complex bodily organizations," adds the hylomorphist. "There is no need to admit the separate existence of such incomprehensible and unverifiable things as minds," they all chorus together.

Behavioral scientists are not as yet in complete accord on these issues. Behaviorists are convinced that all behavior can be explained as the result of bodily stimulation, whereas self-psychologists seem to feel that the self, that modern analogue of the mind, must be invoked if we are to understand man's behavior.

³ Again the student must be warned against a possible misinterpretation of Freud. Freud claimed to be a materialist. Nevertheless he is here treated as a psychophysical dualist because a good deal of what he said is impossible to state in other than dualistic terms. The id, ego, etc., are employed by Freud as explanatory constructs rather than as descriptions of kinds of behavior. Yet they are not identified with any organ of the body.

REFERENCES

Aristotle: "De Anima," trans. by J. A. Smith, in W. E. Ross (ed.), *The Works of Aristotle Translated into English*, Oxford University Press, London, 1931.

Descartes, René: "Meditations of First Philosophy" and "The Principles of Philosophy," trans. by E. S. Haldane, and G. R. T. Ross, Dover Publications, Inc., New York, 1955.

Dewey, John: *Human Nature and Conduct*, Vintage Books, Random House, Inc., New York, 1957.

Holland, James G., and B. F.

Skinner: *The Analysis of Behavior*, McGraw-Hill Book Company, New York, 1961.

Moustakas, C. E. (ed.): *The Self*, Harper & Row, Publishers, Incorporated, New York, 1956.

Plato: *Phaedo*, trans. by R. Hackforth, Cambridge University Press, London, 1955.

Titus, Harold H.: *Living Issues in Philosophy*, 3d ed., American Book Company, New York, 1959.

Watson, John: *Behaviorism*, The University of Chicago Press, Chicago, 1959.

SELF-REVIEW QUIZ

1 The theory that a man consists of two things, mind and body, which are somehow joined together during life is known as _____ _____.

2 If the mind and body are said to affect each other, the theory is _____.

3 If the mind and body are said not to affect each other but only to be correlated, the theory is _____.

4 Descartes defined minds as (a) _____ things and bodies as (b) _____ things.

5 According to Descartes, we think with the (a) _____. According to the theory known as (b) _____, we think with the brain.

6 If two variables are correlated with each other, then it is always true that one is the effect and the other is the cause. (T or F)

7 The statement that mind is adjectival rather than substantival expresses the point of view of the American philosopher, Dewey. His theory is known as _____.

8 Aristotle's view that man is formed matter is known as (a) _____. The soul, on this view, is which: (b) the form or (c) the matter?

9 According to Aristotle, the reason anything functions as it does is that it is _____ as it is.

10 Watson's theory that psychology should give up the notion of mind and study behavior instead is known as _____.

11 Watson's reason for his view is that the alleged existence of such nonmaterial things as minds is not _____, either in principle or practice.

12 If Watson and Dewey are right, to know that $2 + 2 = 4$ is which? (a) to have ideas in one's mind; (b) to be able to add two and two and get four; (c) both.

13 In general, according to Dewey and Watson, knowledge consists of the capacity to _____ in appropriate ways to certain stimuli.

14 In general, any theory according to which there are no minds but only bodies is known as _____.

15 The principle of respondent conditioning asserts which? (a) That when food is repeatedly paired with a bell, an animal will come to think of the food when he hears the bell; (b) that the bell will eventually elicit a response similar to that elicited by the food; (c) both.

16 The principle of operant conditioning asserts which? (a) That an animal will learn to jump through a hoop because he knows in his mind that he has been given food for doing this before; (b) that the presentation of food when he jumps through a hoop will increase the frequency with which a deprived animal will jump through a hoop; (c) both?

17 The principles of operant and respondent conditioning are principles of a _____ psychology.

18 The doctrine that the notion of a self is required to explain some of man's behavior is held by (a) _____. (b) Indicate at least one kind of behavior, which according to them, cannot be explained without the self.

Summary of
the Program

Max O. Hocutt

When the subject under discussion is human behavior,
three questions are of interest: (1) How do men behave?
(2) Why do they behave as they do? and (3) What can
be done about their behavior? Most of us are naturally
more interested in the third, practical, question. The behavioral scientist, on the other hand, is primarily concerned
about the first two—and they are more fundamental. We
must accurately describe behavior and adequately explain
it before we can successfully undertake to change it, if
changing it is our desire. If knowledge is power, the
greatest knowledge, which is knowledge of what men do
and why they do it, is the greatest power; and those who
have such knowledge are the most powerful among men.
Consequently, if our interests are truly practical, we shall
learn all we can about human behavior. Every leading
politician, advertiser, industrialist, and educator recognizes the necessity of such knowledge. The purpose of this
book is to help others recognize it as well.

More exactly, the point of the book is to indicate something of what is known about the behavior of men as well
as to suggest what is not, but needs to be, known. The last
aim is as important as the first. Although the preoccupation
of civilized man has always been man himself, we have
only comparatively recently begun to study ourselves with
the same critical tools which we have, for a longer time
and with such spectacular results, applied to the rest of
nature. Since the subject is more difficult, our ignorance is
enormous. Accordingly, the book begins with a brief
presentation of some of the methods which it is essential
to employ if we are ever to arrive at anything like the
truth about human behavior (Part I). We must gather
accurate and relevant empirical data; we must draw our
generalizations from sufficient samples randomly chosen;
and we must test our theories by means of experiments
carefully conducted under controlled conditions. In short,
we must proceed in the manner of every properly conducted science.

It is a premise of the book, as it is of modern behavioral science, that men are organisms. This, of course, is a truism. But even self-evident truths are, unfortunately, not immune against being forgotten, and in the emphasis upon human superiority, this truth is often forgotten. The book remembers it in two units of essentially biological materials, including discussions of the genetic mechanisms of inheritance, homeostasis, and the nervous system. The importance of biology is that form determines function. This means that the description of a man's biological makeup and of its development gives us clues to his behavior. In general, heredity sets limits on, and defines opportunities for, growth, which the environment may or may not favor; but not much detail is known regarding the specific effects of genetic variations. The endocrine system operates much like a feedback mechanism, which, in order to maintain optimal efficiency and avoid death, motivates responses that keep the relations between the internal and external states of the body within certain narrow ranges. The autonomic nervous system is an integral part of this process. The diverse functions of the central nervous system may be roughly summarized by saying that the central nervous system (particularly the cortex) integrates stimulus inputs and relates them to appropriate effectors.

The biological emphasis of the book is continued in later chapters, which trace the development of the organism from conception to puberty (Part IV). Considered here, among other topics, are Freud's theory of developmental determinism, the Spitz-Ribble hypothesis, and maturation. Freud maintained that infantile experiences are decisive in the formation of adult personality. According to him, parental mismanagement at the oral, anal, or genital stage will result in personality fixation—that is, in neurotic oral, anal, or genital behavior in later life. Freud's theories, which were based on his clinical experience, require experimental verification. The Spitz-Ribble hypothesis concerning the effect on later adjustment of tactile, auditory, and kinesthetic stimulation or deprivation has some experimental warrant, although the experiments have, so far, been mostly performed using infrahuman species. Maturation is the process of developing whatever structure is essential to performing a given function. Its importance is illustrated by the fact that behaviors such as walking and talking appear almost automatically upon sufficient growth but cannot be induced to appear before then.

A section in the book on learning deals with the environmental influences on behavior, or, more precisely, with the acquisition of response dispositions under appropriately controlled stimulus conditions (Part III). Two principles of learning are discussed, respondent conditioning and operant conditioning. Respondent conditioning is a matter of pairing an unconditioned stimulus with a conditioned stimulus until the conditioned stimulus alone becomes sufficient to elicit the response. (The book details the importance of respondent conditioning in emotional behavior.) The principle of operant conditioning is that the consequences of a response constitute punishing or reinforcing contingencies which affect the probability of the emission of that response on subsequent occasions. Different schedules of reinforcement, such as fixed- and variable-ratio and -interval schedules, have different effects on both the frequency and the persistence of responses. (This section of the book illustrates operant-conditioning procedures by referring to the classroom and to child rearing as well as by experiments with laboratory animals. Operant conditioning models also appear later in the book in an analysis of parent-child relationships.) Both respondent and operant conditioning apply to the learning of stimulus generalization and discrimination and to response differentiation and chaining.

Still another part of the book is about personality theory and the mechanisms of adjustment (Part V). Here the book operates on a somewhat different level, both more exalted and more vague. The concern is not so much with specific responses and their acquisition as with the integration of many characteristic habits into a unified whole. The question is, what are the principles of personality organization and disorganization? Freud saw the personality as a kind of uneasy accommodation between life instincts on the one hand and death instincts on the the other; between the ever-struggling id, ego, and superego; and between the conscious and the more powerful unconscious. Conflict that is too severe to be solved is, he said, repressed, and the consequence is neurotic anxiety. As therapy, Freud recommended dredging repressed fears and desires up out of the unconscious. Freud's theories are tension-reduction theories. Other personality theorists explain personality in terms of goal direction or self-direction. If some psychologists are right, instead of merely responding to biological needs, we set goals for ourselves and work toward them. Some of our motives (e.g., the need for esteem) become functionally autonomous of the primary needs which originally led to their formation. Part of this process is awareness of our selves and of appraisals of our selves by others. Another part is the postulation of an ideal self as a goal for self-actualizing activity. Mechanisms of adjustment, such as rationalization, repression, projection, and identification are devices employed by us whenever the disparity between what we want to be and what we believe ourselves to be becomes too painful to accept.

It will be evident that *Human Behavior* not only covers many topics but that it also embraces different points of view. This diversity is an accurate reflection of the complexity of human behavior and a proof that there is no unanimity on the question of its best interpretation. A final part (Part VI) deals with the philosophical questions which this situation implies: Is a science of behavior adequate which attempts to explain behavior solely in terms of the structure of a material organism and its interaction with a physical environment, or is it also necessary to invoke immaterial entities such as minds and selves? The fact that Part VI does not settle its own question mirrors the state of the behavioral sciences at the present time. Some behavioral scientists answer one way and some another.

Thus the book moves from biology through psychology to philosophy. Its unity is that the question of how best to describe and account for human behavior is always in view. The book covers much ground, some of it superficially. This inadequacy is unavoidable. Even with the book's large scope, it does not treat all that must be treated if human behavior is to be sufficiently understood. In particular, it leaves out social sciences such as sociology and anthropology. Since man is largely a social animal, this is a significant omission. But not everything can be said in one book, and the authors are now preparing a companion volume on social behavior which will discuss what limitations of space have made it expedient here to ignore.

Answers to
Self-review Quizzes

Part I

1 (a) practice
   (b) principle
2 (a) direct
   (b) indirect
3 (a) private
   (b) public
4 (c) confirm or disconfirm
5 (a) sample
   (b) population (or universe)
   (c) generalization (or induction)
6 (a) random sample
   (b) biased sample
7 representative sample
8 (c) probable
9 (b) in a systematic manner
10 hasty generalization
11 variable
12 (a) positive (direct) correlation
   (b) negative (inverse) correlation
13 experiment
14 (a) alcohol
   (b) experimental variable
15 control
16 (a) independent
   (b) dependent
17 disconfirmed

Part II, Unit 1

1 the maintenance of the value of a metabolic factor within narrow limits—a "steady state"
2 If it is known (from knowledge of parents) that a gene is present once, it is dominant if it is apparent and recessive if it is not.
3 mutation, gametogenesis, recombination
4 one; two; one

5 four; AB, Ab, aB, ab
6 as a particular configuration of DNA molecules, which serve as directions for development
7 a number of gene pairs affecting the character
8 Females have 24 pairs of chromosomes, while males have 23 pairs plus 1 which differs—i.e., females XX, males XY.
9 because their heredity is the same, and observed variation can be attributed to the environment
10 They always interact. A common form of the interaction can be stated: Heredity determines that, if the environment permits, characteristic X will develop.
11 It is the genetic material, and its internal structure is the genetic code.
12 because breeding experiments are not possible
13 by inference from experiments with plants and animals and by statistical analyses of populations
14 It is highly probable in those areas in which its resemblance to lower forms is clear; probability is determined by statistical techniques in population analyses. Inferences have been validated by observation more often than not.
15 Because the potential for, and limitations of, behavior are functions of the genes

Part II, Unit 2

1 a change in the environment
2 through specialized cells called receptors
3 Motor neurons carry impulses into the central nervous system; sensory neu-

rons carry impulses away from the central nervous system; and connecting neurons carry impulses within the central nervous system.

4 The intensity of stimulus required to elicit a response. The threshold determines which stimuli an organism can perceive and permits differentiation among stimuli of varying intensity.

5 Nerve cells differ in threshold, and more intense stimuli cause more nerve cells to fire.

6 A gap between two nerve cells; it confers a directional property on a fiber.

7 It is the reflex center which connects various levels of body, and the sides of body, and which transmits impulses to and from the brain.

8 loss of vital functions, e.g., of breathing, of heartbeat

9 loss of balance and muscular coordination

10 loss of higher mental powers, of perception, of voluntary movement

11 viscera—e.g., digestive system, heart, diaphragm

12 (a) heart—speeded up by sympathetic impulses and slowed by parasympathetic impulses—rate adaptive
(b) stomach—activity increased by parasympathetic impulses and decreased by sympathetic impulses—rate adaptive

13 The retina contains a pattern of discharging nerve cells which is correlated with the sight; the cortex has a pattern of activated nerve cells which is correlated with the sight.

14 slower and longer-lasting

15 It is necessary, but it is not sufficient. Some behavior is either too complex for our understanding of the nervous system, or the relation between the behavior and the nervous system is not clear.

Part III, Unit 1

1 stimulus discrimination

2 perception

3 the tendency to respond the same way to stimuli with similar properties

4 (a) illumination, or illuminating properties
(b) hue, brightness, and saturation

5 context

6 sound waves, or air vibration

7 (a) pitch
(b) loudness

8 consonants

9 deprivation, disease, traumatic injury, brain damage, fatigue, ingestion of alcohol or drugs

10 pituitary and adrenal glands

11 alarm reaction, resistance stage, and exhaustion stage

12 subjective, or experienced

13 preparatory set

14 learning

Part III, Unit 2

1 classical (respondent); instrumental (operant)

2 conditioned reflex

3 autonomic

4 (c)

5 (a)

6 (a) the cessation of the learned response; (b) discontinuing of pairings of CS and US; counterconditioning

7 the principle of spontaneous discovery

8 (a) $S^d \cdots R \to S^r$
(b) S^r, or reinforcement

9 (a) the number of responses (lever presses) the animal makes (or, simply, response rate)
(b) resistance to extinction of the learned response (lever pressing)

10 A negative reinforcement is a stimulus which, when it is terminated, strengthens an existing behavior. (See frames 97 to 98 for examples.)

11 (a) primary
(b) secondary

12 (a) FI means that the S^r is presented regularly at predetermined time intervals, e.g., every 5 seconds, or every 3 minutes, etc.; FR means that the S^r is

presented for a fixed amount of work, e.g., every 5 lever presses, or $100 for every 2 cars sold.

(b) VR means that the same S^r is given for different amounts of work, e.g., every 3, then 5, then 6, then 2 presses; or a $100 bonus for every 2, then 3, then 5, then 2 cars sold.

13 (a) 2; (b) 1; (c) 3
14 avoidance conditioning
15 response differentiation
16 chaining

Part IV, Unit 1

1 zygote
2 germinal stage
3 (a) endoderm—lungs, gastrointestinal tract lining, endocrine glands
(b) mesoderm—muscles, skeleton, circulatory and excretory organs
(c) ectoderm—hair, teeth, nervous system, sensory cells
4 embryonic
5 forty weeks
6 deafness, mental deficiency, visual defects, heart defects
7 obstetrics
8 (a) suctorial—sucking response
(b) plantar—toe extension
(c) grasp—(self-defining)
(d) Moro—arm and leg extension, then return
9 differentiation
10 Integration increases with development.
11 (a) sequences
(b) rate
12 imprinting

Part IV, Unit 2

1 At different maturational ages, pleasure is derived from stimulation of different parts of the body.
2 oral-receptive; anal-expulsive
3 No. However, the reader should remember that research about such complex behavior is difficult to pursue and that results are based on human interpretation.

4 Marasmus and anaclitic depression. Spitz's studies have not been repeated; thus the validity of his claims has not been established.
5 rejection, overprotection, and overindulgence
6 identification
7 The types of parent behavior expressed toward the child. "Democratic," permissive, and controlling home atmospheres were described.
8 The latency period (roughly, between age six years and puberty) presumably is a period of repressed sexual activity. Research on American children does not support Freud's claims.
9 younger siblings
10 middle-class status
11 (a) verbal
(b) corporal or physical
12 responsible self-direction

Part IV, Unit 3

1 (a) adolescence
(b) puberty
2 (a) reproduction
(b) body changes associated with but not involved in reproduction
3 androgen (male), estrogen (female)
4 (a) identification
(b) social stimulation and reinforcements
5 age, socioeconomic status, physical maturity, mental age, availability of contact (any three)
6 (c) religious affiliation
7 Relationships are low between these variables.
8 high school
9 a reasonably high degree of relationship
10 (a) competitive dating
(b) continuous, single dating
11 (a) latchkey
(b) fourteen and seventeen
12 courtship
13 (b) Birds of a feather flock together.
14 size of family, socioeconomic status, religion, and age at time of marriage (any three)

Part V, Unit 1

1 (4)   **2** (1)   **3** (3)   **4** (3)   **5** (2)
6 tension reduction, self-direction, goal direction
7 id, ego, superego
8 conscience, ego ideal
9 life, death
10 conscious, preconscious, unconscious
11 reality, neurotic, moral
12 The concepts are vague; the observations are not made under carefully controlled conditions; the observations are made primarily on abnormal patients; the emphasis is on hereditary influences.

Part V, Unit 2

1 (b)
2 functionally autonomous
3 (a)
4 (c)
5 (a)
6 process activity, modal needs, effect needs
7 (a) biological tension
   (b) symbolic value
   (c) teachings of parents and others
   (d) functional autonomy
8 (a) personal experiences
   (b) reactions of others to us
9 reduce biogenic drives, become more independent of surroundings, make optimum use of abilities, create, grow to higher level of effectiveness
10 comprehensiveness, accurate predictions, logical consistency, testable postulates

Part V, Unit 3

1 defending against anxiety, deceiving the self, circumventing problems
2 denial of reality, distortion of reality
3 threats from the outside world, inner promptings of the id, self-condemnation of the superego
4 blocking of goal-directed behavior, conflict of motives

5 Individuals repress thoughts and feelings which are painful; repressed thoughts and feelings find expression in dreams.
6 hatred toward parents, rejection of parents, self-rejection, chronic fears, passivity
7 attributing undesirable traits to others, denying possession of undesirable traits
8 sensitivity to criticism, overreaction to flattery, withdrawal
9 It helps the person over the first shock of a problem; it enables him to escape the routine of living and perhaps provides opportunities to develop new resources for problem solving.
10 (a) 5   (f) 6
   (b) 2   (g) 1
   (c) 8   (h) 4
   (d) 3   (i) 9
   (e) 10   (j) 7

Part VI

1 psychophysical dualism
2 interactionism
3 parallelism
4 (a) thinking
   (b) extended
5 (a) mind
   (b) epiphenomenalism (materialism will do)
6 false
7 functionalism
8 (a) hylomorphism
   (b) the form
9 formed (organized)
10 behaviorism
11 verifiable (observable will do)
12 (b) to be able to add
13 respond (behave)
14 materialism
15 (b) that the bell will eventually elicit a similar response
16 (b) that the food increases the frequency of response
17 behavioristic
18 (a) self-psychologists
   (b) You might mention either self-actualizing, unique, or value behaviors.

NAME INDEX

SUBJECT INDEX